# Advertising Works 22

Proving the payback on
marketing investment

Case studies from the
IPA Effectiveness Awards 2014
Open to all agencies, media owners and
clients worldwide

## Edited and introduced by
## Lorna Hawtin
Convenor of Judges

IPA

warc

First published 2015 by Warc
85 Newman Street, London W1T 3EU
Telephone: 0207 467 8100
Fax: 0207 467 8101
Email: enquiries@warc.com
www.warc.com

A CIP catalogue record for this book is available from the British Library

ISBN: 978-1-84116-227-0

Typeset by HWA Text and Data Management, London
Printed and bound by CPI Group (UK) Ltd, Croydon, CR0 4YY

# Contents

# Foreword

**Lindsey Clay**
Chief Executive, Thinkbox

Thinkbox is now in its tenth consecutive year as the proud sponsor of the IPA Effectiveness Awards. We have sponsored these prestigious gongs every year since we were set up. Supporting them was one of the first things we did.

We have treasured this because the IPA Effectiveness Awards are special; no other comes closer to what we are about. They recognise advertising campaigns that work; they celebrate what we are supposed to do: change behaviour, build and maintain strong businesses, and expand the economy. These are the awards to win because they get to the heart of what advertising is all about.

They are also incredibly hard to win. They demand the highest standards of proof and recognition must go not only to the winners, but to all those clients and agencies that invested the time, money and effort in entering. It may be little comfort to those that did not win but, by entering and sharing the insights gained from what you did, you will have helped others to better understand and get more from their advertising investment.

Of course, most congratulations should go to the winners. We have been huge fans of adam&eveDDB and Foster's Grand Prix-scooping 'Good call' campaign since the beginning. It ticks every box: a strong brand idea led by powerful, emotional TV, which is then brilliantly integrated across platforms. It has reinforced the learning from Les Binet and Peter Field's work on the IPA databank that the most accurate predictor of effectiveness is likeability. So we shouldn't be surprised it is supremely effective.

Grey London should also take a particularly enormous bow for winning the Effectiveness Company of the Year award. A brilliant effort.

Advertising is an investment that can be judged in many ways; was it popular, did it win creative awards, are people talking about it or sharing it with friends? These are all valid, but nothing is as important as whether or not the advertising was effective. Did it actually achieve something? If not, you have to question what the point was in the investment. Get as many shares and likes as you want; if sales, profit or changed behaviour don't follow they are ultimately meaningless. That is why the IPA Effectiveness Awards, and the body of evidence they provide, are so important and why we will continue to support them.

# Sponsors

The IPA would like to thank the companies listed here for their sponsorship of the 2014 competition. We are particularly grateful to Thinkbox, its overall sponsor, for their continuing support, which extends into other initiatives such as brand films and publications.

**warc**

**Arthur J. Gallagher**

**Ipsos**

**newsworks**

**campaign**

IN ASSOCIATION WITH

**thinkbox**

# Acknowledgements

Many people worked hard to make the Awards a success, especially the following:
Karen Buchanan, Chairman of the IPA Value of Creativity Group, Lorna Hawtin, Convenor of Judges and Bridget Angear, Deputy Convenor of Judges.

At the IPA, the team were:
Yasmin Elsworth, Tottie Faragher, Suzanne Fox, Helen Goddard, Tessa Gooding, Conor Harte, Roger Ingham, Jonathan Kemeys, Jaxey Lewis, Matthew Ogborn, Kathryn Patten, Najeeb Qaisrani, Mark Rasdall, Louise Rome and Sylvia Wood.

We also owe a debt of gratitude to:

## The IPA Awards Board

| | |
|---|---|
| IPA Chairman of VCG, Karen Buchanan | Publicis |
| 1980/82 Convenor of Judges, Simon Broadbent (d) | |
| 1984/86 Convenor of Judges, Charles Channon (d) | |
| 1988/90 Convenor of Judges, Paul Feldwick | |
| 1992/94 Convenor of Judges, Chris Baker | |
| 1996 Convenor of Judges, Gary Duckworth | |
| 1998 Convenor of Judges, Nick Kendall | |
| 2000 Convenor of Judges, Tim Broadbent | |
| 2002 Convenor of Judges, Marco Rimini | |
| 2004 Convenor of Judges, Alison Hoad | |
| 2005 Convenor of Judges, Les Binet | |
| 2006 Convenor of Judges, Laurence Green | 101 |
| 2007 Convenor of Judges, Richard Storey | M&C Saatchi |
| 2008 Convenor of Judges, Neil Dawson | SapientNitro |
| 2009 Convenor of Judges, Andy Nairn | Lucky Generals |
| 2010 Convenor of Judges, David Golding | adam&eveDDB |
| 2011 Convenor of Judges, Charlie Snow | DLKW Lowe |
| 2012 Convenor of Judges, Marie Oldham | Havas Media |
| 2014 Convenor of Judges, Lorna Hawtin | TBWA\Manchester |
| 2016 Convenor of Judges, Bridget Angear | AMV BBDO |
| IPA Director General, Paul Bainsfair | |
| IPA Director of Communications, Tessa Gooding | |
| IPA Head of Awards and Events, Kathryn Patten | |

Acknowledgements

## The IPA Value of Creativity Group (January 2015)

| | |
|---|---|
| Chris Hirst | Grey (Chairman) |
| Bridget Angear | AMV BBDO |
| Les Binet | adam&eveDDB |
| Lucas Brown | Total Media |
| James Devon | MBA |
| Neil Godber | JWT |
| Agathe Guerrier | BBH |
| Rachel Hatton | Dare |
| Lorna Hawtin | TBWA\Manchester |
| Gavin Hilton | VCCPme |
| Simon James | Sapient Nitro |
| Richard Morris | Vizeum UK |

# The Judges

**Lorna Hawtin**
*Convenor of Judges*
Disruption Director,
TBWA\Manchester

**Bridget Angear**
*Deputy Convenor of Judges*
Joint Chief Strategy Officer,
AMV BBDO

## INDUSTRY JUDGING PANEL

**Dominic Box**
Managing Director
Tangible Branding

**Janey Bullivant**
Founding Partner
The Effectiveness Partnership

**Maggie Collier**
Co-founder and Chief Executive
Flamingo

**Clive Cooper**
Founding Partner
Yourfuture

**Chris Fill**
Director
Fillassociates

**Jonathan Harman**
Managing Director, Media
Royal Mail

**Judy Harman**
Planning Director
Newsworks

**Brian Jacobs**
Founder
BJ&A

**Sara Marshall**
Managing Director
Deeks Consulting

**Deborah McCrudden**
Managing Director
Ipsos ASI

**Colin McDonald**
Owner
McDonald Research

**Bob Morrison**
Founding Partner
Elephants Can't Jump

**Andrew Phillips**
Director
Big Island

**Tony Regan**
Founder
Brand Performance

## CLIENT JUDGES

**Lord Davies**
Vice-chairman, Corsair Capital
Chairman of Judges

**Abigail Comber**
Head of Marketing
British Airways

**Sucheta Govil**
Global Head of Marketing
AkzoNobel

**Nicholas Hall**
Head of Broadcast and Delivery
Gocompare.com

**Cameron Hughes**
Head of Brand
EDF Energy

**Andrew Mallery**
Marketing Director
Mercedes-Benz UK

**Stephen Smith**
Chief Customer Officer
Asda

**Jeremy Tester**
Deputy Managing Director
Sky Media

**Troy Warfield**
Chief Commercial and Licensee Officer
Avis Budget Group EMEA

# Introduction

**By Lorna Hawtin**
Disruption Director, TBWA\Manchester

Let's face it, writing an IPA award is not for the faint-hearted.

It's difficult to get the data. Hard to find the time; let alone diagnose, strategise, create and implement the campaigns that warrant an entry in the first place. And then you've got to persuade those around you that it's worth the paper it's written on even before it gets in front of some, let's face it very cynical, sticky judge types.

So why is it important to get involved?

Of course there's recognition and reward; a warm feeling of success that tells both colleagues and competitors that you're someone to be reckoned with.

Then there's corporate reputation. Who doesn't want to work for, and with, companies that are successful and skilled? An IPA effectiveness award is rigorous proof of just that.

But for me it's really about the impact that sharing your experiences can have on a broader community and on how it solves its client's problems in the future. It comes down to legacy.

Every single author adds to the rich library of 1,400 cases spanning 34 years. No other creative industry in the world has such a detailed and rigorous record of how the business and consumer relationship has evolved: an incredible asset and one which strategists across the globe are increasingly taking note of.

Much has been written recently on the power of stories and their significance for the communities in which they are shared. Stories are a culture's means of passing on the most valuable lessons and values from one generation or group to another. Without stories, it would be almost impossible to help our youngsters engage in the information that is crucial for their survival and success. So to me, these papers are vital because they're not just 'case studies'; they're *our* community's *stories*.

The ebbs and flows of business and brand fortunes are vividly laid out before us in every IPA submission. We read of seemingly insurmountable odds, devious insights, ingenious ideas, astounding climaxes, turning points and twists. Stories of come-back kings, returning rebels, Davids versus their very own Goliaths, Trojan horses and even

Pied Pipers; all culminating in the diligent detective work required to demonstrate communications payback and return on marketing investment.

The key question though, is not whether we all enjoy a good story – that goes without saying. Our goal here must be to see whether we can determine what separates a great story from a merely good story. After all a great story really changes its audience in some significant way and has a lasting value beyond the immediate telling.

Those which we celebrate here offer us gripping tales of survival, resurgence quest and loyalty, brilliantly well told and all with an implicit 'moral' or learning. In the following sections we hope to tease out some of those lessons. By doing so, we hope to see not just the impact of what is *changing* in our world, but more importantly draw attention to and underline the importance of those things that *remain constant*: the power of emotional insight, creative ingenuity, the desire to make your mark, and ultimately the possibility of triumph against great odds.

If you want the story of a declining favourite who finds an intelligent way to turn around their fortunes, pick up the Grand Prix-winning Foster's tale, or the Mercedes-Benz, Garnier, Premier Inn, ITV, Everest or Fairy stories. These tell how once market-defining brands have gone on the offensive, returning to communications to reinforce price premiums, fight off competitors, target fresh segments or simply re-engage with complacent audiences.

If the tale of the plucky rebel looking for renewed purpose is more your kind of story, why not try the ONLY, easyJet or first direct cases? These stories tell how the original rebel and category reinventor finds itself no longer quite as new and interesting, no longer the cheaper option, no longer the innovator – but not yet the undoubted leader either. Learn how these brands dig deep into the roots of their organisational and brand values to find the solution to their problem.

Or perhaps you are interested in how to lead the consumer and create new behaviours. Read cases that use a Pied Piper strategy, be it Transport for London's campaign to mitigate the potential travel chaos of the 2012 Olympic Games, the British Heart Foundation's aim to equip the nation with the skills to perform hands-only CPR, the New Zealand National Depression Initiative's goal to get people to self-treat rather than ignore the symptoms, or the Fire Service's need to get people to check their smoke-alarm batteries.

Thinking about brand and campaign strategy in terms of character and narrative is much more than a retrospective tool. Doing so can miraculously suggest the strategic twists required to move the story of your brand forward. The challenge therefore becomes to fill one's head with as many of these brand archetypes and stories as possible; giving yourself the richest palette from which to paint your own plot lines. So don't get bogged down in the challenges that you might be facing today. Instead, pick up one of these IPA Effectiveness stories and start to see your problem as a great story in the making.

# SPECIAL PRIZES

**Grand Prix**
Foster's

**The Channon Prize for Best New Learning**
Olympic Delivery Authority & Transport for London

**Best International**
National Depression Initiative

**Best Multi-Market**
ONLY

**Best Small Budget**
Pancreatic Cancer Action

**The Broadbent Prize for Best Dedication to Effectiveness**
Sainsbury's

**Effectiveness Company of the Year**
Grey London

**Effectiveness Network of the Year**
OMD

.

# GRAND PRIX

**adam&eveDDB for Foster's (pp. 9–38)**

# GOLD AWARDS

**M&C Saatchi for Olympic Delivery Authority & Transport for London (pp. 55–103)**

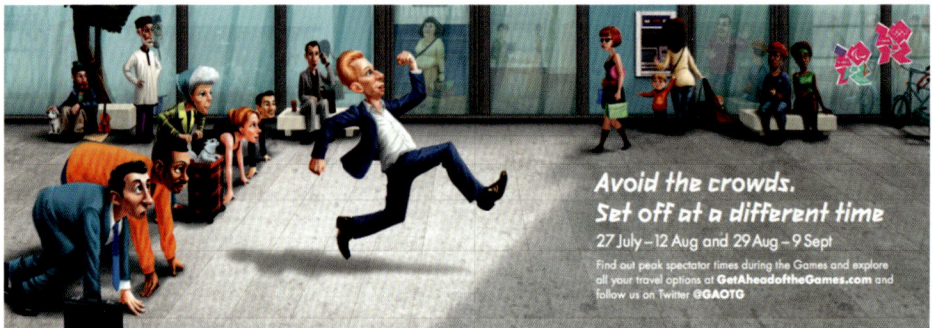

**Grey London for British Heart Foundation (pp. 115–143)**

Manning Gottlieb OMD for Specsavers (pp. 145–181)

**UncleGrey and Grey London for ONLY (pp. 197–215)**

## Publicis London and Manning Gottlieb OMD for Dacia (pp. 245–275)

**DACIA**

Hello.

We're Dacia. We make cars.

Cars that favour function over frivolity.

We've made an enemy of the unnecessary.

Because we believe you should only pay for what you need.

We make a simple range of cleverly designed, quality vehicles.

Our prices are clear and straightforward, whether you buy online or at our nationwide retailers.

Maybe that's why we're the fastest growing car brand in Europe, and have been since 2004.

Now we're here in the UK.

And delighted to introduce you to the new Dacia Duster 5-seat SUV range that starts from only £8,995.*

You do the maths

Duster

*Car shown is a Dacia Duster Laureate dCi 110 4x2 at £12,995 with optional Styling Pack at £655 and optional metallic paint at £470. Prices correct at time of print.

5 YEAR WARRANTY

DACIA
GROUPE RENAULT

The Dacia Duster | Pre-order at dacia.co.uk

The official fuel consumption figures in mpg (l/100km) for the Dacia Duster dCi 110 4x2 are: Urban 49.6 (5.7); Extra Urban 61.4 (4.6); Combined 56.5 (5.0). The official $CO_2$ emission is 130g/km. All Dacia prices are quoted at Manufacturer's Recommended Retail Prices.

■ *Standard HP offer: Cash Price £8995, customer deposit £744, 60 monthly payments of £169, Representative APR 9.9%. 5yr warranty for £5 offer: Cash Price £9390. £395 charge for cash customers or £300 charge (equivalent to just £5 a month over the 5 year term) for finance customers. Customer deposit £744, 60 monthly payments of £174, Representative APR 9.0%. On all agreements a £99 arrangement fee is payable with the first monthly payment plus a £149 Option to Purchase fee is payable with the final payment. Subject to status. Guarantees or indemnities may be required. You must be at least 18 years old and a UK resident (excluding Isle of Man and Channel Islands) to apply. Finance provided by RCI Financial Services Ltd, PO Box 149, Watford WD171FJ. At participating dealers only.

**AMV BBDO for Mercedes-Benz (pp. 293–311)**

**FCB New Zealand for National Depression Initiative (NDI) (pp. 329–344)**

THE JOURNAL
DM TO GP PRACTICES

**Team Darwin for Pancreatic Cancer Action (pp. 345–365)**

# SECTION 1

# Staging Comebacks

# How to stage a comeback

**By Bridget Angear**
Joint Chief Strategy Officer, AMV BBDO

Let's go back to 1968. Elvis Presley, despite huge success in both his music and acting careers, had seen his popularity wane in the past few years.

Since leaving the army in 1960, he'd been churning out commercially viable but musically uninspiring movie soundtracks which the public was beginning to lose appetite for. The arrival of fresh, authentic and cool bands such as The Beatles served to further position Elvis as over-produced, over-staged, and overblown.

In 1968 his manager Colonel Tom Parker fixed for him to take part in a television Christmas special for the TV network NBC. An event that the network and the Colonel envisioned would be similar to an Andy Williams-like (traditional folk singer) sequence of Christmas carol performances.

With the benefit of hindsight, how could this have been anything but another nail in the coffin of Elvis's career?

But then fate intervened. Responsibility for the show was given to a young TV producer called Steve Binder who argued that the special was an opportunity to re-establish the singer's reputation after years of formulaic movies and recordings of variable quality. He noticed how Elvis and the other musicians would spontaneously unwind by jamming and improvising old blues and rock 'n' roll numbers and it occurred to him that this would be a great way to present The King – informal, 'unplugged' and natural.

The rest, as they say, is history. The show has subsequently become known as the '68 comeback special and is credited with re-vitalising Elvis's career.

I think there are some remarkable parallels that can be drawn between Elvis's comeback and brands that have done the same.

One thing is most certainly true: we all love a comeback. We are rooting for them to succeed. Deep in our psyche is the belief that there is more to admire in someone who has seen the error of their ways and repented than someone who has never needed to repent (the parable of the prodigal son comes to mind). And so we're on the side of comebacks, cheering for them and willing them to succeed.

Marketing people also love a comeback. A lot of the brands that stage fight-backs had their heyday in the golden era of TV when one single advertisement could reach over half the UK's population. Therefore it's not surprising that if this latent awareness can be harnessed and turned into positive sentiment, it's going to be a lot cheaper than starting from scratch. I can still sing all the jingles from the confectionery brand commercials that called to me in my youth.

Maybe this is one of the reasons we have seen a lot of brand relaunches in this year's IPA submissions. Many are brands that today's marketeers would have remembered fondly from their youth and would therefore be keen to return to their former glory. Perhaps this year's glut shows us a post-recession trend, with confidence returning, to reinvest in existing brands rather than creating new ones.

Dormant affection is a powerful tool if it can be unlocked. But it can only work if the product itself can also be made relevant. Many brand relaunches fail because the expectation is that the communications alone can save the brand and that no other changes are necessary. Almost all of the cases in this book highlight the need for more fundamental changes.

I'd like to propose five lessons that I think can be learned from reading these cases.

## Lesson Number One: All comebacks need a saviour

There has to be someone who is prepared to be the challenger voice if a brand is going to confront its issues and be prepared to change. Elvis needed Binder. 'Basically, I told him I thought his career was in the toilet', Binder recalled in an interview almost four decades later. This challenger voice is often someone new to the brand. A person who can come in with fresh eyes, see all the implicit assumptions being made and the ones that need to be overturned.

It cannot be a coincidence that a lot of the brands mentioned in these pages, including easyJet and ITV, had new management and marketing teams leading their revitalisation programmes. All change programmes need a change team. It doesn't have to be an entirely new team. But change requires at least one individual who is willing to kill the sacred cows; plus several other members of the team who are willing to accept the need for change.

## Lesson Number Two: Look back to look forwards

In all turnaround stories there has been a willingness to re-create the future by going back to the past. In 1954, when Elvis walked in off the street to Sun Records and cut his first track it was just him, his voice and a guitar. The '68 comeback special was a return to his pared-back, natural state.

When Old Spice burst back on to our screens in 2010 with Isaiah Mustafa it was with essentially the same proposition that had made it famous in the 1970s – an aftershave for a man's man.

EasyJet launched in 1995 as a budget airline, pioneering no-frills flying. But over the subsequent two decades they had become better known for hidden extras and poor service than for low cost travel. A new management team were willing to address these issues and in so doing pull themselves away from the category.

They understood that 'Generation easyJet' were smart, savvy shoppers looking for value, not mugs willing to put up with anything as long as it was cheap.

The Foster's 'Good call' campaign saw the brand return to its humorous, irreverent Aussie bloke roots initially made famous by Paul Hogan in the 1980s.

The ITV re-positioning was described as 'the most ambitious brand revitalisation programme in broadcast history' which, despite our industry's love of hyperbole, might for once not be too much of an over claim. In one single day, every single way that ITV was presented was transformed. The logo, identity, brand behaviour and advertising all changed. And yet in essence all of this pointed the brand back to where it had started as a brand at the heart of popular culture.

## Lesson Number Three: Find the brand's single point of weakness and do the exact opposite

Or in other words, work out the brand's Achilles heel and confront it head on. Prospects who sat in a Mercedes-Benz said they felt ten years older than they actually were. They said the car made them think it should be a reward at the twilight of their career rather than an accompaniment during life's earlier, more dynamic moments. They said the car made them think they had reached the peak of their career and were on the downward trajectory. Not ideal when the brand's main competitors were seen as cars for those rising up the career ladder. Mercedes confronted this negative perception with both its models and its communications, repositioning itself as younger, sexier and aspirational.

Cuprinol was seen as a functional product bought by men wanting to protect their exterior wood from the elements. But it had run out of fence panels to paint with this strategy. So they did the opposite. They repositioned it as a product for women wishing to create a beautiful outdoor space and unleash their creative talents on their garden.

Garnier Ultralift was in a category where the dominant codes were white lab coats and scientific claims. Having lost a third of its sales in four years it needed to do something differently. The brand bypassed the lab coat lecture approach and did the opposite, getting real women to experience, measure and judge the results of the product.

## Lesson Number Four: Fortune favours the bold

Of all the lessons, I think this is the most important lesson. I am talking about a particular type of bravery because I actually think it's fairly easy to be brave when you have nothing to lose. When you are at rock bottom, as they say, you can only look up. If you ask yourself 'what's the worst that can happen?' and the answer is 'not much', change is relatively easy. But in all these cases, things were OK. Not great, but not disastrous either.

All these brands did have something to lose. Sales to their existing customers. And this is when change is hardest. In most cases there had been a softening of sales and some kind of decline in consumer regard, but not enough to panic.

Cuprinol could have bided its time and waited for the housing market to pick up once again, knowing that sales would respond to an increase in house buying and selling. Mercedes could have decided to accept that its drivers were getting older and taken advantage of the 'grey pound'. Both brands decided not to accept their fate, but to alter it. Change in these situations requires some kind of sacrifice.

ITV broadcast some of the biggest and most loved shows on television, with 90% of the population watching them every month. They could have been happy with that. But there was one piece of data that troubled them. One third of viewers thought that ITV 'didn't have anything for them', and it was this perception that they decided to redress.

ONLY knew it needed the approval of the fashionistas. The usual way to court this fickle audience was with expensively produced glossy 'look books' that usually took the lion's share of a brand's marketing budget. ONLY jeans decided to do something different and instead built their own interactive digital catalogue made up of specially shot films that told a story as well as showing the clothes.

Elvis could have carried on churning out his formulaic songs. Sure his fans might have begun to buy fewer discs, but he would still have been trousering plenty of cash, with plenty of people around him telling him everything was OK. But he chose the harder path. It was a path that required courage, because if he failed, his career would really have been washed up.

Just like the brands in the cases that follow this chapter. They too took a decision that OK was not OK, believing they could do better if they took the risk and changed something.

## Lesson Number Five: Repositioning requires investment

It's relatively easy to get a short-term sales uplift as a result of an increased focus and investment behind communications, but much harder to sustain it over the longer term. Repositioning requires investment, often maintained over a period of time and often extending beyond communications.

Premier Inn's turnaround has been sustained for six years, delivering incremental revenue to the brand for every one of those years and a return on marketing investment of close to £4 for every £1 spent.

Mercedes-Benz had been growing steadily year-on-year for the previous decade, but a corporate goal to smash through the magic 100,000 car sales a year mark drove the business to invest in the long-term.

Fairy Liquid was sitting comfortably on a value market share of 50%. The brand could easily have been treated as a cash cow, being milked and not invested in. But instead, P&G did the opposite. They invested in the brand's communications and saw value share surpass 60% and a return on investment of £2.16.

In a lot of these cases, the product itself had to be re-engineered before the brand could be re-positioned. Mercedes brought out new, sportier models reflecting their ambition to court a younger target audience, and Premier Inn upgraded its beds in order to justify the proposition 'a good night's sleep'. These brands understood that the product had to be fit for purpose in order for the communications to succeed.

All of the brands celebrated here must have had to put the case for investment to their executive board. And all of the brands were successful in making the case for that investment as otherwise they would not be here.

They went on to justify that investment, delivering strong returns back to their respective businesses as a result.

I think as a body of work they go to prove that there's nothing sweeter than a comeback. Seeing a brand succeed, falter, and then given a second chance is a story of redemption we all wish a happy ending to. I hope these stories will inspire more of us to make the case for similar ailing brands in our care. As I think they go to prove, we all really do love a comeback.

# Foster's

## Tackling men's worries, with a 'no-worries' attitude

**By Toby Harrison, Les Binet and Sarah Carter, adam&eveDDB**

Contributing authors: Jon Fox and Andreas Georgiou, Holmes & Cook; Simon Moorhead, adam&eveDDB; and Louise Flin Holmes & Cook

Credited companies: Creative Agency: adam&eveDDB; Media Agency: MediaVest; Econometric modelling agency: Holmes & Cook; Client: Heineken UK

**Editor's summary**

Forty years old and once an advertising icon, Foster's had lost its way and lost touch with its drinkers.

The agency decided to look beneath the ritual of male camaraderie so that Foster's could learn to reconnect with a new generation of UK men. They found that the modern man no longer subscribed to the 'tribal drinker' ethos, and amidst the banter and fun of drinking, their mates were acting as a sounding board for how to deal with the issues of the day. Critically, humour was an important part of how they helped soothe each other's insecurities.

By changing the way beer brands talked to blokes and exporting Australia's famed 'no worries' attitude through a TV-led campaign, Foster's moved from third place to market leader, delivering £32 of revenue per £1 spent on advertising.

**What struck the judges about this case was how it managed to grow a brand in a declining market at a premium; combining a clever marketing idea with a strong insight and a highly engaging creative idea. The fact that they managed to topple the market leader at the same time is testament to the business power of this thinking.**

## Introduction

Forty-year-old brands in mature markets don't often experience a growth surge that topples a long-term brand leader. But this is the story of a brand that did.

Every successful beer brand has always intimately understood their male drinkers and built their communication around this understanding. However, Foster's had lost touch with the new generation of UK men – a generation who were now 20 years younger than the brand from down-under. Life had moved on for them, and in ways that weren't all positive. Foster's had failed to spot this …Until 2010 when, strewth! – by changing the way beer brands talked to blokes, Foster's catapulted from third place to market leader.

With every £1 spent on advertising generating £32 of revenue, this is potentially the most effective beer campaign ever entered for an IPA award.

## 'The good-old Amber Nectar'

To many, Foster's is the quintessential Aussie lager. Created by the Foster brothers in Melbourne back in 1888, Foster's grew to become one of the most popular lager brands in Australia – with a premium image and price tag to match.

But the real success came when Foster's moved overseas. Imported into Britain in 1971, Foster's was the first Australian beer widely available here, and soon gained a cult following. Britain's Courage breweries were quick to spot the trend, and acquired a license to brew Foster's locally from 1981. But the real breakthrough came when they advertised their new brand.

Those were the halcyon days of British beer advertising, and Courage set the pace with award-winning campaigns for Courage Best, John Smith's Bitter and Hofmeister Lager.[1] But their 1980s ads for Foster's, featuring Australian comedian Paul Hogan, were perhaps their best. Hogan's irreverent, laid-back humour epitomised the likeable Aussie stereotype of the time, and connected brilliantly with British blokes. The highlight was the 'Ballet' spot, voted one of the most popular ads of the twentieth century[2] (Figure 1).

Affinity for the brand translated directly into sales, and Foster's was soon the most popular lager in Britain.

## Trouble brewing

Thanks to the Paul Hogan campaign, the 80s and 90s were a great time for Foster's. But sadly, in 2010, when our story begins, things were looking bleak.

For a start, the market was now shrinking. Recession, rising beer duty, and increased competition from wine, spirits and cider had all taken their toll. Beer sales were falling by 5% a year.[3]

Lager, the 'poster boy' of the beer category and biggest volume contributor, was suffering badly. Over six years from 2004 to 2010, lager volume dropped by 19%[4], which meant Britons were drinking 1.3 *billion* fewer pints a year – the equivalent of wiping out the top two lager brands combined (Figure 2).

## Figure 1: Foster's 'Ballet' featuring Paul Hogan

## Figure 2: The lager market was in decline

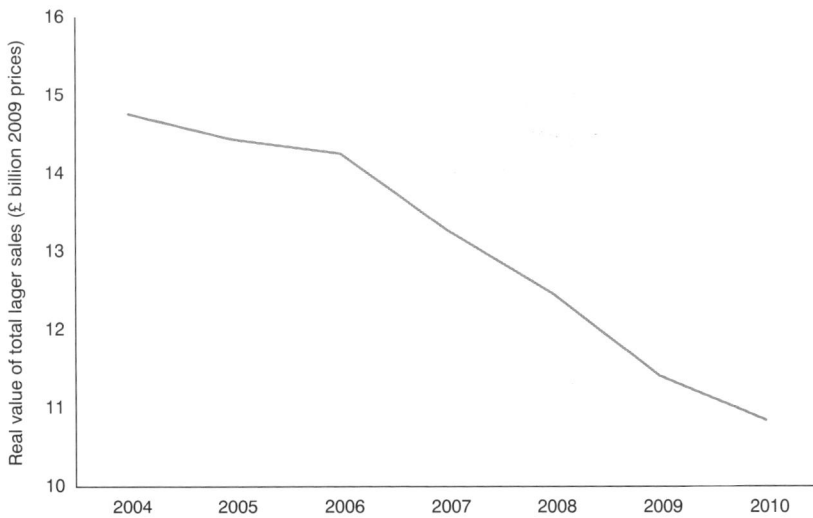

Source: Mintel

## Last orders in the on-trade

Traditionally the 'on-trade' had been the most important sales channel for beer brands, and like most of its rivals, Foster's always focused their business plans around the central role of pubs.

But in 2010, the pub trade was far from booming – due to higher taxes, smoking bans, an ageing population and a general trend towards in-home entertainment. As a result, between 2005 and 2008, 40% of all drinkers were visiting the pub less frequently, or *not at all*.[5] Then, recession hit, and between 2008 and 2010, on-trade volumes fell by more than 18%.[6]

Young blokes, the engine room of the lager category and Foster's core target, were deserting the pub, choosing to save money by drinking at home instead. In 2010, over half of Foster's core customers were regularly drinking at home.[7]

With 'locals' shutting at an alarming rate of 30 per week,[8] publicans looked to the breweries to cut costs and win back customers. It was a difficult situation for Foster's: either take a reduction in price in a shrinking market, or potentially lose distribution.

It became clear to Heineken (who had acquired Foster's in 2008) that a change in attitude needed to be adopted against what would be 'loss-leading' accounts. They walked away from several big pub contracts, leading to a substantial decrease in distribution in the on-trade.

The on-trade was becoming a less profitable channel, so in 2010, Heineken took the brave decision to broaden its focus and channel more energy into a new strategic battleground: the off-trade.

## The new battleground

Traditionally, the off-trade (shops that sell alcohol) had been of secondary importance. But the trend towards home consumption was changing all that. Now the off-trade was accounting for an ever-increasing proportion of volume that would soon be as big as the on-trade (Figure 3).

The off-trade had started to become more profitable too, with healthy margins now possible due to economies of scale. Off-licenses and supermarkets offered lucrative potential ... but it wasn't going to be a cakewalk.

## A brand in a bit of strife

Concentrating on the off-trade made strategic sense. But sadly, Foster's wasn't in the greatest shape to compete there. Recently, Foster's had been losing market share. Once the number one brand in the category, it had lost connection with drinkers, and with it, its number one position to Carling.

## Supermarkets with superpowers

Brand strength is vitally important when tackling the off-trade. For Foster's, any brand weakness would leave it painfully exposed there. Because lurking amidst the

## Figure 3: Off-trade share of the lager market

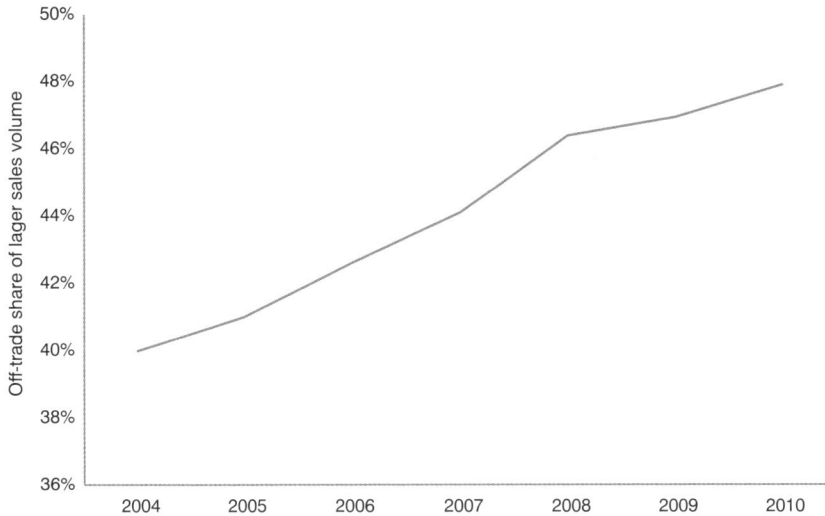

Source: Mintel

independent off-licenses were the big four supermarkets who wielded huge buying power – and influence.

A brutal judge of brand strength, supermarkets saw almost all the lager brands as substitutable, resulting in standard lager brands being cycled through a discount 'merry-go-round'. Volumes would receive a short-term uplift, but the long-term effect was an erosion of perceived brand value. Retailer 'price compression' was eroding off-trade margins for all mainstream lager brands, including Foster's. If Foster's couldn't build a more meaningful consumer connection, then the off-trade could offer no hope to the brand.

## A new focus for the business

In 2010, Heineken set a bold new course for the business.

■ The focus, now, was to dominate the *off-trade* without slashing prices vs the competition.

## Help was coming, but it was going to be a long wait

Within lager, there are two categories:

■ 'premium' lagers: with higher alcohol contents (over 4% ABV),[9] demanding higher prices;
■ 'standard' lagers: weaker and cheaper.

Foster's is a standard lager. This worked well in the 80s and 90s, but modern drinkers were now choosing stronger 'premium' beers, often imported from abroad.

In response, Heineken was working on a new premium lager with an ABV of 4.8% – Foster's Gold – to extend Foster's into new 'upmarket' drinking occasions.

But while Foster's Gold could help in the long term, it wouldn't be enough. Launch date wasn't until mid-2011, and projected sales were modest compared to Foster's core product. For the foreseeable future, Foster's would have to rely on the core product to be the driver of sales and profit.

## Getting strong in the core

However, the core was the problem. Once the powerhouse of the UK lager market, Foster's was now in a state of 'double jeopardy':

- it was losing share
- in a declining market.

By 2010, off-trade sales were falling at a rate of almost 8% a year[10] (Figure 4).

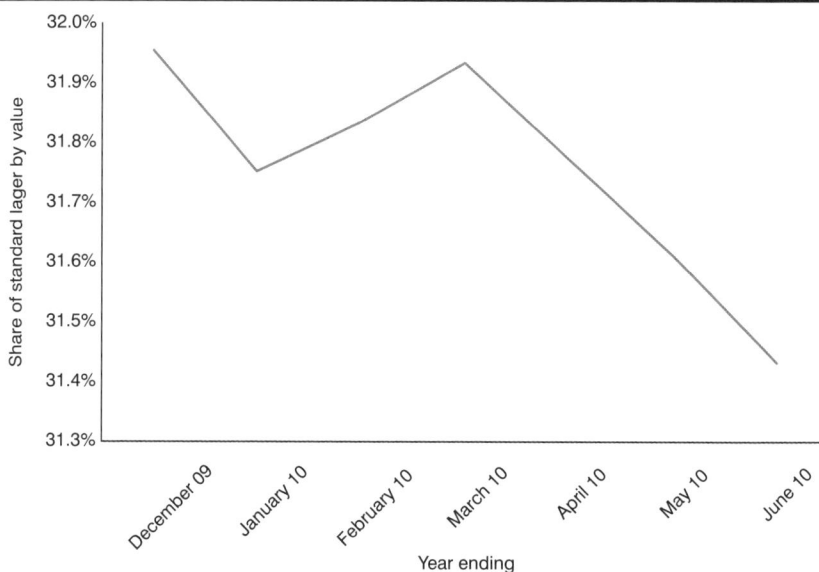

Figure 4: Foster's was losing market share

Source: IRI, off-trade

Turning this round wouldn't be easy, but Heineken believed in Foster's potential, setting tough new business objectives to restore it to number one, within two years.

## Business objectives

1. Make Foster's the number one volume brand of standard lager in the off-trade by 2012.
2. Pave the way for the successful launch of Foster's Gold in 2011 to deliver 160KHL[11] = 3.8% share of bottled lager by 2012.

## The role for advertising for Foster's

Rising beer duty and inflation would mean that Foster's would have to increase prices in order to maintain a profit margin. However, the IPA's own research has shown[12] that increasing both volume and price together is very tricky to pull off.

It can only be achieved through brand building – strong brands are less price sensitive, and require less discounting in order to drive sales volume (Figure 5):

### Figure 5: Brand building is the key to lower price sensitivity

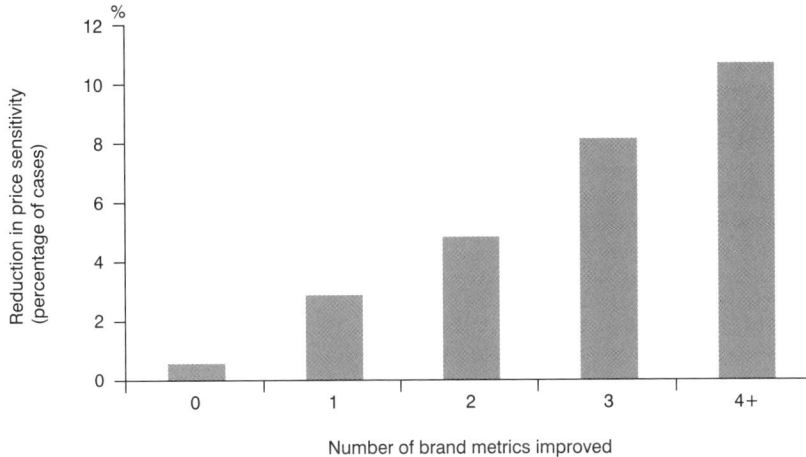

Source: Binet & Field 2013

The most important ingredient in this process is *emotional* bonding. If people really like a brand, they're willing to pay more for it.

Sadly, that's where Foster's was most in trouble. Back in its heyday, the Paul Hogan campaign had built huge emotional bonds with young UK blokes, allowing Foster's to dominate the market. However, since then, Foster's advertising had steadily lost this emotional connection (Figure 6).

Lager drinkers felt little connection to this brand now. Foster's communications had become as unmemorable as the rest of the category.

The communications challenge was clear:

- rebuild the emotional bond with lager drinkers
- so they would actively choose Foster's in retail outlets.

It was early 2010. Heineken knew they required a breakthrough creative solution, and they needed it urgently. Heading into the summer, with a football World Cup only 20 weeks away, a massive volume opportunity beckoned.

To get Foster's fighting fit and fast, Heineken called a pitch.

## Reconnecting with the young British blokes

In the 30 years since Foster's heyday, British blokes had changed – a lot. But curiously in the world of beer advertising no one seemed to have noticed. Back-slapping

Figure 6: Foster's 'Hitchhiker and the Tycoon?' TVC, from 1990, featuring Burt Lancaster and the 'Pass it on' tagline.

'Don't you just love it?' TVC 1992 with Paul Whitehouse, and 'Robot' TVC 2005 featuring the 'Think Australian, Drink Australian' tagline.

blokey 'pub-bravado' ruled still. Men were men. In-jokes, not insecurities, were the advertising order of the day.

adam&eve were invited to pitch, and began by looking more deeply at the core Foster's target – named by Heineken segmentation as the 'Tribal Drinker'. These men aged 18–34 were the type of blokes who lived for Friday and Saturday nights. Fuelled by banter and spontaneous fun, for these few precious hours, they could be with their mates and truly be themselves.

Over a series of weekends, the agency got up close and personal, witnessing the target's true behaviour in 'the wild'. The real breakthrough, though, came when they gave bartenders in the few pubs the target still frequented 'eavesdropping duties'. They listened in to the topics of conversation and kept a diary of what blokes were *really* talking about.

Watching young blokes 'at play' in pubs, they seemed superficially pretty happy with their lives. But from the eavesdropping of the publicans, and when they were talked to individually away from their friends, a very different picture emerged.

## Life as a bloke was getting tougher

Modern life wasn't easy for young blokes. They were at a point in their lives where they were facing many dilemmas: should they move out of home? How could they afford it? Should they get serious with a girlfriend? How could they compete with the sexual prowess they witnessed in pornography? How could they get more impressive abs? And what about performance at work?

## 'Troubled' drinkers

They seemed to be less *'Tribal Drinkers'* – and more accurately *'Troubled Drinkers'*. Laden with angst that they kept hidden from the rest of the world, their superficially larky get-togethers were actually a coping mechanism. Amidst the banter and fun of these occasions, mates were acting as both a support group and sounding board for how to deal with these issues. Critically, humour was an important part of how they helped soothe each other's insecurities and diffuse the awkwardness of them.

## Blokes were copping it

But no brands seemed to have noticed this. Young blokes[13] felt that no commercial portrayals of men were accurate, and that 'blokes were being beaten up' by both the media and marketing. They were stereotyped as either the bumbling boyfriend or the beer swigging party guy. And they didn't like it.

No brands really seemed to understand our target or the difficulties they were going through. And even fewer accurately reflected who they were.

Could Foster's be of help?

## Unlocking the emotional connection in 'Australian-ness' – our new strategy

The best beer advertising does one simple thing: it gives an emotional 'free sample' of the brand. adam&eve's new understanding of these men revealed a potential way in: could Foster's use its uniquely Australian personality to help soothe the insecurities of Troubled Drinkers?

## Australia was Paradise…lost

The 'ideal' that was Australia in Hogan times had lost its lustre for modern blokes. The tyranny of distance that had once kept the 'great southern land' shrouded in a glorious mystique was no longer a reality. The veil had been lifted; thousands of Brits had now experienced Australia for themselves. "Oz" was deserts, sharks, spiders. And Sydney's Cronulla riots showed Australians as dumb, drunk and racist – not surf gods. To top it all off, they weren't even better than us at cricket any more.

## But…

To our blokes the best part of Australia was still *the attitude* it had always 'exported': a laid-back, no-worries sense of positivity.

This attitude was still really compelling to them and was an Aussie equity that adam&eve felt Foster's could actively use to help bond with blokes again.

## You'll be a'right mate

If 'Troubled Drinkers' were using social drinking occasions to assuage their angst and issues, then *Foster's could help tackle the worries of young blokes with its 'no worries' attitude.*

It was a bold strategy that flew in the face of 'traditional' lager advertising. Where other brands play to men's bullet-proof bravado, Foster's was going to remind them of their vulnerability. But if it could be pulled off, this could rebuild the genuine emotional bond with 'Troubled Drinkers' that Foster's so desperately needed.

Teams were briefed and fingers were crossed (Figure 7).

### Figure 7: The Creative Brief

client: Heineken UK          first review: 17.2.2010
brief: Foster's Lager        client pres: 23.2.2010
date: 15.2.2010             Budget:      1m

adam
&eve

**Background**
Foster's, like all beer brands, is hurting especially hard right now. The brand has lost it's connection with young British drinkers and is losing share in a shrinking market.
**the problem:** people see all the brands in the Lager category as roughly the same. They buy whatever's on offer in the supermarket, rather than a brand they like.
our challenge: get people to choose Foster's, even when it's more expensive

**Target market:** Foster's drinkers are young men who live for the weekends. Being with their mates, having a few beers and taking a piss out of each other for a few hours is when they feel like they are on their best form, and it's the only time they feel they can truly be themselves.
**Insight:** Beneath the bravado, they are actually pretty worried. They are transitioning into a life stage where they have more responsibility and with this comes a variety of tricky social dilemmas.

what's it all about?

Foster's no-worries, optimistic outlook on life helps you
see the opportunities in an uptight world.

**RTB: Foster's is...**a brand with a refreshing Aussie attitude. that means it's funny, laid back, sociable, sunny and uncomplicated. it's about making the best of things. it's about living in the moment. it's about mates. it's about taking life as it comes. it's about finding comedy in the every-day. it's about finding it easy to have a laugh. it's not about being lazy or uncaring. it's not about being idiotic or crass. it's masculine without being macho or misogynistic.

One creative idea emerged that had huge potential. *Foster's would create a help-line to deliver a dose of 'Aussie positivity' to their mates over in the UK.*

Heineken agreed and awarded the pitch to adam&eve.

## The 'Good Call' campaign

The idea was to link Troubled Drinkers here in the UK to the 'Aussie paradise' that was the spiritual home of Foster's – via a pair of stereotypical Aussie larrikins, Brad and Dan. These two mates would, from their idyllic beachside hut, field calls from the UK and provide an agony uncle service – all in the spirit of mateship.

Through each piece of communication, Foster's would deliver a pint-sized dose of guidance and a positive, sunny solution to UK men's dilemmas.

The 'Good Call' campaign was born.

Importantly, the ads were made for real blokes. Rather than casting bronzed Aussie surf gods, two normal guys were chosen instead. This would help build the emotional connection Foster's needed (Figure 8).

Figure 8: Brisbane school friends and debating team-mates Tom Oakley and Luke Toohey were cast as Brad and Dan

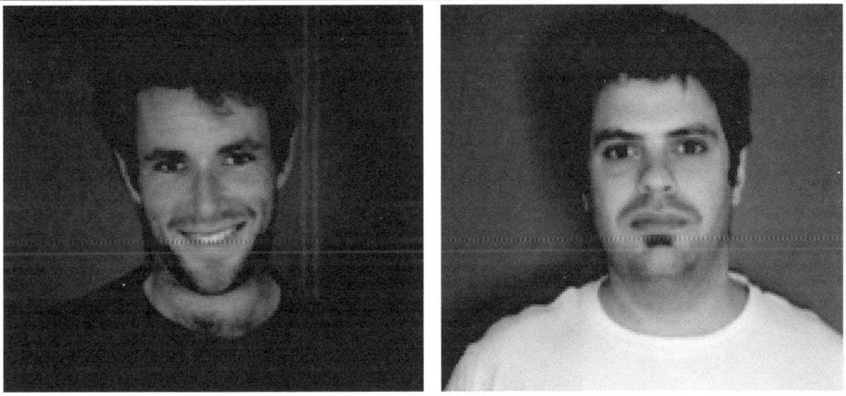

In the summer of 2010 the new campaign began.

Brad and Dan began their helpline to UK blokes via a series of three television commercials, posters, a website overhaul, a comedy sponsorship programme and a regular dilemmas column in *Shortlist* magazine.

Could two Aussie mates start to turn round the business in the UK?

There was a lot riding on it.

GOLD
GRAND
PRIX

# The first 'Good Calls'

## Figure 9: 2010 TV advertising – Girlfriend's mum

In this commercial we see Brad and Dan help a UK caller who is worried that his girlfriend is going to end up looking like her mum.

We open on the beach hut. The phone rings and is quickly answered. 'Hi, it's Ben from Southend', welcomed as 'Benno!' by the Aussie lads. Ben is at his girlfriend's parents' house for lunch.

Ben, slightly panicked, is set away from the table as food is being served, and discreetly whispers down the phone 'Is my girlfriend definitely definitely going to look like her mum?'.

Brad and Dan acknowledge the tricky and familiar guy dilemma. But they quickly reassure Ben with humorous advice to put a positive spin on the situation: 'Don't worry about the future, just enjoy the now'. Brad then follows up: 'Who knows, she [the girlfriend] might turn out to be a Vorderman!'

Notably calmer, Ben is elated with the advice, in particular the thought of Vorderman. His new enthusiasm and raised voice quickly returns to a hushed 'Thanks guys!' as he notices he's attracted the attention of the mother in question. The commercial ends with Foster's can and pint on the hut table and voiceover: 'Good call!'.

## Figure 10: 2010 TV advertising – Tattoo

In this commercial we see Brad and Dan help a UK caller wrestling with whether or not to get his girlfriend's name tattooed on him.

We open on an establishing shot of the beach, the phone rings and Brad and Dan quickly answer: 'Hi, it's Craig from Leicester', they reply: 'G'day Craig–o'.

Craig is outside at a smart back garden BBQ, stood on one side. He shares a dainty wave with his girfriend as he asks: 'I'm thinking of getting my girfriend's name tattoed on me, is that a good idea?'.

Dan asks: 'What's your girlfriend's name, Craig?', 'It's Trudy Holloway!', Dan recoils at the  name, but quickly replies with a uniquely Australian positive perspective. They advise caution with getting any 'tough sticker' as they are hard to rub off, as Brad reveals his 'Atomic Kitten' tattoo. They suggest using her nickname, which Craig reveals to be 'Peanut'.

Brad and Dan instead suggest Craig to get a tattoo of 'I love Peanut' – 'That way if, heaven forbid, you and the lovely Trudy do split you've just got a tattoo expressing your love for a delicious small, salted bar snack – and we all love peanuts!'. Craig is delighted with the solution and thanks our guys. The commercial ends with Foster's can and pint on the hut table and voiceover: 'Good call!'.

## Figure 11: 2010 TV advertising – Leaner

In this commercial we see Brad and Dan helping a UK caller who is having his personal space invaded.

We open on the beach, but this time Brad and Dan are sat out front with a barbie on the go. The phone rings and it's 'Tom from High Wycombe'. Brad and Dan greet him as 'Tommo!'

Tom is in the pub and quickly explains that his brother's mate stands too close when he talks. Brad and Dan are of course well versed in the problem: 'Ah, a space invader!'. Tom is flustered and explains the measures he's already taken to try and deter this 'leaner'.

Dan and Brad impart their usual wisdom, sharing the only and final solution to Tom's dilemma: 'You've got to become a shouter – just shout at him like he's in the next state'. We see Tom wince on the phone as Brad blares down the line as an example.

Tom is eternally grateful and seems set on his next course. The call ends and cuts back on Brad and Dan who share a quick exchange: 'Your uncle was a space invader' – 'Your auntie was a shouter'. The commercial ends with Foster's can and pint on the hut table and voiceover 'Good call!'..

# Weekly 'Good Calls'

**Figure 12: 2010 shortlist partnership**

A Shortlist partnership saw a weekly page dedicated to our new Foster's characters Brad and Dan, to answer and impart with more 'Good call' advice for real UK male dilemmas and write-ins to help further drive and reinforce the new Good Call campaign.

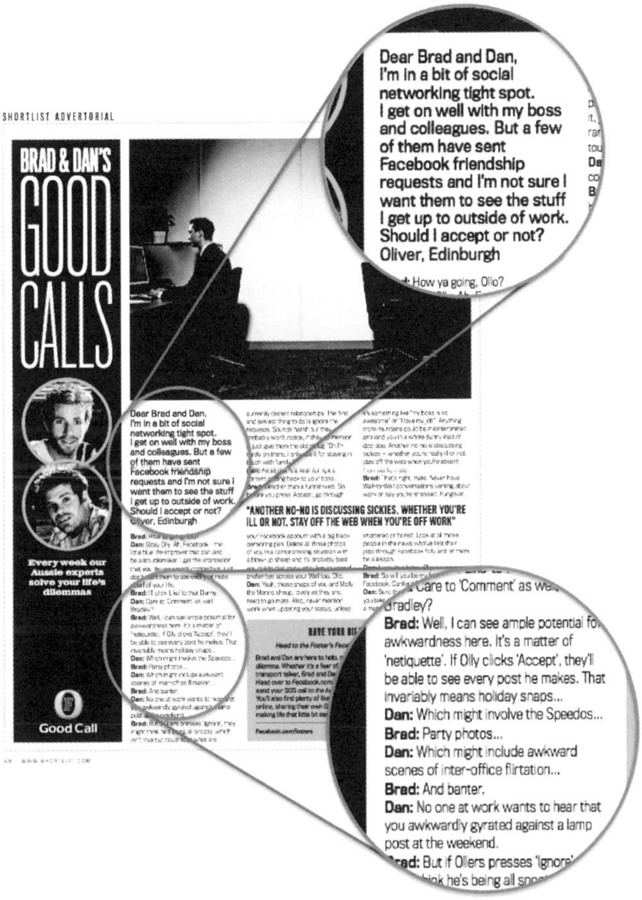

# From football to funny

adam&eve only began working with Foster's in April 2010 – a mere 16 weeks before the start of the football World Cup. As part of the pitch process, Foster's had made it clear that their intention was to have a new campaign in place just in time to slake the thirst of the football-mad British public.

Although watching football and drinking lager go hand in hand, Foster's would struggle to translate its new brand position into the world of football. Australia wasn't exactly well known for football, and against its key rivals of Carlsberg and Carling, Foster's had no credibility to be involved in the game.

Music and sport were the traditional arenas where beer brands had invested in sponsorships. However, these types of agreements are both costly and notoriously tricky to negotiate due to the amount of competition. Additionally, they rely upon an existing article to sponsor, such as a tournament, event or artist. Finding a match that perfectly suits the brand ideals is difficult and often leads to a compromise in some form. If Foster's were to create an alignment with a property, it would need to look elsewhere.

But there was another option – comedy. It presented a rare opportunity for sponsorship; few brands were associated with it, it gave permission for 'a drinking occasion' and it was an equity that the brand had strongly delivered against during its heyday.

In combination with the 'Good Call' campaign, Foster's began to associate itself with 'funny'. In the summer of 2010, Foster's became patrons of the long-standing Edinburgh Comedy Festival and sponsored a host of specialist comedy venues across the nation (Figure 13).

Figure 13: 2010 Foster's Edinburgh Comedy Awards winner Russell Kane phones his mum to tell her the news

Additionally, Foster's partnered with Channel 4 to provide 'idents' in and around comedy programming.

## Foster's = funny

In 2011, Foster's moved from sponsor to creator. Housed on the new 'FostersFunny. co.uk' website, original content from Alan Partridge, Reeves and Mortimer and The Fast Show debuted exclusively (Figure 14).

## The 'Good Call' centre

The concept of Foster's 'Good Call centre' began to take on a life of its own. Within months of the campaign launch, a Facebook petition appeared, urging Foster's to set

Figure 14: 2011 'Foster's Funny' website with bespoke content created for Foster's

up a real-life call centre. And in early 2011, they did just that. The Good Call centre was a digital experience that allowed fans to 'dob in a mate' with a dilemma, and get a tailor-made response sent back to them by Brad and Dan (Figures 15 and 16).

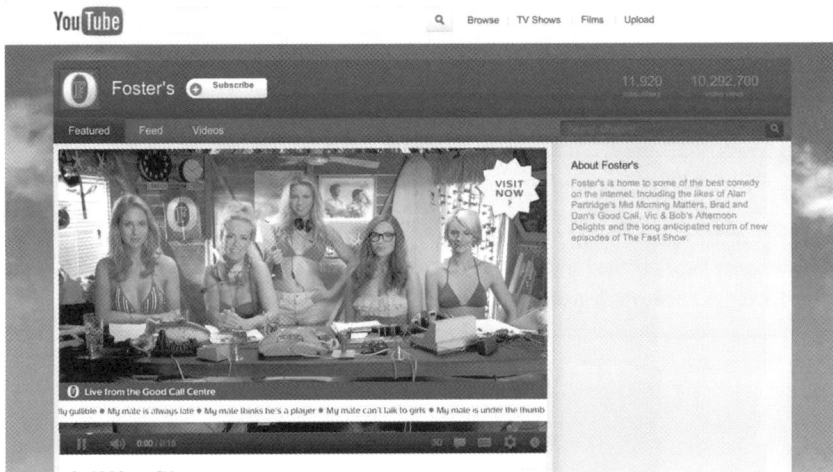

Figure 15: 'The Good Call centre' digital experience

## Figure 16: 2010 online experience – The Good Call centre

By popular demand, Foster's created and served their very own Good Call centre experience to tackle a variety of popular male dilemmas via an interactive online video. In turn, users could pick and choose a dilemma relevant to their mate, before sharing Brad and Dan's witty advice via social media channels.

The experience starts at a new beach hut with four Foster's girls, manning the lines of our make-shift switchboard. The hut is adorned with all types of decorative beach pieces, much like the main Foster's hut.

Each line represents a category for different male issues: Image / Girls / Ignorance / Personality. Depending on category choice, the relevant Foster's girl then reads out three 'man problems' to choose from. For example, under 'Imagery', the user could choose from 'my mate has rubbish dress sense / obsessed with pumping iron / has a bad haircut'.

Once picked, the user can type in his mate's name [Martin] – once confirmed, the girl on the line passes to another accomplice who in turn rushes the choice issue over to our famous Foster's beach hut. Brad and Dan await and depending on the choice of male issue, they serve the appropriate advice with a personalised greeting – 'G'day Marto!'.

The experience plays out Brad and Dan's quick-witted advice, at any time offering to share on that mate's Facebook page, which in turn is viewed and interacted with by others.

## A campaign with flexibility

Brad and Dan had provided a new, likeable face for the Foster's brand, and in 'Good Call', they had also found a creative idea with great flexibility. The boys were adaptable enough to use for the launch of Foster's Gold in 2011.

And they even travelled back in time to 1888 to reinforce the brand's historical credentials too (Figure 17).

Figure 17: '1888' TVC from 2011 featuring Brad and Dan as William and Ralph Foster

In total, Brad and Dan have appeared in some guise or another in a total of 23 ads.

## Media

The Good Call campaign began in May 2010 and has run for four years (Figure 18 and Table 1).

Figure 18: Media plan

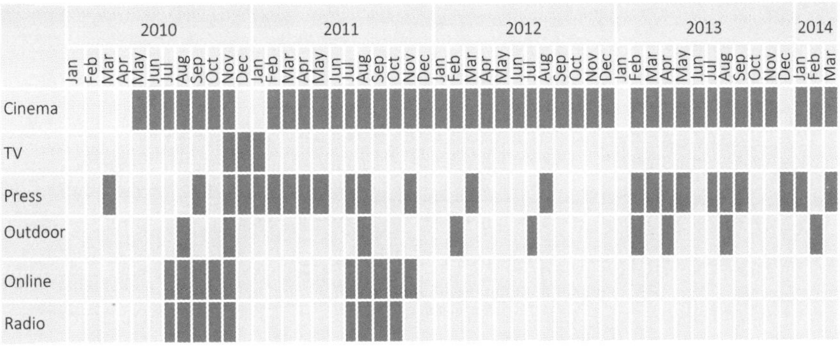

Source: Nielsen Ad Dynamix

| Table 1: Foster's ad spend by year | | | | |
|---|---|---|---|---|
| Ad-Spend | 2010 | 2011 | 2012 | 2013 |
| TV | £4,649,053 | £6,817,948 | £5,195,806 | £4,936,561 |
| Cinema | £456,114 | £104,091 | £0 | £0 |
| Press | £126,786 | £215,160 | £16,933 | £910,980 |
| Outdoor | £234,539 | £586,341 | £1,861,118 | £1,673,885 |
| Online | £127 | £232,542 | £0 | £0 |
| Radio | £24,195 | £3,079 | £0 | £0 |
| Total | £5,490,814 | £7,959,161 | £7,073,857 | £7,521,426 |

Source: Nielsen Ad Dynamix

## The results were ripper...

In 'Good Call', Foster's had developed a campaign that finally connected again with young UK blokes, addressing their insecurities in a way that they loved. And it paid off brilliantly on the shelves of retailers too.

## Pommie blokes loved the new campaign

The idea immediately got the attention of Foster's target audience. Communications awareness increased dramatically as soon as the new campaign went on air, and Foster's has been the best-known lager campaign in Britain ever since[14] (Figure 19).

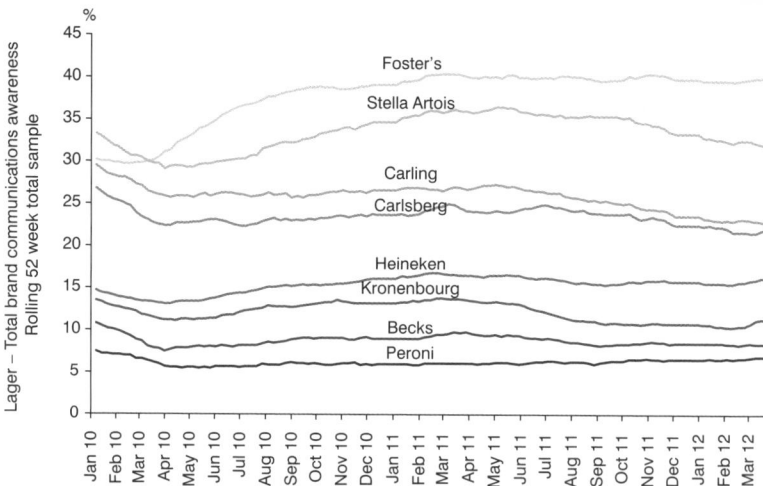

Figure 19: Lager total brand communications awareness (%)

Source: Millward Brown (no comparable data for 2013). Base: bought long alcoholic drinks last seven days

And it was clear that the idea was immediately loved too[15] (Figure 20):

## Figure 20: Tweets to @FostersUK in response to the campaign

Even the blokes who didn't like beer liked the ads (Figure 21)!

## Figure 21: Tweet to @FostersUK in response to the campaign from a non beer-drinker

Foster's began to be voted the best advertising in the category. As the campaign went on, Foster's started to leave their rivals far behind (Figure 22).

## Figure 22: Brands that have good advertising

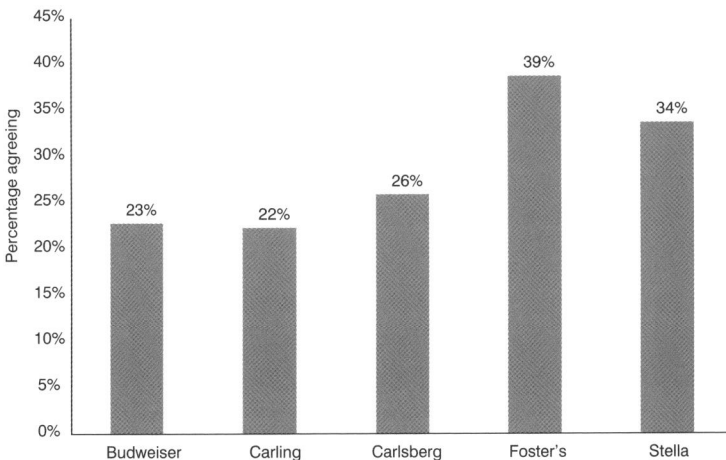

Source: Millward Brown 12 months ending April 2012 (no comparable data for 2013). Base: bought long alcoholic drinks last seven days

29

## Another round please mate

Punters were eager to get more of it online. The number of people searching for the brand doubled (Figure 23).

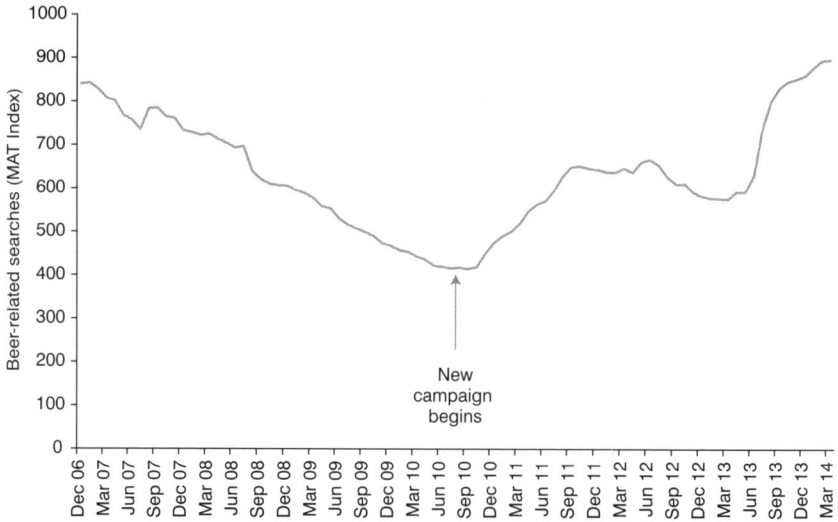

Figure 23: Google searches for Foster's

Source: Google Trends

And search for the ads on YouTube grew by 700% (Figure 24).

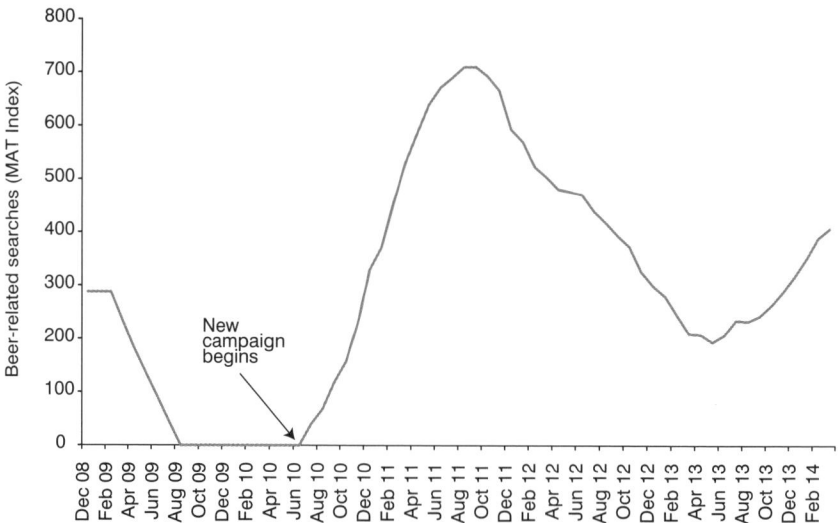

Figure 24: YouTube searches for Foster's

Sourcce: Google Trends

The Good Call website also received over 600,000 unique views, with 232,000 interactions to send a response to a friend.

## Comedy went off like a frog in a sock

Sponsorship deals often feel a bit forced, with no natural link between brand and content. But the Foster's comedy sponsorship was a marriage made in heaven. People had no trouble linking the humour in the Foster's ads to the comedy programmes they were watching. And as the campaign wore on, association between Foster's and comedy got stronger and stronger (Figure 25).

Figure 25: Five brands that you associate with comedy

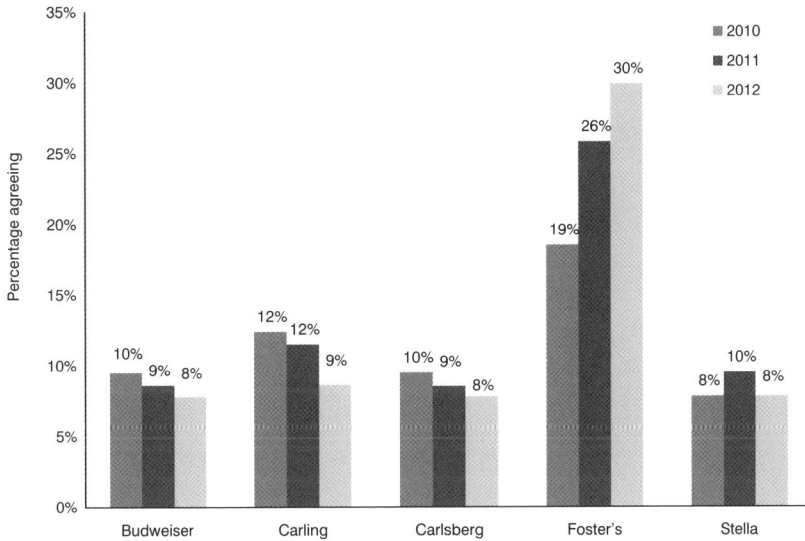

Source: Millward Brown (no comparable data for 2013). Base: bought long alcoholic drinks last seven days

## Much-needed brand refreshment

Prior to 'Good Call', Foster's had begun to look tired and out-of-date. But the new campaign changed all that. Now the brand seemed much more modern and popular (Table 2).

Table 2: Quality perceptions and appeal improved – Change in brand image scores 2012 vs 2010

| | Foster's | Carling | Carlsberg | Stella | Budweiser |
|---|---|---|---|---|---|
| A brand that is setting the trends | +25 % | −5% | +6 % | +3% | −3% |
| An up to date brand | +19 % | −2% | −1% | 0% | +1% |
| Most popular brand | +16 % | −11% | −2% | −7% | +13 % |
| Getting more popular nowadays | +28 % | +9 % | +5% | +5% | +9 % |

Source: Millward Brown (no comparable data for 2013). Base: bought long alcoholic drinks last seven days

And this had a halo effect on quality perceptions, which improved significantly, even though the product was the same as ever. As a result, people found Foster's more appealing, which would allow the brand to support the price rises that would be needed to protect margins from rising duty and inflation (Table 3).

| Table 3: Foster's seemed more modern and popular – Change in brand image scores 2012 vs 2010 | | | | | |
|---|---|---|---|---|---|
| | Foster's | Carling | Carlsberg | Stella | Budweiser |
| Higher quality than other brands | +21% | +13% | 2% | −7% | +1% |
| Higher opinion of than other brands | +11% | +9% | −1% | −5% | 0% |
| Appeal to you more than other brands | +6% | 0% | −1% | −3% | −2% |

Source: Millward Brown (no comparable data for 2013). Base: bought long alcoholic drinks last seven days

## More tinnies sold

Blokes were lapping up the ads, but most importantly, they were lapping up Foster's lager too. As soon as the ads ran, sales rose, and they have continued to do so (Figure 26).

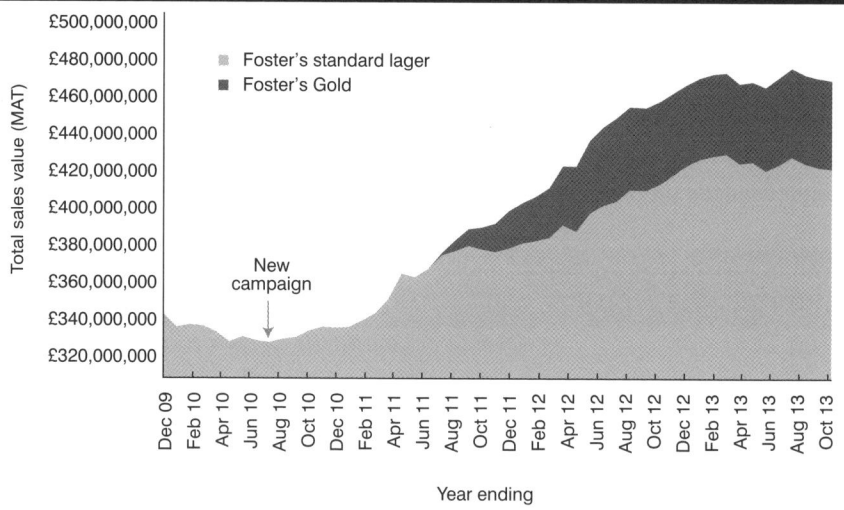

Figure 26: Sales increased as soon as the ads went on air

Source: IRI, total off-trade

As planned, the bulk of the extra sales came from the standard product, although the launch of Foster's Gold added extra impetus from the second year of the campaign.

This was an impressive feat, given that the market was still shrinking. In fact, Foster's was the *only* standard lager to increase sales during this period (Table 4).

| Table 4: Sales growth 2009–2013 | | |
|---|---|---|
| | Change in sales value | Change in sales volume |
| Foster's | +20% | +7% |
| Carling | –1% | –13% |
| Carlsberg | –3% | –4% |
| Stella 4% | –24% | –34% |
| Total market | +3% | –9% |

Source: IRI, standard lagers off-trade

And increasing volume in a declining market is even more impressive when you consider that Foster's was more expensive than other standard lagers throughout the duration of the campaign (Figure 27).

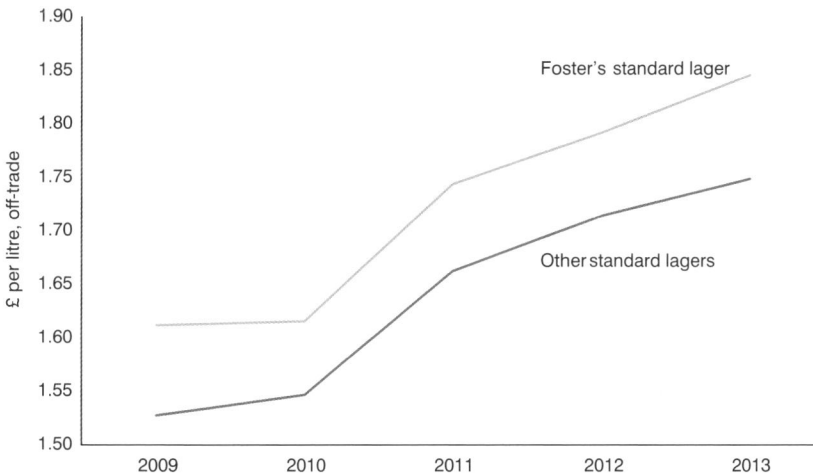

Figure 27: Average price per litre, standard lager, off-trade

Source: IRI, off-trade

## Onya Foster's. Job done!

In the three years after 'Good Call' began in 2010, Foster's grew from third place in the off-trade, to an outright number one in both volume *and* value (Figure 28).

## Figure 28: Foster's is now the no.1 brand

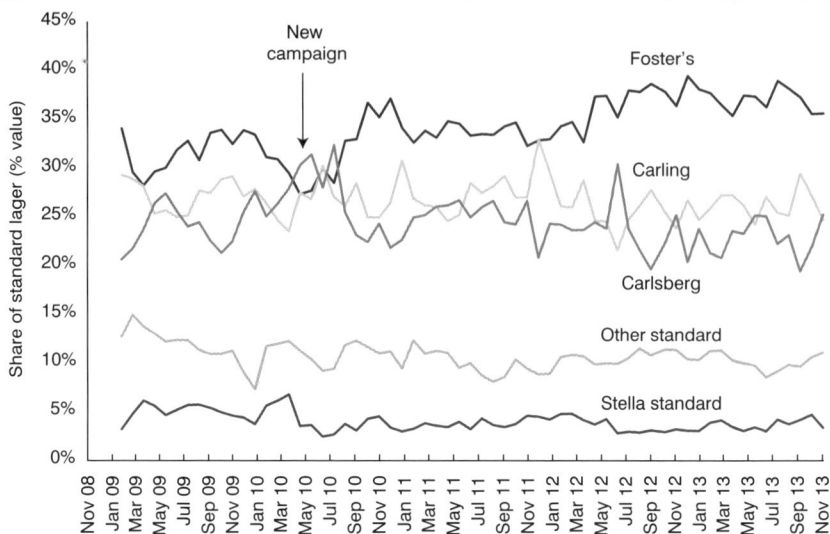

Source: IRI, total off-trade

This was achieved without extra discounting. In fact, average price paid had *increased* 14%.

And 'Good Call' also paved the way for a successful launch of Gold. By April 2012, Gold had secured share of 5.5%, smashing the target of 3.8%.

All our targets had been met.

## Fair dinkum ads that worked their socks off

In order to quantify the effect of their marketing activity for Foster's, Heineken recently commissioned a major econometric analysis from consultancy Holmes and Cook. This shows that advertising has been the main force driving off-trade sales of standard lager since 2010, accounting for nearly 70% of the growth. The launch of Foster's Gold accounts for most of the remainder (Figure 29).

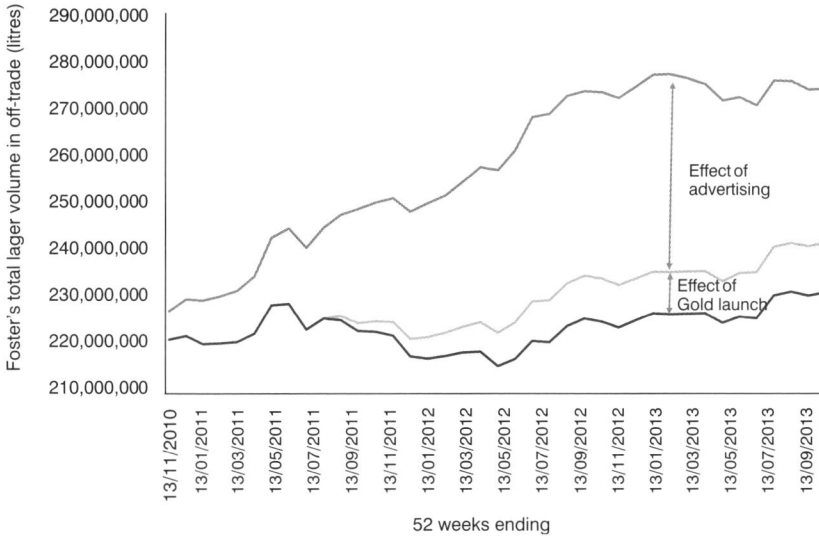

Figure 29: The effect of advertising (total off-trade)

Source: Holmes and Cook econometrics (off-trade)

## Did other factors help?

The 'Good Call' campaign has clearly revitalised the brand. But were there other factors at play? Let's look at the likely suspects.

### It wasn't the market

As shown above, the market continued to shrink during the period of the campaign, depressing the sales of all standard lagers *except* Foster's.

### It wasn't the product

The launch of Foster's Gold helped from 2011 onwards, but sales started rising over a year before that. The bulk of the extra sales came from the standard product, which was unchanged.

### It wasn't distribution

Foster's didn't go into any new shops – in fact, brand distribution fell very slightly, and the range of products on the shelf contracted slightly too (Figure 30).

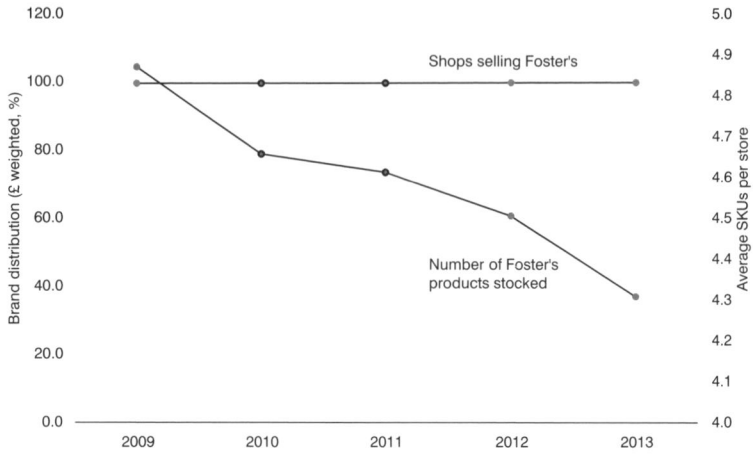

Figure 30: Distribution of Foster's standard lager

Source: IRI, major mults

## It wasn't price cuts or promotions

Price promotions play a big role in the off-trade, and they are an important tool in Foster's armory. But they cannot explain Foster's volume growth since 2010, because prices *increased* during this period, both in absolute terms and relative to the competition (Table 5).

### Table 5: Growth was not achieved by discounting

|  | 2010 | 2011 | 2012 | 2013 |
|---|---|---|---|---|
| Avg. price paid for Foster's standard lager | £1.62 | £1.74 | £1.79 | £1.85 |
| Avg. price paid for other standard lagers | £1.55 | £1.66 | £1.71 | £1.75 |
| Difference | £0.07 | £0.08 | £0.08 | £0.10 |
| Difference in percentage | 4% | 5% | 5% | 6% |

Source: IRI, standard lager, off-trade

In fact, econometrics has shown that changes to prices and promotions have actually *reduced* volume growth (although as intended, higher prices have helped maintain margins), as shown in Table 6.

### Table 6: Rising prices have slowed volume growth

|  | Actual growth achieved | Growth assuming price and promotions fixed |
|---|---|---|
| Total Foster's volume growth, 2010–2013 | +22% | +46% |

Source: Holmes and Cook econometrics, off-trade

*There wasn't less competition*

Competition was as tough as ever, and none of Foster's rivals was de-listed or withdrawn from the market.

*It wasn't just a matter of spend*

Ad spend has varied from year to year, but overall, Foster's share of voice has remained fairly constant (Table 7).

| | Foster's annual ad spend | Other lager brands ad spend | Foster's share of voice |
|---|---|---|---|
| **Table 7: Share of voice remained constant** | | | |
| Pre 'Good Call' 2009 | £7.2m | £46.8m | 15% |
| Post 'Good Call' 2010–2013 | £7.0m | £46.0m | 15% |

Source: Nielsen Ad Dynamix

## A very profitable investment

Econometrics shows that advertising has been the biggest single factor driving the growth of Foster's since 2010. And Holmes and Cook's models also allow us to quantify payback. Overall, they show that every £1 spent on advertising since 2010 has generated £32 in sales revenue.[16] Heineken cannot disclose their profit margins, but they assure us that this is more than enough to be profitable. In fact, a comparison with other IPA papers suggests that this is potentially one of the most effective beer campaigns ever entered for the IPA Awards (Table 8).

| Beer brand | IPA Year | Revenue generated per £ spent |
|---|---|---|
| **Table 8: Comparison with other IPA winners** | | |
| Foster's | 2014 | £32 |
| Stella Artois | 2000 | £12 |
| Budweiser | 2002 | £6 |
| Bud Ice | 1998 | £5 |
| Stella Artois | 1996 | £5 |
| Marston's Pedigree | 1994 | £4 |
| Stella Artois | 1992 | £2 |

## Conclusion: 'Good Call' let British blokes know that a 'no-worries' Aussie brand really understood them

Not all emotional advertising has to make you cry to get you to buy.

Breaking the mould of traditional beer advertising with the help of some sun-drenched, laid-back Aussie humour, re-established a powerful connection between a new generation of pommie drinkers and a brand old enough to be their dad.

It was a brave move. But it put a fair-dinkum brand right back on the map for British blokes.

## Notes

1   See for example our previous IPA papers for John Smith's (1982, 1984) and Hofmeister (1984).
2   Channel 4, '100 Greatest TV Ads' poll (April 2000).
3   Real sales value, 2006 to 2010. Source: Mintel.
4   Source: Mintel.
5   Source: BBPA study 2011.
6   Source: Mintel Beer in the UK report 2013.
7   Source: Mintel Drinking in the home report June 2013.
8   Source: BBPA statement 30/9/2010.
9   ABV = Alcohol by Volume.
10   Annualised volume decline, year to June 2010. Source: IRI.
11   KHL = Thousand hectoliters.
12   'The Long and the Short of It' by Les Binet and Peter Field, IPA 2013.
13   Source: Askmen.co.uk great male survey 2009 – 67% indicated no portrayals of men were accurate.
14   Millward Brown tracking is only available up to 2012, as Heineken switched to a new data provider.
15   Source: Twitter.
16   Source: Holmes and Cook econometrics, revenue-based ROI, on- and off-trade combined.

# ITV

## Brand revitalisation: winning back the hearts of the nation

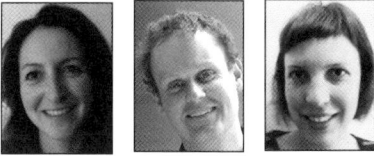

**By Clare Phillips, Rufus Radcliffe and Elinor Bateman, ITV**

In 2012, like all terrestrial channels, ITV was losing market share as digital channels entered the market. It was awash in viewing performance data and, while it understood what its audiences had watched the night before, it didn't know what role the channel brand played in their viewing decision-making or how they felt about the brand. Research showed it was seen as overly commercial, too focused on entertainment and not a beacon of quality.

Despite ITV broadcasting many popular and loved shows, its audiences felt little for the ITV brand. Whilst 90% of UK viewers watched ITV every month, a staggering one third thought that 'ITV didn't have anything for them'. This meant that the brand was a barrier to watching; it was harder to launch new shows, it wasn't getting the credit for the shows and viewers didn't routinely consider watching.

These low expectations were a real problem, so in January 2013 it relaunched its brand in a comprehensive manner. A powerful thought to underpin the new brand was needed: an idea the entire organisation could get behind. Audience immersion sessions told it that, at its best, ITV tells stories viewers all care about so it defined ITV's position as 'The Heart of Popular Culture'.

The broadcaster's challenge was to persuade the nation to fall back in love with it by turning viewers and customers into fans. Brand driver analysis proved that genre advertising paid back more to the brand than single titles, because they communicated 'range' as well as delivering on 'something for me'. This was an approach undertaken, and during 2013 it developed campaigns for drama, factual, comedy, entertainment and news.

It also developed a new tone of voice – one that was human, warm, modern and welcoming. There was more non-TV activity. Posters and cinema acted as 'flares' communicating quality. Its logo was redesigned and a new brand architecture was created. On social media, it unplugged the computer that had been announcing programme times replacing it with a human team who shared in the emotions of its programmes alongside its audiences, speaking as fans to fans.

On 14 January 2013 the new identity, including new channel identities, programme end boards and ITV office branding across the world, was unveiled. It wasn't a cosmetic change that ITV underwent, it was a cultural shift in ITV's relationship with its audiences – viewers, customers and advertisers. To demonstrate this change to its advertisers, it shared the new identity with its key media agencies and clients at the 2012 'Upfronts' in time for 2013 trading, but months before unveiling to the public.

The revitalisation of ITV was extraordinarily successful and the impact almost immediate. Audiences loved the new brand – nearly three-quarters of the nation were aware of the logo five weeks in, it's now at 98%. Love for the brand rose nearly 40%, overtaking its commercial broadcast rival C4. Critically, people agreeing that 'ITV does nothing for me' halved from 30% to 15%, while spontaneous consideration for ITV increased by 13% from 52% to 59%. In 2013, ITV main channel share increased for the first time in 20 years, while BARB analysis showed that 15.4 million ITV medium viewers watched one more minute (+4%) of ITV every day in 2013. This equated to the one more programme a month ITV had aimed for.

The brand revitalisation also created dramatic improvements amongst its clients and advertisers. In 2013, ITV delivered 370 brand new advertisers to TV, a growth of 35% year on year. ITV spot advertising grew by £52 million (+3%) and non-spot advertising by 14.6 million (14%). The share price rose 74% over the year, out-performing the FSTE 100 six times and FTSEurofirst Media, three times.

# Premier Inn

## Changing the face of budget hotels

**By Jeremy Poole, RKCR/Y&R**
Contributing authors: Eleanor Grant, RKCR/Y&R

In 2007 branded budget hotels had become a commodity market, with consumer choice driven by two functional factors of location and price. For Whitbread to achieve profitable, sustainable growth with Premier Travel Inn, it needed to overcome the following challenges:

- build awareness of the brand;
- raise expectations of the brand and improve perceptions of value for money;
- broaden relevance for a greater number of people;
- widen its suitability for a greater number of occasions.

Premier Travel Inn wasn't going to be a destination hotel, but it could still promise customers something powerful and emotive: the perfect ending to their action-packed day, or the perfect start to their busy day ahead.

With this simple promise established at the heart of the brand, the task was to design a superior experience around it that would totally change people's expectations of budget hotels. What would be created was a new kind of budget hotel: a premium budget hotel.

Additionally a new identity and brand name were established and a commitment to using communications to boost the Premier Inn brand was decided on.

In 2008/09, the first role for communications was to introduce the Premier Inn brand. Launch advertising focused on rational points of product superiority, underpinned by a reassurance on price, summed up in the strapline 'Everything's Premier but the Price'.

These points of difference were highlighted by Lenny Henry. Lenny was the perfect choice for the role. He brought celebrity sparkle to the brand, making it feel like a serious player in the market, as well as a sense of warmth, accessibility and familiarity.

In 2010/11, following the financial crisis, Premier Inn recognised that consumers were adapting their travel habits, taking more breaks in the UK and trading down to lower-cost hotels. The role for communications at this point was to encourage people to opt for the consistent quality offered by Premier Inn rather than risk a poor experience at another hotel.

A further phase of activity – 2011–13 – set out to make Premier Inn top of mind when planning a night away from home, using the emotive promise of a good night's sleep guaranteed. Communications brought to life recognisable moments when people would be in need of a good night's sleep and asserted that, at those moments, they could always rely on a Premier Inn.

In order to reframe expectations of the brand and improve value perceptions, it needed to use communications to actively influence consumers at the point when their perceptions of hotel brands were being formed. This meant communicating further upstream in the decision-making process. TV was the perfect channel to do this and has been the lead medium throughout the campaign.

The advertising broke in March 2008 and immediately generated cut-through, salience and created a sense of positive energy around the brand. There was positive endorsement of the choice of Lenny as brand spokesperson, indicating he brought the right sort of values to the brand. By early 2009, there was qualitative evidence of some distance between Premier Inn and other budget hotels and signs that quality perceptions had shifted.

Tracking shows the advertising has out-performed competitors in budget and mid-market (Hilton and Marriott) sectors. Premier Inn has achieved a shift in emotional resonance, with a stronger, closer brand connection than any other major national hotel brand.

The changes in brand perception that have been outlined are reflected in the shift in brand preference, from a distant competitor in 2007 to Britain's number one brand for leisure and number two for business. Overall Premier Inn is the first or second choice for more hotel users than any other brand.

# Cuprinol

## Cheer it up! How Cuprinol added colour and value to the garden woodcare category

**By Rob Ward, 18 Feet & Rising**
Contributing authors: Kathryn Ledson, AkzoNobel; Sara Donoghugh, Pearl Metrics; Mark Woor, AkzoNobel

In 2012 garden woodcare was dominated by a high-volume, low-value segment – water-based fence treatment. Cuprinol products were significantly more expensive than Ronseal and Own Label, which aggressively traded share points through deep and frequent price promotions. Yet in the eyes of consumers, there was little differentiation between the leading brands Cuprinol and Ronseal.

This lack of perceived differentiation in the category made consumers more willing to opt for cheaper Own Label alternatives. Especially as both B&Q and Homebase were such well-established DIY brands.

Against a backdrop of low consumer interest, commoditisation, aggressive credible competitors and appalling weather, Cuprinol was struggling to maintain a price premium and had been losing volume and value share. The challenge was how to drive value and engagement back into the category, justifying Cuprinol's premium price position and ultimately achieving a value target growth of 8.8% for the brand in 2013.

For over a decade, Garden Shades had been a sleeping giant: a product that not only protected wood, but coloured it, allowing consumers to decorate the wood in their garden. Despite achieving 100% distribution, awareness was low (in 2012, 28% prompted for Garden Shades versus 77% for Cuprinol). Cuprinol believed that, with the right communications support, 2013 was the year to unlock the potential of the dormant Garden Shades to revitalise the brand and the category. It had the potential to shift consumer perceptions of garden woodcare, but there were three key tasks it needed to address: engage a new audience; reposition the brand; and stand out creatively.

It targeted female influencers as its new audience. The garden was increasingly seen as another room that can be decorated – a space to feel proud of and show off when guests come round for a BBQ. And females expressed more pride and emotional attachment to their gardens and wanted to experiment with the look of them.

It repositioned the brand with a platform called 'Cheer it Up!' – one that could integrate all marketing channels: packaging, point of sale, website, social, PR and above the line.

Given the small budget, it needed a creative idea that would generate disproportionate buzz for a brand and category that is rarely talked about. Cuprinol's British heritage and eccentric personality were good foundations from which to build. The answer was a sad, unloved crying shed that was cheered up.

With a total media budget of only £1.1 million, repositioning the brand and category was going to be a challenge. In line with industry best practice it chose a combination of TV and digital. TV for its emotional power and brand-building potential, and digital for activation.

It needed consumers to feel differently about the brand and category, hence using the emotive qualities of TV, and it needed digital to give consumers a little nudge. Research had revealed that whilst this new positioning had the potential to inspire, some consumers required a little nudge to change their behaviour, so there was a large focus on digital messaging to promote buying 3 testers for £1.

Results justified the investment. Brand awareness rose, particularly amongst its female target, helped by a strong social buzz unprecedented for Cuprinol advertising. Consideration rose by 15 percentage points to 72, closing the gap with Ronseal. Cuprinol's advertising emotionally engaged and prompted into action a new female audience willing to pay a premium to be part of the burgeoning 'garden inspiration' trend. Consequently, it managed to achieve a value growth of 23.1%, smashing its target of 8.8%, while payback was an impressive £3.20 incremental profit for every £1 spent on communications.

# Garnier UltraLift

## The Garnier UltraLift challenge: swapping lab coats and jargon for tangible proof

**By Ant Harris and Tony Quinn, Publicis London**
Contributing author: Vasileios Kourakis, L'Oréal

In the late noughties, the anti-ageing category hit crisis point. With more and more anti-ageing products launching, professing miracle cures and magic ingredients, the language of science lost its impact. In 2009, Garnier UltraLift was struggling to overcome public doubts, with 57% of women believing that anti-wrinkle cream claims were 'overhyped'. Much of the suspicion stemmed from the BBC's 2007 *Horizon* story, which implied most anti-ageing creams didn't work. As a result between 2007 and 2010 volume sales of UltraLift fell by 30%.

Thus Garnier's major challenge was how to communicate the effectiveness of UltraLift in a way people would actually listen to – before it was too late for the brand. They had to: stem the dramatic decline in volume and value sales of the entire UltraLift range; communicate the fact that UltraLift actually works, in a way that a sceptical public are actually prepared to take note of and act on; drive positive sentiment and word-of-mouth recommendation in a category surrounded by scepticism.

The brand knew UltraLift worked and it had the clinical results to prove it. But consumers in research said that they pay little attention to clinical results – especially in ads paid for by cosmetics companies. So Garnier had to find a way to show, not tell. They had to provide tangible real-world results. Most people didn't know that the effects of anti-wrinkle cream do not show until after 14 days of product usage. They'd use it for a few days, feel that it's not working, and become disillusioned. Thus Garnier's brief was to find a way of getting people to see and feel the full 14-day benefits of the product for themselves, as tangibly and as physically as possible.

The campaign became known as the UltraLift challenge and the brand encouraged people to put the product to the test for 14 days, to deliver a verdict on it, and then to use their comments and verdicts to drive the conversation forward and spark further trial. Because the changes take place gradually and one wouldn't notice much difference from one day to the next, it needed a way to make it easy to compare Day 1 with Day 14. The comparison mechanism was a deceptively simple, super-low-tech device called 'The Wrinkle Reader'. Its very simplicity and physicality was a perfect antidote to the suspicious 'over-sophistication' that had generated such consumer scepticism in the first place.

The trial phase took place in June and July 2011. It was the largest self-selecting trial Garnier had ever attempted. TV, online advertising, PR, and CRM activity drove people to the UltraLift homepage where they could order a free sample kit and Wrinkle Reader. The trial phase delivered exactly the kind of recommendations Garnier was looking for. It meant that when the results phase of the campaign went live in November, Garnier was able to put real consumers who had experienced the positive effects of UltraLift at the heart of the campaign. They were happy to share their discovery with other women, and talked with such enthusiasm for the product that the campaign felt genuine and thus persuasive. TV and print were used to showcase their views, the most believable evidence to the target with all the footage in the commercials unscripted, natural, and believable.

The results were remarkable and reversed UltraLift's sales decline. It was a campaign that more than paid for itself, with a revenue ROMI of £1.91 for every pound spent. Phase 1 of the campaign introduced the sample kit and Wrinkle Reader: 239,000 sample kits were requested, (of that 171,000 of the trial participants were new to the Garnier database) and 80% said that they had seen visible results. Phase 2 of the campaign drove positive sentiment and significant uplifts in perceptions of UltraLift having believable claims, the best anti-ageing benefits and products that were scientifically proven to work. Eighteen months into the UltraLift challenge, unit sales were 40% higher than before the campaign began.

# SECTION 2

# Behavioural economics

# Framing and re-framing, nudges big and small: effectiveness and behavioural economics in modern advertising

**By Nick Southgate**
Behavioural Economics Consultant

## Introduction

IPA member agencies have always been choice architects. Agencies always knew that not all ways of communicating the same information are created equal. Behavioural economics offers an academically rigorous account of why the effects campaigns draw upon are real and powerful and run far beyond just creating awareness and information.

A better understanding of these effects allows us to look for more ways of applying them. You can simplify the process by applying two broad behavioural economics principles.[1] First, people think in comparisons instead of judging absolute values (e.g. it is easier to know one thing is longer than another than to know either thing's actual length). Second, any effort, however small, can influence a decision (e.g. when people can't find something in a shop they often prefer to leave empty-handed than make the effort of asking for help).

The importance of comparisons and efforts when understood through a behavioural economics lens leads to powerful campaigns. The evidence for this is now accumulating in the IPA Effectiveness Awards Database. The 2014 crop adds several useful and illuminating case studies to that list.

## Clarity of purpose and quality of data

As Binet & Field have shown, campaigns that have behaviour as a hard target are more effective than those that target soft interim or proxy measures.[2] This should be no surprise. Businesses ultimately profit only when people *do* something. Identifying this behaviour gives campaigns greater clarity of purpose. Behavioural economics' focus on behavioural outcomes encourages this clarity.

The London 2012 TfL paper demonstrates this clarity well. It shows the shift from a simple information campaign to a multi-layered, multi-touchpoint behavioural intervention. It is precisely and exhaustively aware of what was required of Londoners to change their travel behaviour and help the 2012 Olympics be a success.

It is also exemplary in pulling apart actual and claimed behaviour in its analysis. Such rigour is not new to IPA papers. However, as the TfL paper shows, a digital age provides new sources of data based on actual behaviour, where previously measures of claimed or intended behaviour would have to have been relied upon (in this case, Oystercard data provides actual journey details). Such data was unimaginable when the first IPA papers were written, whereas now the technical possibilities of data will only grow while the costs involved in collecting it fall. IPA papers will adapt to take advantage of this and further strengthen the logical and evidential link between campaigns and final outcomes.

## The rediscovery of positioning

The original arguments for positioning were made as long ago as the early 1970s by Al Ries and Jack Trout.[3] The truism for Ries and Trout was that no-one remembers number two on a list – only number one. Consequently, they advised brands to position themselves in a category – even to the point of inventing one – so they were number one. Better to be a big fish in a little pond and try to grow the pond. In other words, a brand's standing is a comparison to its category, not a matter of its absolute values.

The Dacia launch paper demonstrates how good positioning is the difference between success and failure. Dacia is the most successful launch of a new car marque in the UK since Daewoo in 1995 – itself an IPA Effectiveness Awards Winner in 1996 and a paper cited by the authors of the Dacia paper.[4]

Daewoo succeeded by creating its own market for an unknown, low-cost, car marque. The campaign focused on real drivers by letting 100 people test drive the car instead of automotive journalists. The buying experience emphasised fixed prices, no salesman and standard warranties – all pain points for consumers. Dacia confronted the same issues in a 21st century context.

The success of Dacia is, in essence, proof of the correctness of behavioural economics. Classical economics does allow for many factors in purchases decisions, but gives a strong priority to price and value. Yet Dacia knew that their low prices were as much a blessing as a curse. Behavioural economics explains this – and suggests what to do about it.

First, price is a signal in and of itself. Good cars are expensive, therefore cheap cars tend to be bad. The cheapest cars are likely to be the worst. The campaign needed to make cheap an untarnished virtue.

People also care what other people think, especially experts. Dacia is easy meat for cheap minutes on *Top Gear* even though we all know Jeremy Clarkson is not the target market. Dacia needed to find its own audience and give them confidence to buy.

People also think in comparisons. The Dacia hails from Romania and is easily grouped with other lost-cost, low-quality imports, from the Trabant to Ladas and Škodas. Škoda shed this reputation by making much of their acquisition by Volkswagen, a brand synonymous with quality engineering.

However, Dacia couldn't take this route by appealing to parent brand Renault without risking cannibalising a parent struggling at 18th place in the UK market.

Dacia needed to give people another useful comparison to make that would frame the low-cost car market positively and give people confidence to buy.

The 'You Do The Maths' campaign does this elegantly. It provides people with a way to think about a complex decision that they find convincing, intuitive and defensible – essential ingredients of a confident decision.

Research showed that people know they end up paying more for extras they don't really want or use. Eastern European cars have always had a cult following amongst people who celebrated the combination of Spartan fittings and low prices. The 'You Do The Maths' campaign updates this for a modern, post-recession period and makes buying cheap the smart move. The result was 21,852 car sales – 12,852 over the baseline target.

Behavioural economics has already inspired other award-winning campaigns that position price and value creatively, for example Aldi's 'Like Brands' campaign[5] and thetrainline.com.[6] It is an area where we will see more creative – and effective – examples in the future.

## Heuristics, ways of thinking and ways of doing

Dacia gives people a new way to think about a category, ultimately leading to different decisions and better sales for Dacia. The British Heart Foundation and Fire Safety campaigns are examples of giving people a new way to think about a behaviour.

Both create what behavioural economists call 'heuristics'. These are rule-based ways of making decisions. The rules may not always provide an optimal solution, but they provide with minimal effort, a near-optimal solution on most occasions.

Public health and safety campaigns have often sought to create or spread heuristics: The Green Cross Code, 'Clunk Click Every Trip', 'Think Once, Think Twice, Think Bike', 'Eat Five A Day', etc. Giving people a way to think about something makes it easier for them to act.

Two papers this year validate this approach with impressive results.

The BHF paper demonstrates how people can be aware of a potential solution but lack confidence to act. Everyone knows that people having a heart attack can be helped by cardiopulmonary resuscitation (CPR). Yet universal awareness did not lead to universal action. People think CPR is something for trained people to do. Could a TV ad train a nation to do CPR and make them act?

The 'Stayin' Alive' campaign fronted by Vinnie Jones showed you can. First, it simplifies the behaviour (where to push on the chest, how hard and how often). Second, it removes the most crucial barrier people face – not knowing how often to pump the chest. The correct rate is 100 times a minute. This is an almost impossible instruction to follow. However, human beings are instinctively rhythmic. Almost everyone knows the Bee Gees hit 'Stayin' Alive' – which has a tempo very close to 100bpm. Following the rhythm of 'Stayin' Alive' is a simple instruction to follow. Creativity converts folk knowledge into a life-saving skill – one that has already directly saved at least 30 lives and will save countless more in a nation better equipped to act fast.

Fire Safety also created a heuristic by creating a new connection to drive behaviour change. People know to install a smoke alarm. They probably know it needs to be tested to be sure the battery hasn't run out. Yet testing the battery is one of those small yet tedious tasks people typically put off.

The campaign insightfully identified the beginning and end of British Summer Time as an occasion when people already go around the house changing and checking their clocks. It is essential to know what time it is as compliance with this behaviour is near universal. While they are making this effort and have the steps out anyway to do it, why not suggest that they check their smoke alarm as well? It worked: when the clocks changed, people who'd seen the advertising were three times more likely to test their smoke alarm as well.

Both campaigns understood that behaviour can be changed by removing barriers that might seem trivial in the context of the 'real' problem. Neither the risk of fire nor the thought of not being able to help a dying loved one can be turned into a motivation as effective as removing the barrier of getting the steps out or knowing how to perform CPR with confidence. Behavioural economics is a body of evidence both campaigns could use to justify these creative and lateral approaches.

## Nudges across journeys and touchpoints

Behavioural economics famously produces nudges. Broadly these are small changes in choice architecture that can have large impacts on behaviour.[7] These impacts can be large, as with, for example, the oft-cited change from an opt-out to an opt-in for organ donation.[8] The BHF and Fire Safety Campaigns are examples of single nudges seeking such large changes.

However, in marketing, shifts of even 1% can be crucial to the bottom line. Could it be possible to add up a series of small nudges into a big campaign success?

The digital age has made multi-touchpoint campaigns the norm. An early pioneering paper using behavioural economics, the 2010 TDA paper, described using a series of nudges to keep a candidate in play through the often complex and convoluted process of deciding to switch careers to teaching – a process they dubbed 'The TDA pinball'.[9]

The TfL London 2012 paper, already discussed, also uses this approach. The campaign did not just provide general information. It also broke information down into easy-to-act-on behaviours for individual lines, stations and routes. No-one was left unclear on their options. Each targeted communication provided the thousands of changes necessary to build into millions of changed journeys across the network.

Another is the Everest paper, which used an apt analogy from Dave Brailsford, the Team GB Cycling Performance Director. Brailsford knew that performance enhancement would come from finding a series of 1% improvements in diet, training regime, etc. Not from any single 'silver bullet' solution.

The Everest team took that dictum to heart and restored a brand to its heyday. They looked for small but useful behaviour changes at each part of the customer journey. Direct mail shots were simplified to make appointment booking easier. Segmentation divided those looking for quality and value from those simply shopping on price. Analysis of the media strategy justified the effort of using more bespoke channels over blanket door-drops and cold mail-shots. Each nudge added a few per cent to the response rates, and a thousand or so appointments. Collectively this smart thinking about small differences was enough to reverse a steep 25% year-on-year decline in appointments and see Everest grow in a market that is otherwise declining.

## The future for behavioural economics in the IPA Effectiveness Awards

The IPA Effectiveness Awards, at their best, show the connection between creativity and business outcomes. The collection of papers cited here show how behavioural economics both stimulates that creativity and makes its connection to business results clearer.

The precise focus on behaviour inevitably leads to more clarity on required business outcomes. Alone this would be a significant contribution. However, it is the contribution to the quality, confidence and application of creativity that makes these papers fascinating.

There is a willingness to find big ideas that go to the heart of an issue – be it seeing the value of cheap cars, carrying out CPR or checking a smoke alarm – that is encouraged by having theory on hand that supports how these insights work better than previous approaches based on information and education.

Finally, and perhaps most importantly, there is a granularity encouraged by focusing on behaviour. Everything that can change behaviour at any touchpoint is worth doing to bring about overall success. This embraces and guides us in a digital age of multiple channels and once again proves how wide reaching and powerful the application of agency creativity can be.

## Notes

1 See the IPA Publications *We're All Choice Architects Now* (2010) and *Let's Get Practical* (2011), IPA, London.
2 Les Binet & Peter Field (2007) *Marketing in the Era of Accountability*, IPA, London, Figure 4, p. 20 shows that in all cases where only hard objectives (like behaviour change) are set, the effectiveness success rate is 50%, compared to only 11% when only soft objectives (e.g. attitude or awareness) are

set. For not-for-profit, the comparison is 30% for hard objectives, 7% for soft objectives. Table 7, p. 21, shows that those setting one hard objective are 28% more likely to report a large business effect, and 41% more likely to accountable. For those setting four or more objectives, these figures rise to 76% and 66%.

3 And gathered in Al Ries & Jack Trout (1981) *Positioning: The Battle for Your Mind,* McGraw-Hill, New York.

4 Rachel Walker & Chris Forrest (1996), 'Advertising That Builds Strong Consumer Brands? That'll be the Daewoo', IPA Effectiveness Awards, Silver Winner.

5 Ian Lloyd Jones and Sibel Akel Saoulli (2012) 'Aldi: The Like Brands Campaign', IPA Effectiveness Awards, Gold Winner.

6 Susan Poole (2010) 'Thetrainline.Com – Back On Track: Using Communications To Change Entrenched Behaviour', IPA Effectiveness Awards, Silver Winner.

7 Although Thaler & Sunstein provide a more technical and restrictive definition that strictly rules out any closed or mandated choices (e.g. removing an option) or where the effort of avoiding a nudge is unduly high (e.g. Thaler has stated that having adult content as an opt-in from ISPs impose a too high cost of potential embarrassment to count as a nudge).

8 Rates above 90% result from the opt-out model. The Netherlands is the most successful opt-in at 28%, even after running a direct marketing campaign that reached every single adult in the country. See Dan Ariely (2008), *Predictably Irrational,* HarperCollins, London.

9 Dom Boyd, Alex Vass, Ami Smith & James Caig (2010) 'TDA Teacher Recruitment: Best in Class: How Influencing Behaviour with a New Media Strategy Helped Nudge Teacher Recruitment to Record Levels', IPA Effectiveness Awards, Gold Winner.

# Olympic Delivery Authority & Transport for London

## London 2012: Securing Gold

**By Richard Storey, M&C Saatchi**

Credited companies: Creative Agency, M&C Saatchi; Media Agency, Walker Media; Client, (Travel Demand Management), Olympic Delivery Authority / Transport for London

### Editor's summary

The stakes were high. In the run up to the Olympics, London anticipated an unprecedented transport surge and modelling showed that the transport network would not cope with demand, even after a £6.5bn infrastructure upgrade. Previous Games in Atlanta showed how much damage could be done if transport ground to halt so a 'Travel Demand Management' programme was devised, investing 0.3% of the Games' budget to encourage London to 'Get Ahead of the Games' by changing its travel behaviours. This resulted in 77% of 'Background Demand' users modifying their travel behaviour, thousands of businesses implementing contingency plans and 11.2m Ticket Holders journeying as recommended, thereby preventing operational melt-down. The £30m expenditure effectively safeguarded £16.5bn of benefits; a 550:1 ratio of the value of success to the investment required to achieve it.

**This fascinating case impressed the judges in the rigour and attention to detail applied across the audience journey, both before and during the Games itself. The complexity of the challenge and the scale of the pressure was palpable, but the results showed how multiple behavioural changes across multiple audiences were clearly achieved.**

It may seem inevitable now that Mo Farah would stride to double Olympic gold in front of his home crowd. Just as Usain Bolt would cruise to three golds. But few would question these successes were the result of meticulous preparation. So it was with the 2012 Games themselves. This paper describes one unglamorous but vital component of the meticulous preparations for *'the greatest peace-time challenge London has ever faced'*.[1]

Hosting the equivalent of 26 World Cups simultaneously, London anticipated an unprecedented transport surge. Even with a £6.5bn infrastructure investment, modelling showed the network behind 'the first ever public-transport Games' would not cope with demand.

But cope it did, admirably. Thanks to 77% of 'Background Demand' users modifying their travel behaviour, thousands of businesses implementing contingency plans and 11.2m Ticket Holders journeying by recommended means.

All this would not have 'just happened' by itself.

Rather, 0.3% of the cost of the 2012 Olympics was invested in a Travel Demand Management[2] communications programme, encouraging public, business and spectators to *'Get Ahead of the Games'* by changing their travel behaviour.

This prompted a variety of changes to travel patterns, mitigating the Olympic travel surge and preventing major operational issues. As a component of success, rather than a discretionary investment, the £30m expenditure effectively safeguarded £16.5bn of benefits; an efficiency ratio of 550:1.

## Preparing to win

In 2005, as London[3] won the right to stage the 2012 Olympics,[4] it began preparing for the outcome we now take somewhat for granted. It's easy to forget triumph was by no means guaranteed. Two key factors were judged capable of derailing the Games; terrorism and transport.

Over £1bn was duly invested in security. This paper concerns the £6.5bn invested in transport to successfully stage the Games, whilst keeping London open for business. Specifically, it examines the relatively small but essential investment in Travel Demand Management (TDM); communications directing travellers to modify their journeys, preventing network overload.

We begin by examining TDM's critical role in ensuring a successful Games.

## A critical issue

As London tendered for the Olympics, most commentators agreed transport would lose it the bid, while officials argued a credible transport plan was key to winning:

*London Olympic bid 'is doomed'.*

Daily Telegraph, January 2003

*Creaking transport network will lose us the bid.*

Daily Mail, September 2004

*Without excellent transport, the Games will be at risk of failure. London's reputation will depend on ensuring appropriate transport infrastructure is in place.*

> House of Commons Transport Committee, 'Going for Gold' Report of Session, 2005

*The provision of adequate transport represents the biggest challenge to London's bidding and hosting of the Games.*

> Recommendation 3: London Assembly, Culture, Sport and Tourism Committee report, January 2003

History shows the International Olympic Committee (IOC) was convinced by the officials. However, they explicitly acknowledged transport as critical.

## Figure 1: Congestion map showing London and key Olympic sites

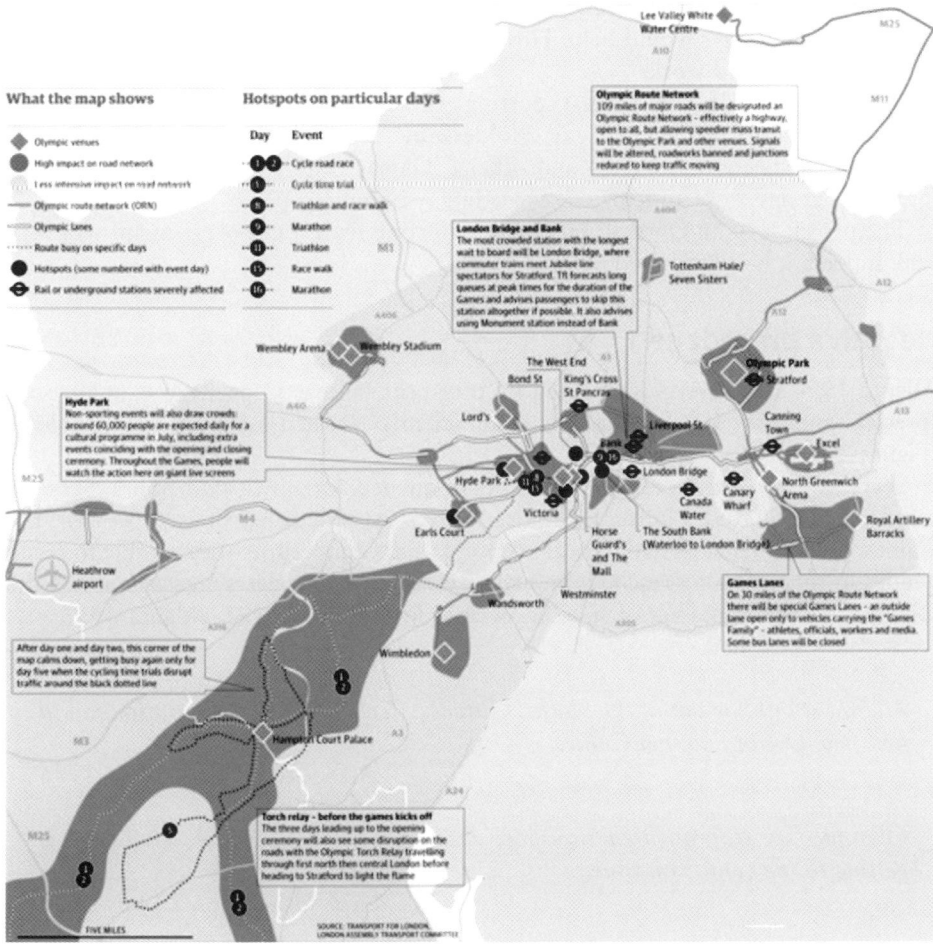

**What the map shows**

- Olympic venues
- High impact on road network
- Less intensive impact on road network
- Olympic route network (ORN)
- Olympic Lanes
- Route busy on specific days
- Hotspots (some numbered with event day)
- Rail or underground stations severely affected

**Hotspots on particular days**

| Day | Event |
| --- | --- |
| 1 2 | Cycle road race |
| 1 | Cycle time trial |
| 8 | Triathlon and race walk |
| 9 | Marathon |
| 11 | Triathlon |
| 13 | Race walk |
| 16 | Marathon |

**Olympic Route Network**
109 miles of major roads will be designated an Olympic Route Network - effectively a highway, open to all, but allowing speedier mass transit to the Olympic Park and other venues. Signals will be altered, roadworks banned and junctions reduced to keep traffic moving.

**London Bridge and Bank**
The most crowded station with the longest wait to board will be London Bridge, where commuter trains meet Jubilee line spectators for Stratford. TfL forecasts long queues at peak times for the duration of the Games and advises passengers to skip this station altogether if possible. It also advises using Monument station instead of Bank.

**Hyde Park**
Non-sporting events will also draw crowds around 60,000 people are expected daily for a cultural programme in July, including extra events coinciding with the opening and closing ceremony. Throughout the Games, people will watch the action here on giant live screens.

After day one and day two, this corner of the map calms down, getting busy again only for day five when the cycling time trials disrupt traffic around the black dotted line

**Games Lanes**
On 30 miles of the Olympic Route Network there will be special Games Lanes - an outside lane open only to vehicles carrying the "Games Family" - athletes, officials, workers and media. Some bus lanes will be closed

**Torch relay - before the games kicks off**
The three days leading up to the opening ceremony will also see some disruption on the roads with the Olympic Torch Relay travelling through first north then central London before heading to Stratford to light the flame

Lee Valley White Water Centre

Tottenham Hale/ Seven Sisters

Olympic Park / Stratford

Wembley Arena / Wembley Stadium

The West End / Bond St / King's Cross / St Pancras

Canning Town

Excel

Lord's

Liverpool St

North Greenwich Arena

Hyde Park

London Bridge

Canary Wharf

Canada Water

Royal Artillery Barracks

Victoria

Earls Court

Horse Guard's and The Mall

The South Bank (Waterloo to London Bridge)

Heathrow airport

Wandsworth

Westminster

Wimbledon

Hampton Court Palace

FIVE MILES

SOURCE: TRANSPORT FOR LONDON, LONDON ASSEMBLY TRANSPORT COMMITTEE

*During the bid, substantial transport plans have been clearly confirmed. Provided [the programme] is delivered fully and the ORN implemented, the Commission believes London would be capable of coping with Games-time traffic and that Olympic and Paralympic transport requirements would be met.*

IOC technical report[5]

*London's bid shows commitment and conviction to solving critical transport issues. It is essential these plans are implemented in full.*

IOC press release[6]

This was no idle scaremongering. London was uniquely vulnerable. The third most densely populated Olympic city, its roads were heavily congested. Declaring London *'the first public transport Games'*, spectators' cars were banned from venues.

Events were planned at multiple venues across a city already heavily reliant on public transport (Figure 1). Carrying over 25m journeys daily, the network operated close to capacity. And its infrastructure was difficult and costly to expand. School and summer holidays would help. However the Paralympics corresponded with the return to school and work.

Hosting the world's two largest sporting events would mean unprecedented travel uplifts. Not just from 11.5m Ticket Holders, but accompanying friends and family, non-ticketed spectators,[7] media and official 'Games Family'. Over 3m incremental journeys per day were anticipated, exceeding maximum capacity.

The prospect of an Olympic city unable to cope with transport demand was very real. Indeed, it had happened before.

## Negative precedent

Atlanta 1996 was severely impacted by transport failure. Capacity was incorrectly forecast and the travelling public insufficiently warned of potential problems (Figure 2).

Severe overcrowding resulted. Travellers queued for up to two hours. Services were heavily delayed. Normal operation of the city was compromised, as were the Games. Some events opened to near-empty stadia. Competitors were unable to reach venues in time, causing rescheduling and cancellations. Athletes checked-out of the Olympic Village, anxious of missing events. Publicly criticised, Atlanta 1996 was irrevocably tarnished.

*Atlanta stumbling out of the blocks. Glitches: Technology, transportation fail in first few days of Summer Games.*

Associated Press, 22 July 1996

*Olympics an 'unmitigated transport disaster'. Athletes' biggest challenge is getting to the venues on time.*

New York Times, 23 July 1996

Figure 2: Commentators' criticism of Atlanta 1996[9]

*Fix transit glitches, IOC tells Atlanta. Angry IOC's message to organizers 'You've got to fix transport'.*

The Inquirer (Georgia), 22 July 1996

Even the IOC was equivocal. These were the only Games not declared '*Best Olympics ever*'. Tellingly, President Samaranch merely affirmed Atlanta '*exceptional*'.[8] Official reports later criticised Atlanta's transport.

Figure 3: Future Olympic bidders cautioned about Atlanta's performance[10]

*Whilst Atlanta largely met its obligations in terms of transportation of Games Family, this came at the cost of significant disruption to the City ... A clear lesson future Games must benefit from.*

IOC, Atlanta 1996 Final Report

One of the attractions of hosting the Olympics is to 'showcase' the city and nation globally. Atlanta's problems were instead reported as showcasing the 'state of the nation'(Figure 3).

*Atlanta took the hit for a lot of trends reflected throughout the United States. The Olympics were like a backstage tour of America, laid open for the world to see.*

New York Times, 6 August 1996

## Learning the lessons

Subsequent Games learned from Atlanta, allocating increased resources to travel planning.[11] They had to, as the IOC effectively made TDM mandatory for host cities.

*Requirements include Travel Demand Management. Strong communication campaigns should be implemented to inform constituents of transport issues, alter travel behaviour and moderate travel demand.*

IOC Host City Contract[12]

*TDM programs and public mobility behavioural changes are fundamental and solutions should be supported by extensive communications programs*

IOC Host City Contract[13]

## Planning for success

Committed to avoiding an Atlanta scenario, £6.5bn was allocated to permanent transport improvements prior to London 2012.[14] These would be supplemented with Games-time enhancements, including the Javelin, Park-and-Rides, direct coaches, more and longer Overground trains and longer operating hours.

This effort would be optimised by thorough maintenance and incident response, to avoid lost capacity at the critical time. These three strands would ensure maximum feasible capacity for Games-time (Table 1).

The question was, would this be enough? Increased investment was considered, but rejected as uneconomic. Incremental spend on London's legacy network would yield progressively limited returns. Crudely, you can only run so many trains through the Tube without re-digging it. Attention turned instead to modelling and managing the demand side of the equation.

| Table 1: Net available capacity, Summer 2012 | |
|---|---|
| | **Games-time capacity vs. 2011** |
| Underground | +11 % |
| DLR | +25 % |
| Overground | +9 % |
| Buses | +7 % |

## Modelling demand

The irregular nature of Olympic events, plus London's transport idiosyncrasies, meant developing an ultra-granular demand model.[15] Patterns were established by transport node, by fifteen minute interval.[16]These snapshots were aggregated to give daily reports for each line and node (Figure 4).

The top-line picture was clear. Even allowing for increased capacity, the network would be critically incapacitated by Olympic demand. London would literally grind to a halt.

> *Without additional measures, the anticipated uplift will result in severely congested roads, station closures, infrastructure strain and failure, significantly increased journey times, spectators missing their events and commuters not able to get to work.*
>
> ODA, TDA Business Case, 9 May

## Modelling the solution

IOC conditions demanded a solution. Reducing Olympic attendees would be both unlikely and undesirable, so the imperative was to manage non-Olympic travel.

Modelling highlighted extreme concentration of visitor flows at venues and interchanges. While 65% of public transport and 70% of roads would *not* be significantly affected, 300 junctions and 187 public-transport 'hotspots' most definitely would be.

The solution prescribed both reducing demand and spreading it onto less congested routes and times. Geographic targeting would be critical to focus on those journeys impacting hotspots. This indicated three critical audiences.

### Audience one: Background Demand

All regular London travellers were still making non-Olympic journeys, whether by public transport or car. The solution required 30% of them, on any given day, to change their travel habits. Research[17] showed, despite any Olympic positivity, each was personally reluctant to do this.

> *Patriotism's all very well, but it's my journey to work we're talking about.*
> Define qualitative research respondent[18]

## Figure 4: Example outputs of demand modelling

### London's road network without TDM

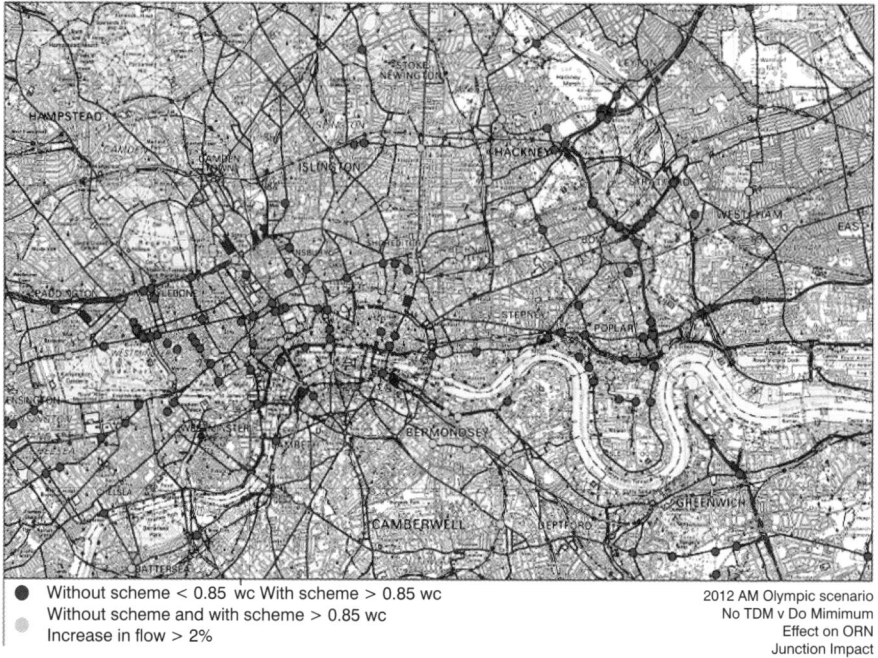

● Without scheme < 0.85 wc With scheme > 0.85 wc
● Without scheme and with scheme > 0.85 wc
○ Increase in flow > 2%

2012 AM Olympic scenario
No TDM v Do Mimimum
Effect on ORN
Junction Impact

### London Bridge Station without TDM

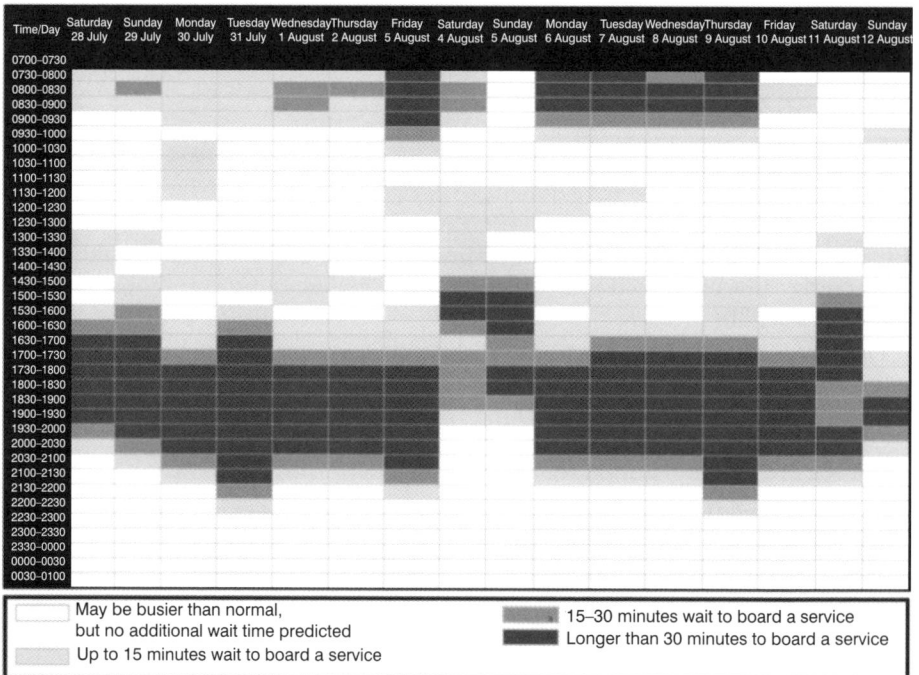

May be busier than normal,
but no additional wait time predicted

Up to 15 minutes wait to board a service

15–30 minutes wait to board a service

Longer than 30 minutes to board a service

Unmotivated to help the broader Olympic effort, most were 'happy' with their usual journey. It worked for them and many felt they had little or no practical alternative. Most were unaware of the likely scale and reach of Olympic disruption. Their journey went nowhere near Stratford. Why should it be affected?

Just 11% agreed they would re-plan their usual journey.[19] Most claimed they would 'wait and see', which would lead to calamitous overcrowding on Day One. We needed to encourage them to make alternative plans.

### Audience two: Businesses

Their role was twofold. The solution required those with London workforces to support their employees' travel changes. This would require adapting working practices, times, policies, etc.

Those with road-based supply chains would be affected by restrictions and potentially contribute to congestion, unless they made provisions to operate differently.

Most businesses had little awareness of likely Games impact. Just 3% had a plan and only 18% were preparing one.[20] 'Business as usual' was their priority.

We needed them to plan for the inevitability it would not be.

### Audience three: Ticket Holders

To ensure this discrete audience received a first-class experience, we needed them to comply with recommendations on how to reach their event. This wasn't as straightforward as perhaps assumed. The car could not be the default choice. Plus, the recommended journey was not necessarily obvious.[21]

Ticket Holders' familiarity with London was extremely varied. Visitors had little idea how to reach their venue. Londoners had mistaken assumptions about the best method.

Whilst more amenable than Background Demand, spectators were far from compliant. Just 22% claimed they were likely to follow transport advice given by London 2012.[22] We needed them to.

## Push and pull

The detailed nature of the problem meant each customer needed highly specific information to best decide which, if any, changes to make.

The programme strategy therefore focused on using marketing communications to 'push' travellers and businesses to on-line planning tools. Using these to assess for themselves likely Games impact and possible options would effectively 'pull' them into better journey choices.

### Addressing the audiences

Different channels were prioritised for each audience. Advertising targeted Background Demand, utilising owned (on-system and CRM), earned (PR) and paid-for media.

Face to face events and direct communications (direct mail and e-CRM) reached businesses. The approach was to 'reach the few to influence the many', with activity targeting key intermediaries and nominated Olympic Liaison Officers.

Mailings and e-CRM reached Ticket Holders directly, as names and details were known. Signage and Games-Makers were vital on the day.

Despite these discrete methods, there was considerable overlap. Today's Ticket Holder would be tomorrow's Background Demand. Either could be Businesses' employees. So a single integrated plan was created.

### Communication strategy

Contrary to initial assumptions, research showed personal risk of disruption was a more effective message than broader Games success.[23]

Reluctant audiences could be encouraged to act if they registered the following sequence of messages:

*The Games will generate widespread travel congestion*

*Your journey / business could be affected*

*You can avoid this by re-planning journeys / business practices*

*There are options (the four 'R's) that may work for you*

*Further information, tools and tips are available*

*(Approaching Games-time): Now's the time to act*

The challenge was to balance negativity with positive prospects. Creative development duly steered the approach away from 'big scare', to an implicit personal benefit,[24] as expressed in Figure 5.

**Figure 5: Campaign theme**

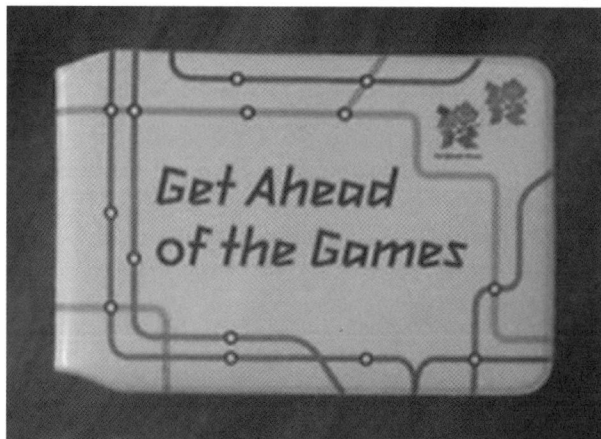

# Behaviour-change journey

That programme strategy defined the following behaviour-change journey and resulting campaign structure (Figure 6).

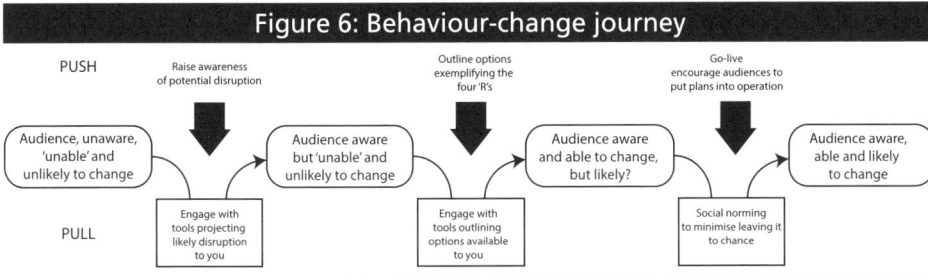

Figure 6: Behaviour-change journey

## Campaign structure

Background Demand activity was deployed in three phases (Figure 7):

- raise awareness: Highlight the disruption the Games would cause;
- outline options: Exemplify the *'Four 'R's'*;
- go live: Encourage travellers to put plans into operation.

## Four 'R's

The campaign proposed four options, prescribed by the modelling (Figure 8).

- *'Reduce'*: Behaviour resulting in fewer journeys being made, in particular working from home.[25]
- *'Re-time'*: Avoiding peak hours, by staggering travel times.
- *'Re-mode'*: Switching to less busy (potentially quicker) modes, particularly cycling, walking and bus.[26]
- *'Re-route'*: Taking a different route on the same mode, particularly avoiding Jubilee and Central lines.

## Specific messages

Numerous specific themes were also developed within the campaign (Figure 9).

- *Roads:* Warning of congestion and announcing the ORN and PRN.
- *Road races:* Warning of road closures and diversions.
- *Hotspots:* Location-specific warnings of especially crowded stations.
- *Other venues:* Activity for Weymouth, Eton Dorney, Lee Valley, Hadleigh Farm, Football venues, Wimbledon, etc.

## Figure 7: Examples of the three phases

Raise awareness

Outline options

Go live

  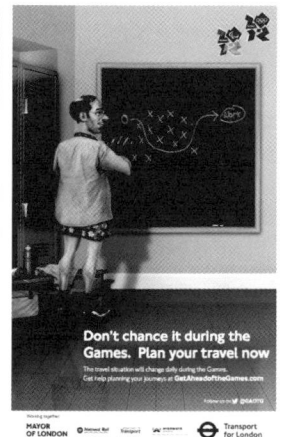

## Figure 8: The fours 'R's

Reduce

Re-time

Re-mode

Re-route

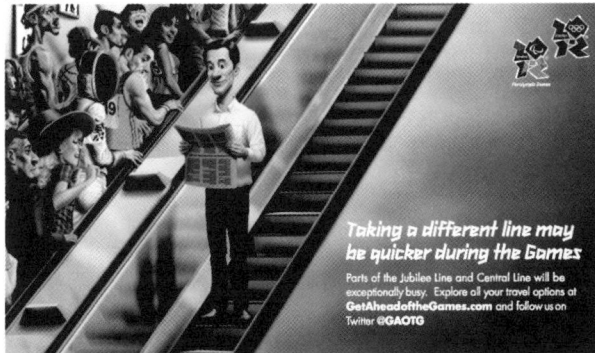

## Figure 9: Examples of specific messages

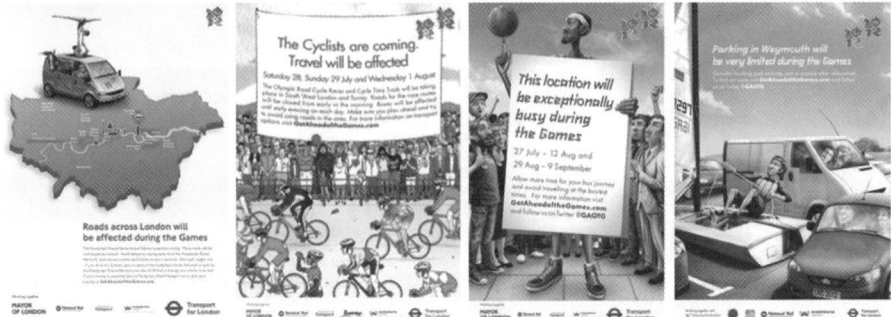

In all, some 106m e-mails were sent to most at-risk customers (Figure 10). All activity drove response to www.getaheadofthegames.com, where information, tips and travel planning tools were hosted. Travellers were also encouraged to subscribe via Twitter for real-time updates (Figures 11 and 12).

## Figure 10: Examples of e-mail and PR activities

Example email: one of 106 million sent across the program

Example PR stunt, exemplifying the potential congestion

Figure 11: www.getaheadofthegames.com

Unprecedented collaboration meant these assets were shared across travel industry platforms.[27]

With the Olympics over, there was a 15-day hiatus, during which travellers needed to be tee-ed up for the Paralympics.

### Business campaign

Business activity deployed a similar structure, adopting business vernacular and practices. Its 'keep on running' theme was positive and benefit orientated, in line with overall strategy. To accommodate planning, consultation with key businesses and intermediaries began in 2010.

Awareness was raised via a conference in November 2010, followed by several high profile events, direct mail, including a letter from Lord Coe, and paid-for advertising in business environments. Options were outlined to nominated Olympic Liaison Offers, via toolkits and action-planning workshops.

With front-weighting proving effective, encouragement at 'Go-live' was restricted to lightweight advertising, an event hosted by the Secretary of State and face-to-face visits in hotspots. Specific advertising and bulletins were targeted at businesses making freight deliveries.

At the same time, data released to satnavs and the freight industry alerted drivers of congestion. The London Lorry Control Scheme was also relaxed to allow 'out of hours' deliveries (Figure 13).

## Figure 12: Leaflet and #GAOTG Twitter feed

### Don't get caught out on the roads

Predicted impact on roads. Saturday 28th and Sunday 29th July

#### Avoid driving on the following days:

**Central London**
Sat     21–27 July:    Olympic Torch Relay
Thurs   2 Aug:         Triathlon Technical Rehearsal
Sat     4 Aug:         Men's 20km Race Walk
Sat     4 Aug:         Women's Triathlon
Sun     5 Aug:         Women's Marathon
Tues    7 Aug:         Men's Triathlon
Sat     11 Aug:        Men's 50km Race Walk
Sat     11 Aug:        Women's 20km Race Walk
Sun     12 Aug:        Men's Marathon
Fri     24–29 Aug:     Paralympic Torch Relay
Sun     9 Sept:        Men's and women's Paralympic Marathon

**Central London and Surrey**
Sat     28 July:       Men's Cycling Road Race
Sun     29 July:       Women's Cycling Road Race

**South West London and Surrey**
Tues    31 July:       Time Trial Technical Rehearsal
Wed     1 Aug:         Men's and Women's Road Cycling Time Trial

**Brands Hatch**
Wed     5 - 8 Sept:    Paralympic Road Cycling

Road event days will mean road closures and restrictions.
In some cases roads will be affected from early in the morning
to early evening.
**Use our roads tool at GetAheadoftheGames.com**

### Walking times for Tube journeys

There are 47 tube journeys that can be walked in under 10 minutes

Zone1

### Ways to avoid station hotspots:

**Try walking or cycling**
Avoid congestion on public transport by cycling
or for short journeys it may be quicker to walk.

**Travel at a different time**
Leaving work or home earlier or later to miss the busiest
times will make your journey easier. The key times
to avoid are 7–10am and 4–8pm, when large numbers
of spectators will be on the move at the same time as
regular travellers.

**Avoid unnecessary journeys**
Don't travel unless you have to. Combine trips and
reduce the number of journeys you make to avoid
crowds and delays.
Whatever you do, leave the car at home. Driving into
and around central London should be avoided.

**For more information visit GetAheadoftheGames.com**

← → C ⌂ 🔒 Twitter, Inc. [US] https://**twitter.com**/GAOTG

Search 🔍    Have an accou

**GetAheadoftheGames** @GAOTG · 1 Sep 2012
2 of 2 - If you don't have accessibility requirements, use Ham&City line to West
Ham or National Rail services from Liverpool St.
Expand

**GetAheadoftheGames** @GAOTG · 1 Sep 2012
1 of 2 - Javelin Service from St Pancras to Olympic Park is very busy.
Expand

**GetAheadoftheGames** @GAOTG · 1 Sep 2012
The DLR, Central and Jubilee lines will be busy throughout the day.  Visit
GetAheadoftheGames.com for more info
Expand

**GetAheadoftheGames** @GAOTG · 1 Sep 2012
Canada Water and Mile End will be particularly busy in the morning.  f possible,
try to avoid these stations at busy times.
Expand

**GetAheadoftheGames** @GAOTG · 1 Sep 2012
Follow @GAOTG and @TfLTravelAlerts to find out what's happening on the
transport network and keep your travel plans up to date.
Expand

**GetAheadoftheGames** @GAOTG · 1 Sep 2012
To avoid hotspots and see how your journey may be affected, visit
GetAheadoftheGames.com.
Expand

## Figure 13: Example of freight activity

Freight delivery activity

### Ticket Holders

Activity was geared to providing relevant travel information from early in the ticketing process. Games Travel Pages ensured potential purchasers could make informed decisions before applying for tickets. Travel advice was subsequently directed to successful purchasers via e-mail.

Reflecting the key imperative of encouraging public transport, rather than car usage, One-Day Travelcards and travel information were despatched along with each ticket. The first ever Spectator Journey Planner was created, providing nation-wide transport information in a single portal and directing spectators away from hotspots.

On the day, signage and Games-Makers and an app directed spectators seamlessly (Figure 14).

Figure 14: Example page from the Spectator Journey Planner

Example page from the Spectator Journey Planner

## Successful outcome

Confounding a national tendency towards pessimism and disparagement, something remarkable happened in Summer 2012. The Olympics passed without major incident or disruption. In fact, media, competitors, spectators and other nations universally declared them a huge success, without dissent.

> *The brilliance of the London Games was not all about sport. It was about putting the country on display and they have done just that.*
> Toronto Sun, Canada, September 2012

> *London, you didn't half do a brilliant job. It might just represent a new PB for the Olympics.*
> Sydney Morning Herald, 13 August 2012

> *Can we have London hosting all future Games?*
> TV4, Sweden, Sept 2012

Contrary to prior concerns, transport was heralded a success.

> *Overall Games success was underpinned by effective transport.*
> Final Report of the IOC Co-ordination Commission, August 2013

> *What we expected: Chaos, the Underground grinding to a halt and the Olympic Park marooned miles from Central London. What we got: Surprised Londoners and spectators finding their way around with remarkable ease.*
> The Independent, 13 Aug 2012

> *By any reasonable measure, the Games were a success and delivered value for money. Crucially, they passed off without major transport disruption or security incident.*
> National Audit office. Post Games Review, December 2012

Indeed, on Day 4, some media mischievously accused activity of being over-effective.

> *All quiet on the west end front.*
> The Economist, 3 August 2003[28]

> *Publicity around public transport has been very effective, probably too effective.*
> Bryan Roberts, Kantar Retail[29]

This un-dramatic outcome belied an unprecedented travel surge across London (Figures 15 and 16).

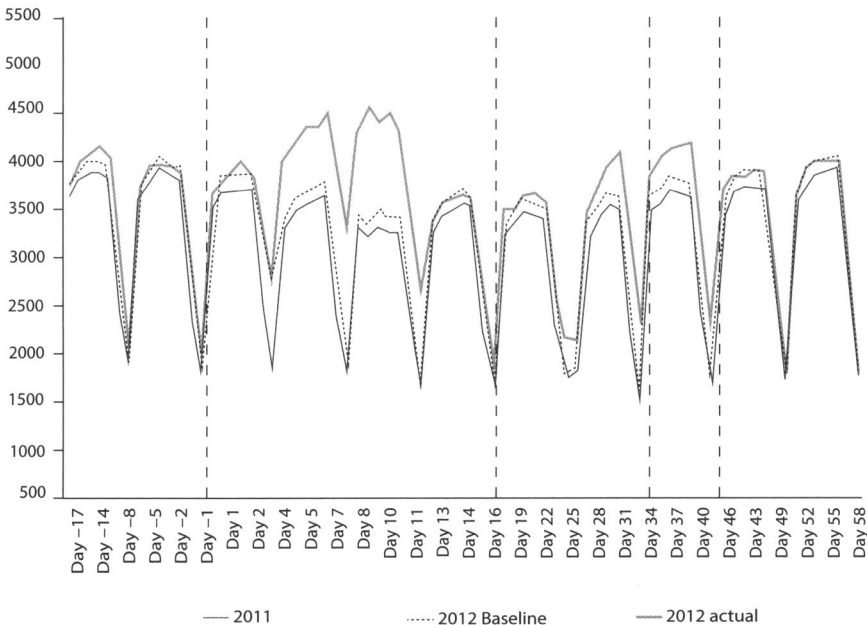

Figure 15: Daily journeys on Underground

— 2011    ····· 2012 Baseline    — 2012 actual

Source: TfL Customer Experience

73

**Figure 16: Daily journeys on Docklands Light Railway**

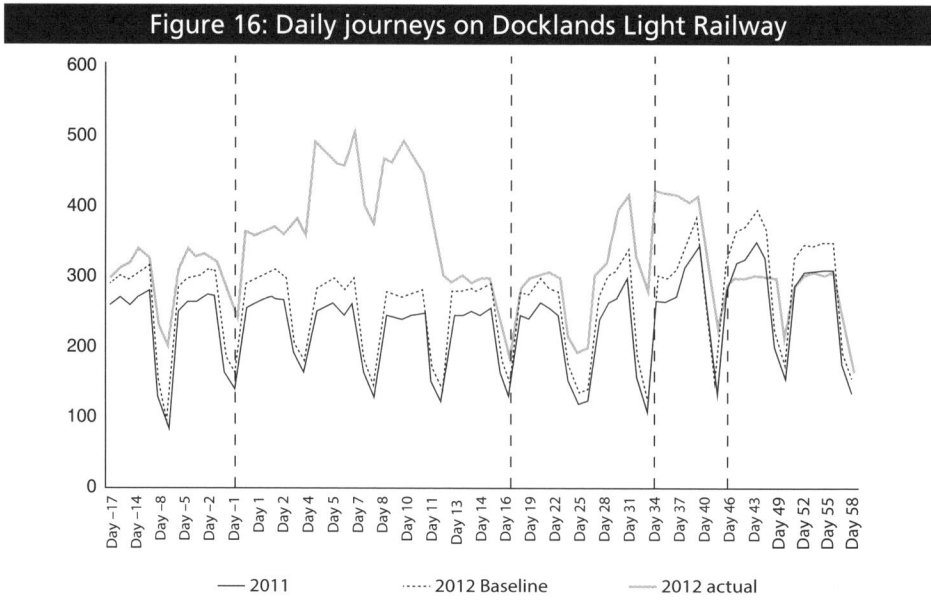

Legend: —— 2011    ⋯⋯ 2012 Baseline    —— 2012 actual

Source: TfL Customer Experience

## Travel surge

At Games-time, London was in fact busier than it had ever been, carrying 1.7m extra journeys each day (Figure 17).

**Figure 17: Uplift in total London journeys**

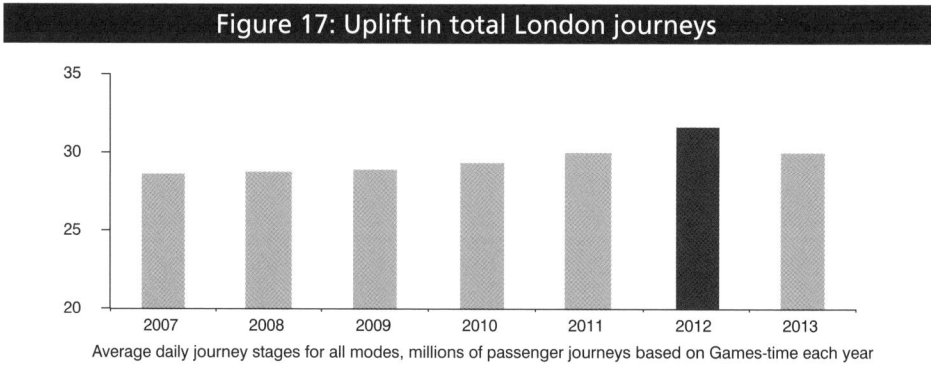

Average daily journey stages for all modes, millions of passenger journeys based on Games-time each year

Source: Transport for London

As anticipated, much of the uplift was carried by rail-based modes, which bore a 29% uplift[30] (Figure 18).

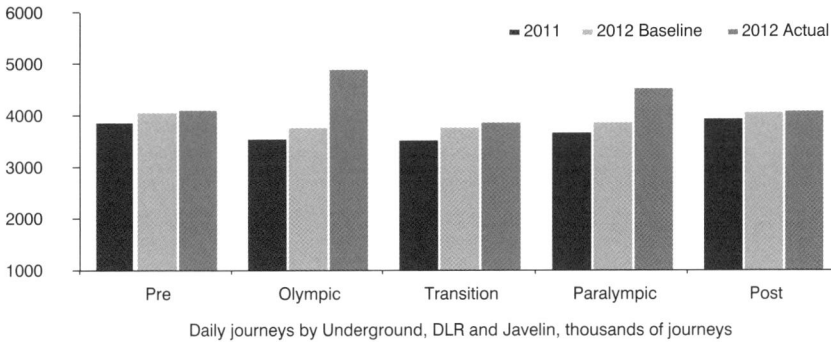

Figure 18: Uplift in rail-based public transport

Legend: 2011, 2012 Baseline, 2012 Actual

Categories: Pre, Olympic, Transition, Paralympic, Post

Daily journeys by Underground, DLR and Javelin, thousands of journeys

Source: Transport for London, London Rail

As predicted, concentration was acute at key hotspots and times. Venue Tube stations experienced an 83% uplift. River services rose 44%. Demand on the DLR doubled. August 7th was the Underground's busiest day ever in 149 years. August 3rd from 18.00 to 18.30 was the busiest 30 minutes London Bridge ever experienced.[31]

However, whilst significant, these uplifts were manageable and the networks coped.

## Incident-free

Despite record demand, reliability was maintained or improved. Over 99.5% of scheduled services ran during the Games.[32] Journey times were on-par or better than normal summer services (Table 2).

### Table 2: Service reliability measures, major modes

|  | Benchmark | Olympic | Paralympic |
|---|---|---|---|
| **Underground** | | | |
| % good service | 71% | 80% | 89% |
| Average wait time | 2m 23s | 2m 18s | 2m 17s |
| Average journey time | 15m 5s | 125m 2s | 14m 41s |
| **National Rail** | | | |
| Public performance measure | 94.9% | 97.3% | 94.8% |
| **Overground** | | | |
| Public performance measure | 96.9% | 98.2% | 98.5% |
| **DLR** | | | |
| Reliability score | 97.5% | 99.1% | 98.7% |
| **Buses** | | | |
| Excess wait time | 0.92m | 0.81m | 0.95m |
| **Road** | | | |
| Average traffic speed | 41 km/h | 42 km/h | 41km/h |
| Journey time reliability | 91.2% | 91.% | 89.5% |

Source: Transport for London

We now see how response to TDM helped achieve this.

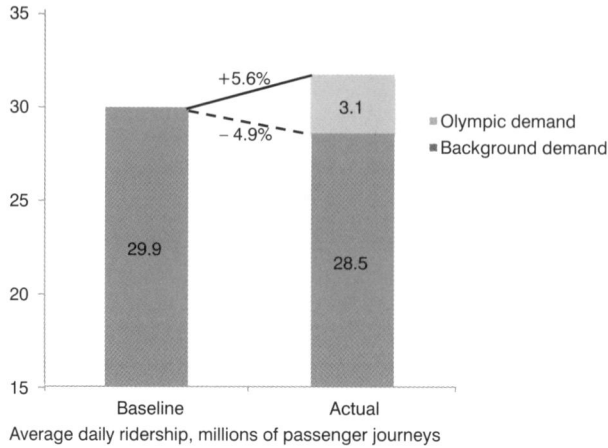

Figure 19: Reduced Background Demand mitigated Olympic effect

Average daily ridership, millions of passenger journeys

Source: Transport for London

## Background reduction

Two effects occurred simultaneously during the Games. The surge was limited to 1.7m extra journeys by a corresponding 1.4m *decrease* in Background Demand (Figure 19).[33]

Without that reduction, the total increase would have been almost double at 10.5%, or 53m additional journeys over the 17 days of the Olympics (Figure 20).

The same pattern was repeated 17 days later for the Paralympics, with total daily uplift restricted to 1.2m, via a 900,000 background decrease (Figure 21).

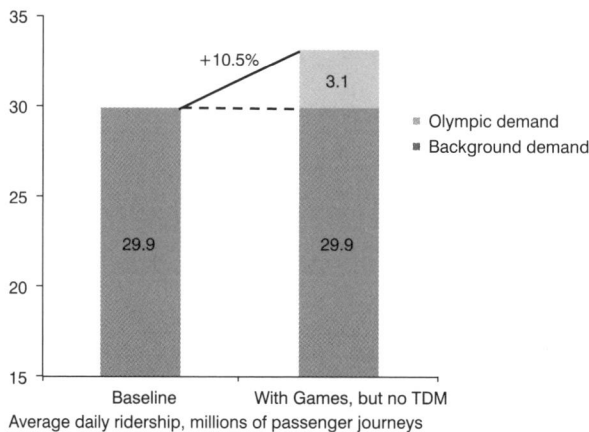

Figure 20: Total demand increase without TDM

Average daily ridership, millions of passenger journeys

Source: Transport for London

As modelling predicted, curtailing total journeys was vital to safeguard hotspots. A 1.4m reduction in background journeys equated to significantly lower road congestion, 39% less Jubilee Line Background Demand and 41% less on the DLR.[34]

### Clearing the roads

Contrary to popular expectation, but in line with TDM advice, car use during the Games dropped (Figure 22).

As a result, Olympic Routes performed better than planned. ORN and PRN journeys were 30% faster and more reliable than normal London journeys.[35] This enabled London to exceed IOC contractual obligations.[36]

## Figure 21 Reduced demand mitigated Paralympic effect

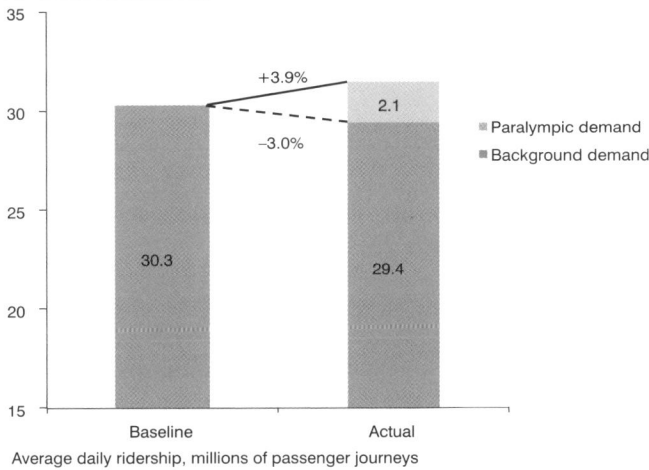

Average daily ridership, millions of passenger journeys

Source Transport for London

## Figure 22: Reduction in car usage during the Games

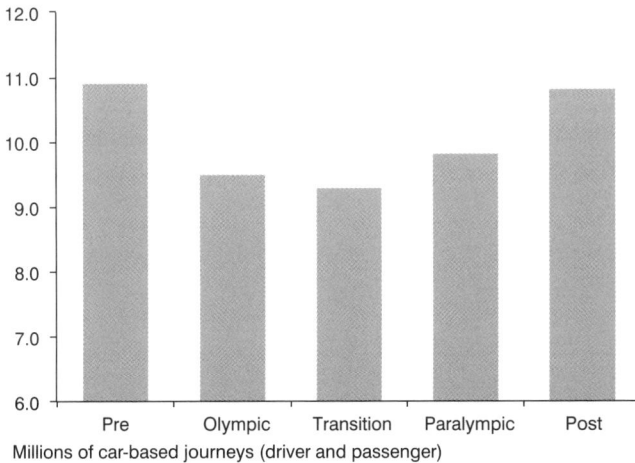

Millions of car-based journeys (driver and passenger)

Source: Transport for London

## Figure 23: Travel mode used by spectators to reach venue

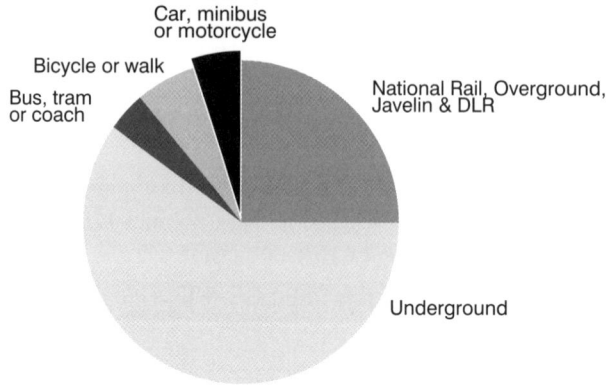

Car, minibus or motorcycle

Bicycle or walk

Bus, tram or coach

National Rail, Overground, Javelin & DLR

Underground

Source: TfL Spectator survey, July 2012

Several factors contributed to this. Ticket Holders heeded our advice, with less than 5% driving to venues[37] (Figure 23).

Background car drivers drove less. During the Games, road traffic dropped 8% below the seasonal norm, unlike before or after. Following TDM advice to avoid busy areas, Central London journeys were reduced at twice the rate of Outer London (Figure 24).

There was also a demonstrable reduction of freight. Indicative data show 10% fewer long vehicles on the road during the Games.[38] Car users' switch to other modes is reflected in increased public transport share of travel during both Games (Figure 25).

## Figure 24: Reduction in road usage below seasonal baseline

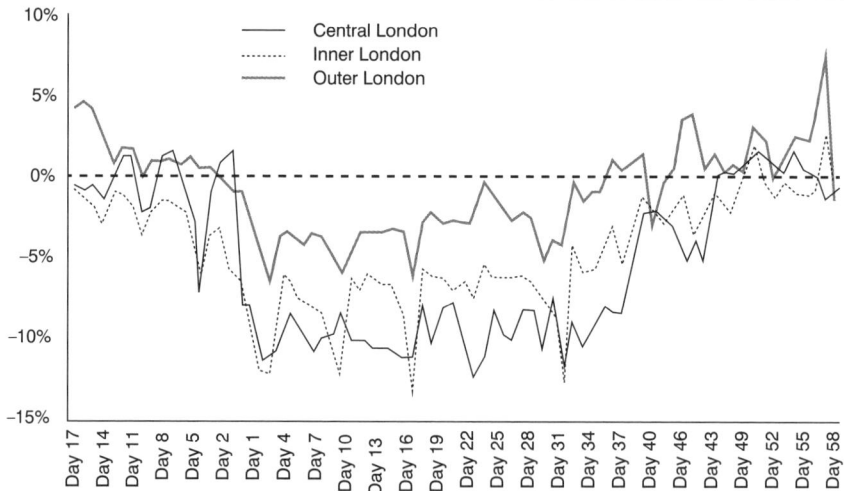

— Central London
········· Inner London
— Outer London

Average daily traffic flows on London roads, % change vs baseline

Source: TfL Suface Transport

## Figure 25: Switch to public transport during the Games

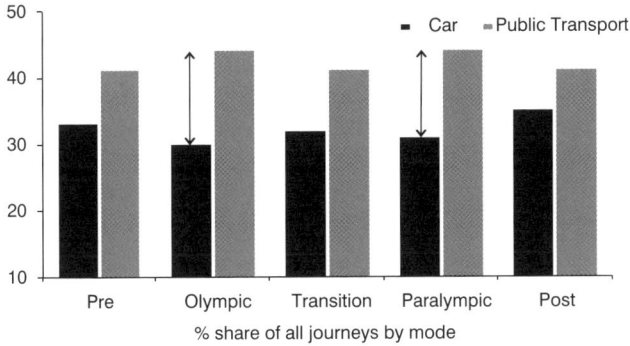

% share of all journeys by mode

Source: Transport for London

### Clearing the Underground

The majority of Olympic journeys were made on the Tube, meaning total usage was up 35% during the Olympics (14% Paralympics).[39] However, this masks a 760,000, or 24%, decrease in Background Demand journeys.[40] This is clearly visible in journey patterns by station type.[41] Fewer journeys were made at commuter stations, whereas significantly more were made to venues (Figure 26).

## Figure 26: Change in Underground journeys by station location

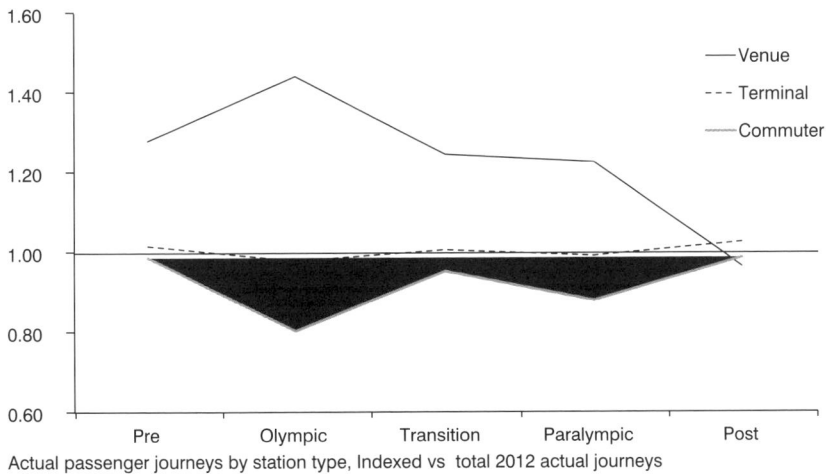

Actual passenger journeys by station type, Indexed vs total 2012 actual journeys

Source: Transport for London Group Planning

We can also treat Oystercard usage as a proxy for regular background travel, since Olympic spectators were issued with Travelcards for their event day.[42] This shows a clear pattern of reduction during the Olympics and Paralympics (Figure 27).

**Figure 27: Reduction in regular Oystercard Underground journeys**

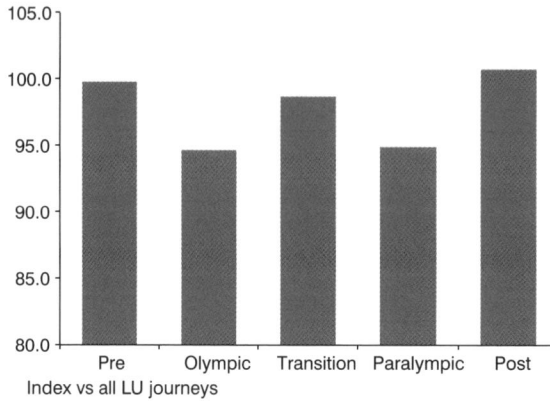

Index vs all LU journeys

Source: Transport for London Group Planning

'Reduce' was just one of the four 'R's. We now examine evidence the others were adopted.

## Re-timed journeys

In addition to fewer cars using the road, there are clear indications of remaining drivers re-timing their journeys during Games-time. Road journeys made at peak times were reduced by 1.1m, with 1.2m more taken instead before 7am (Figure 28).

**Figure 28: Time shift of road traffic**

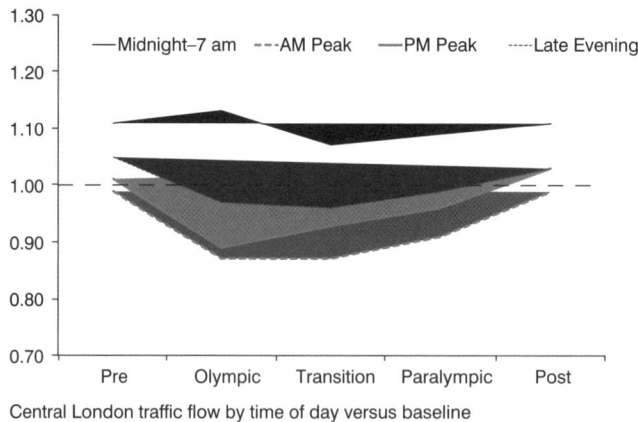

Central London traffic flow by time of day versus baseline

Central London saw more pronounced re-timing than elsewhere, clearly reflecting TDM advice (Figure 29).

## Figure 29: Olympic road traffic time shift by location

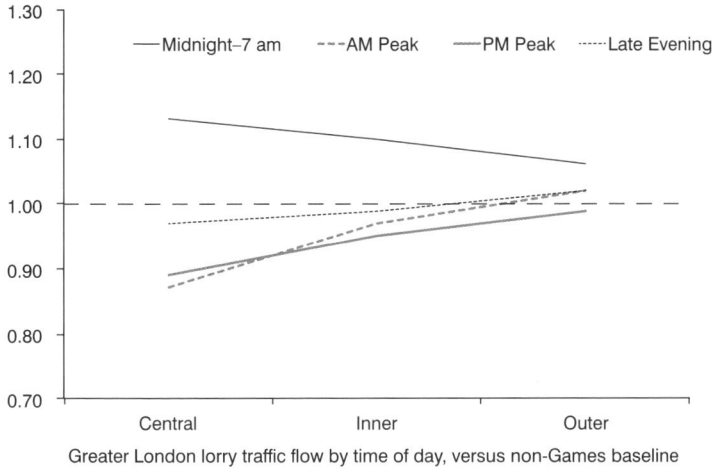

Greater London lorry traffic flow by time of day, versus non-Games baseline

A similar picture is visible with freight. There was a shift away from predominant daytime traffic, towards night (pre-6am) and evening (post-6pm) deliveries[43] (Figure 30).

## Figure 30: Time shift of freight traffic

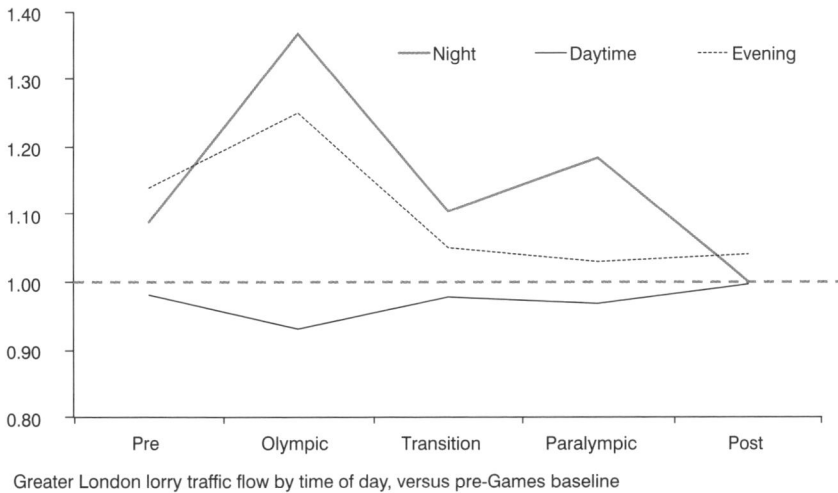

Greater London lorry traffic flow by time of day, versus pre-Games baseline

Source: Tfl Suface Transport, ANPR camera data

On the Underground, we can see re-timing of background journeys away from peak, towards mid-day and evening, again using Oystercard usage as a proxy for non-Olympic demand (Figures 31 and 32).

## Figure 31: Re-timing of background Underground journeys

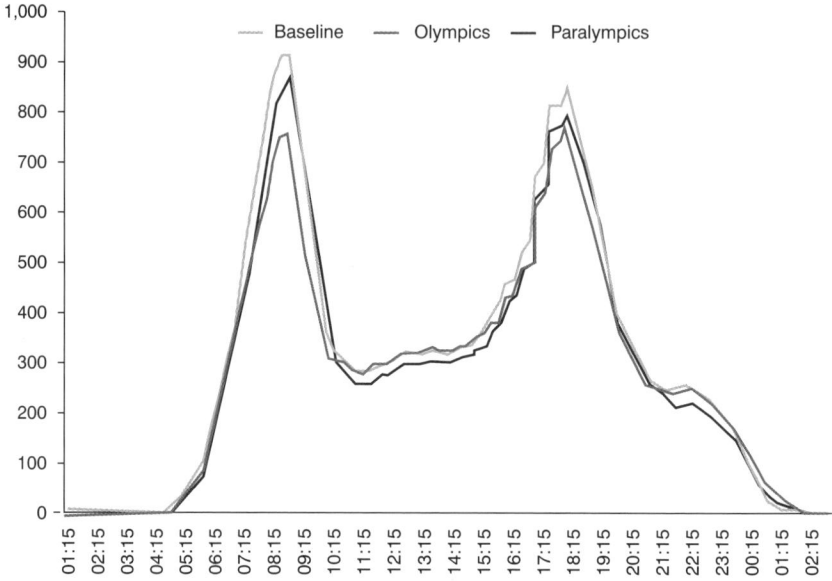

Source: TfL Customer Experience

## Figure 32: Re-timing of background Undergound journeys

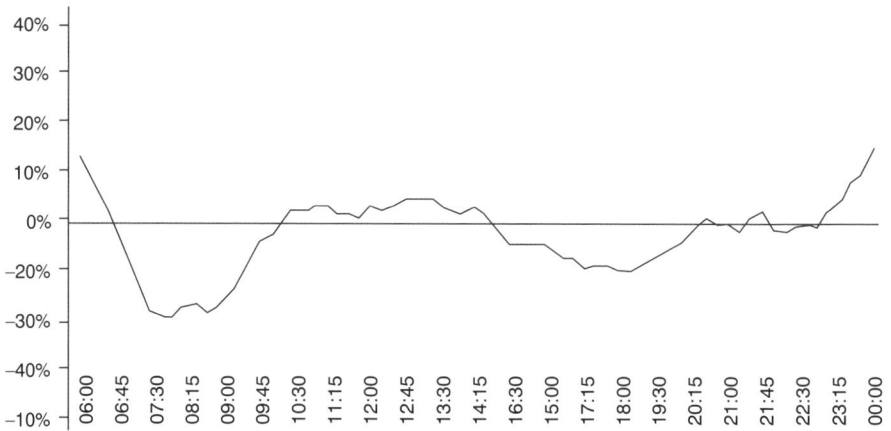

Oystercard entries and exits, indexed vs pre-Games baseline

Source: TfL Customer Experience

This effect is most pronounced at commuter and terminal stations, with 19% peak-time reduction. This further indicates a TDM-specific, rather than a London-wide effect (Figure 33).

## Figure 33: Re-timing of background Underground traffic by location

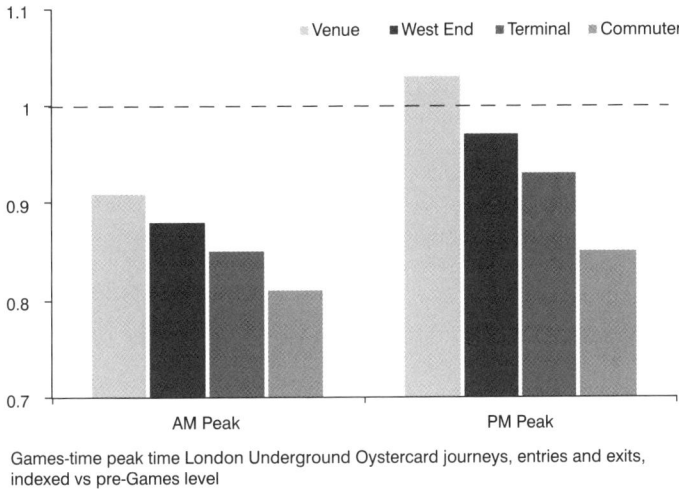

Games-time peak time London Underground Oystercard journeys, entries and exits, indexed vs pre-Games level

Source: TfL Customer Experience

Canary Wharf is of particular note. As a major employment centre on the Jubilee Line and DLR, it was responsible for significant Background Demand. Major employers were heavily targeted with a working hours message. Traveller activity was also up-weighted, focusing on re-timing.

As a result, Oystercard patterns reveal significant forward-shifting of rush hour peaks (Figure 34).

## Figure 34: Re-timing of background Underground journeys

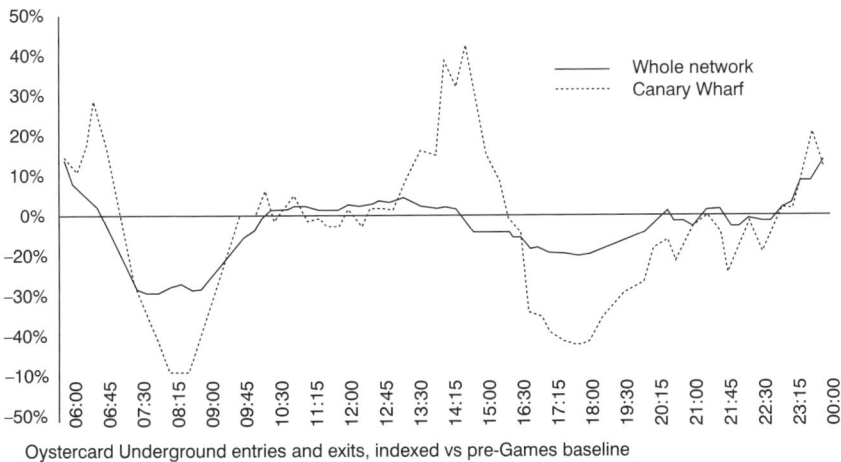

Oystercard Underground entries and exits, indexed vs pre-Games baseline

Source: TfL Customer Experience

## Re-moded journeys

TDM advocated switching from congested modes (road, Underground, rail) to less busy alternatives. We have already shown reductions in non-Olympic journeys on congested modes (Figure 35).

Simultaneously, there were uplifts on modes with 'spare' capacity; buses (+5%), walking (+9%) and cycling (+25%) (Figures 36, 37[44] and 38[45]).

**Figure 35: PR stunt encouraging commuters to walk, run or jog**

**Figure 36: Increased bus journeys**

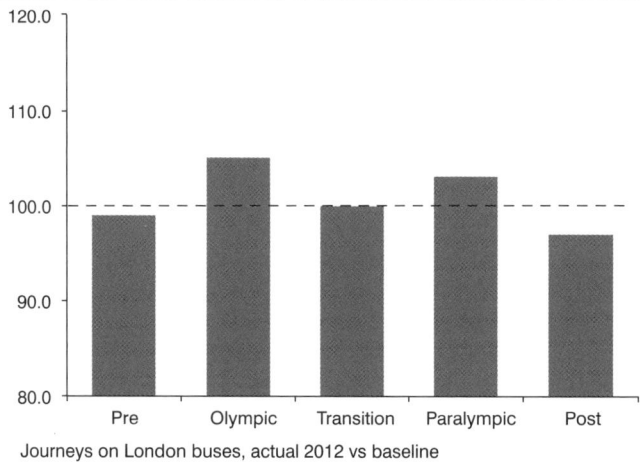

Journeys on London buses, actual 2012 vs baseline

Source: TfL Customer Experience

## Figure 37: Increase in walking journeys

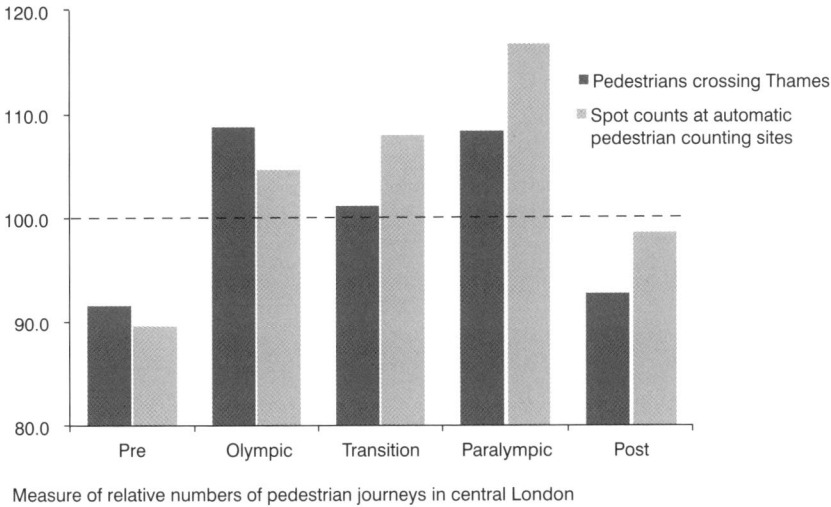

Measure of relative numbers of pedestrian journeys in central London

Source: Transport for London Group Planning

## Figure 38: Increase in cycling journeys

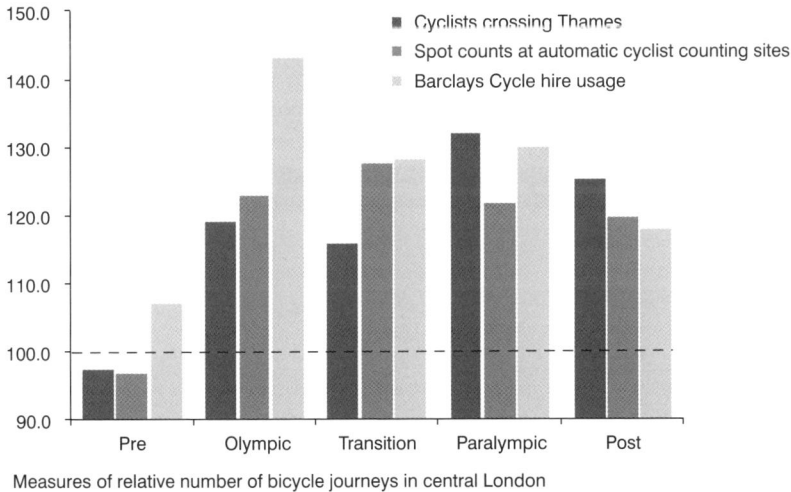

Measures of relative number of bicycle journeys in central London

Source: Transport for London Group Planning

Weather was normal for both Games, but unseasonally poor before (and after) Games-time, accounting for lower pre and post levels of walking and cycling.

Significantly, cycle journeys closer to the Olympic Park rose substantially more than elsewhere (Figure 39).

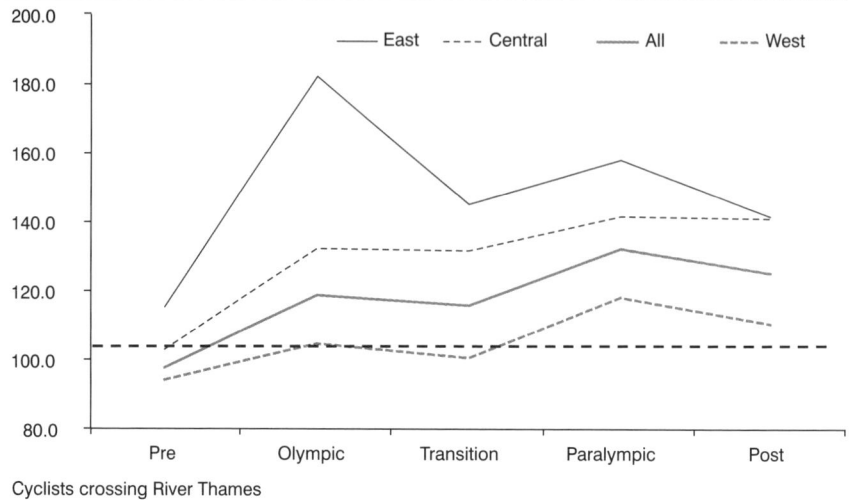

Figure 39: Increase in cycling journeys by location

Cyclists crossing River Thames

Source: Transport for London Group Planning

## Re-routed journeys

As re-routing remains within the same mode, it is not directly visible in total passenger numbers. However we can see its effect in Underground line usage. Again using Oystercards as proxy, we see Background Demand on Central and Jubilee lines reduced more than other lines, following 'Re-route' advice (Figure 40).

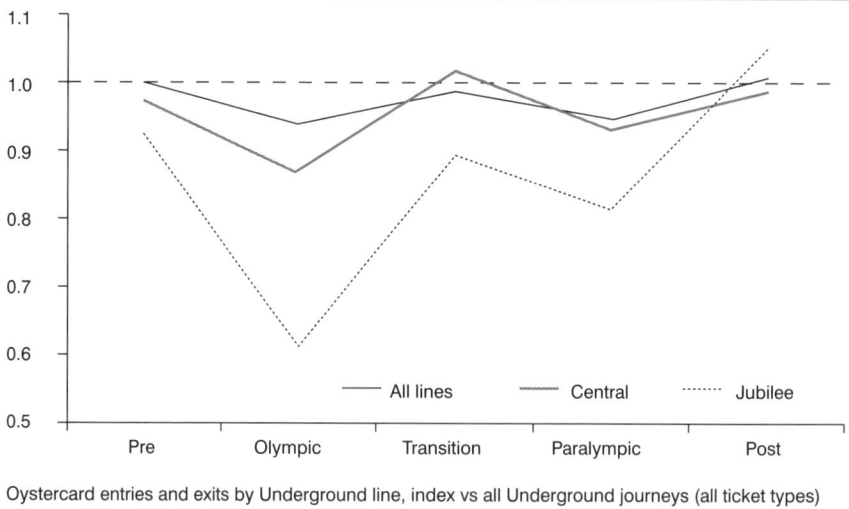

Figure 40: Background journeys by Underground line

Oystercard entries and exits by Underground line, index vs all Underground journeys (all ticket types)

Source: TfL Customer Experience

## Claimed behaviour

Hard journey data show total travel increased, but non-Olympic travel reduced, re-timed, re-moded or re-routed, exactly as TDM prescribed. We now examine claimed behaviours corroborating the campaign effect.

## Background behaviour

Claimed behaviour exceeded TDM objectives. On any given Olympic weekday, 3m regular London travellers (35%) changed their travel via reducing, re-timing, re-moding or re-routing. For the Paralympics that figure was 2.6m, equivalent to 31%[46] (Figures 41 and 42).

**Figure 41: Change in regular travel on a typical Olympic weekday**

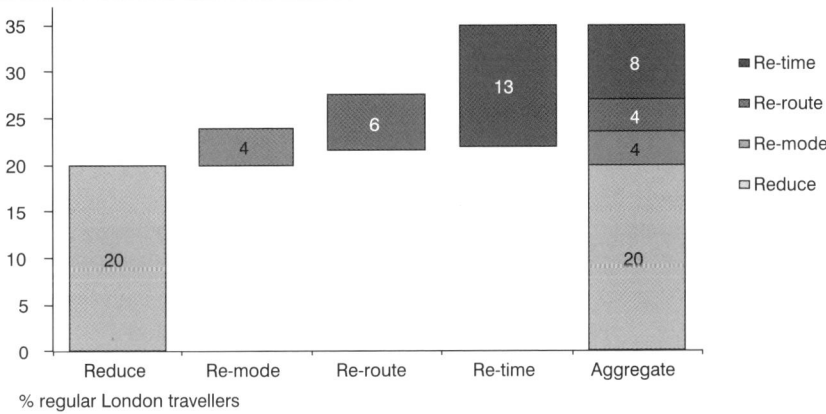

Source: Transport for London Journey Maker Survey 2012

**Figure 42: Change in regular travel on a typical Paralympic weekday**

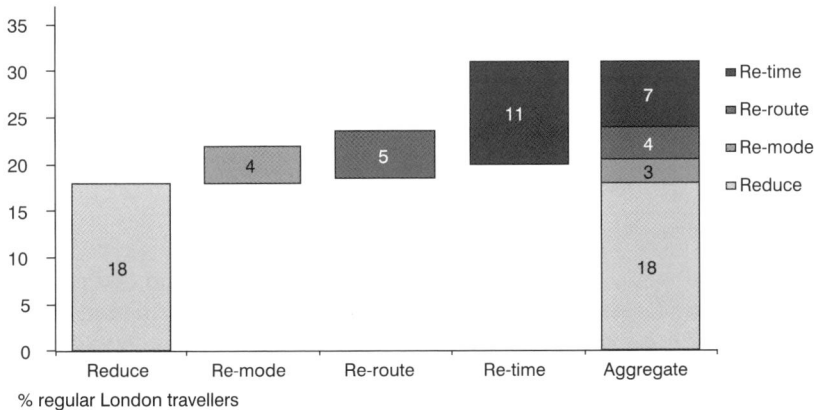

Source: Transport for London Journey Maker Survey 2012

Across the Olympics as a whole, over three quarters of regular travellers made any change (Figure 43).

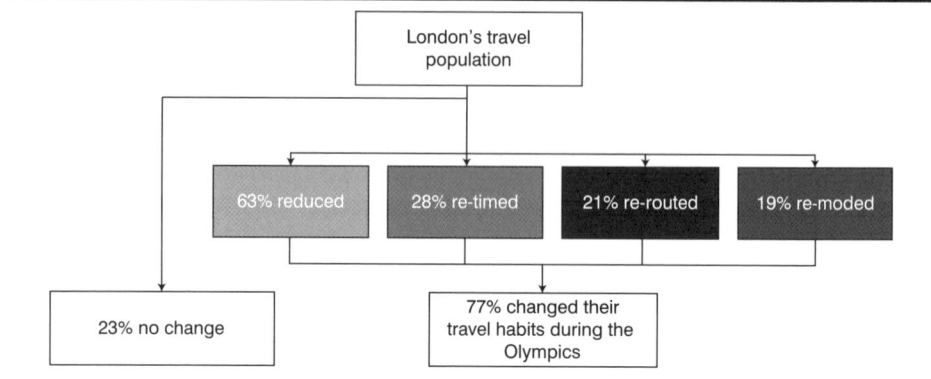

Figure 43: Change in travel behaviour across both Games

Each of the four 'R's was observed, with 'Reduce' being most common, matching actual journey data. This coincided with business travellers making greater use of remote-working tools (Figure 44).

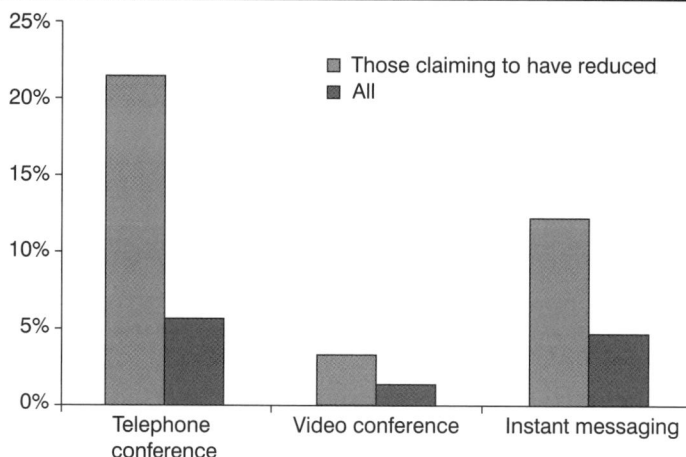

Figure 44: Increased use of remote working tools

Source: TfL Personal Travel Panel

Claimed travel mode shifted from Underground to walking and cycling, as per re-mode advice. A modest shift is also visible from private car, to bus and rail (Figure 45).

A share of 22% of workers claimed to have re-timed travel, leaving for work earlier than usual, with 6% later. Going home, 15% travelled earlier and 7% later (Table 3).

Research specifically amongst hotspot station users showed greater change. While 92% expected that station would be busier than normal, 99% considered in advance how to make their work journey and 43% made changes.[47]

## Figure 45: Change in travel mode across both Games

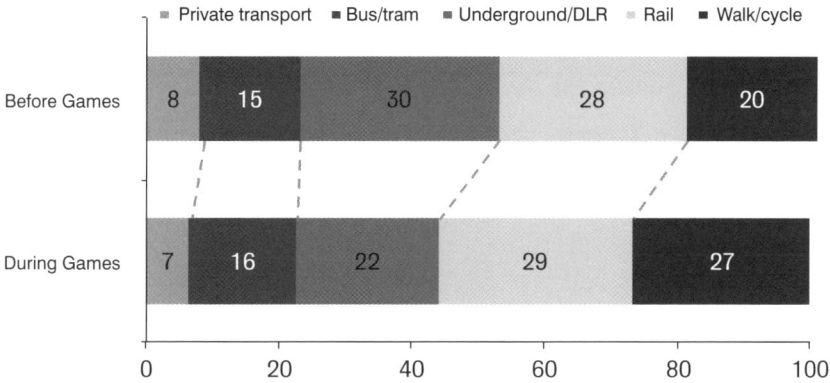

■ Private transport  ■ Bus/tram  ■ Underground/DLR  ▪ Rail  ■ Walk/cycle

Before Games: 8 | 15 | 30 | 28 | 20

During Games: 7 | 16 | 22 | 29 | 27

0    20    40    60    80    100

Source: TfL Personal Travel Panel

## Table 3: Re-timing of commuter trips during the Games

|  | Commuters who changed to an earlier travel time | | Commuters who changed to a later travel time | |
|---|---|---|---|---|
|  | Outward | Return | Outward | Return |
| Before the Games | 07:40 | 17:15 | 08:15 | 18:00 |
| During the Games | 07.15 | 16:15 | 09:00 | 16:45 |

Source: TfL Personal Travel Panel

Significantly, the origin of those making changes was evenly distributed. This rules out the possibility of response being due to Central London residents simply experiencing and reacting to greater levels of congestion.

## Businesses' behaviour

Behaviour was consistent with travel patterns established earlier and TDM messages. By June 2012, 98% of larger businesses had travel plans encouraging staff to avoid busy routes, minimising travel at busy times and promoting walking and cycling. [48]

A separate survey shows 57% of all businesses claiming to have changed travel procedures (72% amongst larger businesses). The changes focused on three of the four 'R's, with reducing and re-timing most common[49] (Figure 46).

The specific nature of changes made supports this, with only 3% of changes having a net increase effect, the remainder support Reduce, Re-time and Re-route, in that order (Table 4).

## Figure 46: Majority of businesses changed their travel procedures

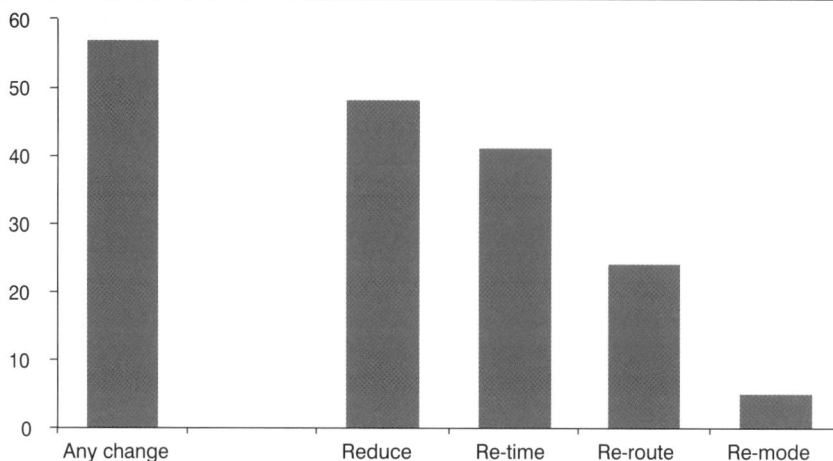

Source: Transport for London, Olympic Business and Freight Survey

## Table 4: Nature and effect of business changes made

| | Incidence | Effect |
|---|---|---|
| Flexi-time | 71% | Re-time |
| Taking leave | 20% | Reduce |
| Working from home | 15% | Reduce |
| Flexi-days | 14% | Reduce |
| Part-time staff changes | 11% | Reduce, Re-time |
| Split shifts | 9% | Re-time |
| Working from other locations | 6% | Re-route |
| Extra staff/all leave cancelled | 3% | Increase |
| Other | 1% | ??? |

Source: Transport for London, Olympic Business and Freight Survey

## Freight behaviour

The majority of freight operators claimed to have made changes to their deliveries (Figure 47).

A long list of changes to delivery practices shows the extent to which operators considered the implications of road impacts. Most changes supported Reduce, Re-time or Re-route, as below (Table 5).

## Spectator behaviour

Ninety-five percent of spectators claimed to reach their venue by public transport. This resulted in high levels of spectator satisfaction with their journey.

## Figure 47: Majority of freight operators changed travel procedures

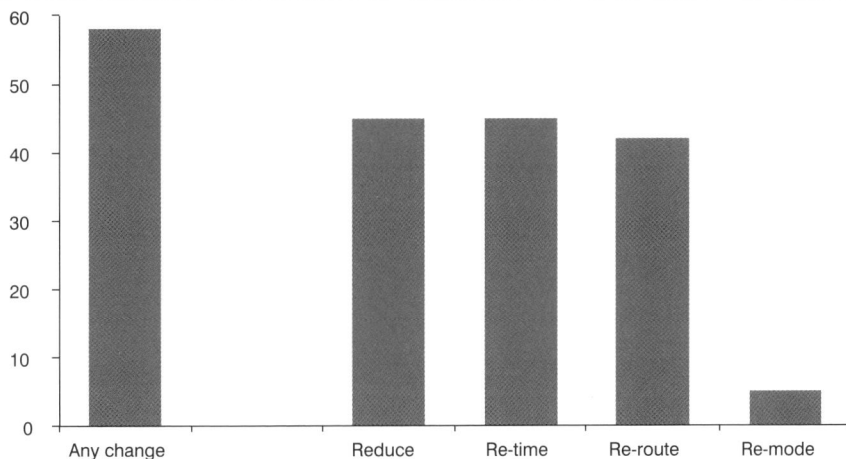

Source: Transport for London, Olympic Business and Freight Survey

## Table 5: Nature and effect of changes made

|  | Incidence | Effect |
|---|---|---|
| Alternative routes avoiding congestion hotspots | 58% | Re-route |
| Alternate routes avoiding restrictions | 57% | Re-route |
| Change delivery/collection time | 48% | Re-time |
| Ensure deliveries right first time | 47% | Reduce |
| Driver/staff start times | 41% | Re-time |
| Change delivery/collection day | 38% | Reduce |
| Out of hours operations | 36% | Re-time |
| Driver/staff shifts | 34% | Re-time |
| Consolidated journeys | 28% | Reduce |
| Stockpiling | 25% | Reduce |
| Postpone non-essential deliveries | 25% | Reduce |
| Re-route from alternative destination | 23% | Re-route |
| Pre-order and pre-deliver | 22% | Reduce |
| Staff leave | 17% | Reduce |
| Sharing resources | 13% | Reduce |
| Temporary stockroom | 10% | Reduce |
| Staff working from home | 8% | Reduce |
| Walking deliveries | 3% | Re-mode |
| Cycle deliveries | 3% | Re-mode |
| Used other modes | 1% | Re-mode |

Source: Transport for London, Olympic Business and Freight Survey

## TDM Causal Effect

So far, proof of TDM effectiveness has centred on observed outcomes matching campaign inputs. Audiences behaved in ways they were not anticipating, or keen to consider prior to the campaign. We now show evidence TDM activity prompted this change of mind.

Across all three audiences, awareness of likely disruption increased, leading to increases in planning and intent to implement changes. Significantly this change occurred across the campaign period, suggesting it was premeditated, and not a last minute panicked response (Figures 48,[50] 49 and 50).

### Figure 48: Changes in intent – Background Demand

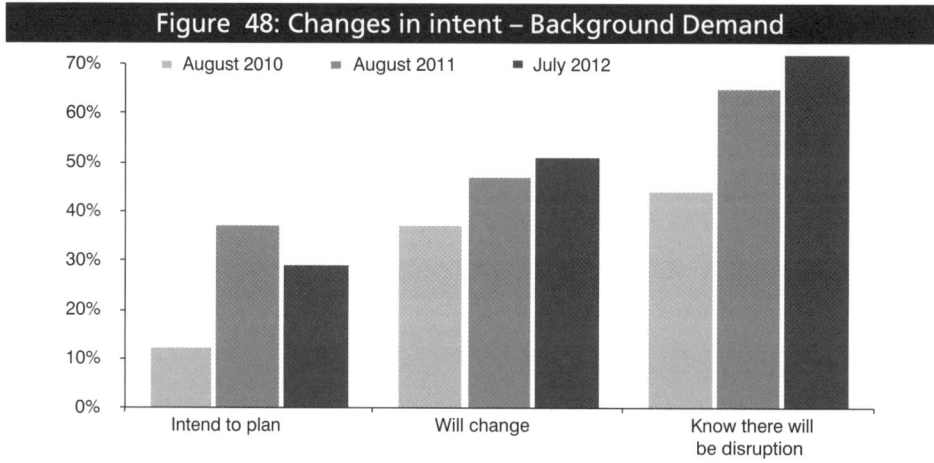

Source: Tfl, London Journey Maker

### Figure 49: Changes in intent – Businesses

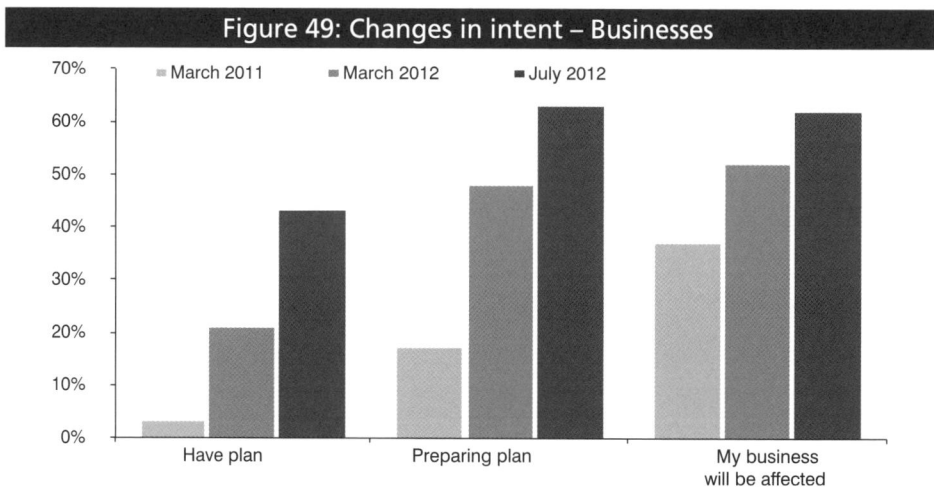

Source: Tfl, London Journey Maker

## Figure 50: Changes in intent – Spectators

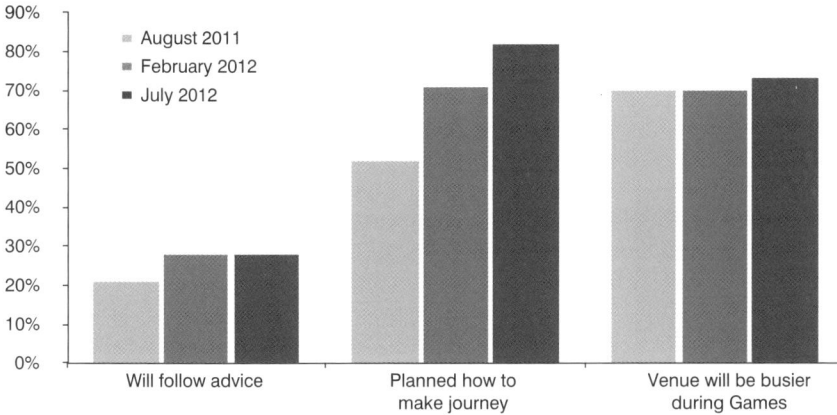

- August 2011
- February 2012
- July 2012

Categories: Will follow advice · Planned how to make journey · Venue will be busier during Games

Source: TfL, Games Spectator Survey

Premeditation is also evident in uptake of planning tools. Over two thirds of regular travellers used the GAOTG website. Usage appears to drive both higher (claimed) incidence of changed journeys and more types of changes undertaken (Figures 51 and 52).

## Figure 51: Engagement with tools drove change

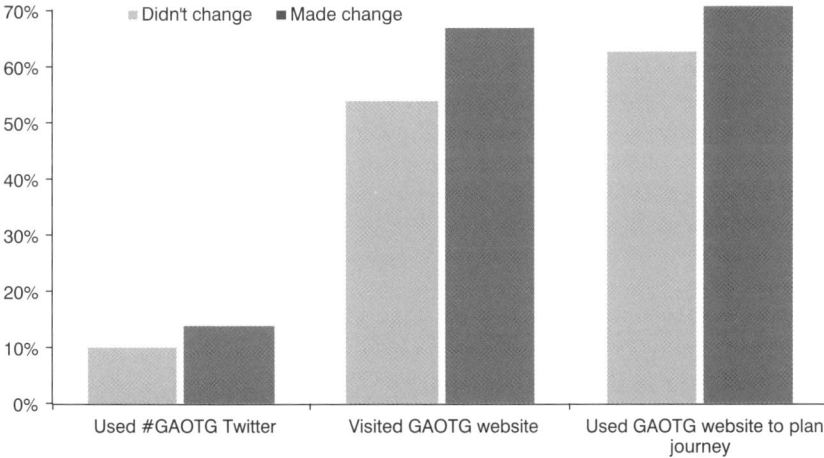

- Didn't change
- Made change

Categories: Used #GAOTG Twitter · Visited GAOTG website · Used GAOTG website to plan journey

Source: Tfl, London Journey Maker

## Figure 52: Visiting GAOTG website correlated with extent of change

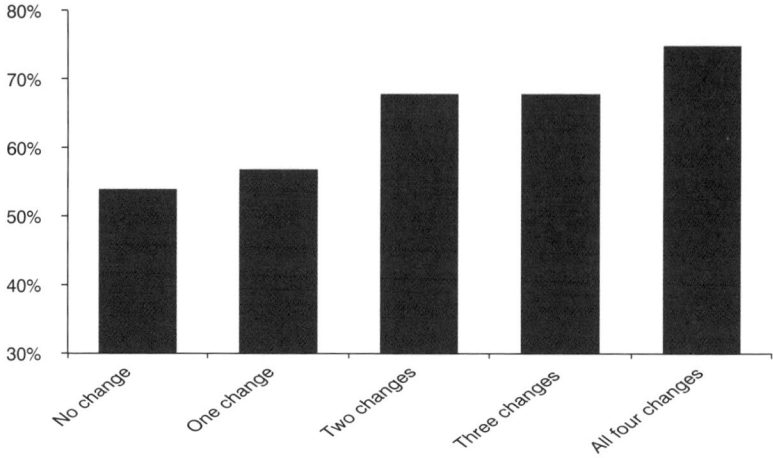

Source: TfL Personal Travel Panel

Awareness of GAOTG advertising built throughout, reaching 60% amongst regular London travellers. Outside London, with more limited exposure, awareness reached just 21% (Figure 53).

## Figure 53: Awareness of GAOTG advertising

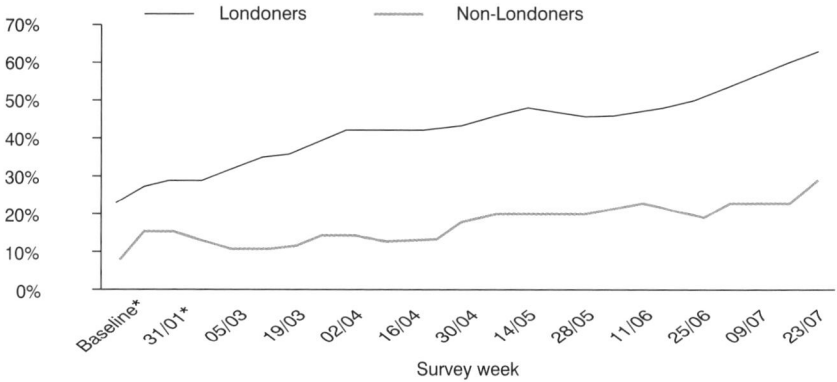

% claiming to recall GAOTG advertising, regular London travellers vs national source

Source: TfL GB Ad-tracker Survey

Significantly, campaign recall shows clear registration of the need to plan and the on-line help available (Figure 54).

Businesses also engaged with on-line tools, prompted by high awareness of TAB communications, especially amongst large Central London businesses (Figures 55 and 56).

## Figure 54: GAOTG message recall

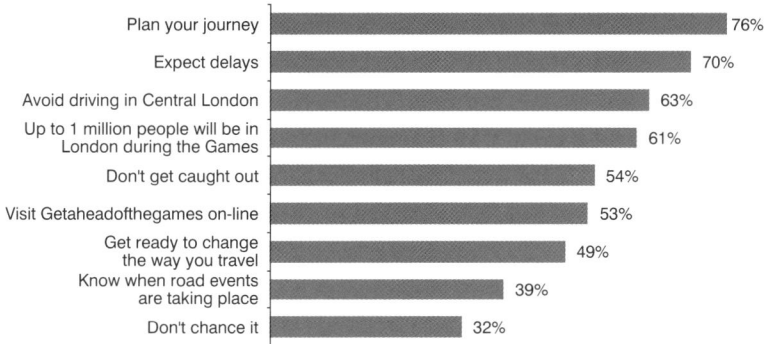

| Message | % |
|---|---|
| Plan your journey | 76% |
| Expect delays | 70% |
| Avoid driving in Central London | 63% |
| Up to 1 million people will be in London during the Games | 61% |
| Don't get caught out | 54% |
| Visit Getaheadofthegames on-line | 53% |
| Get ready to change the way you travel | 49% |
| Know when road events are taking place | 39% |
| Don't chance it | 32% |

% prompted recall of GAOTG messages, regular London travellers

Source: TfL GB Ad-tracker Survey

## Figure 55: Business use of online planning tools

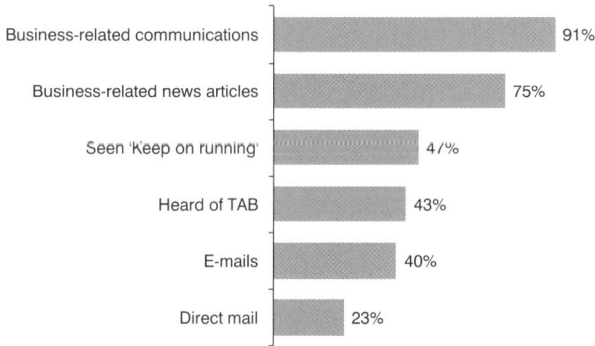

| Tool | % |
|---|---|
| Business-related communications | 91% |
| Business-related news articles | 75% |
| Seen 'Keep on running' | 47% |
| Heard of TAB | 43% |
| E-mails | 40% |
| Direct mail | 23% |

Source: TfL London Business Monitor

## Figure 56: Awareness of business communications

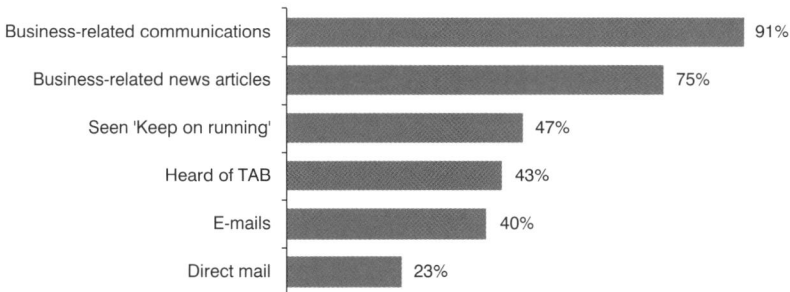

| Item | % |
|---|---|
| Business-related communications | 91% |
| Business-related news articles | 75% |
| Seen 'Keep on running' | 47% |
| Heard of TAB | 43% |
| E-mails | 40% |
| Direct mail | 23% |

Prompted recall of TAB initiatives, large London businesses

Source: TfL London Business Monitor

Spectators also used planning tools in substantial numbers: 82% claimed to have pre-planned by July, with 55% visiting the Getting to the Games section on the website.

## Worth doing?

Having established TDM was effective, we now examine the more profound question of whether it was financially worthwhile.

Unlike most commercial IPA Effectiveness cases, this was not a discretionary investment aimed at driving profitable growth. Investment was mandatory, not discretionary. Its objective was reduction, not growth. And its motive wasn't boosting profit, but eliminating failure.

This scenario dictates an alternative to ROMI for establishing 'worth'. Ratio of Success Achieved (ROSA) considers the cost of a component relative to the overall outcome it helps ensure.

This prompts three fundamental questions:

1.   Were the Olympics themselves 'worth' hosting?
2.   How much of their success was the TDM campaign responsible for?
3.   How efficient was it in ensuring that success?

## Value of the games

Of the countless qualitative assessments of the value of London 2012, two stand out. Firstly, the extensive 'legacy' benefits – central to London's bid – are now widely reported 'on track'.[51]

Secondly, the UK public overwhelmingly feels the Games were worth hosting, in marked contrast to popular opinion prior to bidding (Table 6).

| Table 6: Public attitudes towards the London 2012 Games | | |
|---|---|---|
| | 2005 | 2012 |
| I am in favour of London hosting the Olympics | 37% | |
| The amount spent on London 2012 was worth the money | | 79% |
| London 2012 was worth the investment | | 69% |

Sources:  BMRB, ICM/The Guardian, ComRes/BBC

It may be disingenuous to seek a quantitative value for the Games. It is certainly difficult. Nevertheless, the two substantial independent post-Games assessments anticipate likely returns of £16.5bn and £28bn to £41bn.[52]Final published costs are quoted as £8.77bn.[53]

## TDM's contribution

Here, an analogy establishes how much of that anticipated return TDM might reasonably claim to be responsible for. Car insurance is generally regarded as an unfortunate cost. Other than satisfying themselves they aren't overpaying for it, most people rarely concern themselves with what it's 'worth'.

Without insurance however, a car cannot be legally driven, rendering it effectively worthless. The value of the insurance in that sense equates to the value of the car (both likely selling price and utility to the owner).

Likewise, as an essential component in the delivery of the Games, the TDM campaign can lay some claim to *all* the benefits of the Games. When insuring a car, a key consideration is the relative value of the vehicle versus the cost of the insurance. As this ratio drops and approaches 1:1, the viability of that car becomes questionable.

On that basis, the pertinent consideration is the ratio of the total value of the Games to TDM cost.

## TDM cost

The total cost of the TDM campaign was £30m.[54] When considering the campaign, other means of achieving the same effect were dismissed as having too great a human and political 'cost'. These included odd and even number-plate car restrictions, enforced business closures, mandatory changes to working hours and changes to public holidays.

More pertinently, the £30m cost of TDM was weighed up against further investment in infrastructure. Investment above £6.5bn was considered and rejected, on the basis of demand reduction being a more efficient means of coping than capacity increase.

Certainly, TDM was over a hundred-fold cheaper than increasing capacity further, effectively saving £1.5bn–£3.5bn.

## ROSA

Ratio of Success Achieved (ROSA) considers the cost of the campaign versus the total value of the outcome.

Taking the lower figure for anticipated benefits, £16.5bn was effectively safeguarded by a component costing £30m, a ROSA of 550:1, comfortably above the viability threshold.

## Conclusion

Olympic success depends on preparation. London's preparations included pre-empting and preventing extreme transport overload and delays. The substantial investment in increased capacity was essential and left a valuable infrastructural legacy.

In comparison, managing demand was relatively cheap. It also allowed capacity investment to be capped at £6.5bn. London coped with its unprecedented Olympic surge in part because underlying demand was managed precisely in the four ways prescribed.

In retrospect it is perhaps unsurprising the campaign worked as intended, such was the rigour that went into determining the desired behaviours. As a mandatory component of the Games' success, TDM produced a stellar 550:1 ROSA.

Not bad for a nation prone to downplaying and undermining success.

The final words are best left to LOCOG Chairman and four-time Olympic medal winner, Lord Coe:

*When our time came, Britain, we did it right.*

Lord Coe, LOCOG Chairman, 12 August 2012.

## Appendix 1: Glossary of terms

With apologies for the extensive use of acronyms and terminology in the paper, this glossary should help the reader navigate what was a complex logistical exercise.

| | |
|---|---|
| ATM | Active Travel Management: programme of works, such as alterations to traffic signals, designed to manage vehicle flows on the London road network, co-ordinating with the establishment of the ORN and PRN. Being largely road orientated, ATM was intended to work in concert with TDM, but not replace it. |
| DCMS | Department for Culture, Media and Sport, the department of the UK Government holding ultimate responsibility for the successful staging of the Games. |
| DLR | Docklands Light Railway: mass transit rail system serving many of the Games venues in the East of London. |
| Four 'R's | Term describing the four behaviour change objectives prescribed by the demand modelling. Whilst never externally communicated as such, they were 'Reduce', 'Re-time', 'Re-route' and 'Re-mode'. |
| Games | For the purposes of this paper this term is used as shorthand for the London 2012 Summer Olympic and Paralympic Games, more formally known as The Games of the XXX Olympiad. |
| Games Family | Collective term for athletes, coaching teams, other team officials and accredited media. The Olympics attracted 17,800 athletes and a total Games Family of 44,800. For the Paralympics, these figures were 4,000 and 9,000. Games Family were entitled to drive in Games Lanes. |
| Games Lanes | Under London's Host City Agreement, the 30 most critical miles of the ORN were marked out with dedicated lanes. Rather like bus lanes, these were restricted at key times to officially accredited Games Family Vehicles and emergency vehicles on-call. Non-accredited vehicles using active Games Lanes received a £130 fine. Unlike bus lanes, the times Games Lanes were operative were variable, controlled according to background levels of road traffic. |
| Games Makers | Official term for London 2012 volunteers; 100,000 took on various roles from scanning tickets, cleaning toilets, providing physiotherapy and helping backstage at Opening and Closing Ceremonies to directing spectators. |
| Games-time | The active periods of the Olympic and Paralympic Games; 27 July –12 August and 29 August–9 September 2012. |

| | |
|---|---|
| GAOTG | Get Ahead of the Games; key theme of the TDM campaign. The website www.getaheadofthegames.com was the key referral point of all regular traveller communications. The hashtag #GAOTG was also the Twitter handle used during the campaign. |
| Javelin | Not the athletics event, but a high-speed shuttle service operated during Games-time between St. Pancras International and Stratford International, serving the Olympic Park. |
| Jubilee Line | London Underground line running from Central London to Canary Wharf and on to Stratford, site of the Olympic Park. Along with the DLR, projected to experience the greatest growth from Olympic traffic. |
| LOCOG | London Organising Committee of the Olympic and Paralympic Games: organisation overseeing planning and development of the Games. Jointly established by the DCMS, Mayor of London and the British Olympic Association. LOCOG was structured as a private company limited by guarantee and worked closely with the publicly funded ODA. |
| LLRS | London Lorry Control Scheme: set of rules governing the driving of heavy goods vehicles over 18 tonnes into and across London. Night-time hours of restriction are typically 9pm to 7am, but were relaxed during the Games, to facilitate Re-timing. |
| National Rail | Rail services operating nationally. Some of these services are 'commuter' trains into London. Most non-London UK Ticket Holders travelled to London using National Rail services. See also Overground. |
| ODA | Olympic Delivery Authority. Non-departmental public body of the DCMS, responsible for delivering Olympic venues, infrastructure and legacy. Effectively our client for this project. |
| ORN | Olympic Route Network. Network of dedicated roads linking Games venues. Roads in the network are subject to modified traffic regulations and kept free of obstructions and road works. Some 30 miles of the ORN in London had dedicated Games Lanes. See also PRN. |
| Overground | Rail network serving London. Part of the National Rail network, but under franchise control of Transport for London. TfL therefore has a greater quantity and quality of data for passenger movements on this section of the rail network. |
| Oystercard | A smart card used for travel across London's public transport network. The card is 'touched in' and 'touched out' to allow access to the service. This generates rich data for TfL on actual travel patterns by individual user. The majority of regular travellers use a plastic Oystercard pre-loaded with cash and/or period travel pass. Olympics Ticket Holders were issued with a complementary paper Olympic Travelcard for use on the day of their event only. This allowed TfL to analyse journey flows by Olympic versus regular travellers. |

| | |
|---|---|
| PRN | Paralympic Route Network; the PRN was effectively a smaller version of the ORN. |
| ROSA | Term introduced in this paper. Ratio of Success Achieved divides the value of the success by the cost of an element helping ensure it. ROSAs approaching 1:1 represent questionable value. |
| TAB | Travel Advice to Businesses; a sub-campaign within the overall TDM campaign. |
| TDM | Travel Demand Management, the subject of this paper. Defined as the application of strategies and policies to reduce travel demand, or redistribute demand in space or in time. The IOC demanded London implement TDM activity across both roads and public transport network. Interventions can be physical/policy based or communication/advice based. Aside from ATM alterations to road flow via traffic-light phasing, LOCOG rejected the use of other physical interventions, such as alternate odd and even car number plate restrictions, in favour of communications. |
| TfL | Transport for London, the local government body responsible for implementing transport strategy and managing transport services across London. Operating in an integrated framework, it co-ordinates all modes of transport from walking and cycling to driving and 'public transport'. |
| TLRN | Transport for London Route Network. These are roads owned or managed by TfL. They represent 5% of London's roads, but 33% of its road traffic. Special provisions have been made to encourage cycling on these roads and across London. |
| Traffic | Note that, depending on context, this term may mean road traffic, or numbers of passengers on public transport modes (otherwise referred to as 'passengers', 'journeys' or 'demand'). |
| Travelcard | Ticket allowing unlimited use of London public transport, within certain zones and time periods. Travelcards can take both paper and electronic form. Regular travellers predominantly use electronic versions, loaded on their Oystercard. More occasional users tend to purchase paper versions, typically in One-Day TravelCard form. The Olympic TravelCard, issued to Games Ticket Holders, was one such paper card. |

# Notes

1 Mayor of London 'Olympic Legacy Monitoring: Personal Travel Behaviour during the Games', Transport for London.
2 A glossary of acronyms and jargon is provided as Appendix 1.
3 'London' is used in this paper as shorthand for London *and the UK*. Although the Games are awarded to a host city, they are staged in its host country. Whilst events were focused on 21 venues across the Capital, venues around the country – notably Eton Dorney, Weymouth and 5 regional football stadia – benefitted from the overall strategy whilst requiring separate provisions of their own.
4 'Olympics' and 'Games' are used to refer to *both* Olympic and Paralympic Games, more formally *'The Games of the XXX Olympiad'*.
5 Report of the IOC Evaluation Commission for the Games of the XXX Olympiad in 2012, March 22 2005 (Technical report, pre the selection of the winning city).
6 IOC press release accompanying the awarding of the Games to London, 5 July 2005.
7 Road races, live sites and cultural events would attract 12m spectators, plus there would be unofficial events and gatherings.
8 *GA Daily News*, August 6 1996.
9 Cartoons from the Opinion Page, *The Atlanta Journal*, July/August 1996.
10 In a move commentators noted as highly significant, Juan Antonio Samaranch did not use his customary plaudit *"the best Olympics ever"*, opting instead for *"exceptional"* and *"well done Atlanta"*. Notably for Sydney 2000 (his final Games as IOC President), he reverted to his traditional *"best Games ever"* accolade.
11 Sydney 2000, Salt Lake City 2002, Athens 2004, Torino 2006, Beijing 2008 and Vancouver 2010 all implemented TDM programmes.
12 IOC Host City Contract (general), Technical Manual on Transport, 2005.
13 IOC Host City Contract (with London 2012), Technical Manual on Transport, 2007.
14 Source: TfL. In the period 2005–2012, £6.5bn was invested to permanently enhance transport infrastructure. This included line upgrades and new trains on the Tube, the extension of the Overground network, capacity enhancements to the Docklands Light Railway (DLR) and remodelling of Kings Cross St Pancras Underground station.
15 This programme of work was a huge integrated effort, utilising the pooled expertise of TfL, ODA, LOCOG, Network Rail and the Train Operating Companies.
16 Data released to the public and shown here was presented in 30-minute intervals.
17 Define conducted four waves of qualitative research to guide development and implementation of the campaign.
18 Define qualitative research, March 2009.
19 Source: London Journey Maker survey, August 2010. Qualitative research suggested car drivers and the most habitual public transport users were most intransigent.
20 London Business Monitor survey, March 2011.
21 For instance, the Olympic Park was served by no fewer than four different stations. Detailed spectator routing strategies meant the recommended station depended on the correct entry gate for each ticket. For 10% of spectators, that meant alighting at West Ham station and walking the 10 minute 'Green Way' to the Park. Eton Dorney was served by three stations, with connecting coach services. Wimbledon Station was not recommended for spectators viewing the tennis at Wimbledon.
22 TfL Spectator Survey.
23 Define qualitative research, 2009–2011.
24 Define qualitative Creative Development research 2009–2010. Early recommendations: 'The Big Squeeze' and 'Beat the Squeeze' were developed into the more implicitly positive campaign slogan ultimately selected.
25 Communications focused on working from home as the most likely 'Reduce' behaviour, but information and tips also advocated taking annual leave at Games-time, whether leaving London or staying at home, possibly to watch the Olympics on television.
26 Buses are less busy over the summer period and were not anticipated to attract significant incremental Olympic traffic. They therefore offered available capacity. Walking and cycling effectively have unlimited capacity. Journeys made wholly or partly on these modes effectively free up capacity on busier modes.
27 GAOTG became a central resource for TfL, National Rail, TOCs, The Highways Agency, travel agents, etc. This allowed these organisations to speak with one voice when it came to planning for the Olympics and to present accurate and useful information. Tools were extensively taken up across these organisations' digital properties – websites, Twitter feeds, Facebook pages, ticket-booking pages , etc.

28  They commented "TfL may have done too good a job in preparing the Capital for the Olympics. Unusually, for a city of individuals not known for their pliancy, millions seem to have observed TfL's plea to 'Get Ahead of the Games'. Transport has for the most part worked well and rush-hour traffic has largely flowed freely. That is to be applauded as a big achievement.

29  He widely quoted in *The Times, Daily Mail, Guardian, Daily Mirror* and *i newspaper.*

30  Source: TfL. Throughout this paper, comparisons are made with 'Baseline' passenger numbers. Separate Baselines are established for each mode, each based on 2011 usage, plus appropriate background growth. Basing them on the equivalent summer period allows for seasonal variation. The Baseline therefore offers *the best forecast of what transport demand would have been in Summer 2012, had London not hosted the Games.*

31  Source: TfL.

32  Source: TfL, 'Enough People Influenced Enough', December 2012. TfL regularly releases a number of network performance metrics for each mode. The key indicator measures are shown here.

33  Source: TfL. All public transport modes. Actual 2012 journeys versus Baseline. As discussed before, the Baseline is based on actual 2011 seasonal usage, plus any appropriate (non-Olympic) growth. Background Demand is calculated by subtracting known Olympic demand from total demand. We go on to show two other methods of inferring Background Demand patterns, using station types and Oystercard data. Both of these indicate the same phenomenon.

34  Source: TfL Travel in London Report 5; Spotlight on the 2012 London Olympic and Paralympic Games.

35  ORN journey reliability 95.6% vs 95% target. PRN journey reliability 97.8%. Journey time is calculated from a number of venue-to-venue travel times. Reliability is based on the number of journeys completed within five minutes of their expected time.

36  As a side benefit, TfL was able to restrict the activation of Games Lanes, opening them to regular traffic for more of the time.

37  TfL Spectator Survey, July 2012. It reported 5% travelled by 'car, minibus or motorcycle'. It is not possible to split this categorisation, but qualitative assessment is that only a small portion of this was by car.

38  Source: TfL. Data for vehicles over 5.2m in length (regular Ford Transit van or larger). The drop is again relative to the long vehicle Baseline.

39  Source: TfL. Rise relative to Baseline (i.e. Forecast usage were London not hosting the Games).

40  Source: TfL. Decrease also relative to Baseline.

41  Stations are categorised into four groups: Venue stations served Games locations; Terminal stations were key interchanges carrying both Olympic and commuter traffic; West End stations covered a mix of general shopping, leisure and work activity; and csommuter stations were in areas mostly serving offices, including the City and Canary Wharf. Not all traffic to venues stations was Olympic, just as traffic to commuter stations would not have consisted entirely of commuters. Nevertheless, the relative patterns are instructive.

42  Paper Travelcards, such as the ones issued as Olympic Travelcards, use a magnetic stripe, whereas Oystercards use a chip. Data for each is therefore collected separately at barriers. Oystercards tend to be used more by regular public transport users. We cannot, however, reliably use Travelcard data as a proxy for Olympic traffic, as many more paper Travelcards are purchased each day than Olympic Travelcards used, for example by less regular public transport users.

43  The decrease of daytime is much smaller than the uplifts in night and evening when expressed as an index, because the base amount of daytime freight is so much larger – it being the predominant time freight is normally delivered.

44  Whilst network usage data effectively measures all journeys, walking data is based on surveys of a representative sample. Two such surveys are referenced here: Count 1 'The River Thames Screenline' measures pedestrians crossing the river Thames at accessible crossing points; Count 2 counts pedestrians crossing a sample of 39 automatic counting sites located in public areas. Despite differences between the two counts, the underlying pattern reported is consistent.

45  For cycling there are three data sources. Count 1 is the same method as for walking. Count 2 is similar to walking, but based on 15 different counting points. Count 3 uses uptake of Barclays Cycle Hire, a system operating across Central London.

46  Source: ODA Journey Maker Survey. Regular travellers in London. Based on London population of 8.5m travellers.

47  TfL Oyster and Hotspot User Survey, 2012.

48  Source: 'Review of Site Specific Action plans', February and June 2012. Businesses with over 250 employees were allocated an ODA travel planner to help them develop an action plan. This was the review of that activity.

49  Source: TFL Olympic Business and Freight Survey.

50  'Intend to plan' declined in the final few months as more travellers actually made plans.

51  Indeed some of that legacy includes lasting travel behavioural change, resulting from TDM, such as increases in cycling and walking.

52  *Economic Impact of the London 2012 Olympic and Paralympic Games*, Oxford Economics; *Post Games Evaluation: Meta-Evaluation of the Impacts and Legacy of the London 2012 Olympic Games and Paralympic Games*, Grant Thornton. Whilst there is no shortage of bloggers and 'experts' claiming the Games were not worth the investment, none quotes a likely return or bases their opinion on statistical economic analysis, as the two reports referred to do.

53  Hugh Robertson, Minister of State, DCMS, Written statement to parliament, 16 July 2013. This represents direct costs. Other investments, such as the purchase of the Olympic Park and indeed, most of the £6.5bn transport infrastructure upgrade are not included in this as they are investments, rather than sunk costs.

54  Source: TfL, 'Enough People Influenced Enough'.

# Public Health England

## Be Clear on Cancer

**By Richard Storey and Katarina Tencor, M&C Saatchi**

Contributing authors: Anna Garratt, Department of Health; James Brandon and Yvonne Ridley, Public Health England; John Paul Cadman, GroupM PRIMUS; Amanda Boughey, Cancer Research UK

Cancer is the highest cause of death in the UK costing £6.4 billion a year in research, treatment and care. Whilst investment is having an effect, UK survival rates lag behind comparable European countries. The need for earlier diagnosis is stark, yet 51% of bowel and 79% of lung cancers are diagnosed late. Correcting this could potentially save a substantial number of lives.

Increasing awareness of symptoms alone would not solve the problem. Cancer is surrounded by a fog of ignorance, fear and denial, which leads people to procrastinate. Clearing this irrationality was critical. Public Health England ('PHE') created a communications initiative to dispel the uncertainties surrounding cancer and normalise seeking GPs' opinions. It looked to drive clarity, straightforwardness and hope, to counter doubt, wariness and unease. This included clarity on symptoms, clarity on action and clarity on the benefit. Appropriately, the initiative was called 'Be Clear on Cancer' ('BCOC').

The cancer space is awash with charitable initiatives for individual cancer types. To maximise cut-through and return, 'BCOC' cast its initiative as cancer-type agonistic, using bespoke colours to span cancer types.

The no-nonsense campaign adopted the tone of a 'good doctor' – authoritative, empathetic and approachable, never skirting around the subject.

To overcome fear and despondency, it deployed a 'good news sandwich', with the possibility of cancer delivered between two pieces of reassurance. First, that having symptoms doesn't mean you have cancer (it's often something else entirely) and second, that earlier diagnosis improves your chances.

With a predominantly older target audience, TV was the key driver behind awareness, supported by print and radio. It used themes of normalisation yet urgency, encouraging those with symptoms to do something sooner rather than later. Ambient ideas were used to deliver cancer-specific messages in an obvious but unavoidable way.

Effectiveness as a mission shaped the campaign in numerous ways. To make best use of resources, cancer types with the potential to save the most lives were prioritised, beginning with bowel and lung cancers.

To ensure best use of public money and assess impact on NHS systems, a 'pilot, evaluate, roll-out' approach was deployed.

Activity was tested locally, piloted regionally, then rolled out nationally, using hard evidence from each stage to justify further investment. Each campaign went through rigorous testing and proof of effectiveness before advancing to the next stage.

A new process of data collection by the NHS allowed 5 million GP visits to be analysed by patient symptom – a first for PHE and a big step forward in the measurement of health-orientated campaigns.

'BCOC' saw as much progress in three months as the previous two years. A pronounced shift in salience and perceived severity of key symptoms led to a 62% and 29% increase of patients aged 50+ visiting their GP for lung and bowel cancer respectively. A subsequent increase of 21.8% and 29.6% in referrals from GPs to specialists demonstrated the campaign's 'quality' of response, indicating that 'at risk' patients (rather than just 'worried well') had reported to their GP.

The acid test of effectiveness, however, is diagnosis. Here too were clear indications, with an increase of 17.8% lung and 11.5% bowel cancer cases diagnosed during the campaign period, representing 696 extra patients diagnosed. From these, over 400 additional cases were caught in early stages.

Not only was the campaign extremely effective according to NICE's valuation of £30,000 per quality life year, through minimising the time needed for care and sick-leave the campaign generated a ROMI to society of £1.26 in the campaign months alone. As a campaign dedicated to prolonging lives, launched under the assumption it costs to do so, seeing a positive economic return was a bonus.

# Department for Communities and Local Government

## Fire safety: how a clock nudged a nation so fire couldn't kill

**By Alice Huntley and Alison Hoad, RKCR/Y&R**

Contributing authors: James Webb and Mary-Ann Auckland, Department for Communities and Local Government; Maziyar Karimian, RKCR/Y&R

In 2008 many people in the UK had smoke alarms that weren't working. The government recommends that you test your smoke alarm at least monthly, but people weren't doing this. A campaign – across TV, radio, digital and print – that year focusing on the dangers of inhaling toxic smoke proved to be relatively successful. A budget of £3.1m was allocated for the first year and after just one burst, people's sense of invulnerability towards smoke from a house fire began to decrease.

However in 2010 substantial cuts were made to government marketing spend across the board. As a sign of the importance of the issue, Fire Kills was just one of three campaigns to survive the cut. But its budget was reduced to less than one third.

The challenge facing the Department was that a new radical approach was needed. Research showed that even though 85% of people agreed attitudinally that 'testing your smoke alarm regularly can save lives', only half as many claimed actually to test their smoke alarm with any regularity. So the Department looked towards behavioural economics and ways to overcome inertia through triggers and nudges. With the decreased budget they needed a strategy of high impact for a short duration.

So, the question was, what would be a specific time and context when people were already carrying out active behaviours and when could they be 'nudged' into testing their smoke alarm?

The answer lay in a national activity that has been taking place twice a year for nearly one hundred years: clock change. Instead of increasing the strength of people's motivation to change their behaviour, it would just make it seem easier to do. And by giving them a specific time and relevant context to act on, it could increase the likelihood that they would actually follow through, and repeat the behaviour.

By concentrating activity into two short annual bursts, it ensured a significant level of cut through with as many people as possible. And unlike some occasions like Mother's Day or Christmas, the clock change dates were relatively free from competition, giving Fire Kills the opportunity to dominate despite a relatively modest media budget.

Radio was the lead medium. It worked by lulling people into the false sense that the advertisement was going to be an information notice about the coming clock change, before shattering this illusion in a chilling switch of message. This radio advert was the second most impactful radio advert that the Radio Advertising Bureau had ever measured.

In print, the campaign centred on a single powerful image of a burnt clock, as if it were forensic evidence retrieved from a home that had been on fire. It visually linked the clock change with fire safety, and added a layer of emotional resonance on top.

Digital activity included Facebook advertising in the week before and after each clock change. To boost the March 2013 campaign, an online video was produced and released on YouTube. PR activity included a 10-minute feature on ITV's *This Morning* about fire safety, linked to the clock change campaign and featuring the campaign's key message – when you change your clock, test your smoke alarm.

Despite a significantly reduced media weight and frequency relative to the previous campaign, the clock change campaign proved to be just as effective, if not more so. Those who had seen the campaign were three times more likely to have tested their smoke alarm. And most importantly, there was a significant (16%) reduction in the annual number of deaths from accidental 'fires in dwellings'. In total, annual fire deaths fell by 41 over the two-year campaign period versus a plateau over the two years before that.

# SECTION 3

# Creating fame

# Being famous

**By Nicholas Hall**
Head of Broadcast and Delivery, Gocompare.com

Your creative agency or your media agency will, at some point in your marketing career, suggest a fame campaign. I know: I've had numerous agencies suggest it over the years, usually coupled with a massive media spend through high-cost media channels. Back in 2009 it was the same at Gocompare.com, but when it was suggested this time, the timing was right and the brand needed one. The category was young and, with no clear brand distinction between the big four, Gocompare.com needed to establish itself as a credible household brand, coupled with a powerful brand icon and high media weights targeting fame channels. In short, we pulled it off and almost overnight established Gocompare.com as one of the leading price-comparison services in the UK. Then came the tidal wave, no, a tsunami of consumer feedback, together with a significant increase in customer traffic – the campaign worked! We got the nation talking about the character and the brand, firmly placing the brand at the top of awareness charts. The campaign was incredibly effective in returning record levels of ROMI for the business and firmly established Gocompare.com as one of the leading brands within the category.

So when reviewing this year's IPA Effectiveness Award submissions, and there were a lot of them, I was pleased to see some submissions included a fame campaign approach, but not all of them approached fame in the same way. Specsavers, one of my favourite brands, has managed to pull off a great marketing trick over their 30 years in business, starting with a simple yet humble campaign focusing on the core aspect of their business – making glasses more affordable for the masses. But it wasn't until 10 years ago that they hit upon something that, in time, would make the brand very famous indeed. It started with a Jerry Springer style talk-show spoof commercial which included the rather catchy line 'Should've gone to Specsavers'. But for some reason the marketing team at Specsavers hadn't realised the potential of this strapline and how it could accelerate the power of their advertising, so they let it drift for a number of years.

It wasn't until 2008, when they brought back the line and coupled it with a series of humorous commercials depicting people in slightly unfortunate situations, did their marketing campaign take off. Fused with their hardworking line and price product advertising, the business saw their marketing performance increase significantly. These series of great adverts borrowed fame from celebrities that included Gordon Ramsey and, ehm, Postman Pat, but more importantly gave the brand permission to move into and engage with consumers in humorous, topical conversations using the strapline 'Should've gone to Specsavers' outside the usual marketing channels. They were quick to capitalise on news events that made headlines, like the famous Olympic 2012 North Korean flag mistake and Chelsea's footballer Eden Hazard's gaff, taking their messaging into print and social media, thus putting themselves into the headlines and being seen as a brand in touch with what's going on in the world. It's still great to see that Specsavers continue to occupy this territory today with a few other selected brands.

On the flip side, Sainsbury's approach was completely different. Their problem was Christmas. A huge challenge for any food retail brand where they traditionally see their sales 20% higher than the average; get Christmas wrong and it has a serious impact on the overall company performance for the whole year. I spent over eight years within a food retail marketing team and the pressure to get every aspect of the Christmas campaign right was immense. What really impressed me was that the marketing team started planning their 2013 Christmas campaign whilst they were delivering their 2012 campaign – now that's advance planning. They also had a very clear idea that moved away from the usual discounting and trying to defend their position from other retail giants and fighting the relentless march of the German discounters. They wanted to create 'Christmas in a day', the real story of Christmas, and play on the emotive side of the season of good will.

Their approach was to analyse previous IPA Effectiveness Awards case studies that had demonstrated the power of emotional strategies and support it with their own research and insight to develop and deliver a campaign that grew their business by more than 5% during this period – very impressive. Their success was down to doing something completely different within their category, creating an emotional fame campaign whilst everyone around them was talking about Christmas ranges and offers. As they gave themselves so long to prepare and develop the campaign it was well thought through and perfectly executed, enabling over 3.18m views of the film and trailers on social platforms. There is no getting away from the fact that this was a very bold move for Sainsbury's, but blending traditional and new digital forms of media and measuring performance across all these platforms gave them the confidence that creating an emotional campaign can deliver hard commercial results for the business.

This now leads me on to a campaign that has fame in its DNA. I am of course talking about Barry the platypus, with his rapping birds, and by now you've probably named the brand – see, fame works! first direct is a brand that has suffered from its success. Back in 1989, when the brand launched to much fanfare from Midland Bank, it was truly carving new ground as the UK's only 24 hour, 365 days a year telephone bank, breaking the mould of traditional banking. I was in retail banking at the time and the initial success of first direct sent a shock wave through retail banking, forcing business change. By 2006 they were in trouble; their customer base had declined and their uniqueness within the market had declined with telephone and online banking now the norm. They had to do something that would again disrupt the category and stop the rot. One thing the bank did have that none of the others had was the first direct spirit – its staff and culture. Quirky and unconventional are not two words you would expect a bank to describe itself with, but first direct does. They took their internal staff values and presented them to the consumer as their brand values. Clear on what they stood for and the type of customer they were looking for, they positioned themselves as 'the unexpected bank'. Using a clear message matrix: distortion (behaving differently), disruption (being different) and dilemma (solving a problem through messaging and incentives), they once again created a campaign that stood out from the crowd, challenging consumers to remember what first direct stands for. Creating a disruptive fame campaign enabled first direct to go back to that core of what the brand stood for and go against banking conventions. Another successful campaign from a brand that was prepared to take a risk and force change within their category.

EDF Energy is another brand shortlisted in this year's IPA Effectiveness Awards which has put fame at the heart of their campaign, again approaching the problem from a different angle and challenging their category. What I really like to see in good IPA submissions is really clear, and dare I say it, concise objectives. First, it makes it a lot easier to judge 'what does good look like' and second, it makes it absolutely clear what the business is trying to achieve. I was surprised at how many submissions have, in my view, unclear objectives – hint to any brand thinking of submitting an entry next year. EDF Energy had two simple tasks: 1) get more customers than anyone else; and 2) keep them in a market where everyone hates energy companies because of the constant price increases and reported exorbitant profits. Following on from these simple, yet clear business objectives, the company identified that it needed a new position within the market, a brand that meant something and most importantly a way of getting that message to the consumer, cutting through the quagmire of negativity that surrounded them. Again, this is another business that turned to the past IPA Effectiveness Award winning papers to gain insight into developing their own campaign, and no better place to start than with a Gold-Award-winning British Gas paper from 2012. The result was to create the first low-carbon energy tariff – the 'Blue + Price Promise' – backed with a customer proposition that, if you could get your energy cheaper with another provider, EDF would tell you and more importantly make it easy to switch, reinforcing transparency and a trust that did not previously exist within the category. This was all topped off with Zingy, a clever brand icon that would bring together the whole campaign across all media formats. The combination of a strong customer-facing proposition with an effective advertising campaign enabled EDF Energy to stand out from the competitive set and allowed them to exceed their business objectives. As the icing on the cake for EDF Energy, Zingy became a social media hit with consumers wanting the physical version and mimicked the character across social networks. I know because I have a Zingy on my desk at work.

This brings me to the last IPA Effectiveness Awards submission I would like to talk about, the British Heart Foundation (BHF). This was always going to be an interesting paper to review: should the charity spend millions on an advertising campaign or directly help front-line services by funding ambulances and other medical equipment? This was a question that popped straight into my mind before turning the first page and, as you would expect from all good IPA Effectiveness Award submissions, this point was addressed in their paper. The BHF detailed at length that their approach in investing in an effective advertising campaign was the best use of their funds. They identified early on that the problem was education and they needed to mobilise the public to take CPR action before the ambulance arrived. To do this they needed a hard-hitting campaign that would get the message across, not only how to perform effective CPR but about having the confidence to act, and gain mass awareness on a national level to save lives – quite a lot to achieve from a modest budget. The clever bit was when the team created a campaign with a high tempo and catchy music track, fronted by the no-nonsense hard-man Vinnie Jones, with a simple yet effective 'Hard & Fast' message. What I really like about this campaign is its simplicity. The creative executions could have been very complex and full of dull medical advice, but the team avoided these pitfalls. The team also knew they didn't have the budget for a high-value media campaign so they went viral, using the power of social networks to spread the message, including developing mobile apps. With any fame campaign you know you have got it right when social networks start to spread the message for you, helping to fuel your PR campaign – which is exactly what happened. The result was a truly impressive gaining national press, media coverage and a host of spoof videos appearing across the web. The campaign also extended into NHS training videos and the term 'You've been Vinnie-d' entered hospital vernacular. The BHF campaign is a clever piece of marketing that used popular culture and media to create an effective yet entertaining campaign.

So, to bring everything together, can a fame campaign be planned? Yes. Are they right for all brands? No. But if you decide on a fame strategy you must ensure it's right for your business, and your marketing objectives. You must be prepared for polarisation – as it can come with the territory. Our Gio Compario character did divide opinion, but it got the whole nation talking about the brand; it wasn't vanilla and, in my opinion, vanilla campaigns are a waste of time and money. Your advertising needs to create an emotive response for it to be effective. And you need to be vigilant as it's just as easy to become famous these days for the wrong things as for the right, as Sainsbury's recently discovered.

But perhaps even more importantly, when you start a campaign of this type you must commit. Keep listening to your customers and be prepared to adapt and evolve the campaign quickly to capitalise on any opportunity to further extend your message because, even though we know it works, unfortunately fame doesn't always last!

# British Heart Foundation

## You've been 'Vinnied': how the BHF taught the UK to save lives

**By Matt Buttrick, Grey London**
Contributing authors: Matthew Gladstone and Lucy Jameson, Grey London
Credited companies: Creative Agency, Grey London; Media Agency, PHD Media; Client, British Heart Foundation

**Editor's summary**

Every year around 60,000 people suffer a cardiac arrest out of hospital in the UK, whilst only an average of 7% (4,200) survive. This is a story of how communications turned Britain into an army of human defibrillators that could step in and perform the basics no matter where the emergency was. The 'You've been Vinnied' campaign brought together Vinnie Jones and the Bee Gees to teach Britain how to tackle a cardiac arrest before the arrival of a paramedic.

The campaign achieved 86% recognition in four weeks, increased people's likelihood to perform 'Hands-only CPR' from 54% to 71%, and 30 lives to date have been directly saved by people who saw the campaign and employed the technique. With the cost to society of each fatality measured at £1.6m, minus the BHF's financial investment, this equates to a saving to society of £48.5m.

**The judges particularly applauded the clear insight and the infectiousness of the creative solution in the face of considerable audience reticence. More importantly however, the paper put together a compelling case for real changes in awareness and behaviour with the potential to impact on survival rates for years to come.**

## Introduction

No one goes to hospital to have a cardiac arrest; they have them at home, on the golf course or in the pub. Typically there's never a paramedic around when you need one.

This is a story of how communications turned Britain into an army of human defibrillators that could step in and perform the basics no matter where the emergency was.

Every year around 60,000 people suffer a cardiac arrest out of hospital in the UK.[1] Shockingly only an average of 7% (4,200) survive to be discharged from hospital.[2] However, if someone can step in before emergency services arrive and perform CPR (getting the blood circulating again by performing chest compressions and rescue breaths), survival rates can double.[3]

The importance of public intervention/training bystanders is made more important due to two key truths:

1. Speed of intervention is critical – performing CPR is about buying time and restoring oxygenated blood to the brain and heart until professional help arrives. For every minute that goes by, a victim's chance of survival drops 10%.[4]
2. Ambulances are struggling to get through – UK ambulances are targeted to be at the scene within eight minutes of a life-threatening call. But only 75% of ambulances make it in this time.[5] Meanwhile, the number of people calling 999 has increased by more than 56% from 4.4m to 7.9m between 2001 and 2010,[6] but the number of qualified ambulance staff since 2007 has remained largely static.[7]

We had to mobilise the public to step in and fill the time before ambulances arrived. Fortunately, the medical community had developed a new simplified 'hands-only CPR' approach; a technique without the need for mouth-to-mouth. We could make bystanders the fifth emergency service. But the barriers were still significant.

### Emergency life support can appear complex

Performing any medical procedure can seem very complicated for ordinary people. This is not made easier if you consider how the process is often laid out to teach people. Complex-looking flow diagrams with multiple options and different versions for adults, children and even pets (Figure 1).

Unsurprisingly, BHF research showed that 73% of adults claimed they were unfamiliar with the CPR procedure while 77% of adults said they simply lacked the knowledge.[8]

### No one is taught CPR

Only a quarter of the UK is trained in CPR[9] so the chances of someone helping are very low. In fact 82% of adults didn't even know if CPR was the right response.[10] With no formal training nationally the UK lagged well behind other Western nations (Table 1).

## Figure 1: Basic life support – adult flow chart

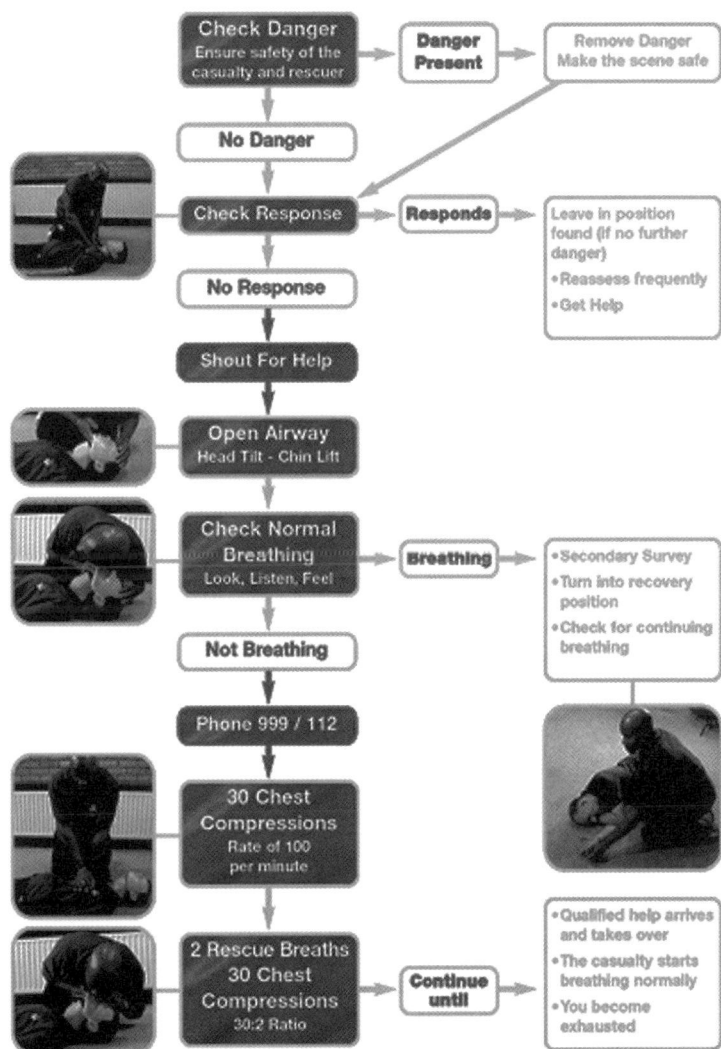

# Basic Life Support - Adult Flow Chart

**Check Danger**
Ensure safety of the
casualty and rescuer

→ **Danger Present** → Remove Danger
Make the scene safe

**No Danger**

**Check Response**

→ **Responds** → Leave in position
found (if no further
danger)
• Reassess frequently
• Get Help

**No Response**

**Shout For Help**

**Open Airway**
Head Tilt - Chin Lift

**Check Normal Breathing**
Look, Listen, Feel

→ **Breathing** → • Secondary Survey
• Turn into recovery
position
• Check for continuing
breathing

**Not Breathing**

**Phone 999 / 112**

**30 Chest Compressions**
Rate of 100
per minute

**2 Rescue Breaths
30 Chest Compressions**
30:2 Ratio

→ **Continue until** → • Qualified help arrives
and takes over
• The casualty starts
breathing normally
• You become
exhausted

Building Safer, Healthier & Better Skilled Communities

**nars**
NATIONAL RESCUE
STANDARD

Contact us:
Call: +44 (0)1922 645097 Email: sta@sta.co.uk Visit: www.sta.co.uk

**sta**

| Table 1: Where CPR is taught – international comparisons | |
|---|---|
| **Denmark** | School pupils aged 12–15 are taught CPR skills. |
| **Australia** | Since 2005 Australian state schools have provided training to all students before leaving Year 12. |
| **United States** | Out of 56 State Governments, 36 have passed legislation to teach CPR in schools. |
| **Seattle, United States** | CPR has been taught in PE lessons for over 30 years. |
| **France** | CPR is a mandatory part of school curricula. |
| **Norway** | CPR is a mandatory part of school curricula. |

Source: BHF (2012) *Policy Statement: Emergency Life Support*

### Fear was holding people back

Emotional barriers were high.

'A fear of making things worse', 'a fear of being judged', 'believing someone else could do better', 'embarrassment', 'uncomfortable with mouth-to-mouth contact' and 'anxiety over the legal consequences' were all identified in research as significant obstacles.[11]

It was little wonder 76% of people admitted a lack of confidence to perform CPR.[12]

### National task – tiny budget

Our budget to overcome all this was tiny. It was significantly smaller than comparable national government campaigns (Figure 2).

**Figure 2: Budgets for national behavioural change campaigns**

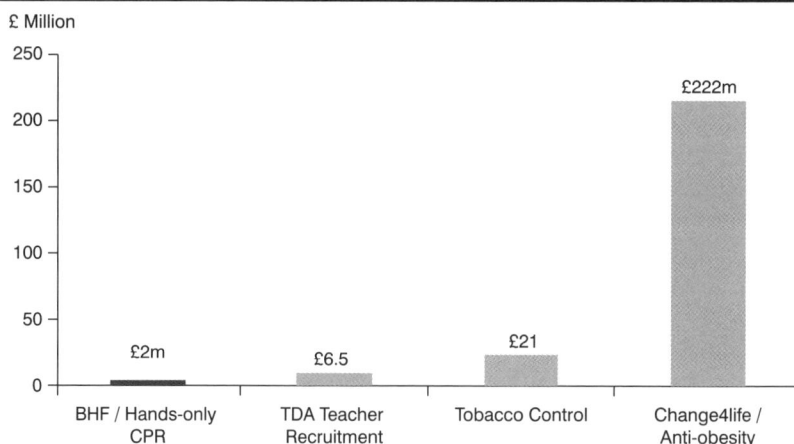

Source: IPA

## Communications objectives

Our communications objectives were:

1.  ensure people knew *how* to perform the new technique;
2.  remove the fear and instil the confidence to act;
3.  register mass awareness of the new 'hands-only CPR' technique at a national level;
4.  save lives.

Initially the answer seemed obvious: a brief about no kissing. You could see the ads.

But would removing one barrier be enough to get a nation stepping forward? Instead we felt communications could do much more.

### Ensure people knew how to perform the new technique

With the British Heart Foundation (BHF) we identified the five steps of the new procedure with no need for mouth-to-mouth:

1.  Call 999
2.  Check the person is breathing
3.  No need for kissing
4.  Push hard and fast in the middle of the chest
5.  To the tempo of 100 BPM.

We needed to teach the behaviour. It was clear we couldn't just stop at awareness. This wasn't traditional AIDA.[13] This was straight to A for 'action'.

We went back to the classics: *Clunk Clink Every Trip* and *Slip! Slop! Slap!*

We noticed that the best public-service communications worked on simplicity and instruction using different 'hooks' that pulled on different senses. Many used a clear visual moment with a snappy sounding phrase. Others offered a simply iconic action that could be easily copied (Figure 3).

**Figure 3: Iconic public service campaigns that hook into different senses**

'Clunk click every trip' was the slogan of a series of British public information films sponsored by the Royal Society for the Prevention of Accidents (RoSPA), 1971

'Slip! Slop! Slap!', Cancer Council Victoria, 1981

Just as an earworm (a catchy tune) infiltrates your brain and doesn't leave you, we needed to create our own simple and sticky piece of communications that stepped people through the procedure.

If we could hardwire it into memory, we'd stand a chance.

### Remove the fear and instil the confidence to act

The communications had to get people over their fear or cardiac arrests would just remain too monumental to cope with.

Traditionally, serious situations require serious thought. But as we began to investigate we found a brilliant seam of advice that suggested fear could be defused through the power of laughter.

American deadpan comic Bob Newhart once said '*Laughter gives us distance. It allows us to step back from an event, deal with it*'. While Mark Twain noted that '*The human race has one really effective weapon, and that is laughter*'. Both were on to something.

We had to make it funny.

### Register mass awareness of the new 'hands-only CPR' technique at a national level

Cardiac arrests are a mass problem. Our audience was a mass audience.

To be effective we needed to be universal and populist. This would simultaneously help the budget go further, but critically it would help gain social approval for the technique. Something that would directly target barriers such as '*lacking confidence in front of others*' and the '*fear of being judged*'.[14]

But more than that, to be noticed we believed we needed to create the total antithesis of a government training film. Something entertaining. Something irresistible. The question we asked ourselves was: What would the 6 o'clock news pick up?

With only £2m for media and production we had to create something with immediate impact. It had to make you take notice. It had to work after just one exposure.

So in summary, this was less like imparting information and more like teaching a dance. More Macarena than medical leaflet if you will (Figure 4).

## The creative work

### Vinnie was born

We set about trampling all over the norms of traditional government advice videos. The secret was to keeping pushing. Picture the scene:

> *Ok, we need a song. It has to be the right tempo. 100 BPM. They use 'Nelly the Elephant' to train nurses? That's funny. No, push it, something everyone knows. Disco? Seriously? Yes. The Bee Gees, wait they did 'Stayin' Alive!' 100 BPM. A gift. Who would get noticed saving a life? A celeb. Not any celeb, a hard man. No, a hard man famed for violence. Someone who could push hard and fast. Vinnie Jones. Doing 'Stayin' Alive'. Brilliant.*

Figure 4:  The Macarena Dance and
UK medical leaflet for hands-only CPR

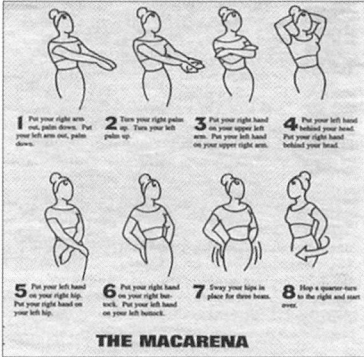

The Macarena Dance by Los del Rio –
iconic international hit from 1995

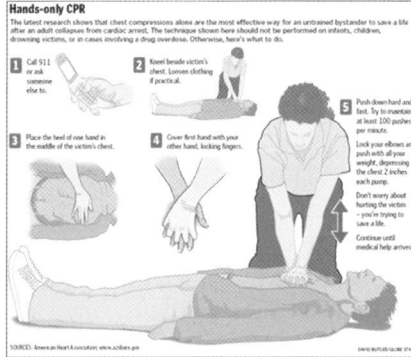

UK medical leaflet for hands-only CPR

We had created a completely different and original type of teacher who could demonstrate how simple 'hands-only CPR' could be, to the tune of a song that everyone knew. We now felt we had some brilliant ingredients: strong characters, snappy dialogue, role-reversal. The comedic and the serious combined. The surprise of the unpredicted (Figure 5).

Figure 5: Hands-only CPR 'Vinnie' TVC

*VO: There are times in life where being tough comes in handy … Say some geezer collapses in front of ya, what do you do? We need a volunteer that ain't breathing … here's one I made earlier. First off you call 999. I know. Then, no kissing. You only kiss your missus on the lips. You push hard and fast here on the sovereign to 'Stayin' Alive'. Remember, call 999, push hard and fast to 'Stayin' Alive'. Hands-only CPR. It's not as hard as it looks.*

We'd created a funny and memorable 'dance' that brought together five elements to maximise cut through:

1. A 100 BPM soundtrack with universal appeal: Stayin' Alive by The Bee Gees
2. A well-known character famous for toughness and hurting people: Vinnie Jones (soccer / Hollywood)
3. A sticky phrase that highlighted the key action and lived beyond the TVC: 'hard and fast'
4. A tone that would challenge traditional government first-aid messaging: the comedic plus serious
5. A script that clearly walked through the five steps of hands-only CPR: see above.

## The channel strategy

As stated, a key objective was to register mass awareness of the new 'hands-only CPR' technique at a national level.

Everything we did with our channel approach was engineered to spread our message as far into UK culture as possible. The creative was a great start but we wanted to make it reach as many potential lifesavers as possible.

Our media objectives were simple.

### Go mass, go viral

The TV buying strategy was designed to maximise 1+ cover, an approach designed to reach as many people as quickly as possible. We ran 480 TVRs in four weeks and 'road blocked' the nation's most popular programmes to ensure we generated maximum fame.

We debuted the ad socially on Twitter with the hash tag #hardandfast. This was then further bolstered with promoted tweets and 37 million impressions booked as rich-display media on national sites such as Yahoo! MSN and AOL.[15] A fully integrated programme of PR and social media activities further amplified the campaign.

### Get the lesson into people's hands

We launched a how-to-do 'hands-only CPR' app through websites such as iTunes and Google Play (Figure 6) and sold a set of limited edition Vinnie T-shirts across the BHF's 700 shops nationwide.

Figure 6: Hands-only CPR

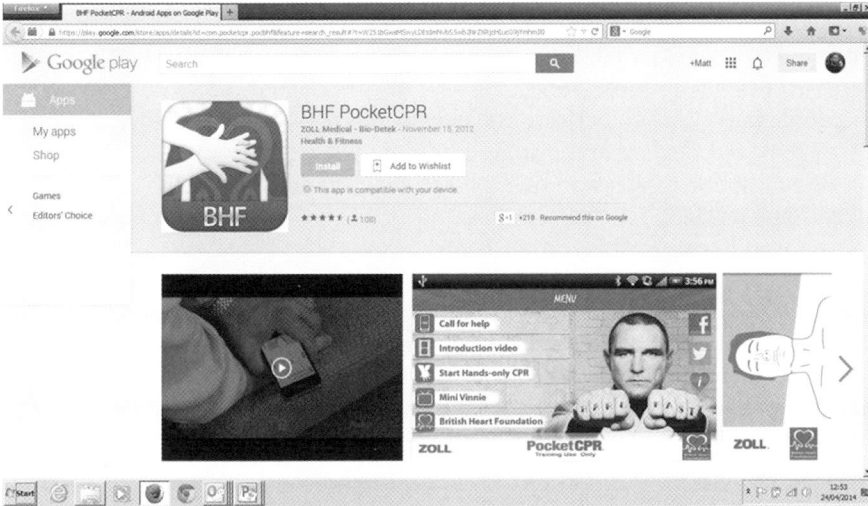

Figure 7 shows a summary of all the activity.

Figure 7: Full communications plan

| | | 2012 | | | | | | |
|---|---|---|---|---|---|---|---|---|
| | | Jan | | | | | Feb | |
| MEDIA | FORMAT | 2 | 9 | 16 | 23 | 30 | 6 | 13 |
| TV | 40" | 150 | 130 | 130 | 70 | 480 TVRs in Total | | |
| Video on Demand | 40" | | 6th - 28th Jan | | | | | |
| Twitter | Promoted Tweets | | 9th - 28th Jan | | | | | |
| Twitter | Promoted Accounts | | 9th - 28th Jan | | | | | |
| Twitter | Promoted Trends | 7th | | | | | | |
| Collective | Video Expandables | | 9th - 28th Jan | | | 8,071,477 Impressions | | |
| AOL | Display | | 9th - 28th Jan | | | 10,894,730 Impressions | | |
| MSN | Mail | | 9th - 28th Jan | | | 13,095,820 Impressions | | |
| Yahoo! | Video Mail | | | 20th | | 5,200,000 Impressions | | |
| Go Viral | Thematic Video Player | | 9th - 28th Jan | | | 136,363 Units booked | | |
| T-Shirts | BHF Stores | | | | | | | |
| Mobile | How-to- Push APP | | | Ongoing | | | | |
| PR | National Media | | | | | | | |

Note: TV shows "6th - 28th Jan" above the bars.

123

## The results

In this section we demonstrate how we achieved our objectives from teaching a new technique to real lives saved:

1.  people knew *how* to perform the new technique;
2.  we removed the fear and instilled the confidence to act;
3.  we registered mass awareness of the new 'hands-only CPR' technique at a national level;
4.  we saved lives.

### 1. People knew how to perform the technique

Post tracking showed barriers were clearly dropping and the right messages were definitely getting through (Figure 8).

**Figure 8: Spontaneous comprehension – main message**

Source: Hall & Partners, post-campaign tracking, February 2012

Nearly half of respondents (48%) *spontaneously* mentioned the 'Stayin' Alive' track (critical as this music provides the right timing for the chest compressions). Meanwhile, 28% *spontaneously* remembered '*Hands-only / no-mouth-to-mouth*' (Figure 9).

## Figure 9: Spontaneous message take out

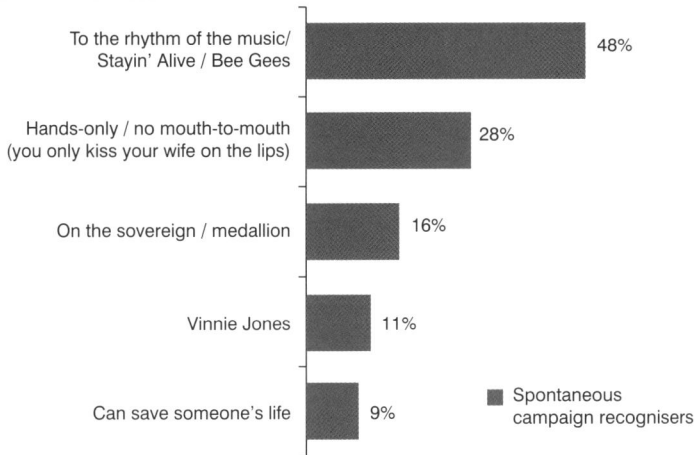

| Category | % |
|---|---|
| To the rhythm of the music/ Stayin' Alive / Bee Gees | 48% |
| Hands-only / no mouth-to-mouth (you only kiss your wife on the lips) | 28% |
| On the sovereign / medallion | 16% |
| Vinnie Jones | 11% |
| Can save someone's life | 9% |

Spontaneous campaign recognisers

Source: Hall & Partners, post-campaign tracking, February 2012

It also showed that we achieved strong message take out: 85% remembered that there was '*no need for mouth-to-mouth*' and 84% remembering to '*press down to the beat of "Stayin' Alive"*' (Figure 10).

## Figure 10: Prompted message take out

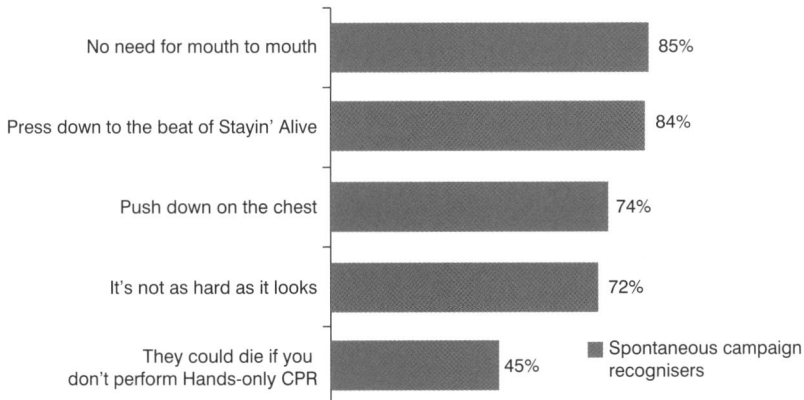

| Category | % |
|---|---|
| No need for mouth to mouth | 85% |
| Press down to the beat of Stayin' Alive | 84% |
| Push down on the chest | 74% |
| It's not as hard as it looks | 72% |
| They could die if you don't perform Hands-only CPR | 45% |

Spontaneous campaign recognisers

Source: Hall & Partners, post-campaign tracking, February 2012

Seventy-nine percent of people even suggested there should be no potential changes to the ad. They had all the information they needed (Figure 11).

### Figure 11: Potential changes to ad

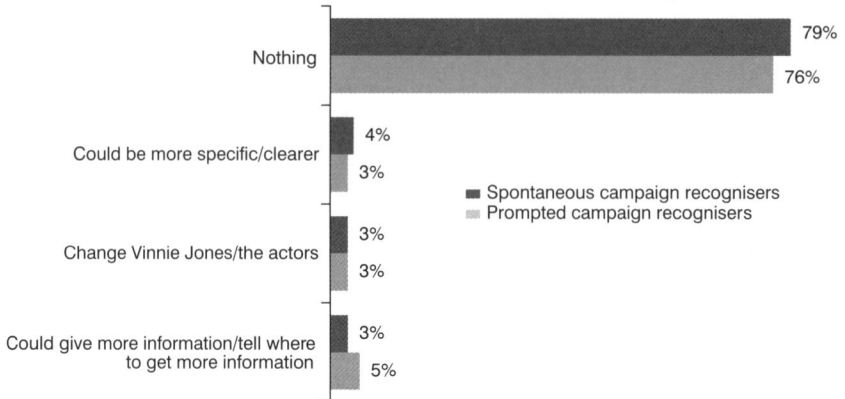

| | Spontaneous campaign recognisers | Prompted campaign recognisers |
|---|---|---|
| Nothing | 79% | 76% |
| Could be more specific/clearer | 4% | 3% |
| Change Vinnie Jones/the actors | 3% | 3% |
| Could give more information/tell where to get more information | 3% | 5% |

Source: Hall & Partners, post-campaign tracking, February 2012

### 2. We removed the fear and instilled the confidence to act

Verbatim comments showed that we had started to correct misconceptions, reduce fear and increase confidence (Figure 12).

### Figure 12: Verbatim comments showed confidence was growing

"My hands would be the only tools I had, i.e. no electric machine like the paramedics have, time is valuable before the emergency services arrived"

"In my experience, mouth to mouth was just as important. I did not know that hands-only could be as effective by itself"

"The procedure is simple and easy to remember, whereas I would not feel confident about giving mouth to mouth without training"

Source: Hall & Partners, post-campaign tracking, February 2012

Fear getting in the way of performing CPR fell following the campaign, including reductions in '*fear of doing harm*' and '*fear of making things worse*' (Figure 13).

**Figure 13: Factors that would prevent respondents from performing CPR**

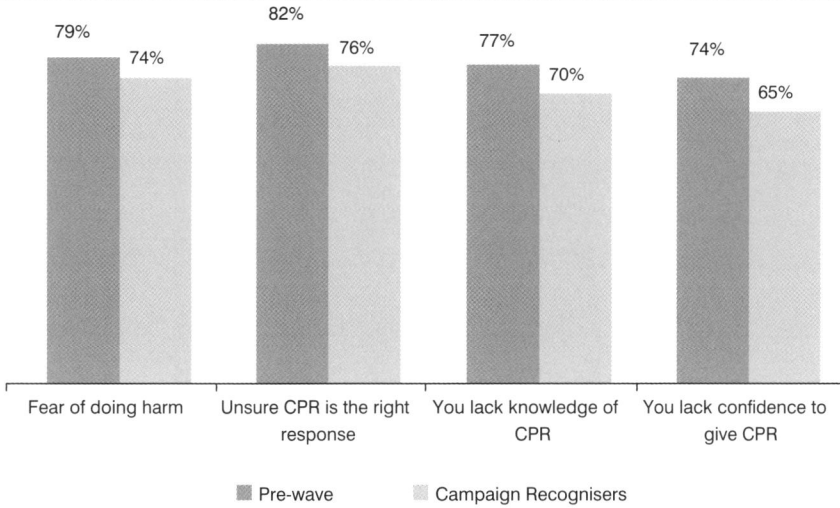

| | Pre-wave | Campaign Recognisers |
| --- | --- | --- |
| Fear of doing harm | 79% | 74% |
| Unsure CPR is the right response | 82% | 76% |
| You lack knowledge of CPR | 77% | 70% |
| You lack confidence to give CPR | 74% | 65% |

Source: Hall & Partners, post campaign tracking, February 2012

The number of people stating they would be confident to perform CPR increased from 23% to 32% after having seen the TV ad (Figure 14).

**Figure 14: Confidence to perform CPR increased**

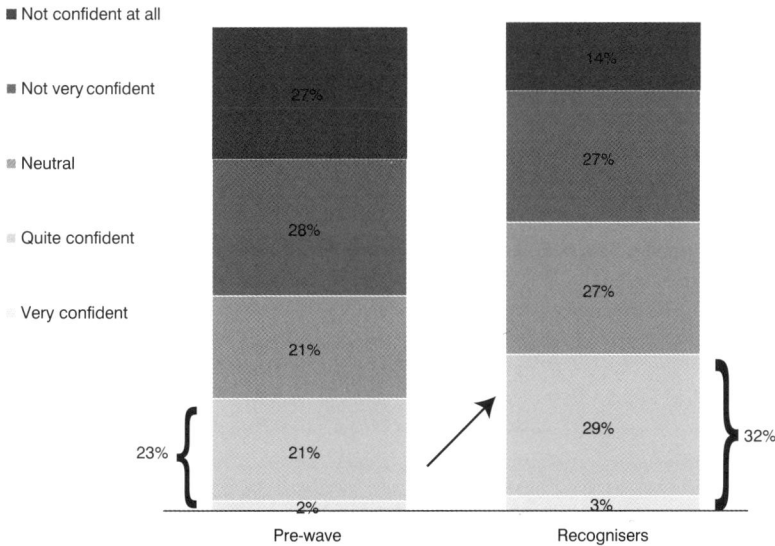

- Not confident at all
- Not very confident
- Neutral
- Quite confident
- Very confident

Pre-wave: 27%, 28%, 21%, 21%, 2% — 23%

Recognisers: 14%, 27%, 27%, 29%, 3% — 32%

Source: Hall & Partners, post-campaign tracking, February 2012

People's likelihood to perform 'hands-only CPR' increased from 54% to 71% (Figure 15).

## Figure 15: Likelihood to perform hands-only CPR

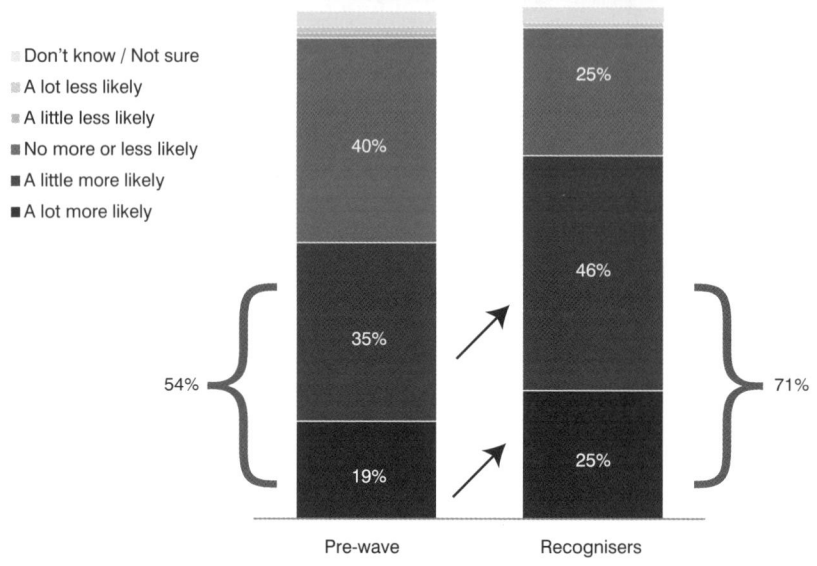

Legend:
- Don't know / Not sure
- A lot less likely
- A little less likely
- No more or less likely
- A little more likely
- A lot more likely

Pre-wave: 40%, 35%, 19% (54%)
Recognisers: 25%, 46%, 25% (71%)

Source: Hall & Partners, post-campaign tracking, February 2012

Post-campaign research also showed that people were even becoming more likely to perform CPR on a stranger (Figure 16).

## Figure 16: Percentage who agree 'Would you be willing to perform CPR on a stranger in public?'

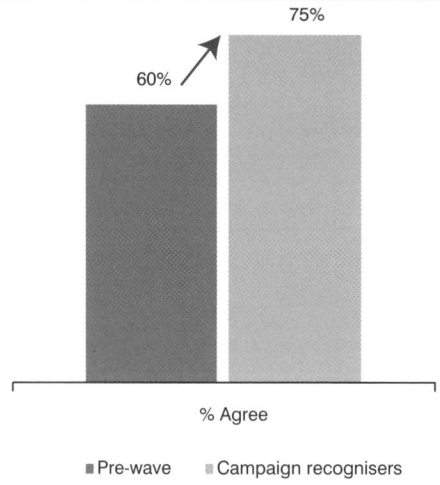

60% 75%

% Agree

■ Pre-wave   ■ Campaign recognisers

Source: Hall & Partners, post-campaign tracking, February 2012

## 3. We registered mass awareness of the new 'hands-only CPR' technique at a national level

Our television ratings ensured we would reach 80% of the population at least once. But it was the campaign's ability to infiltrate mass culture and spark PR that really broadened its impact.

The campaign gained major PR coverage across the biggest online and offline national media channels including the BBC, *The Sun* and *Daily Mail* (Figure 17).

**Figure 17: Major UK PR coverage**

The hands-only TV creative was parodied on the biggest TV shows including 'The Graham Norton Show' (BBC1), 'The Alan Carr Show' (Channel 4) and 'Soccer AM' (Sky Sports) (Figure 18).

**Figure 18: Parody on *Soccer AM* (Sky Sports)**

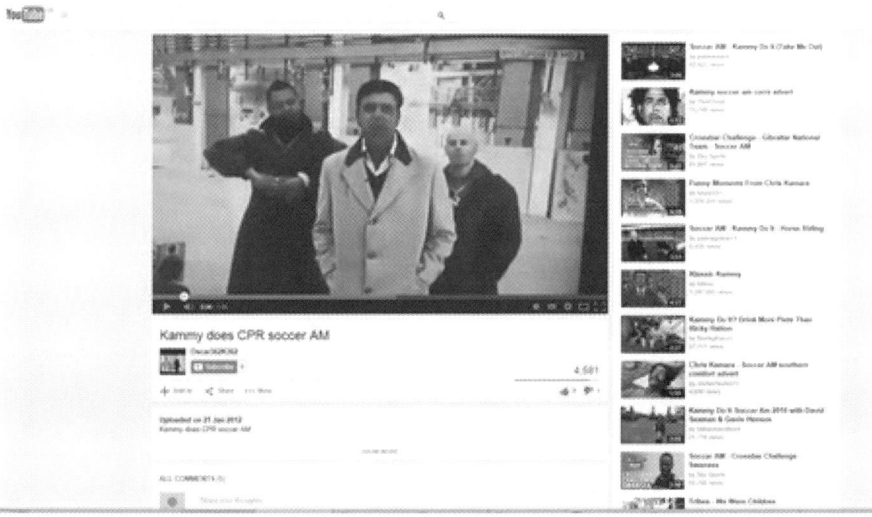

Reconstructed 'hands-only CPR' rescues were also made the feature on two mainstream BBC shows ('Real Rescues' and 'Helicopter Heroes') (Figure 19).

**Figure 19: Reconstructed hands-only CPR rescues appeared on two mainstream BBC shows**

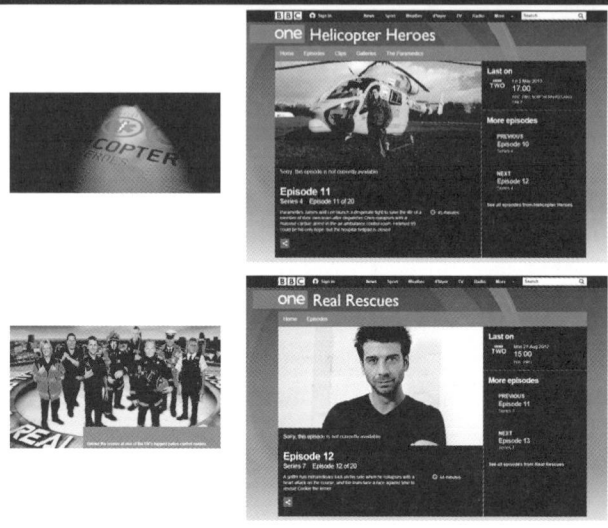

The soundtrack to the ad was even asked as a question in the BBC gameshow 'Eggheads' (Figure 20).

**Figure 20: The soundtrack to the TVC asked as a question on BBC gameshow *Eggheads***

On Twitter #hardandfast trended organically *five times* on launch day (Figure 21). The Vinnie film became the most shared online video in launch week with 72,601 shares across social media in the first 10 days.

### Figure 21:  Vinnie trended on Twitter five times on launch day

It clearly sparked conversation. In fact 21% of people claim they had '*told someone about the ad*' after seeing it (Figure 22).

### Figure 22: Did seeing the ad prompt you to do any of the following

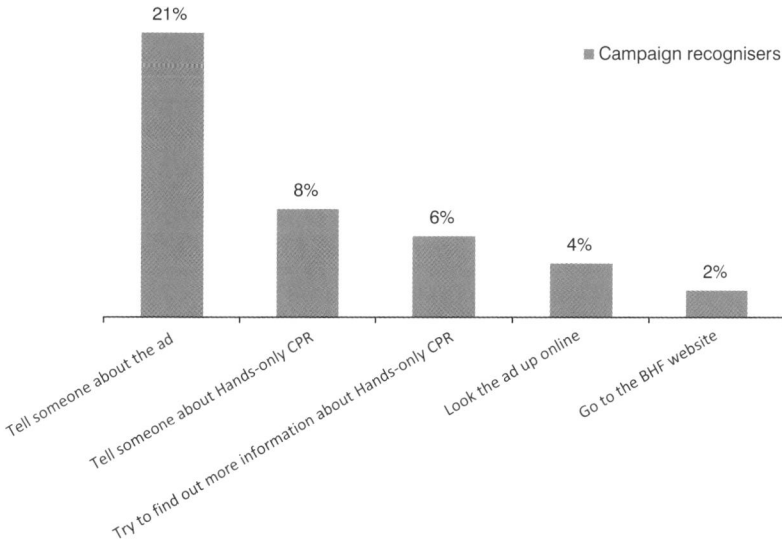

Source: Hall & Partners, post-campaign tracking, February 2012

Meanwhile, our new TV ad punched well above its weight compared to other existing ads running at the same time; it became the second-highest recalled campaign on significantly lower spend (Figure 23).

## Figure 23: UK most-recalled ads, week commencing 8 February 2012

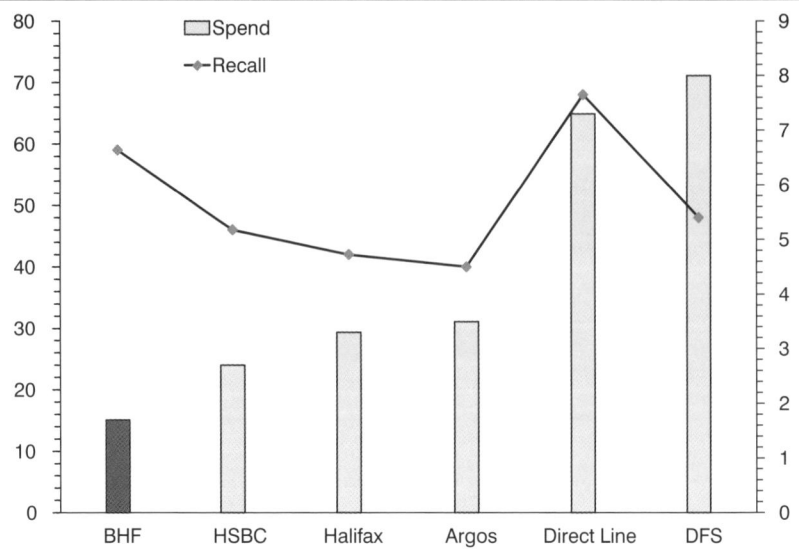

Source: Hall & Partners, post-campaign tracking, February 2012

Post-campaign tracking showed 86% of the UK population recognised the campaign and, of those, 31% spontaneously recalled it (Figure 24).

## Figure 24: 'Hands-only CPR' TV recognition

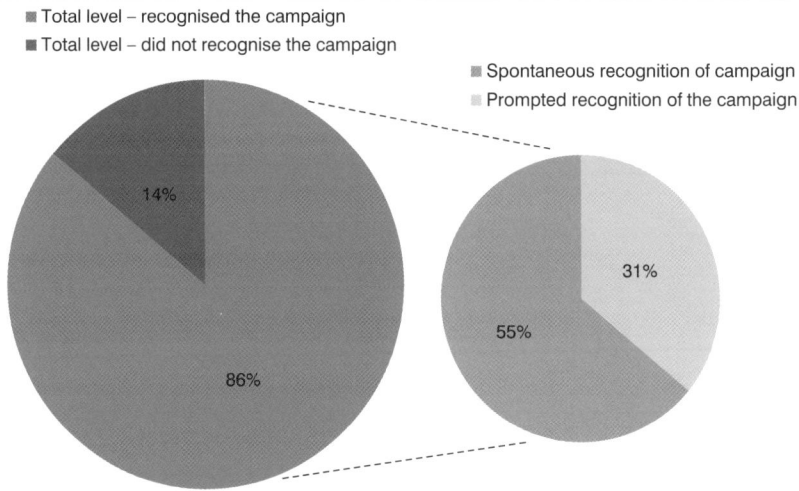

Source: Hall & Partners, post-campaign tracking, February 2012

We achieved 86% recognition in four weeks. By comparison, it took the Department of Transport's Road Safety campaign *Think!* seven years to get to 80% recognition (Figure 25).

**Figure 25: The Department of Transport's 'Think!' road safety campaign took seven years to reach 80% recognition**

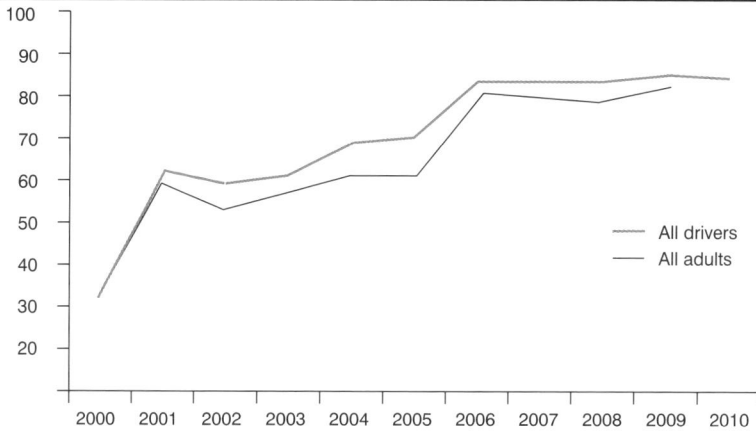

Other UK government campaigns required far bigger budgets to reach comparative levels of campaign awareness (Table 2).

**Table 2: Other UK government campaign budgets**

| UK Government campaign | Media spend | Campaign awareness |
| --- | --- | --- |
| Change4Life 2010 | £222m | 85%* |
| TDA Teacher Recruitment 2010 | £6.5m | 68–77% |
| Tobacco Control 2008–9 | £21m | 82% |

* Average over two periods. Source: IPA

Our combination of entertaining creative, compressed media exposure and waves of subsequent PR had ensured we would hit our objective to register mass awareness of the new 'hands-only CPR' technique at a national level.

Overall post-tracking showed that more people had become more familiar with the 'hands-only' approach than conventional CPR, showing us that we were beginning to teach a new piece of behaviour.

And later tracking carried out a further ten months after the launch in November 2012 showed that familiarity with the 'hands-only CPR' procedure had actually grown, with those saying they were *very familiar* more than doubling from 5% to 12% (Figure 26). Critically this was a period of zero paid media support. The money had stopped but the conversations continued. Our idea had started to live by itself.

**Figure 26: How well, if at all, do you think you know each of the following procedures**

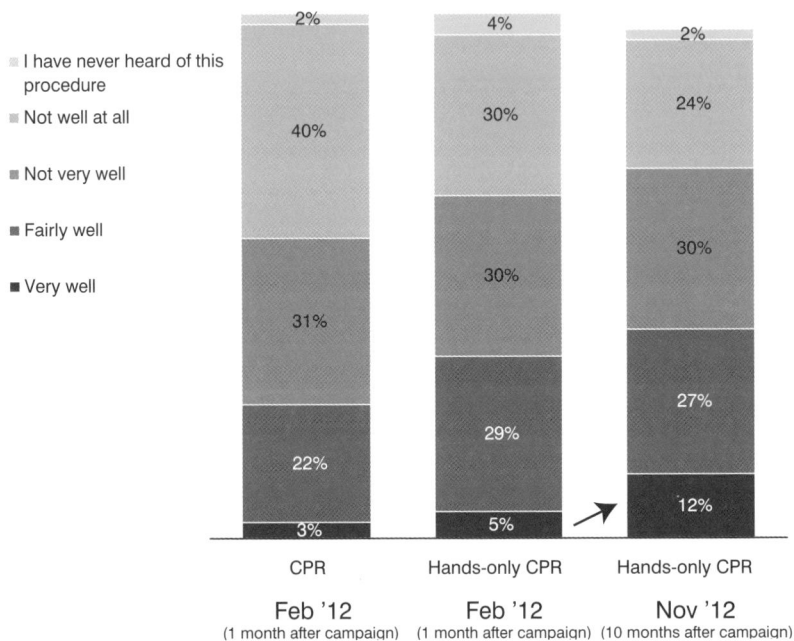

Legend:
- I have never heard of this procedure
- Not well at all
- Not very well
- Fairly well
- Very well

CPR — Feb '12 (1 month after campaign):
- 2%
- 40%
- 31%
- 22%
- 3%

Hands-only CPR — Feb '12 (1 month after campaign):
- 4%
- 30%
- 30%
- 29%
- 5%

Hands-only CPR — Nov '12 (10 months after campaign):
- 2%
- 24%
- 30%
- 27%
- 12%

Source: Hall & Partners, post-campaign tracking, February 2012/Simpson-Carpenter campaign evaluation 2012

## 4. Save lives

Although 60,000 out-of-home cardiac arrests are suffered every year in the UK, this only equates to 164 per day.[16] We were therefore not expecting to see thousands of lives saved as soon as we launched the campaign. This was about equipping as many people as possible in case the day arrives when a cardiac arrest happens near them.

While no national data is collected on the number of bystanders who step in to perform CPR, we do have good London data from the London Ambulance Service that the numbers of bystanders stepping in has increased (Figure 27).

*Bystander CPR figures have increased to the highest level yet, with more than half of patients receiving CPR before LAS personnel arrive on scene.*
The London Ambulance Service Cardiac Arrest Report (Aug 2013)

## Figure 27: Bystanders stepping in to perform CPR

Hands-only CPR Campaign

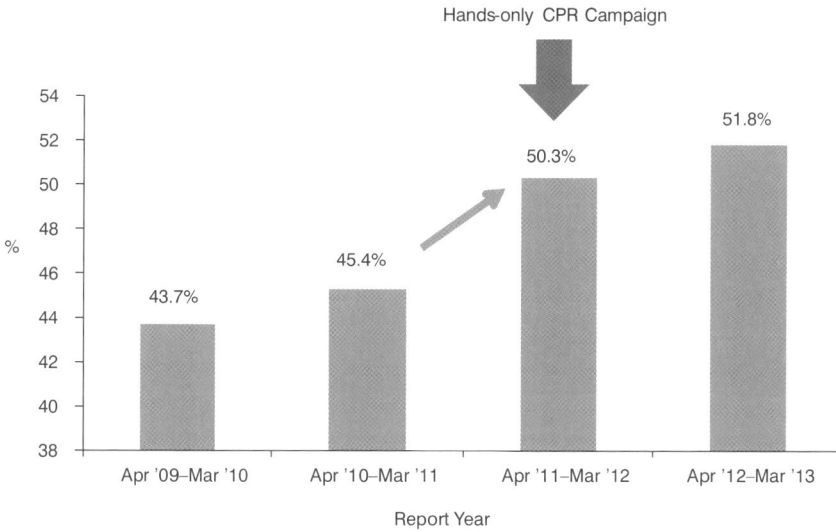

43.7% — Apr '09–Mar '10
45.4% — Apr '10–Mar '11
50.3% — Apr '11–Mar '12
51.8% — Apr '12–Mar '13

%

Report Year

Source: The London Ambulance Service Cardiac Arrest Report (Sep 2013)

Our best source of evidence showing bystanders stepping in were the *real stories* reported in the media (Figure 28).

## Figure 28: News coverage of the real-life saving of Alan Linton

Alan Linton, 42, collapsed in February 2012 from a heart attack as he played golf on Charleston Golf Course, Scotland. His friend Paul Pinkney remembered the campaign and gave chest compressions:

> The ad had been on the week before; it had been on a couple of times. If it hadn't have been for Vinnie Jones you'd have looked at it and gone 'Yeah, whatever' but because he was doing it just sticks in your head.
>     It came straight to us. I was playing the whole thing in my head. We sang it out loud for a bit. It obviously works.[17]

In the *actual* recording of the 999 emergency call, Mr Linton's friend, Paul Pinkney, can be heard recalling the campaign live. He was actually performing what we'd taught (Figure 29).

**Figure 29: The recording of the 999 emergency call showing live recall of the campaign**

| | |
|---|---|
| *999 Call Centre:* | *"Get him flat over on his back and we'll tell you what to do"* |
| *Paul Pinkney, Bystander:* | *"Yep I'm doing it. I'm doing the "Staying Alive" bit"* |

Lettings manager Sharon Shankster from Ealing, West London, said the campaign gave her the confidence to perform the resuscitation for almost 30 minutes until an ambulance crew arrived in January 2012 (Figure 30).

> I haven't had any first aid training but I saw the advert in my head and started doing CPR. I was probably doing it for about 20 to 30 minutes, but it felt like forever. I just knew I couldn't stop. The advert gave me the confidence to act but it all happened too quickly to think about it. You'd think anyone would've done the same thing[18]

Both hospital staff in accident and emergency departments and members of the public who have saved lives have frequently quoted 'doing a Vinnie'.

And although neither the government nor the ambulance service currently measure national CPR attempts, the BHF was been contacted 30 times with stories of successful 'hands-only CPR' attempts – each one thanking the charity for showing the life-saving technique in the campaign (Figure 31).

We believe it is reasonable to suggest that because many people simply don't think to call, this is likely to be just the tip of the iceberg.

## Figure 30: News coverage of bystander Sharon Shankster who saved a life after seeing the campaign

## Figure 31: Lives saved during the 10 months following the campaign

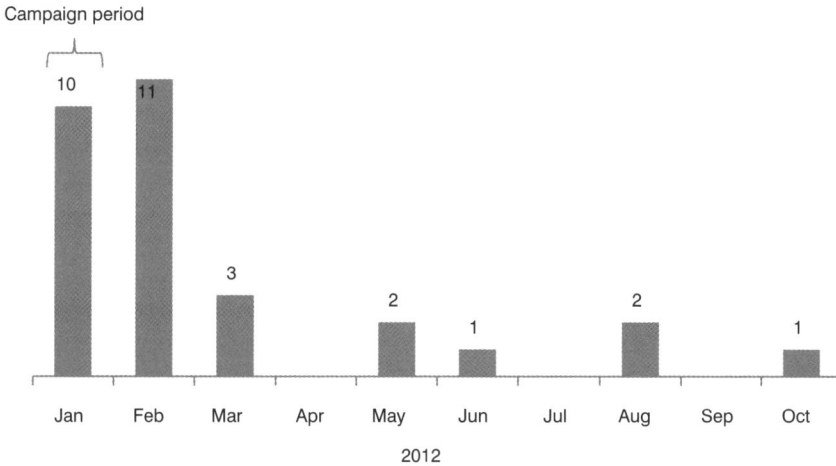

Campaign period

Jan 10
Feb 11
Mar 3
Apr
May 2
Jun 1
Jul
Aug 2
Sep
Oct 1

2012

Source: BHF

Our aim was to recruit an army of bystanders who were more likely to step in during an emergency. How did we do? Post-tracking told us that we had created an extra 6 million people who were now more likely to perform 'hands-only CPR'.[19]

In summary our objectives were achieved (Figure 32).

### Figure 32: Campaign objectives achieved

| | |
|---|---|
| 1. Ensure people knew *how* to perform the new technique. → | 85% aware there is no need for mouth-to-mouth. |
| 2. Remove the fear and instil the confidence to act. → | Claimed likelihood to perform 'Hands-only CPR' up from 54% to 71%. |
| | An army of 6m people now trained. |
| 3. Register mass awareness of the new 'Hands-only CPR' technique at a national level. → | 86% recognition in four weeks. |
| | 34% of the UK population saying they understood the 'Hands-only' procedure well. |
| 4. Save lives. → | Step-in rates reach highest ever at 52%. |
| | 30 recorded lives saved. |

## Discounting other factors

This section usually tries to discount other factors that may have driven sales, such as price promotion, seasonality, fashions or weather.

However, we believe the effect of this campaign can almost entirely be attributed to the 'hands-only CPR' campaign. No other major national CPR campaign had occurred during the time of the activity and no other UK organisation has communicated the issue of 'Hands-only CPR' prior to or during the Vinnie campaign.

'Stayin' Alive' by The Bee Gees was not commercially licensed anywhere else during the campaign period.

## What was the commercial gain?

The British Heart Foundation is a charity. Their ultimate objective is to save lives. We did just that. However, as is the case for most charity organisations, the British Heart Foundation needs to spend its funds wisely. Therefore, we have conducted a series of calculations to demonstrate that the money they used on this communications provided a better return on investment than many of the alternative ways in which they could have spent their £2m media and production budget.

*The case for alternative investment*

What else could the £2m campaign investment have achieved?

1. Bought 2,174 reusable defibrillators; *or*
2. trained just over 66,000 people to be proficient in applying CPR; *or*
3. bought 22 ambulances.

Let's look at each of these approaches in detail.

## 1. Purchasing defibrillators with the campaign spend

First, what would happen if the £2m Vinnie campaign investment had been spent on purchasing defibrillators? Defibrillators are used to give the heart an electric shock and 're-start' it after a cardiac arrest.

The typical starting price for a reusable defibrillator for home or commercial use is £920.[20] So, assuming a cost of £920 per defibrillator, we could purchase 2,174 defibrillators with £2m campaign spend. This works out at only one defibrillator for approximately every 29,000 people.

The question is what impact would purchasing 2,174 defibrillators have on the nation? Unfortunately, 78% of cardiac arrests occur at private residential locations.[21] So, purchasing 2,174 defibrillators would have had a limited impact compared to our campaign, which had much higher reach and in effect turned people into human defibrillators.

Also, people need to be trained to use a defibrillator. So in reality, we would also have had to invest additional funds to explain what the defibrillators were, where they were and how to use them.

## 2. Training the nation in CPR

Another approach would have been to spend the £2m on training the public in basic first aid, to teach them how to apply 'hands-only CPR'. The cost of the most basic online training is £29.99 per person.[22] So our £2m would buy 66,689 places on a first-aid course. Again, this looks superficially appealing, until you realise that the Vinnie campaign trained 25 million people, who are now able to apply 'hands-only CPR' to keep someone alive until the intervention of an ambulance.

Not only that but training courses are – by definition – filled by those who have already expressed an interest in life-saving techniques. The beauty of the Vinnie campaign was that it was reaching out to a substantially larger, more mainstream audience. It would reach many of those whose family might be most at risk of a cardiac arrest (who are often those least interested in being trained, or training their family and friends in how to help in surviving one).

## 3. Purchasing ambulances

The BHF are not responsible for buying ambulances; but to put the campaign in context, it's worth understanding what the cost and impact of improving ambulance response times would have been, instead of training people to do CPR until an ambulance arrived.

In order to have a fair chance of survival (50%[23]) from a cardiac arrest, action needs to take place within five minutes. Currently in the UK, 75% of ambulance response is on average within eight minutes[24] of a call out, so we would need to reduce ambulance response times by three minutes to give a fair chance of survival. At the moment, there are 1,980 ambulances operational within the UK.[25] In order to hit the five-minute response rates, we have calculated that we would actually need an additional 743 ambulances. It would cost an additional £66.8m to supply 743 ambulances. Our £2m spend could only have purchased 22 ambulances. And, this figure does not take into account the cost of training two ambulance staff for each ambulance, one of which would need to be a paramedic.

So, the NHS would have had to have spent £66.8m on ambulances to reduce response times by three minutes. Instead the BHF spent £2m training the public to help keep people alive for the vital minutes until ambulances arrive. By this reckoning, the campaign saved the economy (and the National Health Service) £64.8m, giving a *campaign payback of 1:32,* or for every £1 spent on the campaign, there is a return of £32.00.

### Saving to society

At the very least, we know that 30 lives were saved largely due to the Vinnie campaign. We know this, because the British Heart Foundation was contacted by individuals who told them that they had seen the Vinnie campaign, and as a result applied 'hands-only CPR', keeping a person alive until an ambulance could take over.[26] We suspect this figure is just the tip of the iceberg, but the government does not track bystander CPR rates.

It seems brutal to put a figure on the value of a life, but in the UK, the Department for Transport routinely does just this. If one applies the figures below, on the cost to society of every fatality, then, at the very least[27] (Table 3) the Vinnie campaign has saved society £50.5 million. Taking into account the £2m campaign investment, this gives a saving to society of £48.5 million.

| Table 3: Cost per casualty by accident type | |
|---|---|
| | **June 2011** |
| **Accident/casualty type** | **Cost per casualty (£)** |
| Fatal | 1,686,532 |
| Serious | 189,510 |
| Slight | 12,611 |
| Average for all severities | 50,025 |
| Damage only | |

### Additional effects

Saving 30 lives is not the only positive effect the Vinnie campaign has had:

- during the campaign, 136,000 people signed a petition calling on the government to make it mandatory for all young people to learn CPR;
- the NHS is now using the film as a training video (Figure 33);
- the campaign infographic now appears on ambulances;
- 'You've been Vinnie-d' has entered hospital vernacular;
- 'hands-only CPR' was taught to MPs at all three major party political conferences;
- a follow up 'mini-Vinnie' campaign featuring young kids to train 'hands-only CPR' in schools.

**Figure 33: The NHS is now using the film as a training video**

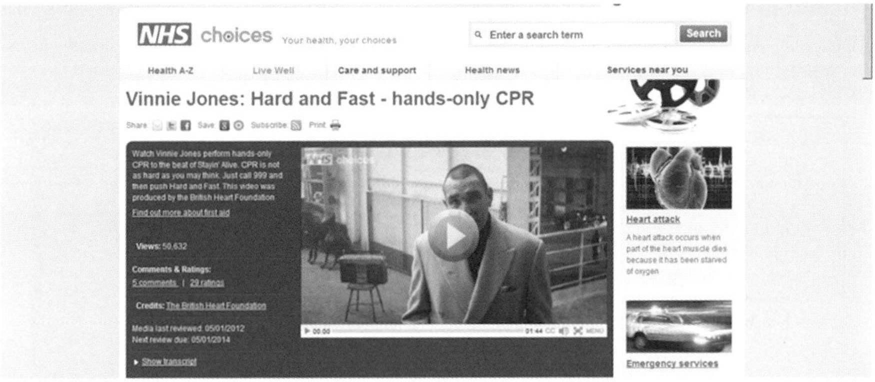

Hands-only CPR was spoken about at party political conferences.

*Many people find giving the kiss of life a daunting prospect; but hands-only CPR is very simple to learn and it could put thousands more life-savers on our streets.*

MP Julian Huppert

During the writing of this paper, Vinnie has continued to push into popular culture. The life-saving advert was recreated in LEGO as part of the promotion for *The LEGO Movie* where famous UK ads were spoofed and pulled together for a special ad break (Figure 34).

**Figure 34: The campaign was one of the ads chosen by LEGO to be recreated for the launch of *The LEGO Movie***

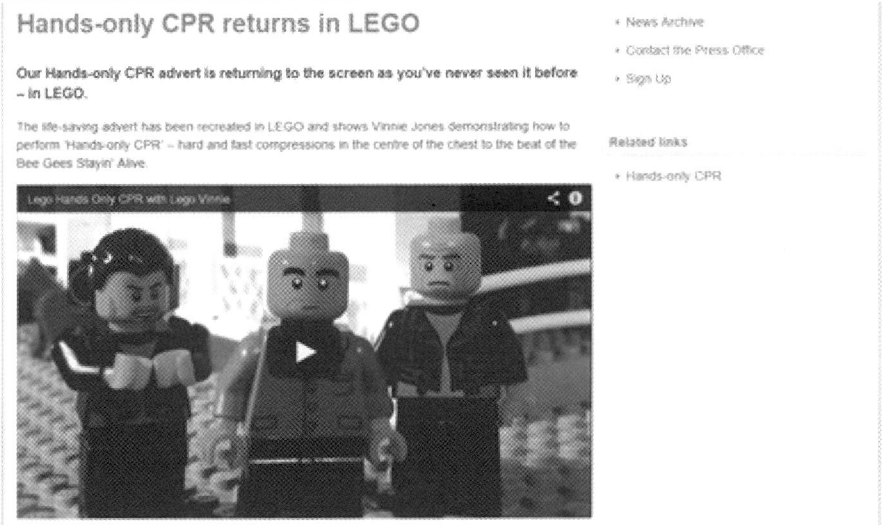

Finally, it's humbling to realise the effect our creativity can have on people's lives, when used in the right way. This is a quote from a couple who felt the effects of the Vinnie campaign first hand (Figure 35).[28]

### Figure 35: Derek Burt who saved his wife after seeing the ad

He said: 'I kept doing CPR for five minutes and phoned for an ambulance. They told me to carry on while they were on their way. Slowly I could see the colour returning to Angela's cheeks, so I knew I must be doing something right.'

She said: 'I just feel so incredibly lucky that Derek saw the ad.'

– Derek Burt, who saved his future wife Angela with 'Hands-only' CPR.

Derek Burt had seen the ad just weeks before his wife Angela had a heart attack

## What can we learn from Vinnie?

*The power of likeability to change behaviour*

- There are a lot of terribly serious things written about behavioural change.
- We flipped the convention, took something scary and made it funny.
- James Belushi, the US comedy actor once declared that *'laughter is a powerful thing'*. We certainly proved it to be a formidable force when welded in the right way. By turning a piece of serious education into a funny dance we helped save 30 real lives.
- IPA dataBANK highlights 'likeability' as a leading indicator of campaign effectiveness in commercial advertising campaigns. We believe Vinnie builds a case for its positive impact on actual behaviour.

*The power of entering popular culture*

- With the right ingredients a campaign can truly infiltrate popular culture.
- If executed correctly it can become self-sustaining, even on a low budget.

*The power of different senses*

- We were struck how 'sticky' Vinnie became. It made us think about *how* people absorb new information.

- Neuro-linguistic programming (NLP) suggests people learn in three key ways: visual (through pictures), auditory (chants and rhythm) and kinaesthetic (gestures and body movements).
- Vinnie combined all three, giving us the opportunity to maximise the learning potential.

So, next time, don't be shy, don't be filled with fear. Instead, have a laugh. Get stuck in and push it. Hard and fast, if you need to.

## Notes

1   Source: Policy Statement: Emergency Life Support, BHF 2012.
2   Source: Policy Statement: Emergency Life Support, BHF 2012.
3   Source: European Resuscitation Council, 2010.
4   Source: Policy Statement: Emergency Life Support, BHF 2012.
5   Source: *Transforming NHS ambulance services*. Department of Health. 2011.
6   Source: *Transforming NHS ambulance services*. Department of Health. 2011.
7   Source: *Transforming NHS ambulance services*. Department of Health. 2011.
8   Source: Hall & Partners post-campaign tracking Feb 2012.
9   Source: Policy Statement: Emergency Life Support, BHF 2012.
10  Source: Hall & Partners post-campaign tracking Feb 2012.
11  Source: Hall & Partners post-campaign tracking Feb 2012.
12  Source: Hall & Partners post-campaign tracking Feb 2012.
13  AIDA describes the communications formula of attention, interest, desire, and finally action.
14  Source: Hall & Partners post-campaign tracking Feb 2012.
15  Source: PHD.
16  Source: Policy Statement: Emergency Life Support, BHF 2012.
17  Source: BBC.co.uk.
18  Source: *Ealing Gazette*.
19  Of the tracked audience of 35–60s, 86% recognised the campaign (18.8m). If we scale this up to an all adult level (based on our media-buying strategy), we achieved 35.9m recognisers. Seventy-one percent of this audience claim to be 'more likely to perform "hands-only CPR"'. This marked an increase of 17% and an absolute number of 6 million people – Source: Hall & Partners post-campaign tracking Feb 2012.
20  Source: Best-selling Phillips HS1 re-usable defibrillator costs £920.00. www.defibshop.co.uk.
21  Source: London Ambulance Service Cardiac Arrest report 2012.
22  Source: https://www.emergencymedicaltraining.com/OnlineTraining/complete-cpr.aspx.
23  Source: For every minute that goes by, a victim's chance of surviving a sudden cardiac arrest drops 10%. Source: British Heart Foundation Emergency Life Support Policy Document 2012.
24  Source: Office of the Strategic Health Authorities, Emergency services review: a comparative review of ambulance service best-practice, 2009.
25  Source: Department of Health and National Audit Office analysis of ambulance service data.
26  Source BHF 2012.
27  In the UK, the Department for Transport routinely puts a value on a life. These calculations include all aspects of the valuation of casualties, including *the human costs*, which reflect pain, grief, suffering; the direct economic costs of lost output, and the medical costs associated with treating an accident. They do not include other costs which are specifically related to road accidents – police time, administrative costs of insurance and damage.
28  Source: *Daily Mail*.

# Specsavers

## Should've gone to Specsavers: a far-sighted view of advertising's role in building a business over 30 years

**By Matthew Philip, Manning Gottlieb OMD**

Contributing authors: Helen Weavers, Real World Planning; Paddy Adams, Manning Gottlieb OMD; Preety Marwaha, BrandScience; Tim Orton, Specsavers Optical Group; Caroline Clear and Tim Pearson, Manning Gottlieb OMD; Sam Dias, BrandScience; David Bratt, Manning Gottlieb OMD

Credited companies: Creative Agency, Specsavers Optical Group; Media Agency, Manning Gottlieb OMD; PR Agency, Beattie Communications; Client, Specsavers Optical Group

### Editor's summary

Specsavers' success is testament to the sustainable power of advertising to grow a business. It's the story of one of the most iconic brands in the UK, and how it grew from a standing start 30 years ago to a £1.8bn international success today.

Having invested nearly £500m in advertising over 30 years, Specsavers commands a dominant share of voice and consistent revenue growth. Their strategy of continuous presence at relatively high spend levels, a broad appeal, commitment to humour as an advertising tool and distinctive, familiar brand assets that build memory structure have all contributed to £1.1bn of incremental profit over 30 years. Rivals have struggled to carve out a distinctive identity in the face of the 'Should've gone…' creative and the brand continues to own the category in the minds of many consumers.

**The judges readily admired the consistency of the communications over decades and its resolve in maintaining such a strong share of voice regardless of market conditions or competitive context. Its courage and commitment being rewarded with enviable results and continued market dominance.**

## Introduction: An overview

This is the story of one of the most iconic brands in the UK, and how it grew from a standing start 30 years ago to a £1.8bn international success today.[1] It is a brand that owes its very creation to a change in legislation allowing advertising in the optical retail sector and owes its subsequent success, to a large extent, to advertising.

This isn't the normal 'problem–solution–results' story; rather it is a story of the power of viewing advertising as a fundamental building block of a successful business, and of the benefits – both direct and indirect – of consistent high spending.

We're going to show you some impressive numbers – how nearly £500m invested in advertising over 30 years, and a subsequent unassailably dominant share of voice, has contributed to extraordinary revenue growth and brought in an estimated £1.1bn of incremental profit.[2] However, we're also going to show you that it's not just the size of the advertising spend alone that has driven that success. This is also the story of the power of one of the best-liked[3] and most recognisable creative ideas in recent memory: *'Should've gone to Specsavers'*.

## Background: Gazing into the past

The optical retail sector was a very different place in the late 1970s and early 1980s – opticians were closer to GPs than business people, their premises didn't resemble shops and there was legislation in place banning them from advertising their products and services. These services were expensive (although majority-funded by the NHS) and their product ranges were limited, dated and uninspired. The market was dominated by independents and a single big chain, Dollond & Aitchison, which accounted for 21% of the market[4] (Figure 1).

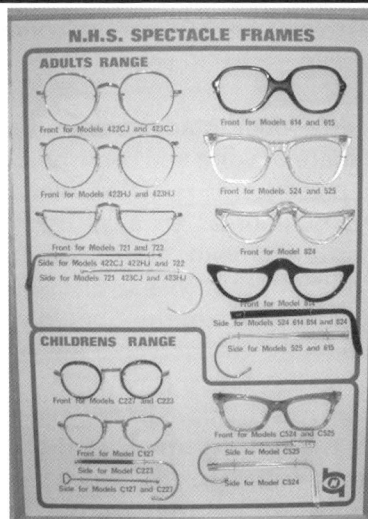

Figure 1: A typical NHS range of specs from 1977; one in three frames dispensed in the UK were one of these styles!

Sources: www.museyeum.org; Fulop & Warren, 'The Marketing of a Professional Service: Opticians', *International Journal of Advertising*, 1992

Then in the mid-1980s, as with so many sectors and industries, Thatcherism changed everything. The Opticians Act 1984 allowed qualified opticians to advertise their services for the first time; this, coupled with the gradual phasing out of NHS specs, led to new entrants in the sector competing on publicity and price for the first time.

One of those new entrants was a business set up by Mary and Doug Perkins, an optometrist couple who had sold a successful chain of opticians in the South West and moved to Guernsey to be nearer their parents. The change in legislation inspired them to return to the business they knew, and they started Specsavers in their spare room (using a ping pong table *in lieu* of a proper desk) with a dream of creating Britain's biggest and best value chain of opticians, providing the best value eye-care to everyone. This meant consistently low prices and a different approach to business (Figure 2).

**Figure 2: Specsavers started its life on this ping pong table**

*We were the first to advertise, have showrooms and let people know what our prices were.*

Dame Mary Perkins[5]

Central to their offering was a commitment to clear pricing, a revolution in the optical industry at the time: the price tag on each frame included the cost of standard lenses, meaning that customers knew exactly what they were going to pay before they got to the till.

Specsavers was from the start a series of joint-venture partnerships, where each Specsavers store is legally a separate business, with 50% of the business owned by the practice partners and 50% owned by Specsavers Optical Group. Each practice pays a fee to the group for services and support, including IT, operations, retail training and marketing. After paying for these services, any profit belongs to the practice partners. In this paper, we will report on combined revenue for all Specsavers stores in the UK.

This business model allowed them to behave like a series of local independent opticians (with all the benefits of trust and personal service that that entailed), with the huge buying power of a much bigger chain. This allowed them to pass any savings on to the customer, ensuring that they lived up to their name – Spec*savers* – from the start.

To state that this model has been successful would be an understatement – in just 10 years Specsavers became the market leader and they have remained there for the two decades since. There are currently 693 Specsavers stores in the UK. Beyond the UK, there are over 800 Specsavers in Ireland, Netherlands, Scandinavia, Spain, New Zealand and Australia, employing over 30,000 people and dispensing over 13m pairs of spectacles each year. In total the business generated revenue of £1.8bn in 2013.[6] Quite an achievement for a company that remains privately owned by the Perkins family and hundreds of store partners!

## Context: Specsavers' history through the lens of their advertising

In the interests of clarity, we're going to chunk Specsavers' advertising up into distinct phases:

### 1. 1984–1993: Looking at the first decade

In 1984, the Perkinses opened the first Specsavers in Guernsey. Soon they broke ground on the mainland, opening a store in Bristol and adding three more opticians by the end of the first year (Figure 3).

Figure 3: One of the first Specsavers stores

In the early years, Specsavers continued to push the optical market forward, notably in 1990 when they introduced their on-going 'two for one' offer, helping people to see glasses as a fashion accessory, not just a necessity.

The market took to advertising quickly, with new chains such as Specialeyes making early forays into press advertising, focusing specifically on price and product (Figure 4).

## Figure 4: A Specialeyes press ad from 1985

Specsavers joined the fray, supporting new stores, running local press advertising that promoted value for money, style and service (Figures 5–7).

## Figure 5: Specsavers press ads from mid-1980s

## Figure 6: Specsavers press ads from late-1980s

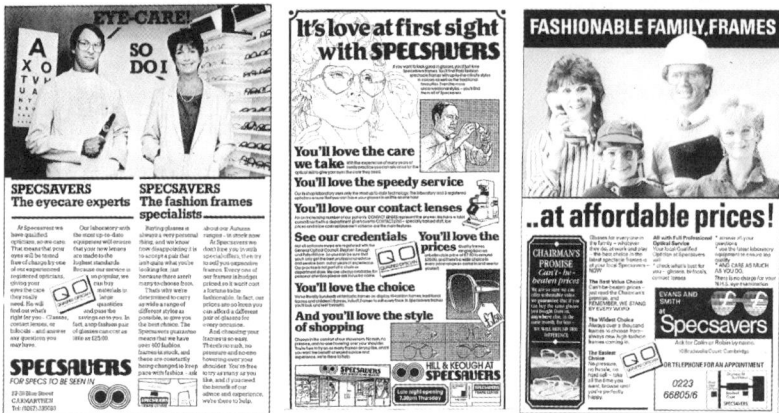

## Figure 7: Share of voice in the optical retail category, 1984–1993

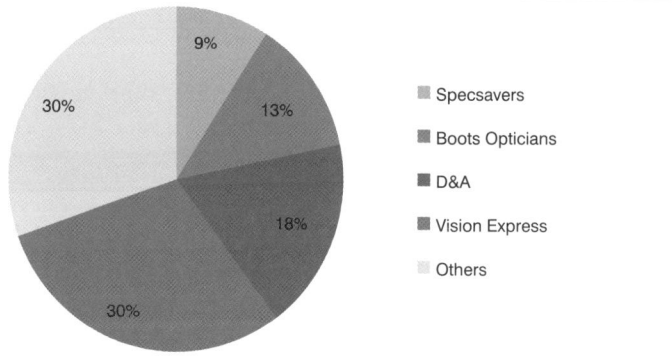

Source: RegisterMEAL, Nielsen

While advertising was beginning to play a key role at local level, spends were comparatively low and growth was primarily being driven by new stores opening (Figures 8 and 9).

In fact, store growth allied to promoting their price positioning was successful enough to allow them to challenge Dollond & Aitchison for market leadership by the end of 1993 (Figure 10).

## Figure 8: Specsavers revenue and number of stores, 1984–1993

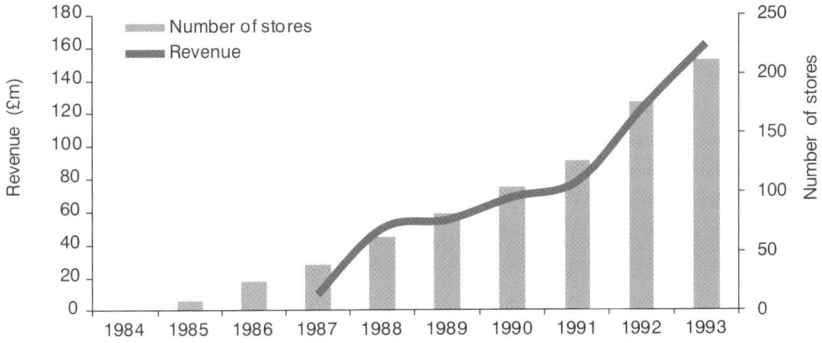

Source: Specsavers

## Figure 9: Specsavers revenue and media spend, 1984–1993

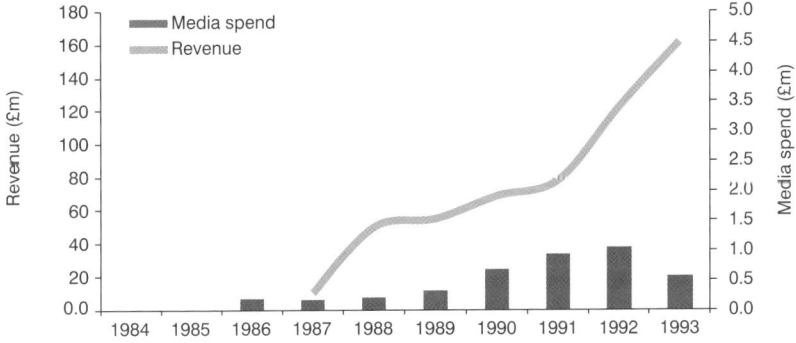

Source: RegisterMEAL, Nielsen

## Figure 10: Optical retail market share, 1993

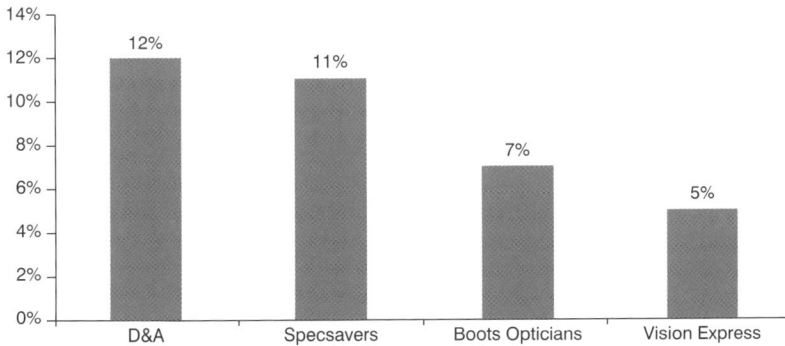

Source: Mintel

## 2. 1994–2002: A national focus

The year 1994 marked a key moment in Specsavers' history. Reaching over 200 stores gave them full national reach, a tipping point in terms of scale, and the decision was taken to expand the marketing budget significantly, jumping from £500,000 in 1993 to almost £4m in 1994. From this point, spend accelerated above and beyond store growth, increasing 34-fold between 1993 and 2001, and driving the total spend of the category up beyond recognition and ensuring that Specsavers was always the dominant spender (Figure 11).

### Figure 11: Optical retail category ad spend 1984–2002

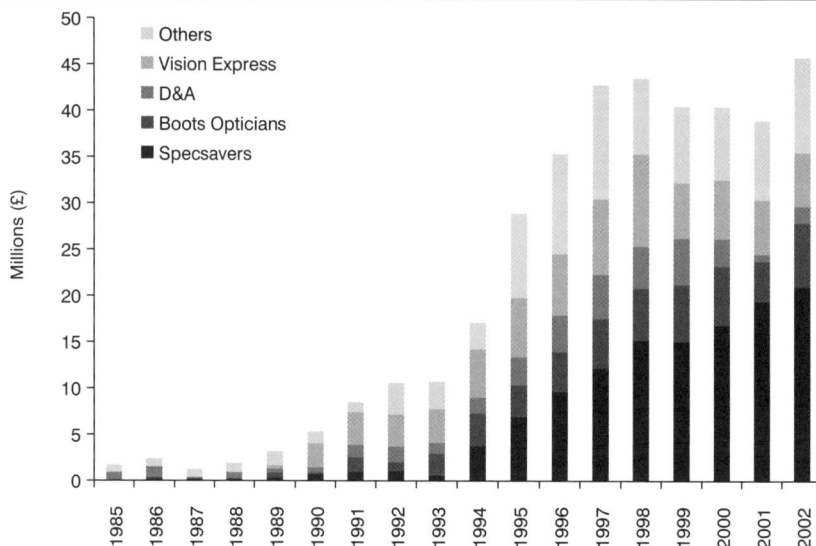

Source: RegisterMEAL, Nielsen

Over this period there was a distinct shift in Specsavers' creative approach.

By this point, Specsavers were firmly established as the category leaders and they broke the rational category conventions in their TV advertising. Press and outdoor remained price-, product- and offer-focused, but their TV executions recognised the power of a big idea in driving brand salience and memorability. Specsavers had always created their advertising in-house, but the team expanded as they created a series of executions talking about the importance of eyesight with a clear emotional hook and the tagline 'Now you can believe your eyes'. This series included 'Physicist', an execution featuring Stephen Hawking which became the first Specsavers advert to be parodied – by Egg, the following year (Figures 12 and 13).

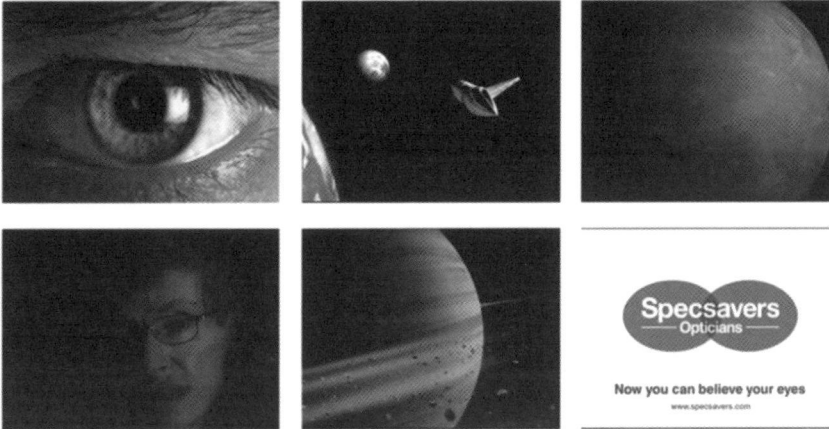

Figure 12: 'Physicist' TV ad

*The scene opens on Stephen Hawking gazing out into the universe from a spaceship. He declares that staring into the universe fills him with wonder and that his eye-sight is important to him.*
**Now you can believe your eyes**

Figure 13: Egg.com parody of 'Physicist'

*The scene opens on Stephen Hawking floating in space, who admits he's starring as the token 'clever clogs' in a shameless plug for Egg. A voiceover claims that with egg you can pick and choose your own investments for yourself. The ad finishes with Hawking declaring that he has discovered that the egg came before the chicken as he crashes into a planet.*

Through 2000 and 2001, Specsavers introduced a narrative approach, running a varied portfolio of ads highlighting different aspects of the business, from contact lenses to style, and seeking to make their 'two frames for the price of one' offer famous (Figures 14 and 15).

## Figure 14: 'Sliding doors' TV ad

*A woman wakes up in bed and drops and loses her contact lenses while getting ready. She sets out for the train station on her commute and just misses her train, potentially missing out on a chance meeting with a handsome stranger. The voiceover announces that Specsavers provide all day, all night 30 continuous wear contact lenses. The camera shows the same woman contentedly sitting on the train the next day.*
**Easyvision all day-all night lenses. £25 per month including aftercare**

## Figure 15: 'Opera' TV ad

*The ad opens with a mysterious female spy stealing some secret plans. She is discovered and followed to an opera house through winding cobbled streets. At the opera she swaps her glasses to change her appearance and slips by her pursuers un-noticed.*
**Two looks for the price of one from £69**

This approach was certainly rewarded with success. As ad expenditure grew, group revenue began to accelerate well beyond store openings (Figures 16–18).

## Figure 16: Specsavers revenue and number of stores, 1984–2002

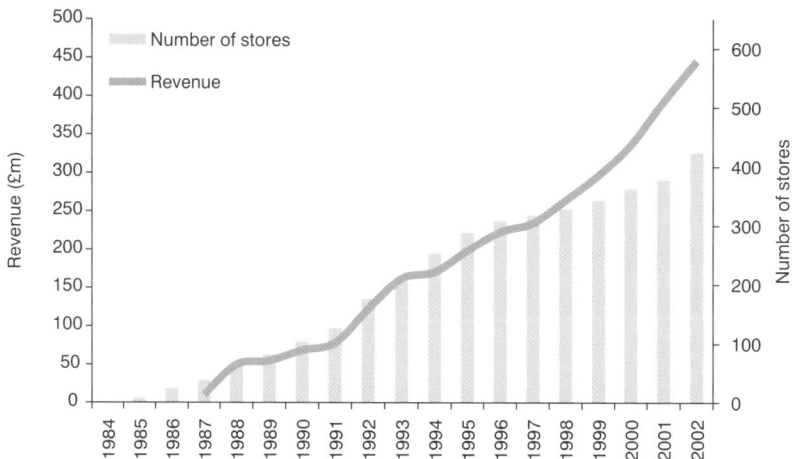

Source: Specsavers

## Figure 17: Specsavers revenue and media spend, 1984-2002

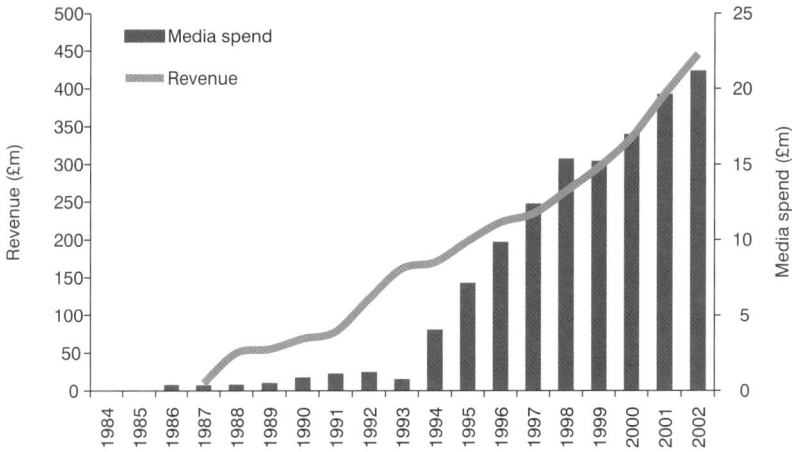

Source: Specsavers, RegisterMEAL, Nielsen

## Figure 18: Optical retail category share of voice, 1994–2002

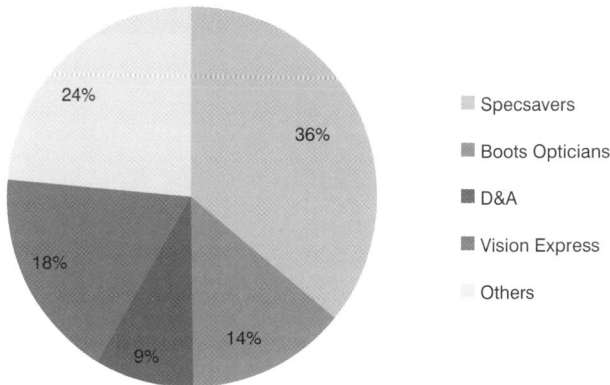

Spource: Nielsen

At the heart of this investment was a reliance on TV, which has taken the majority of Specsavers' above-the-line spend over time (Figure 19).

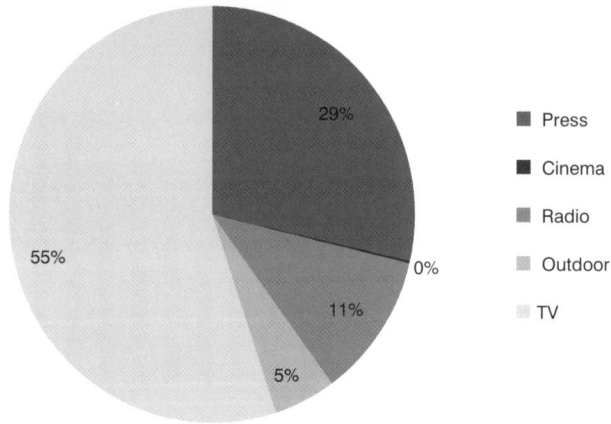

Figure 19: Specsavers media split 1984–2013

29%

55%

0%

11%

5%

- Press
- Cinema
- Radio
- Outdoor
- TV

Source: Nielsen

The result of this growth was that in 2002 market share stood at around double that of the closest competitors (Figure 20).

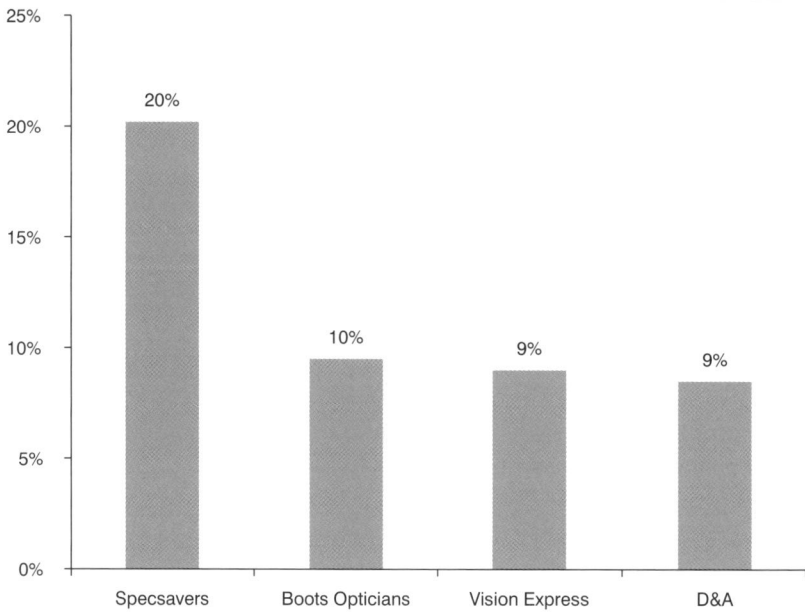

Figure 20: Optical retail category market share, 2002

| | Specsavers | Boots Opticians | Vision Express | D&A |
|---|---|---|---|---|
| | 20% | 10% | 9% | 9% |

Source: Mintel

## 3. 2003–2005: First sight of 'Should've Gone to Specsavers'

By 2003 there was a feeling that while many previous campaigns had been successful, there was no coherent identity to Specsavers' advertising or brand, no common thread that ran through and made the most of their dominant spend.

At the time, there was a set of internal rules that dictated what Specsavers wouldn't put in their advertising: 'No alcohol, no smoking, no nudity, no sex, and *no humour*'.

Rules, though, are made to be broken and the Specsavers creative team, led by Graham Daldry, felt that humour in particular could be a valuable salience driver for the brand. During creative development, they stumbled across a humorous throwaway line that became the very heart of the brand.

*'Should've gone to Specsavers'* had a slightly different meaning first time around; it was most often a joke about having bad specs or losing your primary pair, helping Specsavers to promote their style credentials and their low prices (Figures 21–24).

## Figure 21: 'Breadbin' TV ad

*A family sit at breakfast with the panicking father searching for his lost glasses in the most unlikely of places; the toaster, the bin. His daughter tells him he should have gone to Specsavers where he could have got two pairs of glasses for the price of one.*
**Specsavers. No.1 for Eyewear**

## Figure 22: 'Party' TV ad

*A man in unfashionable glasses flirts with a woman at a party, suggestively enquiring whether she wants to go upstairs, the woman tells him to meet her there in 5 minutes. Upon the man's arrival he finds an empty bedroom with the words 'You should've gone to Specsavers' written in lipstick on the mirror.*
**FCUK, Osiris and Storm designer glasses now only £99 (£30 off)**

## Figure 23: 'Café' TV ad

*Three men sit in a cafe, one of which boasts to his friends that a woman is looking at him. The woman writes a note, hands it to the waiter to give it to the man. The note reads 'Should've gone to Specsavers'.*
**FCUK and Storm Eyewear prescription sunglasses. £30 off – now £99**

## Figure 24: 'Gameshow' TV ad

*The ad opens on a Jerry Springer style talk-show featuring a quarrelling couple. The woman exclaims that her husband wears the worst glasses in the world. The host tells him he should've gone to Specsavers and he is taken away to get new glasses. He returns a new man in stylish specs.*
**FCUK and Storm Eyewear designer frames now £99**

Three years of commitment to this idea certainly paid back dividends. The *'Should've...'* ads were both well recognised and extremely memorable. By the end of 2005, almost 30% of specs wearers could spontaneously remember an execution (Figure 25).

## Figure 25: Specsavers TV tracking, 2002–2005

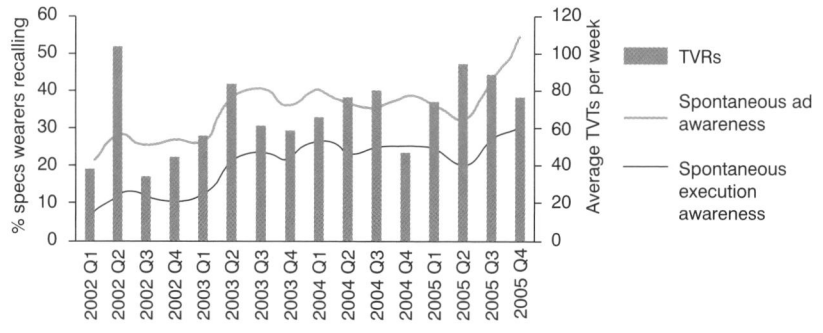

Source: TNS, base c.2,000 specs wearers/6 months

In part, this noticeability was driven by maintaining their dominant share of voice, ensuring that spend always exceeded that of their competitors (Figure 26).

## Figure 26: Optical retail category share of voice, 2003–2005

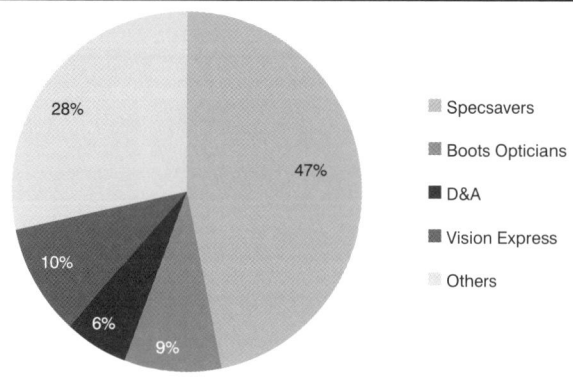

Source: Nielsen

Indeed, *'Should've gone to Specsavers'* had become so well known by this point that Specsavers was even beginning to parody it in their own advertising (Figure 27).

## Figure 27: 'Office' TV ad

*A manager approaches two colleagues in an office. He shows off his glasses, including his second pair, explaining the 2 for 1 offer. He shouts to the office at large that they all 'Should've Gone to Specsavers'. They reply that they all have, holding up their respective second pair of glasses.*
**2 for 1 including varifocals and bifocals from £75.**

And it was clearly having a dramatic effect on business success. During the *'Should've...'* years, sales began to accelerate dramatically beyond store growth (Figures 28 and 29).

## Figure 28: Specsavers revenue and number of stores, 1984–2005

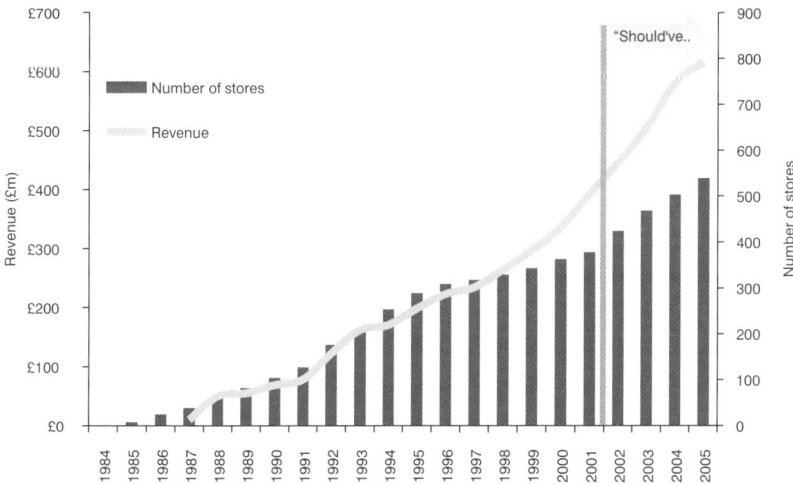

Source: Specsavers

## Figure 29: Specsavers revenue and media spend, 1984-2005

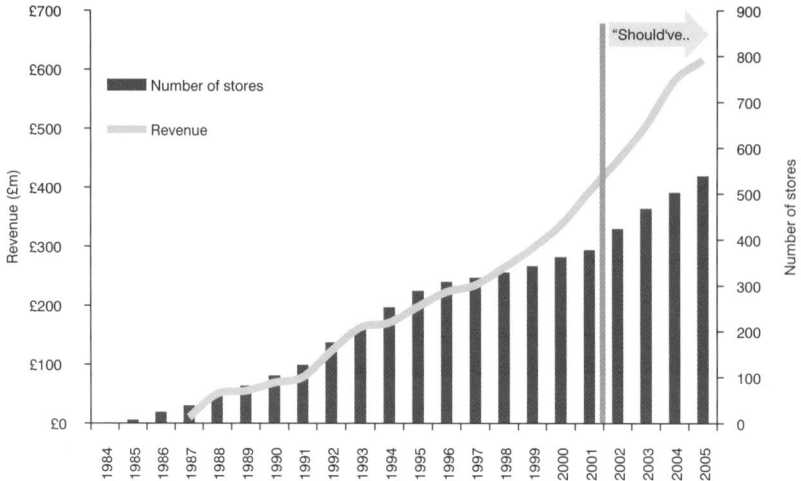

### 4. 2006–2007: Losing focus

By the end of 2005, tracking seemed to be indicating that Specsavers was lagging behind competitors in terms of professionalism, quality and style, and it was hypothesised that the humorous brand communications might be a barrier.[7]

So from 2006 to midway through 2007, the 'Should've...' stories were dropped and replaced with a series of more abstract executions that majored on fashionable frames and a professional approach, bound together with sky-high production values (Figures 30–32).

## Figure 30: 'Dreamboat' TV ad

*A beautiful woman wearing glasses lies resting on a boat in the middle of an ethereal misty lake. She falls asleep and dreams of saving a man wearing glasses in a dark forest. She wakes and finds him beside her in the boat. They kiss.*
**2 for 1 including designer glasses**

## Figure 31: 'Wildside' TV ad

*A man dressed in sunglasses and black coat in the style of 'The Matrix' walks through the streets of a city at night. He is chased and captured by a woman, also in sunglasses, and her gang. She walks away from the scene into the city.*
**2 for 1 including prescription designer glasses**

## Figure 32: 'Juggler' TV ad

*A man juggles on a tight-rope on the side of a snowy mountain, he puts on his glasses, his improved vision allowing him to add more balls to the trick. A voiceover informs viewers that each Specsavers is run and owned by individual opticians.*
**You can have it all at Specsavers**
**30% off glasses for Over 60s**

Despite increasing media investment and achieving a 50% share of voice, the communications tracking wasn't showing positive results. In fact, the advertising was slightly less noticeable – and a whole lot less memorable – than the previous period which involved the *'Should've...'* idea. With fewer people actively remembering Specsavers as a brand, it would surely lead to fewer eye tests and lost revenue, as we will show when we come to discuss the contribution from advertising in the next section (Figures 33 and 34).

## Figure 33: Specsavers TV tracking, 2005–2007

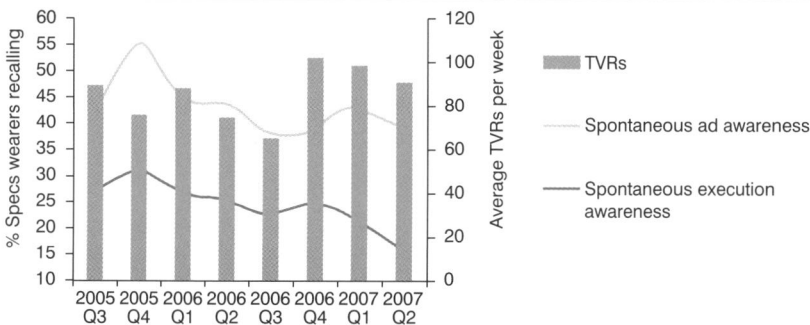

Source: TNS, base c.2,000 specs wearers/6 months

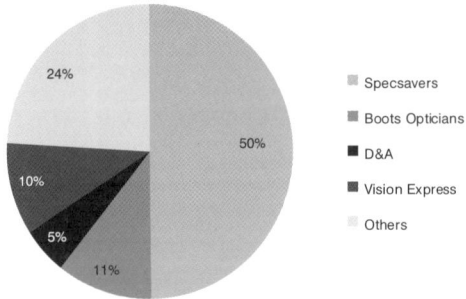

**Figure 34: Optical retail category share of voice, 2006–2007**

- Specsavers
- Boots Opticians
- D&A
- Vision Express
- Others

50%
24%
10%
5%
11%

It was becoming clear that simply dominating spending on advertising wasn't a sure-fire recipe for success.

### 5. 2008–2012: Seeing clearly

By 2008, the continued poor tracking brought clarity to Richard Holmes, Specsavers'Marketing Director, and the team returned to the approach that had made them famous with a new vigour, keeping the high production quality but adding the wit and warmth that defines Specsavers.

But the gag was no longer about bad glasses. The creative team broke the last taboo in optical advertising: *'Should've gone to Specsavers'* became a joke about poor eyesight (Figures 35–39).

**Figure 35: 'Colliewobble' TV ad**

**Figure 36: 'Thunderbirds Are Go!' TV ad**

*Virgil from the Thunderbirds is chased by a villain through a tight, winding underground tunnel, both wearing jet packs. They exit the tunnel, and into bright sunlight. Virgil's lenses darken and he swerves away, avoiding a cliff at the last minute, with the villain smashing headlong into it. Voiceover from Virgil's radio claims 'He should've gone to Specsavers Virgil'.*
**Free Reaction lenses at Specsavers**

## Figure 37: 'Eerie' TV ad

*The scene is set in a small Canadian town in the mountains, but all is not well. In a spooky apocalyptic style all electronic devices turn off one by one: a television, a record player, public fountains, traffic lights. The scene changes to a lumberjack accidently chopping down a power pylon in the woods.*
**Should've Gone to Specsavers**
**2 for 1 including sunglasses from £75**

## Figure 38: 'Postman Pat' TV ad

*The scene opens with Postman Pat and his black and white cat delivering the mail in the morning (just as day is dawning). He gets back into his bright red van and sits on his glasses, breaking them. He continues his rounds nonetheless, but his driving takes an erratic turn, going through fields, gardens, clothes lines, while he accidently delivers vegetables instead of letters.*
**Should've gone to Specsavers Pat!**
**2 for 1 from £69**

## Figure 39: 'Sauna' TV ad

*A man enters a sauna and settles himself down, naked, on a bench. The mist clears to reveal that instead of a sauna, he is in fact sat in Gordon Ramsay's kitchen. Gordon slams his knife down on the table in frustration and the man quickly crosses his legs, embarrassed.*
**Should've Gone to Specsavers**
**Free Varifocal Lenses**

The turnaround in tracking was dramatic, noticeability increased to record levels and memorability shot up markedly (Figure 40).

## Figure 40: Specsavers' TV tracking, 2007–2010

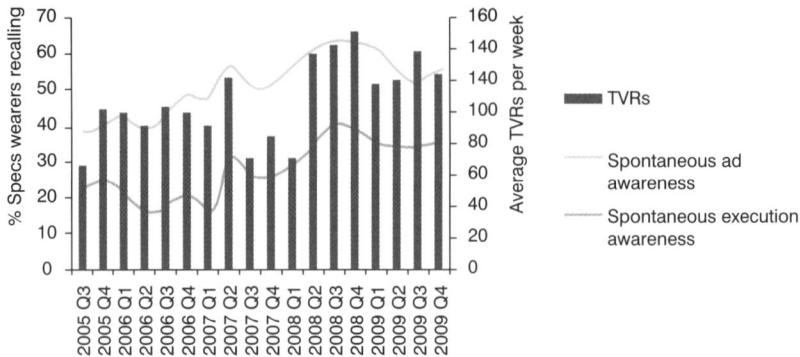

Source: TNS, base c.2,000 specs wearers/6 months

And sales growth was similarly strong, helping revenue to grow at its fastest level ever, well above store growth (Figures 41 and 42).

## Figure 41: Specsavers revenue and number of stores, 1984–2012

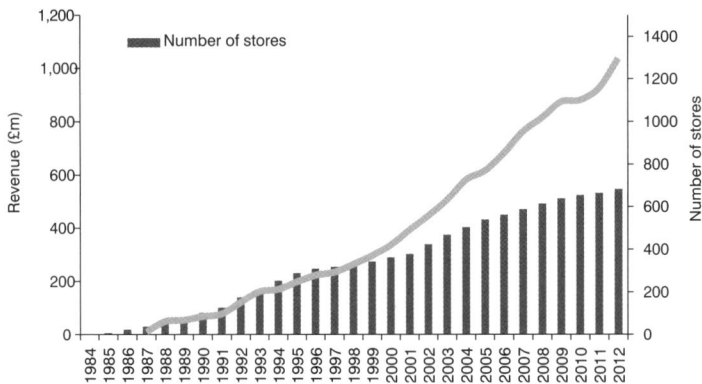

Source:: Specsavers

## Figure 42: Specsavers revenue and media spend, 1984–2012

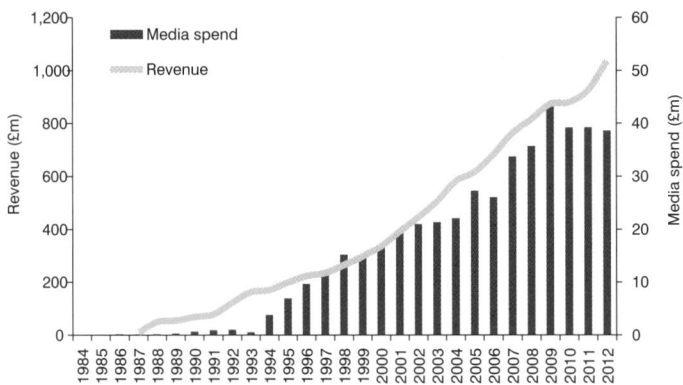

Source: Specsavers

It was becoming clear that *'Should've gone to Specsavers'* was one of the business's most valuable market-based assets, and maintaining memorability of it was central to driving business growth. Research showed that non-customers who recognised *'Should've gone to Specsavers'* felt much warmer and more positive about the brand, and were more open to switching opticians.[8]

### 6. 2013: Focusing on fame

The growth in advertising recognition and business performance gave Specsavers a clear understanding of how advertising helps build fame and grow their business (Figure 43).

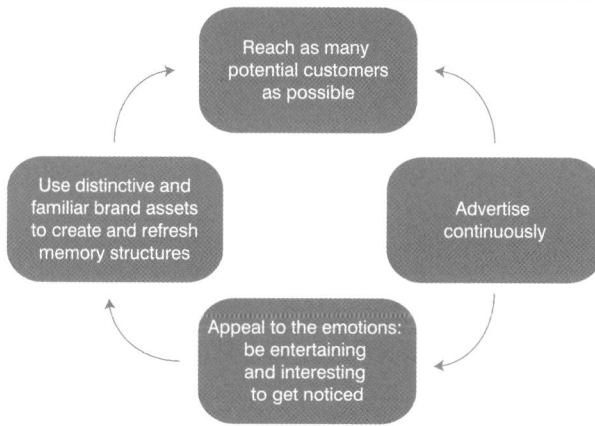

Figure 43: Specsavers communications model

But in 2012 Specsavers faced a conundrum. The 'Should've…' campaign felt like it was working really well, but they began to see a worrying decline in the memorability of their TV advertising. This wasn't due to a drop in media spend – indeed, their share of voice was as high as it had ever been (Figures 44 and 45).

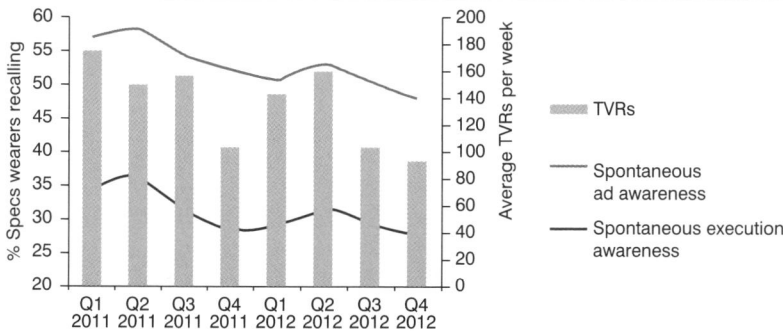

Figure 44: Specsavers TV tracking, 2011–2012

Source: TNS, base c.2,000 specs wearers/6 months

## Figure 45: Optical retail category share of voice, 2008–2013

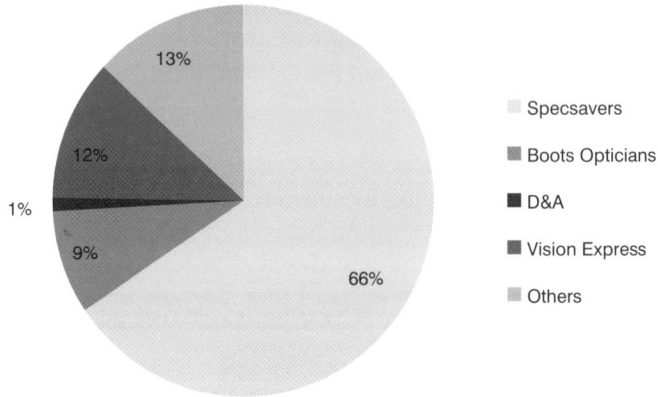

- Specsavers
- Boots Opticians
- D&A
- Vision Express
- Others

13%
12%
1%
9%
66%

Nor was it due to wear-out, despite the weight of media spend behind some of the executions – many of the older ads which were still running in rotation were performing as well as ever (Figure 46).

## Figure 46: Motivation score of various TV executions, 2012

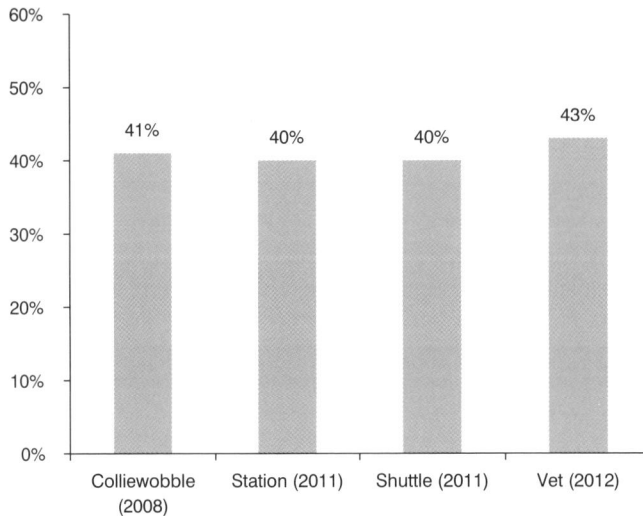

| Colliewobble (2008) | Station (2011) | Shuttle (2011) | Vet (2012) |
| 41% | 40% | 40% | 43% |

Source: TNS brand and communication tracking 2012: they found that despite being five years old, Colliewobble was as liked and as motivating as ever. It also showed that the likeability of almost all 'Should've…' ads hadn't changed significantly and new creatives in the series were performing in line with the older ones

The issue was a shift in media habits amongst Specsavers' core over-45 audience. TV viewing had increased, and consequently the average number of ads they were seeing a day had grown almost 50% since 2002,[9] making it harder than ever to cut through. On top of this, Specsavers were reaching them fewer times in press for the same level of spend.[10]

Also, consumption of video had increased significantly amongst this audience, with double the numbers of 55-year-olds watching catch-up TV than two years before and over-60s increasing the amount of time they spent consuming on-demand videos by 75% in 12 months.[11]

The media approach was changed to reflect this, with an increase in spend on video-on-demand and online video publishing networks (tripling spend in these channels year-on-year).

More focus was put on increasing the fame of the '*Should've…*' campaign[12] rather than focusing on individual executions or offers.

This meant evening out TV ad spend in order to maximise adstock throughout the year (prior to 2013, TV investment had been erratic, with marked differences in TVR levels from one month to the next – this was unnecessary in a market with no seasonality, beyond a dip in December).

Specsavers harnessed the power of social media to make '*Should've gone to Specsavers*' as famous as possible. They knew that people were using the phrase already, but that they could accelerate that usage by reacting to suitable major events as quickly as possible, and seeding '*Should've…*' content socially. Specsavers set up a team to monitor and react to any 'sight gag' opportunities in the news and react to major events by getting a '*Should've…*' gag out at a moment's notice (Figures 47 and 48).

**Figure 47: London 2012 organisers mistake North Korea for their neighbour (national press, Twitter, Facebook)**

에 갔으면 좋았을텐데요 Specsavers

(as they might say in North and South Korea)

Book an eye test at specsavers.co.uk or call 0800 0680 241

Specsavers

©2012 Specsavers. All rights reserved.

**Figure 48: Chelsea player Eden Hazard mistakes a ballboy for a football (national press, Twitter, Facebook)**

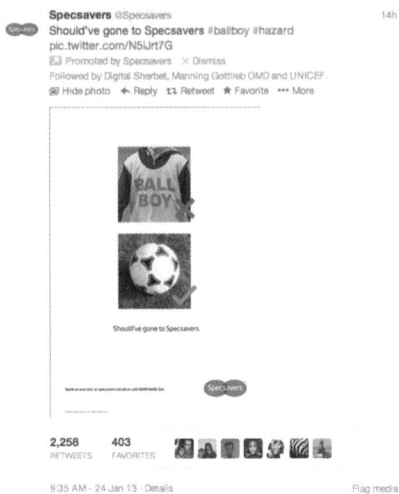

Reacting purely in social media has limited reach, so these gags were brought to millions more people through national press the day after, real-time digital formats and sponsored stories and trends in social media. Through a combination of these and additional shared views, 'Ballboy', for example, was able to reach over 15 million individuals.

Beyond this, *'Should've gone to Specsavers'* doesn't just live in advertising: it's an idea that has truly transitioned into culture, and a go-to phrase for when mistakes are made (Figure 49)!

**Figure 49: *The Times* and *The Sun* take our lead as referee Andre Mariner mistakes Alex Oxlade-Chamberlain for Kieran Gibbs**

The new approach was an immediate success – with no seasonal increase in advertising spend, spontaneous and prompted recall increased markedly[13] (Figure 50).

## Figure 50: Specsavers TV tracking, 2012–2013

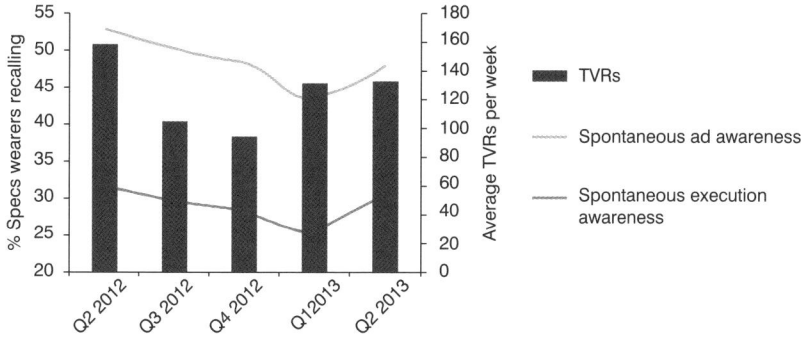

Source: TNS, base c.2,000 specs wearers/6 months

This led to more people taking action – brand searches on Google (a useful proxy for behaviour) increased 12% year-on-year, and eye tests rose 8.6% year-on-year (Figures 51 and 52).

## Figure 51: Increase in branded search volume for Specsavers, 2012–2013

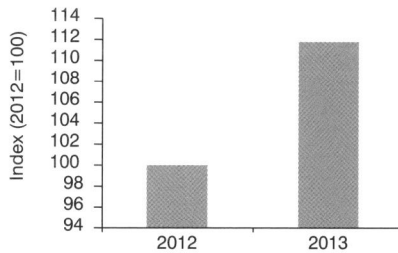

Source: Google Trends

## Figure 52: Increase in Specsavers eye test volume, 2012–2013

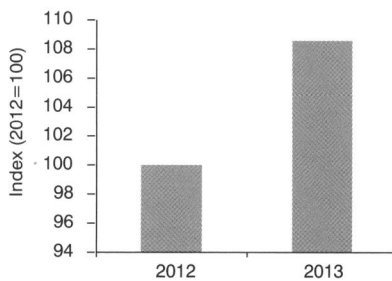

Source: Specsavers

This helped make 2013 Specsavers' best year on record (Figures 53 and 54).

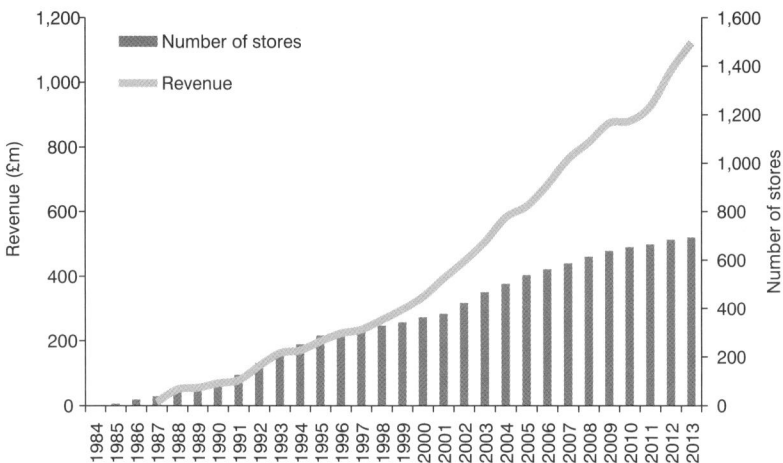

Figure 53: Specsavers revenue and number of stores, 1984–2013

Source: Specsavers

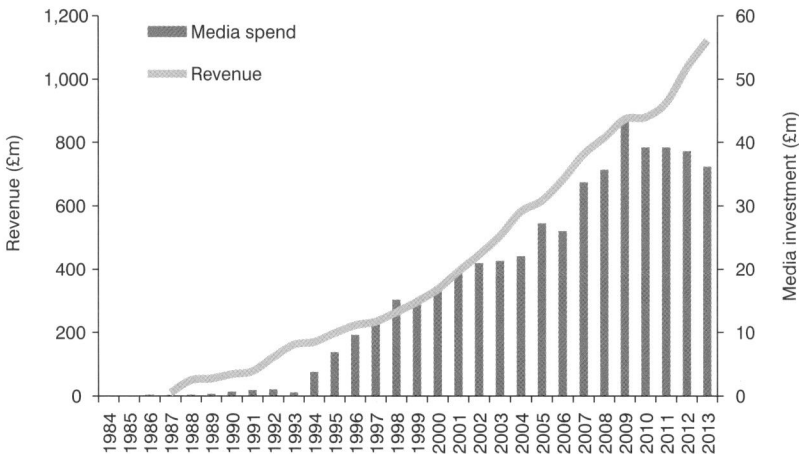

Figure 54: Specsavers revenue and media spend, 1984-2013

Source: Specsavers

## Assessing payback: having a clear view of advertising's contribution

In order to assess the full magnitude of advertising's contribution, it was necessary to build a comprehensive econometric model.

Simplifying the model, we can see that there are two very significant drivers of revenue: store growth and advertising spend. Then there are a myriad of other factors – from growth in the number of people needing sight correction to price inflation – which account for the remainder of the growth (Figure 55).

## Figure 55: Econometric model isolating revenue contribution from different factors

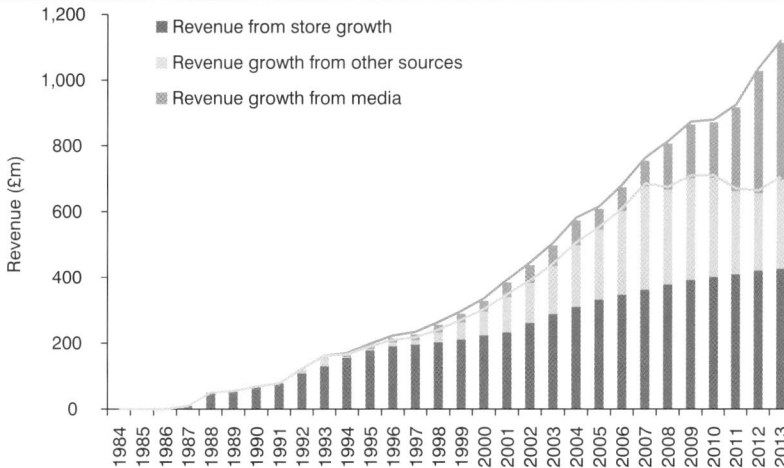

Source: Brandscience

Calculating the revenue contribution of advertising over the past 30 years gives us a figure of £2.1bn from a media investment of £487m.

Understandably, the exact profit contribution from the additional revenue driven by advertising is tricky to assess, and must remain confidential to the business. In order to apply a sensible contribution margin to the proven additional revenue, we will take an established fashion retail ratio of 53.3%.[14]

In total, this approach to estimating profit ROMI indicates that media drove £1.1bn of incremental profit over 30 years, making a net profit payback of £630m, equalling a profit *ROMI of 129%* (Figure 56).

## Figure 56: Specsavers payback from media over 30 years

| | |
|---|---|
| Incremental revenue driven by media: | £ 2,094, 567,659 |
| Marginal contribution to profit: | 53.3% |
| Incremental profit driven by media: | £ 1,116,404,562 |
| Media spend: | £ 486,737,994 |
| Net profit: | £ 629,666,568 |
| Profit ROMI: | 129% |

By interrogating the model further, we can isolate the return from different creative approaches and see the extraordinary power of *'Should've gone to Specsavers'* (Figure 57).

## Figure 57: Revenue return per pound spent by creative period

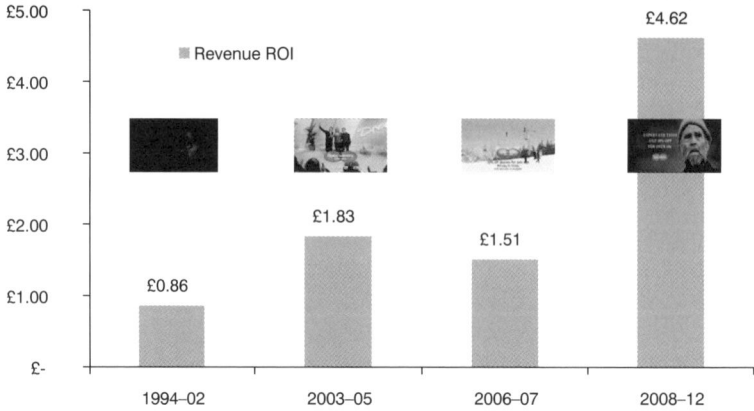

Revenue ROI

£5.00

£4.62

£4.00

£3.00

£2.00    £1.83

£1.51

£1.00    £0.86

£-

1994–02    2003–05    2006–07    2008–12

If we quantify the decision to move away from 'Should've...' in 2006–2007, we can calculate that on a media spend of £60m, Specsavers may have lost £19m of revenue. Clearly when advertising is such a major engine of business growth, decisions like this are not to be taken lightly!

But a valuable lesson was learned, and we can calculate that compared to the previous period, our model shows that the modern incarnation of 'Should've...' delivered an additional £3.11 of revenue per pound spent.

### Putting the results into context

According to the effectiveness ranges detailed in 'Marketing in the Era of Accountability', the Specsavers ROMI result sits around the middle of entries' effectiveness scope (Figure 58).

## Figure 58: IPA Effectiveness Award entries profit ROI range

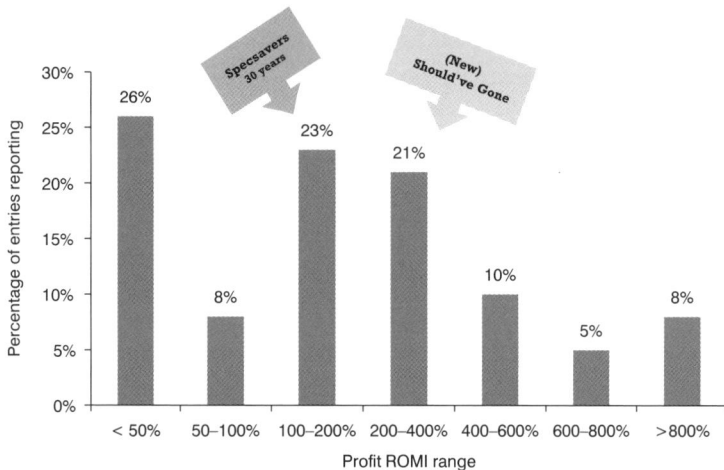

Specsavers 30 years

(New) Should've Gone

30% — 26%

25% — 23%

21%

20%

15%

10% — 8%      10%      8%

5% — 5%

0%

< 50%  50–100%  100–200%  200–400%  400–600%  600–800%  >800%

Profit ROMI range

Source: Binet and Field, *Marketing in the Era of Accountablity*

But we think the results might be a bit better than a mid-table campaign for a few reasons.

- Few other brands in the UK have grown to such a commanding market share:
  - e.g. retail banking – market leader (main current account) is Lloyds with 18%;[15]
  - e.g. supermarkets – market leader is Tesco with 27%;[16]
  - Specsavers' 2012 revenue market was estimated at 39%.[17]
  - However, Specsavers is still growing strongly, and our model shows that as revenue and share reach ever higher levels, an increasing amount of this growth is being driven by advertising. It's likely that advertising may soon be the biggest contributor of business growth to Specsavers.
- While the high street took a battering during the recent economic downturn,[18] Specsavers continued to post astonishing growth, driven increasingly by advertising.
- The IPA EASE database contains just three winners with an investment over £100m who disclose a profit ROI (Table 1).

| Table 1: Profit ROI from IPA Effectiveness Award entries spending over £100m | | | |
|---|---|---|---|
| **Brand** | **Year** | **Budget** | **Profit ROI** |
| VW Golf | 2006 | £124m | 250% |
| Lloyds TSB | 2006 | £142m | 157% |
| B&Q | 2002 | $128m | 8% |
| Specsavers | 2014 | £487m | 129% |

Source: IPA EASE database

Specsavers' return is comfortably within the established range, but also shows that healthy profit can be delivered on much larger spends, furthering the potential for both increased payback and treating advertising as a genuine business investment.

## Eliminating other factors: Framing the contribution of advertising

The business has certainly grown spectacularly and our model suggests that a significant proportion has been driven by consistent investment in advertising. However, it's worth exploring the other factors that may have helped contribute to Specsavers' success.

### Store growth

Store growth has been a very major driver of business growth, but couldn't have accounted for all of the revenue increases. If we look at revenue per store across the period, we can see that it has grown in line with advertising investment (Figure 59).

## Figure 59: Average yearly revenue per store

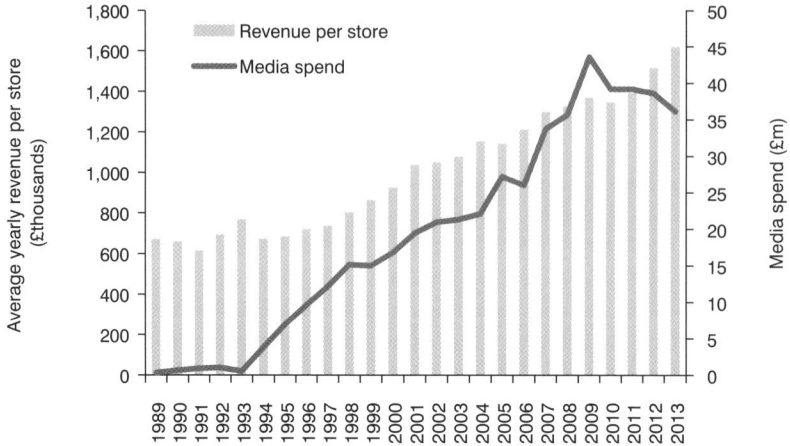

Source: Specsavers

If we take a more detailed look at behavioural measures over the last decade, we can see that the number of eye tests per store has also increased markedly, even as new store openings may cross over into other partners' territories, showing clearly that rate of sale has increased (Figure 60).

## Figure 60: Eye tests per store

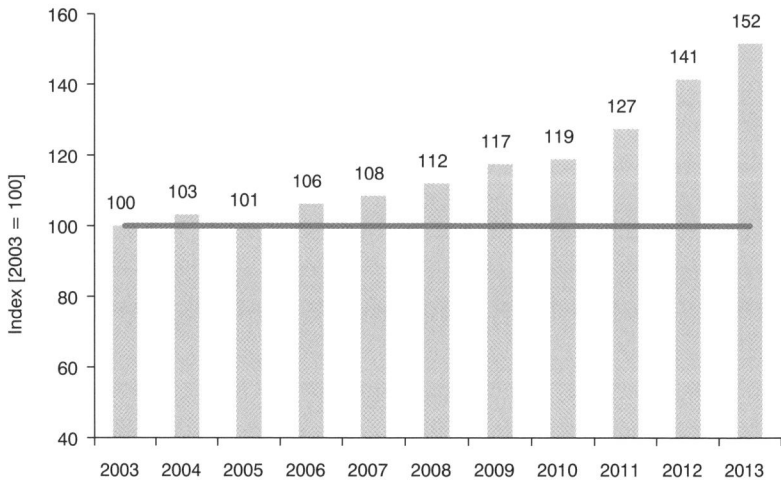

Source: Specsavers

Additionally, we can look at the market share and store numbers of our competitors.

- At their peak in 1991, D&A had approximately 550 stores and an estimated market share of 25% – totalling 0.045 points of market share per store.[19]
- Merging with D&A in 2011, Boots Opticians had 656 stores and a reported market share of 14% – totalling 0.02 points of market share per store.[20]

■ A similar calculation would give us 0.057 points of market share per store,[21] indicating that Specsavers has achieved significantly more market share for the size of its estate than any other optician.

In fact, in 2007, Mintel predicted that market saturation would be the biggest challenge to Specsavers' growth.

*...its sheer scale makes future growth harder to achieve and market share is reaching a plateau.*[22]

And as our model shows, revenue would have plateaued without a continued commitment to salient advertising.

## Market growth

A growing and aging population means that more people than ever before need sight correction. However, if we index Specsavers' revenue growth against the number of people needing eye tests, we can see that Specsavers' growth outstripped market growth many times over, meaning the effect of an increasing user base has been minimal (Figure 61).

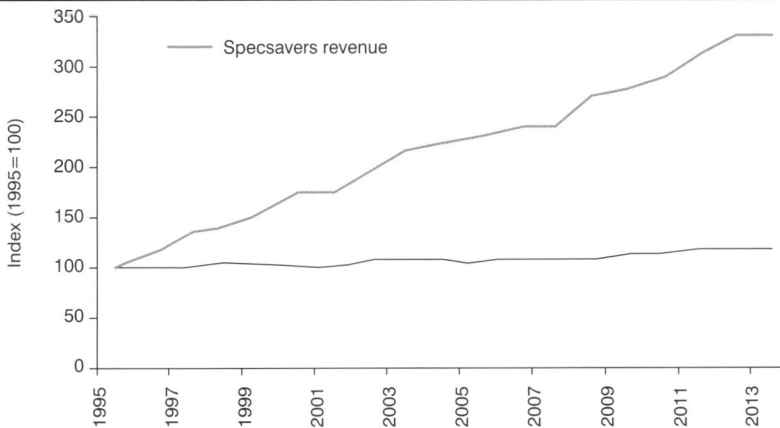

Figure 61: Specsavers revenue growth vs growth of people needing sight correction

Source: Specsavers, TGI

Additionally, if we look at Specsavers' revenue per UK adult needing sight correction, the picture is equally stark, increasing 11-fold since 1991 (Figure 62).

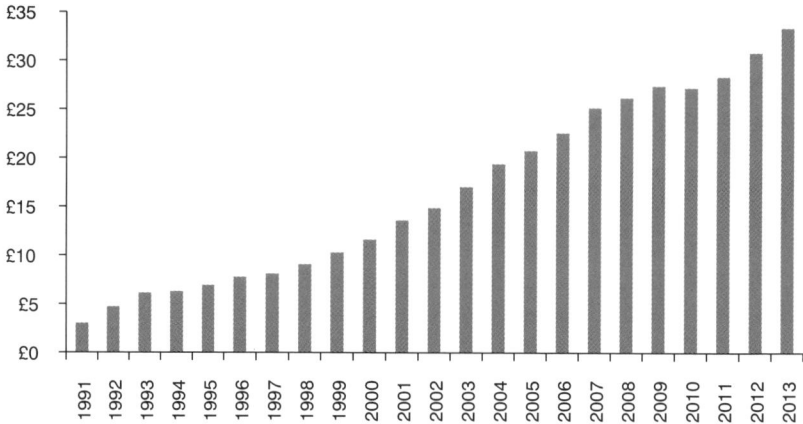

Figure 62: Specsavers revenue per adult needing sight correction

Source: Specsavers, TGI

*Competitors*

Competitors have often mirrored Specsavers' moves in the market. The majority now run similar offers (such as '2 for 1', 'kids go free' and discounts for over 60s), promoting them across all media, and seek to compete on ad spend (Figure 63).

Figure 63: Examples of competitors' offers

The optician market, of course, has been through a period of upheaval, so it's worth checking that the growth wasn't solely at the expense of local independents without the scale or resources of the bigger chains. If we index the market share of Specsavers, the big three chains (Boots, Dollond & Aitchison, and Vision Express) and other smaller chains and local opticians grouped together, we can see that Specsavers took share equally from their bigger competitors as well as smaller ones (Figure 64).

## Figure 64: Optical market share change, 1995–2013

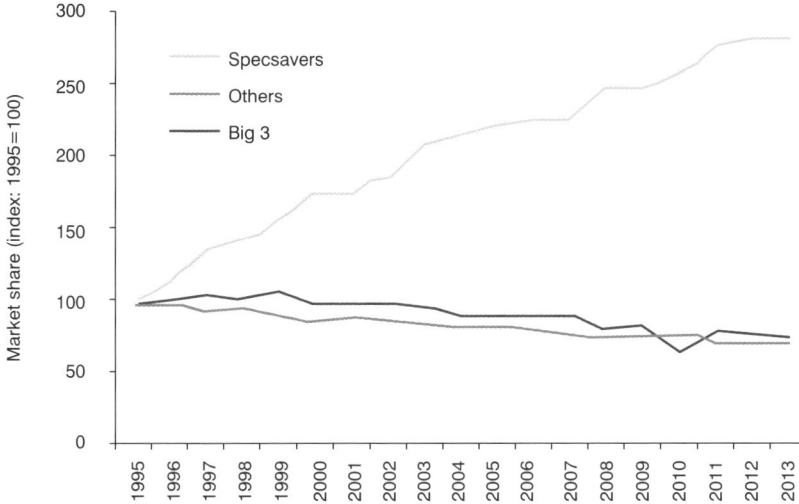

Source: TGI. In order to create a continuous data series for this piece of analysis, we've used claimed usage data from TGI

### Pricing changes

Fair, transparent pricing and great offers have always been at the heart of Specsavers' business model from the birth of the brand.[23] But while offers occasionally change and frame prices do vary, the average price paid by customers has stayed remarkably stable (Figure 65).

## Figure 65: Average revenue per eye test

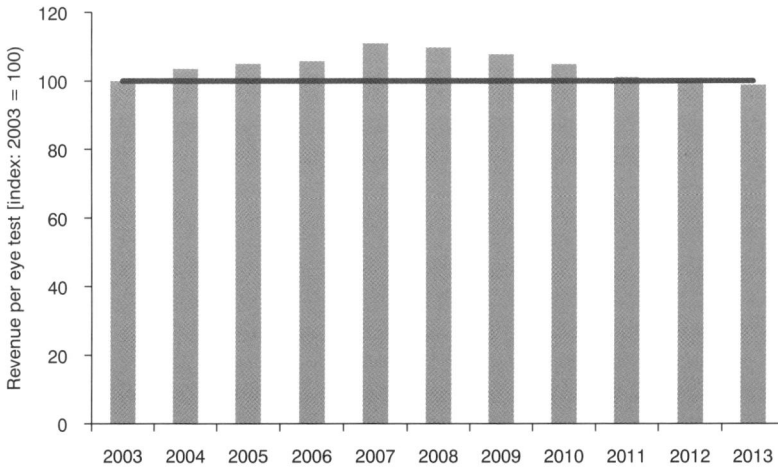

Source: Specsavers

## Other learnings: Looking deeper

*Spending through a recession is a good strategy for growth*

As the downturn hit in 2008, the response from many retailers was to cut spend in an effort to return money to the bottom line. Specsavers saw it slightly differently. They spoke to each Store Partner on the eve of the recession and asked for an increased contribution towards national advertising in 2009, boosting the investment pot by around 20%. This approach paid off, helping Specsavers emerge much stronger than before the recession, while competitors who cut spend, such as Boots and Dollond & Aitchison, lost out (Figure 66).

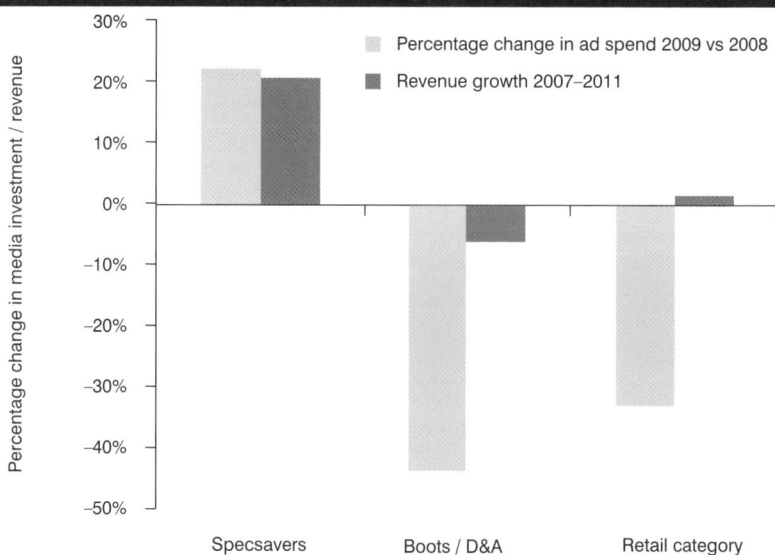

Figure 66: Changes in recession media spend and subsequent business performance

Source: Specsavers, Mintel, ONS, Nielsen

*Heavy brand spending creates a significant barrier to entry*

In 2008, commentators felt that the biggest threat to Specsavers' success was not going to come from other optical chains but from supermarkets:

*Specsavers' greatest threat comes from the growth of Tesco and Asda.*[24]

Walmart, Asda's parent company, is a major player in the US optical landscape so it's perhaps a surprise that they have made such small advances in the UK – Mintel estimates supermarkets' combined 2013 market share at just 3% – the same as six years previously! Particularly when we consider the supermarkets' determined expansion into other categories such as petrol stations.[25]

We believe that Specsavers' presence, fame and continued ad spend makes the optical retail category an unattractive proposition for supermarkets to try to dominate.

*The advertising approach has helped to increase distribution*

When speaking to Specsavers Joint-Venture Partners, it becomes very apparent that the perceived strength of the brand has been a key driver in their decision to join Specsavers (Figure 67).

**Figure 67: Selection of verbatims from Specsavers Joint-Venture Partners**

'Having evaluated other businesses that were available, I remained completely confident that with Specsavers' proven success, established reputation and massive brand awareness, I was guaranteed to rapidly develop a successful business.'

'No other UK optical chain is as well known as Specsavers, and the advertising is a big part of this. I felt it played an important part in which optician people choose and influenced my decision to become a store partner.'

'The decision of opting for a Specsavers franchise has by far been the best choice. It is an established brand with years of legacy behind it… If there was one thing I could change in hindsight, it would be that after years of searching for the right business I can easily say that I 'Should've gone to Specsavers' much sooner and life would have been even more greener.'

Source: Specsavers

From this, we can hypothesise that the brand – built as we've seen through continuous salient communications – has driven at least some of the estate growth.

*Salient mass advertising provided a template for overseas expansion*

The scale to advertise nationally was a key factor in Specsavers' overseas expansion in Australia in 2008. They opened 100 stores in 100 days to get national reach to allow them to use mass media and translated the *'Should've gone to Specsavers'* creative approach directly, using some of the UK's best-performing creatives and a few Australian originals (Figure 68).

Figure 68: 'Big rock' TV ad

**50% OFF**
COMPLETE GLASSES

*A couple sit beside a lake in Australia skimming stones. The man unexpectedly holds out a box containing an engagement ring to propose to his girlfriend. She smiles, takes the box and, mistaking it for a stone, throws it into the lake.*
***Should've Gone to Specsavers***
***50% off complete glasses***

It's been a massive success story, with rapid store openings and dominant advertising spend allowing Specsavers to swiftly capture market share and become market leaders in a matter of just a few years (Figure 69).

Figure 69: Specsavers number of stores, market share and ad spend in Australia, 2007–2010

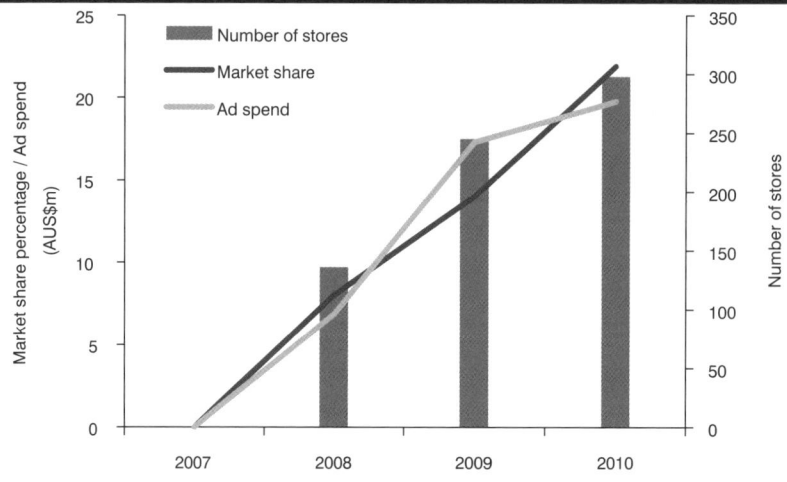

Source: Specsavers

## Summary: Seeing advertising's power clearly

Specsavers' success is testament to the power of advertising to grow a successful business.

It is a story of how continuous presence at relatively high spend levels, a broad appeal that reaches as many potential buyers as possible, and a commitment to distinctive and familiar brand assets that build and refresh memory structure have all contributed to £1.1bn of incremental profit over 30 years.

It is also a story of how the right entertaining and memorable advertising idea, coupled with intelligent media planning, can lead to even greater levels of success.

Finally, it is the story of how advertising can help a brand grow in numerous ways beyond directly driving sales.

## Notes

1  Specsavers annual report 2012–2013.
2  Applying a standard marginal profit contribution from a prior fashion retail entry.
3  Millward Brown tracking shows that 'Should've gone to Specsavers' TV ads typically show 30–50% greater enjoyment scores and 60–90% greater recognition scores than the benchmark.
4  In 1995, 54% of opticians were local independents. Fulop & Warren 'The Marketing of a Professional Service: Opticians', *International Journal of Advertising*, 1992, 11(4): 1–13.
5  Dame Mary Perkins, *Daily Mail* interview, 2011.
6  2012–2013 Specsavers annual report.
7  Source: TNS.
8  TNS brand tracking.
9  Source: BARB.
10 In just three years, the number of heavy internet users amongst this older audience had increased by over a third as the time they spent consuming their favourite press titles in tablet format had doubled (Source: IPA Touchpoints 4).
11 Source: OFCOM Communications Marketplace Report, 2012.
12 IPA Databank learnings have shown that *fame* campaigns have the greatest long-term business effect.
13 The ad-tracking methodology and supplier was changed in Q3 2013, meaning that we can't see whether this effect has continued. However, the new tracking (conducted by Millward Brown) shows that spontaneous ad awareness is currently at 55% and specific ad awareness is at 35% indicating that cut-through may still be rising.
14 This comes from M&S's 2006 IPA Grand Prix Winner, cited from Deutsche Bank. While the businesses themselves differ, they show remarkable similarities in terms of fixed and variable costs when undergoing growth. The optical market is a complex business. While there is a healthy margin on frames, the cost of technical equipment and high-quality staffing means that as volumes increase, larger costs are occasionally introduced into the business. The absolute variable costs (manufacture and distribution of goods) should remain broadly consistent. There are fixed costs in support spends, fees, insurance and utilities. Beyond this some costs, such as floor space and staffing costs may be either fixed or variable depending on the volume of customers served. The average net profit margin of opticians in the UK is 4.5% (Plimsoll, 2014 http://www.plimsoll.co.uk/marketreports. aspx?market=opticians) with the more profitable stores and chains averaging 5.7%. For comparison, Marks & Spencer's net profit margin is commonly between 4.5–6.1% (2010-13 range, annual report).
15 Source: Mintel.
16 Source: Mintel (sales value).
17 GFK.
18 2012 IPA Effectiveness Awards Grand Prix Winner John Lewis highlights many of the retailers who have disappeared from our high-streets since the downturn begun in 2008.
19 Fulop & Warren, 'The Marketing of a Professional Service: Opticians', *International Journal of Advertising*, 1992, 11(4): 1–13.
20 Source: Mintel
21 GFK market share tracking put Specsavers' revenue share at 39% in 2012, at which point there were 684 stores.
22 Source: Mintel.
23 As mentioned earlier, their cornerstone '2 for 1' offer was started in 1990.
24 Source: Mintel.
25 Twenty-seven percent of Brits claim to visit a Tesco petrol station at least once a month (Source: Mintel).

# Sainsbury's

## Christmas in a day: the real story of Christmas

**By Cat Wiles and Craig Mawdsley, AMV BBDO; Rebecca Harper, Blue Rubicon; Imogen Peck, AMV BBDO;Anna Hancock, PHD Media; Mark Given, Sainsbury's; Charlotte Wells and David Wilding, PHD Media**

Contributing authors: Jamie Doubleday, PHD Media; Simon Hall, Google; Aleksander Reichel, Oliver Kunze and Pete Zezulka, AMV BBDO; Nathan Guerra, Google

In the six weeks to Christmas, retail sales at Sainsbury's are 20% higher than average, so it's a critical business time for the brand. The year 2013 was set to be a tough Christmas for the established supermarkets in the face of a tough economic backdrop and the rise of the budget conscious, savvy shopper.

Prior to 2012, the market was dominated by Asda, Tesco, Sainsbury's and Morrisons, but now, previously peripheral competitors were becoming serious threats. However, 75% of category sales were still split between the 'Big 4' and these remaining sales would be fought over more aggressively than ever. Tesco, Morrisons and Asda had outspent Sainsbury's in paid for comms throughout 2011 and 2012 and this trend continued in 2013.

Sainsbury's decided to invest in an emotional connection for its Christmas campaign. This went against the grain of the market, as the rest of the 'Big 4' ploughed their spend into advertising price and promotions. Sainsbury's looked to content both as a way to make its lower budget work harder and to fulfil its brand purpose of helping customers to 'Live Well For Less'.

Its idea was 'Christmas in a Day'. At Christmas most retailers focus on the glitz, glitter and glamour. However, Sainsbury's knew that what matters to people at this time of year are the simple pleasures: eating, drinking and being together.

AMV BBDO identified Oscar-winning director Kevin Macdonald as someone with the expertise to capture the raw authenticity of the season. It asked him to record how Britain really celebrates Christmas, using footage submitted by the public as he had for *Life in a Day* and *Britain in a Day*. The footage was used to make a 48-minute film which formed the backbone of the campaign.

The campaign launch was treated like a film launch, with brand TV ads acting as trailers and using the most engaging, amusing and moving footage to involve people in the story and give viewers a taste of the full-length film. The launch was a 3.5-minute trailer, which took up the entire *Coronation Street* break on 13 November.

Sainsbury's then released further clips from the film at topical and relevant moments: 40 'Christmas Tree' launched earlier in the season when customers were thinking about putting up decorations, whilst 60 'Dancing' appeared later when the festive season was in full swing.

A film poster was made and the film premiered at BAFTA, ensuring full integration with the 'film launch' approach. Once the campaign had broken, Sainsbury's reacted quickly to tap into the overwhelming public reaction to standout stars like 'Spreadsheet Guy' as they clamoured to get hold of his meticulous Christmas spreadsheet.

The campaign achieved its major objective: the business grew by 5.2% like for like and outperformed the competition, delivering a profit ROI of £3.98.

The success in meeting this objective was in large part due to online content which enabled Sainsbury's to show that it understood Christmas better than anyone else, engaging the public and keeping the nation's attention throughout the Christmas period.

Whilst the 3.5-minute advert was only aired four times, it achieved the highest recognition of the 'Big 4', in spite of its low TVRs. The campaign delivered over 235 pieces of media coverage over six weeks, (spanning broadcast, national and regional press and online), with a reach of 131 million and over 92% of sentiment was positive.

Despite being the last to launch, Sainsbury's generated more coverage dedicated to its Christmas campaign than any other supermarket. CEO Justin King proclaimed 2013 the 'best Christmas ever' and the seven days before Christmas as their 'busiest ever' trading week, with over 28 million transactions. Sainsbury's defied analysts' predictions and grew by 5.2%, outperforming the total market and the rest of the 'Big 4'.

# EDF Energy

## Feel better about energy

**By Michael Salter, Havas Media; Shannon Singh and Craig Mawdsley, AMV BBDO**

Contributing authors: Kate Cox, Havas Media; Hammad Mian and Cameron Hughes, EDF Energy

In 2012, EDF Energy needed to differentiate in order to grow and become the brand that customers actively wanted to choose in order to meet its dual objectives to drive acquisition and reduce churn.

Previously EDF had focused on green credentials to differentiate its offer in a hotly contested sector, but money concerns had taken precedence and were overwhelmingly everyone's main concern. This change in the public's priorities meant that EDF's low-carbon energy remained differentiating, but no longer motivating in the way it had been executed up to now. Rather than walk away from the 'low-carbon' USP, it decided to find a way to make it motivating.

So its task to the market that would fuse together EDF Energy's differentiator – low-carbon energy – with consumer concerns – low prices. When EDF Energy's low-carbon energy was connected to a new value proposition – low-carbon energy at no extra cost – it piqued interest. A further challenge came from the dominant market leader, British Gas, with spend regularly surpassing £50m a year (half the total sector spend).

A range of innovative tariffs called 'Blue' were developed to support the positioning of 'Feel better energy'. This umbrella name, 'Blue', would act as a shortcut for any tariffs that were nuclear backed. In addition, the 'Feel Better Energy' claim was strengthened by added service benefits to the low-carbon supply. AMV BBDO discovered a YouTube sensation, Keepon, which became the inspiration for the creative campaign. Keepon is a robot developed for use in the classroom, particularly those with developmental disorders such as autism. The robot acts as a way to help these children interact with the world. The agency worked with one of Keepon's creators to develop a uniquely EDF Energy take on the character, Zingy, keeping the simple, charming 'blank canvas' that made Keepon so universally likeable.

Zingy proved to be a powerful asset EDF Energy could own and use to generate warmth towards them as a brand, despite the negativity of audiences towards the category. A through-the-line campaign launched 'Feel Better Energy' and the new flagship proposition, Blue+PricePromise, in April 2012.

The Zingy launch media plan focused on a heavy advertising presence to drive recognition of the character quickly using a TV-led multimedia approach so Zingy's benefit would be felt in EDF Energy's owned channels such as the website, digital media and social.

It began with a 60-second TV execution followed two weeks later by a 30-second execution. These were pulsed throughout April, May and June and joined by a third execution in May focusing on a new loyalty programme.

A second burst in 2013 followed a similar pattern but with a reduced spend level and only one TV creative. OOH and large format panels became the lead channel, concentrated on commuter opportunities in rail and across the underground. This was also supported with press activity.

The first burst of the Zingy campaign – from April to July 2012 – launched with advertising recognition peaking at 80%. Enjoyment, standout and positivity all outperformed previous EDF Energy campaigns. The second burst – from April to June 2013 – saw spontaneous awareness reach a high of 57% by May which clearly cemented EDF Energy as the third most recalled supplier in the market.

The character swept through social media and achieved the best branding and cut-through of any EDF Energy advertising ever. As a 'feel bad' category, energy suppliers get on average 5% of mentions being positive. After the campaign, 17% of EDF Energy mentions were positive. Zingy was a hit. Seventy-seven percent recognised the character and 67% liked him.

More importantly though was the knock-on effect on business – econometric modelling can prove that the above-the-line advertising was responsible for over 22% of overall acquisitions in 2012 while customer churn had fallen from 13% to 10.6%, and the campaign's overall payback meant that for every £1 spent, £2.36 was generated.

# first direct

## Attracting a new generation of customers

**By Lise Pinnell, JWT**
Contributing authors: Joanne Thornton and Andrew Miles, first direct; Tom
Ellard and Arvind Kapavarapu, Mindshare

After its launch 22 years ago as the UK's first telephone-only bank, first direct was
no longer unique. What was once a competitive advantage, telephone and online
banking, had become the norm. To protect the future health of the business, the bank
needed a change before decline set in. It needed to raise awareness amongst a new
generation of prospects and, more importantly, give them a reason to approach the
bank. Above all, it needed to take stock of what the brand represented within the
new world of banks. Research was carried out which made it apparent that first direct
possessed one thing still unique and still special, which had been part of the bank's
DNA right from the start: their spirit.

The time was right to go back to its core values and remind people why and how
it differed from ordinary banks. It was, and had always been, a challenger brand.

Using this challenger philosophy, it developed the campaign idea of a *The
Unexpected Bank*, which was brought to life with the creative idea of 'spokes-creatures
world'. These creatures would front each new piece of communication activity and
would necessarily be strange and unusual members of the animal kingdom. That's
how Barry the platypus was born – he captured the essence of *The Unexpected Bank*.

In order to shake consumers out of their apathy that all banks are the same, first
direct not only spoke about being the unexpected bank, but behaved in unexpected
ways. In close collaboration with Mindshare, it developed an unexpected behaviours
strategy: the campaign launched with a 10-second TV teaser ad which was unlike
anything banks had ever done before: no offers, services or staff – just beatboxing
birds that encouraged consumers to expect the unexpected.

The subsequent 60-second spot built a strong position and personality for the brand while breaking the traditional 30-second repetition model of banking communications. Unlike many other high street banks who try to avoid inciting online chatter, first direct actively encouraged it. A 'blooper' ad was deployed alongside the cut-down brand ad to refuel online chatter and further humanise the bank.

The success of 'The Unexpected Bank' campaign exceeded our expectations. In fact, at one point we were forced to take the advertising off air in order to stem the overwhelming number of calls to the call centre. Not only did first direct achieve 70,000 new-to-bank customers, it over-achieved on the target by an impressive 24%.

first direct readily admits that the campaign has revitalised the brand. The teaser TV ad generated intrigue and engagement and it achieved its goals of increasing awareness and consideration. It successfully conveyed the brand's unique attitude, outperforming every advertising diagnostic assessment, increased first direct's market share, and attracted new and more profitable customers to the bank.

# SECTION 4

# Global marketing

# Why we need to get better at multi-market campaign evaluation

**By Sucheta Govil**
Global Head of Marketing, AkzoNobel

Never before has the question of global marketing effectiveness been so pertinent.

As a global organisation servicing many consumers across many geographies, how do you speak to the world? One must master a single voice across multiple languages and multiple time zones. More importantly, how do you measure success? Through single global measurement? Multiple source points? Or local-up?

Moreover, news now travels incredibly fast, faster each day, and managing how your communication lands on a global scale across different markets can prove difficult. Equally, what can prove difficult is the measurement of bad news. How do you judge when you need something new?

Understanding local market variations and cultures, speaking the right languages and making yourself heard are all important issues. However, most important of all is knowing, once you have delivered, whether you delivered *well*. A big idea fails if it's incomprehensible when viewed through a different cultural lens, but judging failure is difficult when, as very often happens, measurements are ad hoc rather than existing from the beginning of the development process. Baseline measurement, through to delivery and post-launch evaluation, is key to measuring global communication.

Global marketing and campaign management are vital skills for global organisations and examples like easyJet, Lux, Expedia and ONLY stand out across the many elements of conceiving, planning and implementing for success.

A few common themes jump out when differentiating between those who made the cut in the IPA Effectiveness Awards and those who didn't. Those brands and brand teams who bubble up to the top are much more adept at storytelling in a compelling fashion; they go after key insights that allow for distinctive big ideas to be crafted and curated; they know the power of true segmentation (like in the case of Expedia) and they think multi-market but measure local-up.

easyJet's marketing challenge for the brand lay in the ability to improve perceptions of the brand, particularly among three key new target audiences who would increase average price paid per seat – affluent families, empty nesters and business travellers. Brand building activity was seen as a key means to accelerate the rate and lower the unit cost of acquisition of these valuable customer segments whilst going after huge cost savings. They delivered a brand positioning that raised brand perceptions, internally and externally. The brand campaign 'Europe with easyJet' championed the joy, spontaneity and human connection made possible by low cost air travel, whilst becoming much more aspirational in look and feel.

With regard to Expedia, 'Travel Yourself Interesting' was a strategic idea deeply grounded in both product truth and in a fundamental insight into human nature. As a consequence, it was able to achieve results across borders and across very different market conditions. It turned things around in the UK, where Expedia was the longest-established big player, under attack from a mob of aggressive rivals, and it turned things around in France, where Expedia was a small newcomer struggling to make in-roads. The campaign also created a platform for both future growth and investment in marketing across the breadth of Europe; whilst the campaign continues to be successful in the UK and France, the work has now been rolled out at a pan-European level, spanning Spain, Italy, Sweden, Finland, Denmark, The Netherlands, Ireland, Germany and Norway.

If we move across categories, from airlines and travel across to the East and examine the Japanese haircare market, we find that advertising had to help create, build and defend a Unilever haircare brand, Lux Super Rich, offering a Western dream of beauty. Over time, the brand would evolve its expression as the role of women and beauty evolved in the culture. Western celebrities were symbols of a style of womanhood from a foreign place; a less dutiful land, representing a set of aspirational values for Japanese women to flirt with. As such, the 'Western Beauty Dream' has become the core of the brand and Lux has taken a commanding lead on key dimensions. Lux haircare is also available in China, Hong Kong and Taiwan and it is supported with advertising executions that are largely adaptations of the Lux advertising from Japan.

Increasingly, marketers and advertisers are seeking to identify a communications platform that will inform all creative executions irrespective of media channel or country. But identifying a big idea is a difficult task, even before you contemplate the complexity offered by different countries and cultures. Research of all types – qualitative and quantitative, observational and interactive – can all help inform whether or not an idea is likely to work across cultures. According to Millward Brown, in these days of doing more with less, the message that effective measurement needs to be conducted from the ground up is unlikely to prove popular, but neither does it make it untrue. If you really want to understand how people respond to your campaign ideas, executions and in-market deployment you have to do so at the local-market level. The world is still an incredibly diverse and complex place and if you ignore that granularity it simply opens up opportunities for competitors to take advantage of your blind spots. Global brands are increasingly being challenged in countries like China, India and Brazil by nimbler and more culturally appropriate local brands. Their proximity to their customer gives them important advantages, not least an innate understanding of their culture, the local media and shopping environment. If marketing communication is the equivalent of a brand's conversation with the world, global brands must be well-informed and tapped into local culture if they are to remain successful. They need to measure this success.

This brings us to ONLY jeans, who demonstrated the power of insight and showed how emotional storytelling in the digital space drove commercial success. They took the bold step of *reinventing the fashion catalogue for the age of digital entertainment,* 'entertainment' being the key word.

There is an old saying: 'what gets measured gets managed'. There is no longer any doubt that measurement has now become a vitally important section in the marketing management textbook. Marketers need to join forces with their finance counterparts as the drive for greater accountability across all aspects of business is one reason for the sharper focus on measuring return on investment. And within media, the arrival of digitally delivered communications has led to a torrent of daily data, offering the possibility of continuous analysis.

In a world of multiple choices for brand communications, the industry needs to develop new analytical techniques for multi-channel and global multi-market measurement if it wants a more integrated picture of marketing communications effectiveness.

Traditionally, marketers and companies focus on single source metrics but some successful companies, most notably Mercedes, ONLY, Expedia, Lux and easyJet, have exploited a range of performance measurements, many of them led by the need to evaluate real ROI using hard business measures. The real measurement of ROI isn't about buying cheaper, but achieving greater cut-through and stronger consumer connections. *Better communication, bought better, is the aim.* While this takes longer to achieve and is harder to deliver internationally and globally, the industry needs to move towards the use of ROI analytics as the bedrock of global marketing curation and implementation. The channels used and the way those channels are deployed make a huge difference to real ROI – as measured by sales, market share and profitability – and should be by now a mandatory part of any toolkit. Unfortunately, this still happens only in the minority of cases.

In the end, everyone's interests should be coalesced around the need to improve a brand's business performance through more effective use of media, and the measurement of true ROI should be the key metric.

This approach also changes the dynamics of evaluation. Most performance measurement currently happens after the event, often too late to be of practical use. This has to change, both in terms of strategy and planning development, but also to reflect the changing face of communications delivery. Advertising activity is still too often constructed as a series of campaigns, rather than as a continuous flow. Measurement is treated as a post-campaign activity, rather than an essential continuous set of metrics.

Particularly with the advent of social media, the more enlightened brands now recognise that brand imagery and reputation needs to be permanently supported, as in the case of ONLY and Expedia, with a continuous evaluation of cause and effect.

Marketing will become less driven by blocks of activity – although these will, of course, play an important role – but by a continuous presence, building consumer support via multiple channels. These need to be measured if they are to be managed properly. Online media gives us a glimpse of this future, fast becoming reality. The digital footprints left by tags and cookies and as-yet-uninvented pieces of code provide a new audit trail for measurement.

How exactly can businesses reach and engage multi-market audiences, acquire and retain customers, and drive business growth in the new global multi-platform reality? If we take our successful companies, they developed customer-centric, not platform-centric, marketing strategies brought to life by storytelling (for example, ONLY's 'The Liberation'). Marketers must remember that their objectives ultimately revolve around how they reach, engage and influence *consumers,* not platforms.

The ones which truly stood out created consistent, integrated and platform-agnostic experiences for their customers. While businesses will want to (and should) tailor some experiences to the medium, they should generally strive to build products, content and marketing experiences that operate seamlessly and are complementary across platforms. A holistic approach can create an environment that fosters a 'surround sound' marketing approach that reaches the right people on the right platforms, ultimately generating greater awareness, engagement and conversion.

easyJet, with it's 'Generation easyJet' activity, aimed to show and celebrate the diversity of easyJet's customer base, which ranges from people holidaying or visiting friends and family to a growing number of business fliers. It's a process of storytelling and of building a positive collection of perceptions in customers' minds. Likewise, ONLY produced a story and an interactive movie that gave viewers the opportunity to contribute their own individuality to the storyline and the ability to immediately buy what they saw. Both campaigns created compelling value by building into it the diversity of their own global consumers.

It is my experience that marketers need to start with branding. Branding is the best tool with which to differentiate from competitors, either globally or otherwise, and branding allows a company to encourage demand, chase higher price points and product improvement (even grant permission to enter into adjacent categories). Successful marketers and brands recognise that the external factors that affect branding strategies in customising global brands are culture, political and legal issues, socio-economic reasons, and lifestyle. This is so very apparent in Lux Japan. These factors can make or break the organisation if it is not handled carefully.

Brands help in reducing perceived risks by authenticating the source of the goods and serve as a strong promise of the perceived value of the goods sold. By providing these promises of value through a brand, customers are assured in the purchase decision process that the risk-to-reward ratio of purchasing is higher with a strong brand than that of a similar unbranded product. But as customers associate themselves strongly with the brand, its attributes, values and personality, and fully buy into the concept which is often characterised by an emotional and intangible relationship (higher customer loyalty), it is brands like easyJet who demonstrate the power of putting consumer insight and appropriate segmentation right at the heart of their planning and development.

One of the key issues facing the management of brands today is how to deal with a brand or develop ideas and campaigns as it stretches across multiple societies and geographies. This is a question of how to reach the full potential of a brand in diverse markets. Global and local brand management need to understand each other's viewpoints and also continue to measure the right metrics along the full development cycle.

Global brand standardisation can reap huge benefits in terms of economies of scale: centralised production, increased leverage over distribution partners, one advertising campaign across markets, the same brand extensions everywhere and reductions in brand management, to name a few. But equally, globalisation in this manner cannot stoop to become the lowest common denominator, thereby losing resonance and relevance. Lux Japan has taken the concept beautifully into its market by understanding the power of 'Western beauty'.

Throughout the IPA Effectiveness Awards, it is always the brands that measure along the way, through all stages of development and across the different elements of ROI, that are the ones who can make sure their insights, their segmentation and bold ideas are successful across different channels and different markets.

Brands have become increasingly important components of culture and the economy, being described as cultural accessories and personal philosophies. Brand building is a process of value addition, a technique that projects the image of the product, the company and the country at large. Great campaigns not only demonstrate this across markets but also have the wherewithal to measure and demonstrate shareholder value internally and externally.

easyJet, Expedia, ONLY and Lux defied category conventions and stood apart; they told a compelling story; they were resonant and insightful; and they demonstrated success. And it was easy to understand and acknowledge the success because they had the measurements throughout the journey to prove it.

# ONLY

## Our basket is full: how emotional storytelling in the digital space drove commercial success

**By Lars Samuelsen and Charlotte Porsager, UncleGrey; Matthew Gladstone, Grey London**

Contributing authors: Jimmy Blom, UncleGrey; Lucy Jameson, Grey London; Niklas Soenderskov Andersen and Bettina Schytt Therkelsen, ONLY

Credited companies: Creative Agency, UncleGrey; Creative Agency, Grey London; Media Agency, Vizeum; Digital production, North Kingdom; Film production, Camp David; Sound Design, Dinahmoe; Client, Bestseller

### Editor's summary

Set up in 1995, Danish-based international fashion brand ONLY began to falter after a decade of success and growth. In an effort to reengage with consumers, they took the step of reinventing the fashion catalogue for the age of digital entertainment, using the power of digital to tell stories.

Their approach was to create an immersive and interactive digitally distributed film to showcase and sell their clothes. Viewers could directly interact with clothing featured in the story to create wish lists and shareable content. Ultimately fifteen million people across Europe engaged with the experience, recruiting customers delivering three times the value at one quarter of the cost of previous activities. Annual online sales increased by around 300% in 2012, while offline sales grew by 14.3%, and the campaign is estimated to have yielded a profit ROMI of €18.90.

**As a fight back story in the fast moving and highly competitive fashion business, the judges were really impressed by the innovative use of a very limited budget and how this resulted in a sustantial reawakening of the brand across multiple territories.**

## Introduction

The fashion world is unforgiving. Once a brand falls out of fashion there is often little it can do to regain the excitement it once held. But this paper tells the story of a brand that did just that. It tells how the Danish-based international fashion brand ONLY began to falter after a decade of success and growth, and how its fortunes were then turned round. They were turned around not by fighting back tit-for-tat against the low-cost 'fast fashion' retailers who were undermining its prices and usurping its status. Instead, ONLY took the bold step of reinventing the fashion catalogue for the age of digital entertainment, 'entertainment' being a key word here.

It wasn't just about the technical side of digital – better layout, fewer clicks and so on – it was about the power of digital to tell *stories* that people connect and respond to.

This approach:

- recruited digital customers who were 3 times the value, at one quarter the cost of normal activities;
- created incremental revenue of €38.8 million, with a ROMI of 53.8. Every Euro spent on the campaign brought revenue of €53.80, and (estimated) profit €18.90.

## Where we were in 2011

### The context

Over a decade of growth and success in a volatile market.

*fashion ['faʃ(ə)n] noun 1 a popular or the latest style of clothing, hair, decoration, or behaviour: the latest Parisian fashions. [mass noun] the production and marketing of new styles of clothing and cosmetics; [as modifier]: a fashion magazine.*

In the fickle world of fashion, ONLY enjoyed commercial success for thirteen years.

ONLY was set up by Bestseller in 1995. Bestseller is one of Denmark's largest companies, turning over €2.6 billion with profits of €192.4 million,[1] owning a range of fashion brands. It launched ONLY, focused on denim, T-shirts and tops. Targeted at younger females, its products were sold initially in 'owned' stores in Denmark and later – with success and expansion – through retailers in 23 countries worldwide and with 300 stores in Europe and the Middle East. Until 2008, things looked good.

### The problem

*What comes into fashion can go out again.*

In 2009, ONLY saw its first-ever drop in total sales. Things started going downhill from there. There were two reasons for this.

One was competition. In 2008, in the recession, ONLY faced price competition from 'low-end fast-fashion' brands like H&M, Topshop, Zara, Cheap Monday and Monki.

The other was loss of focus. ONLY's range expanded, its focus became less clear, and its products didn't excite the same levels of interest they had.

The investment in expansion that had been a feature of ONLY's success since the start came to an abrupt halt in 2009, but still the financial position worsened.

## A brand heading towards a crisis

In 2011 the company reviewed. Focus groups confirmed that the brand was lacking an 'edge' and its communications were perceived as generic and old-fashioned. Consumers viewed ONLY's low-priced competitors as more attractive and desirable.[2]

This was bad. If your customers think that your rivals are better and cheaper, the only way is down.

### Figure 1: Total sales

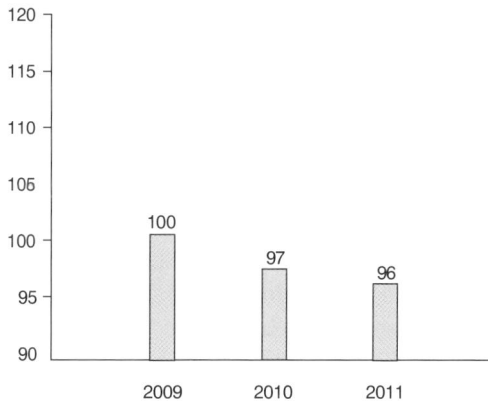

Source: Internal sales data (indexed)

*At that point it was clear that something had to be done otherwise the brand could have spiralled into a terminal decline. It was very hard to imagine a successful ending with the same approach we had been following so far.*

Niklas Sønderskov Andersen, Marketing Manager, ONLY

## The objectives

### Business objective

■ Grow sales by a minimum of 5% in year 1.

### Marketing objectives

■ More customers
■ more spend per customer
■ more purchases via 'owned' channels.

Communications objectives

■ Restore brand relevance and desirability.

## What we did

### The insight

Success in fashion isn't about *the thing*. It's about *being the thing*.

Which is to say, in the fashion business it's less about what your products *are* and more about how your products are *framed* and perceived by the fashionable.

We can all look back on photographs of ourselves in clothes we once wore, and wonder how we ever thought them fashionable. Fashions change. It's not the cut of your jeans *in itself* that makes them cool – it's knowing that they're the ones fashionistas are raving about.

ONLY had practical problems. Its prices were being undercut and its products were failing to excite. But speaking to our target audience,[3] we realised the fundamental problem was deeper than prices and cuts. It was the lack of 'buzz.' If we could rebuild that, then pricing and product specifics would matter less.

To recapture the magic with our audience in places like Aalborg and Dortmund, we needed to get back onto the radar of metropolitan fashionistas.

### The big idea

*To reinvent the fashion catalogue for the digital entertainment age, wowing fashionistas and ONLY shoppers alike.*

Fashion is surprisingly conservative. Even today, most fashion brands rely on traditional media to publicise their products.[4]

'Fast fashion' brands traditionally allocate most of their marketing budgets on beautifully printed 'look-books'.

ONLY was no exception. But the books were expensive, they didn't differentiate the brand or create any extra media interest, nor did they fit with audiences' media habits or with ONLY's increasingly important digital presence.

We had to come up with something different.

### The campaign

We built 'The Liberation', a new kind of interactive digital 'catalogue' made up of a wealth of specially-shot films and other content. It told a story as it showed the clothes.

By reinventing the catalogue we wanted to excite and entertain fashionistas *and* our mainstream audience, and lead them to experience the clothes for themselves.

The content told episodes in the story of a girl in a sleepy town fascinated by three rebellious newcomers. We follow the girls stirring up trouble, letting the viewer interact with the movie, helping the girls get out of town pursued by an angry crowd. The heroines all wear ONLY clothes. You can bookmark for later, pause, take a closer look, even go directly to the shop and buy.

After you watch the content, you will find your own personal store in the catalogue to revisit the clothes you looked at, shop, share, download wallpaper, music etc.

Figure 2: Personalised dialogue

Figure 3: Personalised dialogue

The experience is still live on www.onlybecausewecan.com.

## Campaign implementation
*Constraints:* limited budget – and communications that had to work effectively across nine markets[5].

*The plan:* a digital story organised into five phases over more than 6 months, making full use of the many assets produced.

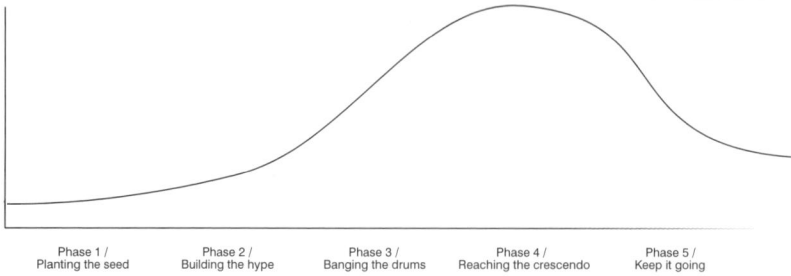

**Figure 4: Campaign overview**

| Phase 1 / | Phase 2 / | Phase 3 / | Phase 4 / | Phase 5 / |
| Planting the seed | Building the hype | Banging the drums | Reaching the crescendo | Keep it going |

Source: UncleGrey Campaign planning

## Phase 1: Planting the seed

- Teaser campaign at Berlin's Bread and Butter fashion fair;
- internal teaser campaign at Bestseller.

**Figure 5: Teaser campaign**

## Phase 2: Building the hype

- Top European fashion bloggers and journalists invited to the shoot to report live from the production. Talent, Film Directors, Marketing Directors, Creative Directors and exclusive content all made available.
- All of ONLY's own channels featured content and interviews from the set.
- nine market blogger outreach.[6]

## Figure 6: Live from the shoot

### Phase 3: Banging the drums

- New teaser released;
- journalists invited to lock-ins, given featured products;
- banner campaign with trailer and launch date;
- ambassador programme across Bestseller brands;
- internal launch across Bestseller brand platforms;
- Lune (who did the soundtrack) performs at Bestseller;
- social media collaboration with Swedish House Mafia.

## Figure 7: PR on teaser

## Phase 4: Reaching the crescendo

- 'The Liberation' launched;
- social media competition, special content released;
- jeans giveaway to first 1,000 users;
- collaboration with Swedish House Mafia;
- competitions on only.com and Facebook;
- full-length film at Danish cinemas with premiere of 'The Hunger Games'.

**Figure 8: The Launch**

## Phase 5: Keep it going

- Digital competition to win a Lune concert ticket;
- additional content distributed to bloggers/select media;
- campaign promoted at advertising award shows;
- Pinterest boards and bespoke catalogues distributed to stores;
- 'The Liberation' pushed to international fashion media as a new take on lifestyle communication – generating new articles, features and blogs.[7]

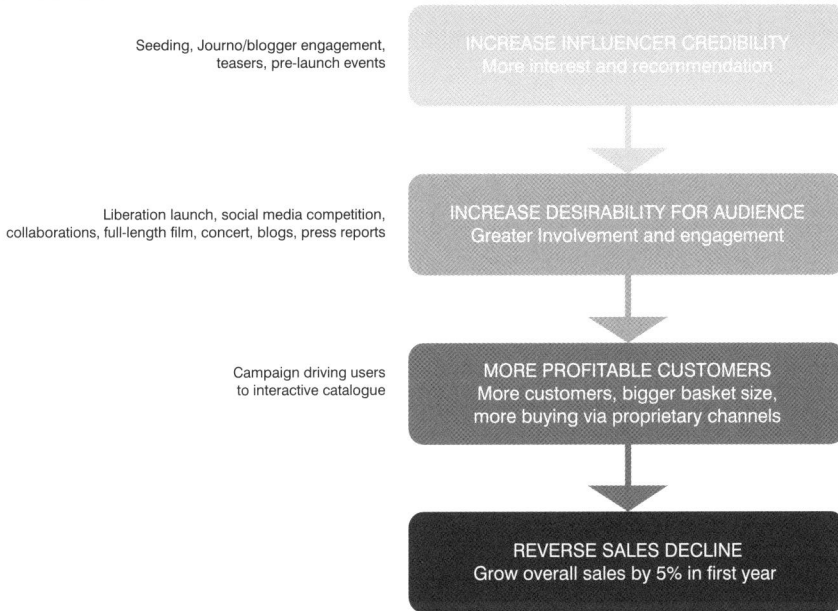

Figure 9: The comms model

| Seeding, Journo/blogger engagement, teasers, pre-launch events | **INCREASE INFLUENCER CREDIBILITY** More interest and recommendation |

Liberation launch, social media competition, collaborations, full-length film, concert, blogs, press reports — **INCREASE DESIRABILITY FOR AUDIENCE** Greater Involvement and engagement

Campaign driving users to interactive catalogue — **MORE PROFITABLE CUSTOMERS** More customers, bigger basket size, more buying via proprietary channels

**REVERSE SALES DECLINE** Grow overall sales by 5% in first year

## The results

*Communications: Restored the 'spark' to the brand*

The campaign…

- connected with fashion influencers;
- created engagement with target audience.

*Marketing: More profitable customers and channels*

The campaign…

- increased online sales rates: more customers and better customers;
- built ONLY a significant new digital revenue stream;
- increased online sales;
- increased offline sales at physical stores.

*Business: Reverse sales decline*

- Reversed ONLY's sales decline in both online and offline.

*Overall: Business health*

- Delivered business growth and reduced costs.

*The results in summary*

| Table 1: The results in summary | |
|---|---|
| **Objective** | **Result** |
| Connect with influencers | ■ More positive influencer commentary: €0.75 million of 'free' blogger/influencer commentary |
| Engage with target audience | ■ Users spent longer on site<br>■ Users viewed more content<br>■ Surge in Facebook 'likes' |
| More profitable customers | ■ Increase web orders: sustained increase in site traffic and conversion rate<br>■ Increase web basket size: 53% increase in basket size at only.com<br>■ Build new web revenue stream: 5,500 actions/buys, 200,000 Euros aditional revenue<br>■ Increase offline sales: signficantly higher sell-through rate for items featured in the campaign (95% versus 70% in Denmark) |
| Reverse sales decline | ■ 14.3% increase between 2011 and 2012, versus a 5% target |
| Deliver growth, reduce cost | ■ The campaign was the largest single contributor to only.com and the web shop. High click-through rate, low cost per click. |

*How the campaign connected with fashion influencers*

'The Liberation' got the fashion industry, journalists and bloggers talking about ONLY in a more positive way. ONLY was able to significantly increase the amount of free press it was able to generate. This had the added benefit of initiating dialogue with key influencers in the fashion industry – significantly increasing earned media impressions.

A Press Point Media Analysis report shows the increased media impressions created across print, online and blogs.[8]

## Figure 10: Press Point media analyses

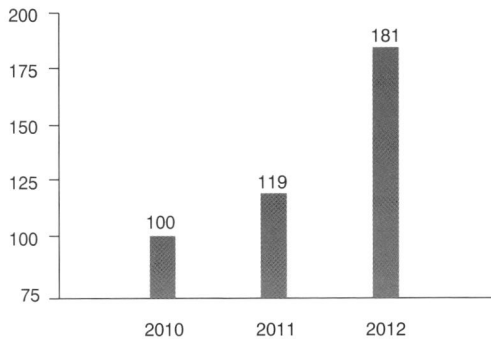

Source: Press Point media analysis 2012

'The Liberation' appeared on all the big fashion outlets like Vogue and Elle, and also on more surprising outlets such as FastCompany and TechCrunch.[9]

*'The Liberation' is a short film/digital catalogue/commercial that grabbed my attention for more then 20 minutes yesterday. Which (if I had to guess) is probably about 20 minutes longer then any commercial has ever grabbed my attention – ever."*

Mike Amps, blogger

*From a PR perspective I would love to see more campaigns that was as easy to get the media interested in as the case with the ONLY project. It is contagious, relevant and has a large degree of WOM built into it.*

Julia Lahme, founder of Lahme PR

Vizeum estimate that the overall free media exposure generated by this project is approximately €0.75 million – and almost all on highly-relevant platforms within the fashion and lifestyle media.

### How the campaign created engagement with the target audience

At 4.06 minutes, the average time spent interacting with 'The Liberation' was significantly higher than the average visit to ONLY's website pre-campaign.

Another sign of high engagement was the high play-to-end rate (how many users chose to see the whole project):

*Play-to-end rate is the highest we have seen for a commercial project. On benchmark for very good performing film trailers we see an average of approximately 60%, but for the ONLY project we saw average of 68% across all regions with Germany leading the pack with 74%.*

Mark Bækgaard, Online Digital Planner at Vizeum

The project more than doubled ONLY's Facebook presence and increased the week-on-week 'likes' growth baseline even after the campaign, outperforming expectations (increase of 25%).

### Figure 11: Development in Facebook likes

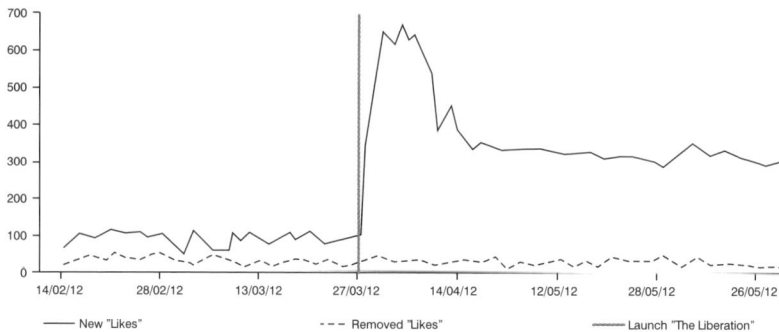

Source: Facebook Insights

*How the campaign increased online 'clicks' sales at only.com: more customers and better customers*

### The campaign

1.  increased traffic to only.com
2.  brought customers who were more profitable, in 2 ways
    a.  more likely to buy (conversion)
    b.  spent more when they did buy (basket size).

### 1. 'The Liberation' generated more traffic to only.com

More than 15,250,000 users accessed/engaged with 'The Liberation'.

The campaign generated more than 3,000,000 unique visitors to only.com during the period it ran.

Once there, they stayed longer: time spent on only.com was 34% higher than pre-campaign visits to the site.

### 2. 'The Liberation' delivered higher quality, more profitable customers

Generating increased traffic is always desirable, but for ONLY it was essential that this traffic would spend money.

a.  During the campaign, the proportion of site visitors buying clothes nearly doubled: the e-commerce conversion rate increased from an average of 1.89% across all markets to 3.51%.
b.  Those people also spent more: traffic delivered from 'The Liberation' generated a 53% increase in basket size, compared to 'normal' buyers in the web shop.

## Figure 12: Increase in basket size

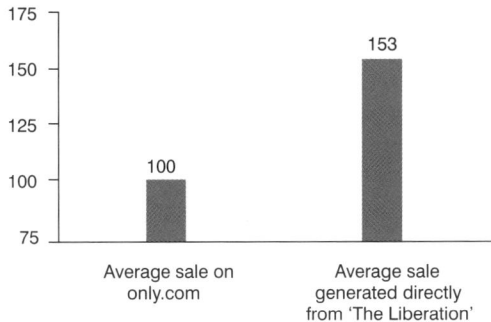

Source: internal sales data

This is a major achievement. It is reasonably easy to 'buy' traffic via Google, but getting 'high quality' traffic – people who actually go on to buy your products in large numbers – is the digital marketing equivalent of gold-dust.

The only difference from 'normal' marketing activities in this period was 'The Liberation'.[10]

### How the campaign built a new digital revenue stream

The campaign actually created a new online commercial platform for the brand. As part of the project consumers were able to purchase featured products directly through the film without having to enter ONLY's traditional web shop (unless they chose to). This was an experimental feature designed to fuel PR and provide the brand with additional knowledge.

More than *5,500 actions/buys* came *directly* through 'The Liberation'.

This provided approximately €*200,000 additional revenue*. Equally importantly it provided input into how digital can generate additional revenue streams.

> *We expected the sales being generated directly in the digital film to be no more than a maximum of 1,000 so we were very pleasantly surprised by the campaign's ability to generate additional online revenue for ONLY.*
>
> Niklas Sønderskov Andersen, Head of Marketing, ONLY

### How the campaign transformed online sales overall

The countries that drove the most traffic[11] to 'The Liberation' saw significant increases in both conversion rates and traffic on only.com, as well as seeing the highest increase in their e-commerce sales.

Germany is one of ONLY's most important markets and the market that generated the most traffic to the project and to the web shop. During the campaign the average conversion rate on de.only.com increased from *2.05% to 3.63%*, significantly increasing the combined online sales of the German market during the campaign.

Similar increases in conversion rates were visible on all of the five markets that saw the most traffic to the 'The Liberation'.

Increased sales index sales for e-commerce

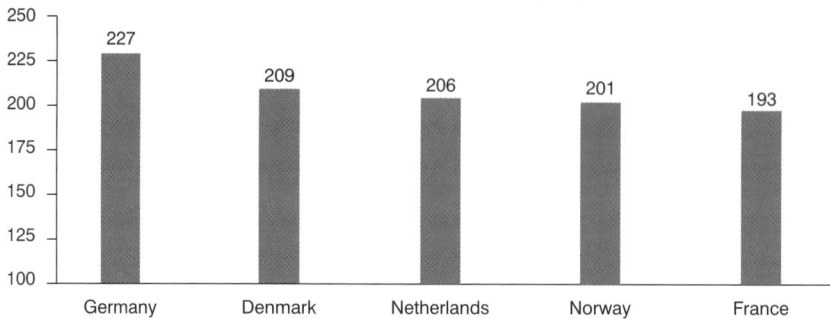

Figure 13: Sales index

Germany 227, Denmark 209, Netherlands 206, Norway 201, France 193

Source: Data provided by ONLY e-commerce manager Rasmus Justesen

*These numbers are very impressive and by far outperform anything we have seen on earlier online activities.*

Rasmus Justesen, ONLY E-Commerce Manager

During 'The Liberation', the online channel's share of total sales rose from 3% to 7.5%, a values increase from €8m to 23.2m.

When the campaign stopped there was a continued uplift in online baseline sales which steadied at around 5.7%, still 2.7% above the former level.[12]

*Online sales increased dramatically around the last week of March and first week of April when the campaign was launched. This increase was sustained throughout the campaign period.*

Rahul Kushai, Performance Management and Analytics, Bestseller

*How the campaign increased the sell-through rate in physical stores – 'bricks'*

To provide metrics we've looked at how the featured items of clothing performed in comparison with items in the same collection that were on sale but not featured in the project.

*Sell-through rate* is the fashion equivalent of retail off-take in FMCG – it measures the % of inventory that is sold through to the consumers, at full price, by retailers.

The campaign increased sell-through rate of the styles featured for all countries: e.g. in Denmark there was a 95% sell-through for the featured styles versus 70% for non-featured styles.

All styles were available in ONLY stores from mid-March. At that point the styles *not* featured in the campaign were outselling the styles to be featured.

But from the campaign launch this was reversed. The sell-through rate for both groups of styles increased, but the featured styles showed a stronger sell-through rate and significantly outperformed the non-featured styles. Featured items generated an average sales index of 183 versus the rest of the collection.

All other marketing of the products was evenly distributed and no other marketing activities were run in the same period.

## Figure 14: Percentage sell-through rate

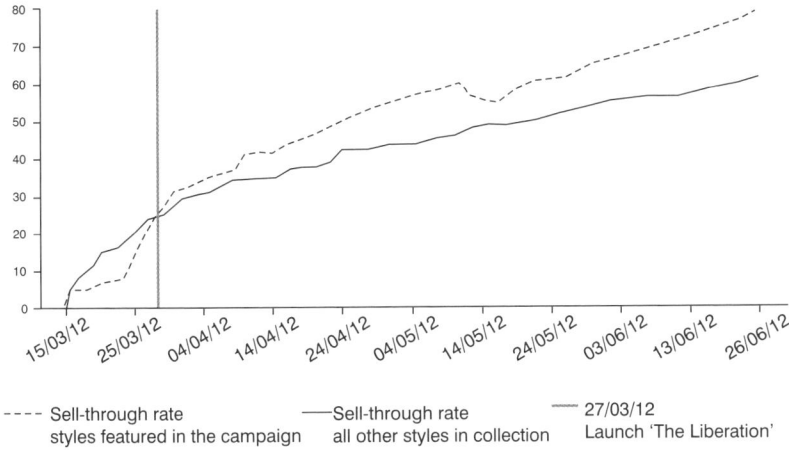

- - - - Sell-through rate
styles featured in the campaign

——Sell-through rate
all other styles in collection

—— 27/03/12
Launch 'The Liberation'

Source: Internal sales data

In sum, the campaign reversed ONLY's sales decline.
Both online and offline sales increased:

- online from €8.1m to 23.2m
- offline, physical stores from €262.9m to €286.5m

## Figure 15: ONLY sales by channel, 2011–2013

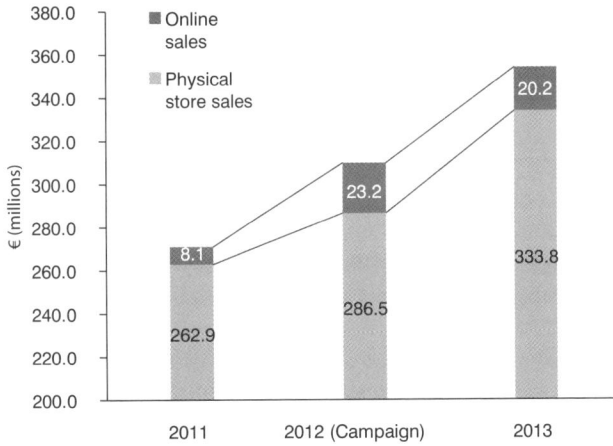

Overall, during 'The Liberation', ONLY went from decline to +14.3% growth, against a 5% target.

## Figure 16: Sales value (euros)

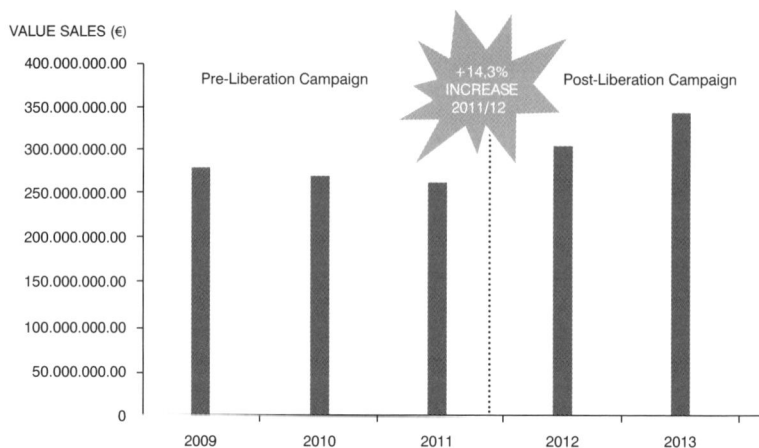

VALUE SALES (€)

Pre-Liberation Campaign — +14,3% INCREASE 2011/12 — Post-Liberation Campaign

Bar chart showing values for years 2009, 2010, 2011, 2012, 2013 with y-axis from 0 to 400.000.000,00.

Source: Internal sales data

*'The Liberation' significantly drove sales across our physical and digital platforms and was an essential part of breaking a stagnating sales curve. At the same time it proved to us that brand building and direct sales could go hand in hand.*

Rasmus Kristiansen, International Sales manager

### How the campaign delivered business growth and reduced costs

As a project which embraced the whole marketing process, 'The Liberation' was able to both increase sales revenue, and, by increasing the proportion of sales via the web shop, to reduce the costs associated with physical shops.

Google analytics data on referrals to the ONLY web shop throughout the campaign showed that 'The Liberation' generated a combined 31% of top 10 referrals and was by far the largest single contributor to the traffic on www.only.com and the web shop.

Liberation had unusually high click-through rate. Video trailers released to promote 'The Liberation' achieved an average CTR of 16.07%[13] compared to an average CTR of 0.23% on ONLY's 'normal' marketing activities. Furthermore, this should be evaluated against a European average of 0.17%.[14]

*This is by far the most effective campaign we have run in terms of its ability to generate traffic to the clients e-commerce platform.*

Mark Bækgaard, Digital Media Planner, Vizeum

Cost per click was reduced. ONLY set a target for CPC on €1. The campaign managed to deliver with a very high efficiency achieving an average CPC of €0.31. *Effectively delivering 3 times more value than the target set by the client.*

# The results in summary

## *Discounting other factors*
### Marketing budget

ONLY devoted no additional resources to this campaign – it simply reallocated part of its existing budget. This meant that the overall marketing budget for 2012 was identical to 2011 and 2010.

### Media spend

ONLY's media spends for the years 2010, 2011 and 2012 were at the exact same level. The different allocation of budget was the primary difference.[15]

### Other advertising activity

'The Liberation' was the only activity for ONLY while the campaign was running.[16]

### Retail presence

Due to the financial crisis ONLY stopped opening new stores in 2011 and 2012.[17] There were no other significant changes in 'owned' or independent distribution.

### Pricing

Items featured in the project were full-priced with no discounts. Approximately 85% of them sold out.[18]

### Collection/products

The number of items featured was the same as in a 'normal' collection from ONLY.[19] There were no unprecedented changes, beyond the usual seasonal variations. The design team was the one that had created the collections for the previous two years, and the same Head of Design had also been leading the department for four years. The companies that produced the garments were the same that had been used for years.

### Promoted items

It was not the case that 'The Liberation' just featured 'best' products that would have sold themselves, without promotion. Sell rates started out *higher* on the products *not* featured in the catalogue than those featured in the catalogue until 'The Liberation' was launched. Then the situation reversed.

## *Payback and ROMI*

'The Liberation' delivered 3m unique site users at a cost of €0.7m. Previously ONLY had to spend €1 to bring each user to its site, so bringing 3m users to the site would have cost 3m euros, not 0.7m euros. This is a saving of €2.3m.

These users were also higher quality:

- double the rate of conversion to sales
- spend 53% more per basket.

From this we estimate each 'Liberation' user was triple[20] the value of an 'ordinary' user.

*In summary: 'The Liberation' brought users who were 3 times more valuable, for approximately 1/4 the cost of normal activities.*

Both online and offline sales increased:

- online:  €8m to 23.2m
- offline, physical stores:  €262.9m to €286.5m.

This gives us the following incremental revenues:

- online sales:  €15.1m
- offline sales:  €23.7m
- total incremental revenue: €38.8m.

This compares with a comparatively low cost of the activity.

- Total media and campaign production:  €0.719m.

This gives the following revenue ROMIs, expressed as return on every €1 invested:

- online sales:  €1: 21
- offline, physical stores sales: €1: 32.8
- total online + offline: €1: 53.8.

### Profit ROMI

We are not able to disclose margins for ONLY or Bestseller, in either channel. However we believe that given the high revenue returns, and the general industry margins of c.35%,[21] 'The Liberation' has been highly profitable for Bestseller.

For example at this 35% margin:

- online profit ROMI: €1: 7.4 (€5.3m profit)
- offline profit ROMI: €1: 11.5 (€8.5m profit)
- total profit ROMI: €1: 18.9 (€13.8m profit).

## Learnings

There are four main lessons:

1.  The power of *framing*. This paper shows that the popularity and appeal of what are essentially the same products can be radically improved by communication that re-engineers the *context* in which those products are seen, and the people they are associated with.

2.  The importance of dealing with the *root cause* of your brand's problem – even when your situation seems to be crying out for short-term 'firefighting'. ONLY's immediate problem was with low-cost fast-fashion rivals undercutting prices and offering rapidly-changing products-of-the-moment. ONLY could have responded by cutting prices, or by changing its collections more often. Instead it focused on the deeper reason for its loss of customers – the sense that

it was no longer the cutting-edge fashionista choice it had once been. Once this was dealt with, the other problems became less pressing.

3.   The role and use of *emotion* in digital media. Because it is new, and because it is technical, discussion of digital tends to centre on technical measures like clicks and digital footfall and dwell time. Which are important. But beyond this, this paper shows digital coming of age as a powerful, emotionally-compelling storytelling medium.

4.   The role of emotion in *reducing cost* of acquisition and *increasing quality* of new customers. This follows from the third learning. A critical driver of success in online businesses and customer acquisition businesses (e.g. online retail, mobile phone companies, subscription-based companies) is the balance between cost and quality of acquisition. Customers who are cheap to acquire often yield less profit. Conversely, profitable customers are often more expensive to acquire. The trick is to find efficient ways of acquiring the profitable ones. 'The Liberation' managed to do this – by providing a highly engaging, emotionally seductive fashion experience to millions of self-selecting potential customers, who were then directly linked to retail, ONLY found a way to get both quantity and quality of customers for a fraction of the going rate.

Emotion pays in digital, as it does elsewhere.

## Notes

1   Source: ONLY, tax year 2012/13.
2   Qualitative Study conducted by Aegis Media.
3   Qualitative Study conducted by Aegis Media.
4   Aegis Media spending data.
5   The media budget (across nine markets) was 249.750 Euro (Vizeum).
6   Developed by Lahme PR.
7   Press Point Media Analysis.
8   ONLY's PR investment has remained the same for the years 2010, 2011 and 2012.
9   Lahme PR Tracking Report.
10   Google Analytics data.
11   Source: Google Analytics.
12   Data provided by ONLY e-commerce manager Rasmus Justesen.
13   Campaign tracking from media agency Vizeum.
14   ADTECH's annual click-through rate analysis.
15   Data provided by ONLY and Vizeum.
16   Niklas Sønderskov Andersen, Head of Marketing, ONLY.
17   Internal data provided by ONLY Retail.
18   Sales data from ONLY.
19   Data provided by ONLY Design.
20   Calculation as follows: 'The Liberation' doubled conversion to sales (2 times) and raised their spend by 1.5 times, meaning that each user who came to the site via 'The Liberation' delivered 3 times more value than the average site visitor.
21   http://csimarket.com/Industry/industry_Profitability_Ratios.php?ind=1301

# easyJet

## Effectiveness, the Luton way: how easyJet grew its brand by cutting costs

**By Michael Lee, VCCP; Bryan Jago, OMD**

Contributing authors: Andrew Perkins, VCCP; Priyang Jha, BrandScience; Henry Bilson, VCCP; Sam Dias, BrandScience; Neasa Cunniffe, VCCP

In 2011, easyJet decided it needed to move on from its 'cheap and cheerful' positioning which had served it so well over 15 years. Over this time, the brand had successfully forged a low-cost positioning, with marketing support almost entirely used to drive short-term direct response. But it was increasingly obvious that this approach needed to change.

easyJet was being squeezed on all sides, rising fuel costs had impacted on profit margins, and the competition was catching up. Ultra-low-cost carriers were able to increase the gap in pricing, and flag carriers had become emboldened to challenge us on price. As easyJet's low-cost positioning was being challenged, an advertising heritage of price promotion had given the brand little else to play with.

It was clear that easyJet needed to invest in its brand. But as a plc whose quarterly sales performance could instantly wipe hundreds of millions off its stock market value, this would also have to be achieved without missing a single quarter's sales target. How could it be done?

The answer lay in easyJet's founding low-cost principles. By applying an efficiency driven mindset to marketing, cost-savings were identified in display and paid search. Freeing up a war chest of funds, this could then be put to good use delivering a brand positioning that would raise brand perceptions both internally and externally.

The new creative platform 'Europe by easyJet' heroed the joy, spontaneity and human connection made possible by low-cost air travel, whilst becoming much more aspirational in look and feel. TV, a medium which easyJet had historically neglected, was now recognised as an essential pillar of its marketing budget investment.

For the first time, the brand was now also in a position to reach out to the audience with the highest standards: business travellers. The growing emphasis on value and efficiency was now as prevalent in the business community as it was in political circles. Therefore, a more modern and nimble approach to business travel became a potent positioning for easyJet to promote. This resulted in a bespoke campaign, launched in mid-2012, running in business print titles and at key business airports.

In Autumn 2013, the campaign evolved to take on an even more aspirational point of view. 'This is generation easyJet' championed the 'get up and go spirit' of the generation of modern travellers easyJet had helped create.

Advertising recall immediately jumped up for the brand as the campaign launched by 6% to 33% in the UK. The campaign also challenged negative perceptions about easyJet; against the old campaign, there was an 11ppt improvement in 'left me with a good feeling about easyJet'.

YouGov BrandIndex data for the UK shows how three key brand metrics – 'impression', 'quality' and 'reputation', have also risen significantly. These were all in decline until the launch of the campaign.

Since the launch, annual passenger numbers for easyJet have leapt by 20% from 48.8m to 60.8m. This has happened at a time when total European air passenger numbers grew by just 8%.

Higher seat revenues have led to profit per seat rising sharply, jumping 46% in 2013 alone.

It has been a remarkable three years for easyJet, a period of unprecedented commercial success, underpinned by a transformation in the positioning of the brand to a genuine middle way between the flag carriers and the ultra-low-cost fliers. This achievement is made all the more exceptional by the achieving of a 15% reduction in marketing budget. Marketing investment itself has contributed a maximum of £454m to market capitalisation since 2009, and a ROMI of 17:1.

# Expedia

## Travel yourself interesting: how advertising helped create a more valuable future for online travel retail

**By Mattijs Devroedt, Ogilvy & Mather London**
Contributing authors: Luis Fernandes and Andrew Warner, Expedia

In 2012, in both the UK and France, the online travel market had become overcrowded and commoditised. Expedia faced numerous challenges to return its brand to front of mind.

Its commercial objective was to reverse the erosion of its margins by increasing both the number and the profitability of customers. For this reason, its behavioural objectives were: to influence consumer behaviour by getting more people to spend more, more often with Expedia; and to influence them to book directly through Expedia's own channels.

In the UK, Expedia wasn't seen to be a popular brand anymore. In France, however, popularity wasn't even relevant; since Expedia was a relatively new brand in this territory, Expedia wasn't even seen as 'professional' yet.

This meant there were two very different brand issues to address, but Expedia had to do it with one creative and strategic idea and without the huge budget of its rivals. It simply didn't have the budget to develop two separate campaigns for the two types of markets.

A major consumer segmentation study convinced Expedia that there existed a targetable audience segment big enough, wealthy enough and with just the right kind of attitude to give it a fighting chance of success. This target audience became known as 'Believers', a significant minority (42.1% in France and 47.9% in the UK) who maintained their travel spend even in recession. They cut other costs to keep travelling. Though smaller in numbers, they represented 79.4% of travel market value in France and 82.3% in the UK. Moreover, they were brand-loyal and had a smaller repertoire of brands of choice.

The brand was specifically looking to actively influence the high-value 'Believers' to book with Expedia more often – and it wanted them to do this directly through its own channels (website or mobile app) rather than via a 'third-party' website like Google or price comparison websites. To do this its strategy was to move away from the clichés in travel advertising (sun, beaches and price deals) to focus on the end-benefit of the effect that travel can have on a person.

Insights gathered through an online research community developed the idea that travel made people more interesting. This kicked off with two TV launch commercials, a series of print executions, billboards and Twitter activity from April to September 2013 across both countries.

The campaign attracted considerable attention despite a low share of voice and it made people sit up and take notice. In the UK – with scores above the category norm on brand linkage, brand recall and message linkage – people took to social media to voice their pleasant surprise with mentions peaking in the week immediately following the launch of the new campaign. In September 2013, the #TYI Twitter campaign also made waves in social media. In less than two weeks, video views accumulated over 420,000 views on YouTube, and its follower base on Twitter grew by 33%. This all contributed to Expedia's gross booking value (the total value generated through all bookings on Expedia) growing by 8% – double the category growth rate and dwarfing its 2013 objective.

In France, where Expedia was trying to get a better foothold, more emphasis was placed on TV. Expedia's customer base grew 30.3% and share of traffic even grew slightly despite increased competitor spend of 47% year on year. Most importantly, perhaps, gross booking value for Expedia grew by an amazing 33% versus a market growth of 8%, outstripping Expedia's expectations for France in 2013.

# SECTION 5

# Econometrics

# Are we creating a black box or thinking outside of the box?

**By Masood Akhtar and Michael Wolfe**
Bottom Line Analytics

Econometrics is often charged with being '*as much a science as an art*'. However, how much of the way we view econometrics is an acceptable creative license, and how much is pure conjecture? Does subjectivity obstruct the systematic process? This chapter argues that econometrics is fundamentally a stochastic process that accepts evidence-based interpretation to add context that is otherwise not found in the data.

Over the last 15 years, markets have become more complex, with consumer segmentation and the advent of social media. The media landscape reflects a more fragmented marketplace, with the rapid increase of digital and social channels, so the level of interaction *between* media channels has increased. Some econometrics practitioners have embraced this new level of complexity as an opportunity to demonstrate the relevancy and power of econometrics to handle this increasingly complex environment, leading to an increase of proprietary metrics and algorithms. This has created confusion for those judging case submissions, as some argue econometrics has become a black box where the detail is cloaked, thus preventing third parties from making informed assessments.

Let us now explore some of the artistry applied within the different stages of an econometrics project's lifecycle and the risks therein.

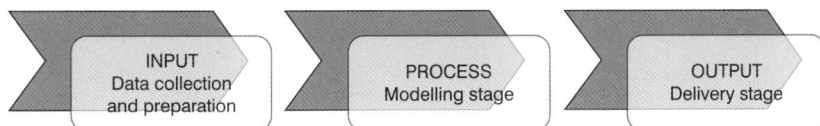

| INPUT Data collection and preparation | PROCESS Modelling stage | OUTPUT Delivery stage |
| --- | --- | --- |

## Creativity at the input stage: Derived metrics and algorithms

Econometrics starts with data collection and preparation. This involves creating a repository of historic brand sales and media data (costs and metrics, like GRPs and impressions). Sometimes there is a need to capture specific effects through the creation of unique metrics that require some degree of derivation. For beverage brand X, one might be presented with a progression of package sizes from 0.2 litres, to 0.5, 1.0, 1.5, 2.0 and 2.5 litres. The hypothesis being that, by trading consumers up to larger package sizes over time, you might drive growth. To measure this you could create a new metric called 'weighted average package size sold'.

Another example might be a client concerned about having too many messages aired at the same time, creating clutter. For this, one might develop a variable based on the number of messages aired, looking at whether this variable had a negative impact on sales above some threshold level.

A third example could be the use of metrics collected through surveys or scored social media commentary, both of which represent the voice of the customer. Such metrics could inject the customer experience directly into the modelling alongside the media mix.

Finally, one might also develop a unique algorithm to capture the long-term brand building effects of advertising and media or use media copy testing score to understand the efficacy of creative elements relative to weight.

These are all examples of *'art'* that enhances the model and is often beneficial to the client.

## Creativity at the process stage: Innovation and renewal

Media effectiveness measurement is going through a period of innovation and renewal for a number of reasons, but largely as a result of the explosion of digital media, and its fragmentation. Consumer behaviour has shifted with social and mobile media, which is reflected in the restructuring of business models. Some traditional offline businesses now also have a large online presence across a number of owned and earned properties, supported by paid media vehicles. Some successful e-commerce businesses are now even experimenting with the possibilities of brick and mortar channels to broaden distribution of new products (i.e. Amazon, Westfield San Francisco Centre, US). All of this is quite some way from the relatively siloed world we lived in 15 or 20 years ago. The renewal in business models, coupled with the changing media landscape, has forced econometricians to think anew, to the extent that we are able to address challenges around measuring media synergies, long-term effects, social media ROI and creative quality.

In the majority of cases, single equation econometric models with unique metrics and algorithms are sufficient in capturing modern complexities. However, the rise in digital media has created an issue often referred to as 'last click attribution problem'. In a multiple channel, digital-only campaign, not all channels will convert into a sale, but they may all have made some contribution pre-sale and therefore assisted in the sale itself.

The emergence of non-stochastic digital attribution methods attempt to measure the contribution made by assisting channels in order for the customer's path to purchase to be defined. However, the majority of these approaches are based on an assumed (mostly arbitrary) credit system, ranging from equal credit to all channels, to more credit offered to channels closer to the converting channel (and vice versa). Of course, the biggest flaw in digital attribution methods is they are limited to assessing digital media channels only.

For traditional econometrics, which attributes credit to media channels based on the last click or channels which correlate the most with sales, this does create a direct challenge – one that some practitioners have been happy to address. More advanced methods in econometrics develop systems of equations representing different stages of the customer journey. They are also able to account for the direct and indirect effects, thus attributing credit based on multiple digital and traditional channels appearing and reappearing along the customer journey.

Other multi-system econometrics approaches are able to model the effectiveness of media on entire categories rather than one brand at a time. This can help to provide a wide-angle view on consumer behaviour (switching and cannibalisation) at the point of purchase, along with the usual sales contribution and ROI insights.

The complexity of modelling has followed the complexities in media execution as marketers are increasingly exploring new methods to engage specific audiences. These include: gamified campaigns to immerse consumers in a game-like manner; innovations in sponsorship; digital offline outdoor media; virtual reality; mobile and online video to extend the reach of TV; and social media campaigns that attempt to drive a positive brand tone or support the customer service functions. New metrics and algorithms alone cannot always capture the effects of multi-channel media campaigns, so some econometricians are utilising other branches of econometrics, which can mean whole new techniques.

## Knowledge-based adjustments at the output stage

An important point to note is that econometrics is driven by techniques that rely on advanced *inferential* statistics. This means the analysis results are averaged, within a range of statistical probabilities, thus giving practitioners some in-built room to manoeuvre. Post-modelling adjustments that challenge the *average* effects are allowable only when there is clear evidence (from external research reports) to support. This represents a situation where external qualitative information is used to adjust modelling results that are *marginally* off. The human dimension is important and can lead to a degree of subjectivity which is a big problem if it is not supported by evidence.

## Subjectivity at the output stage

Econometrics is sometimes marred by allegations of being an art akin to creative accounting – where practitioners fudge modelled results outside of realistic boundaries to suit their own frames of reference and are unwilling to share any technical details for easy assessment. This can be hugely problematic for clients and for the industry as a whole. There are many reasons why this may happen. These include:

■ *Poor model design (too many or too few variables)* can lead to dubious findings and therefore conjecture playing a bigger role in telling the story.

■ *The wrong modelling technique* has been used. Some techniques, such as ordinary least squares (OLS) based regression analysis (still used by the majority), focus largely on the direct effects of media on sales. A key assumption here is that all media activities are independent of one another. Whilst interaction variables (i.e. radio in conjunction with paid search derives a third variable that represents the interaction between radio and paid search) can be created, these techniques are unable to adequately cope with the multitude of interactions and indirect effects we see today.

■ *Not ad-stocking* the data. This is a transformation applied to some media metrics to account for recall, and when not correctly applied it means they see very small or no incremental contribution at all, even when survey research is showing very high levels of ad recall. From a modelling perspective this can wrongly lead to greater attribution to other drivers within the model relative to media, allowing the modelling to become undermined and the narrative to take over.

■ *Backward-looking models.* Econometrics is sometimes seen as a backward-only, explanatory exercise. The assumption is that it can only explain how historic media investments have contributed to brand sales, therefore leaving the forward-looking element open to less than objective methods. However, the predictive capacity of modelling will allow you to have confidence in allocating future budget. Some practitioners do not include an out-of-sample holdout (normally 10–15% of sample) which tests for predictive capability of the modelling. The chart below illustrates the explanatory and predictive portions within a modelled dataset. Framing econometrics as an explanatory-only exercise diminishes its role as a pro-active and forward-looking predictive tool for future strategies and resource allocation.

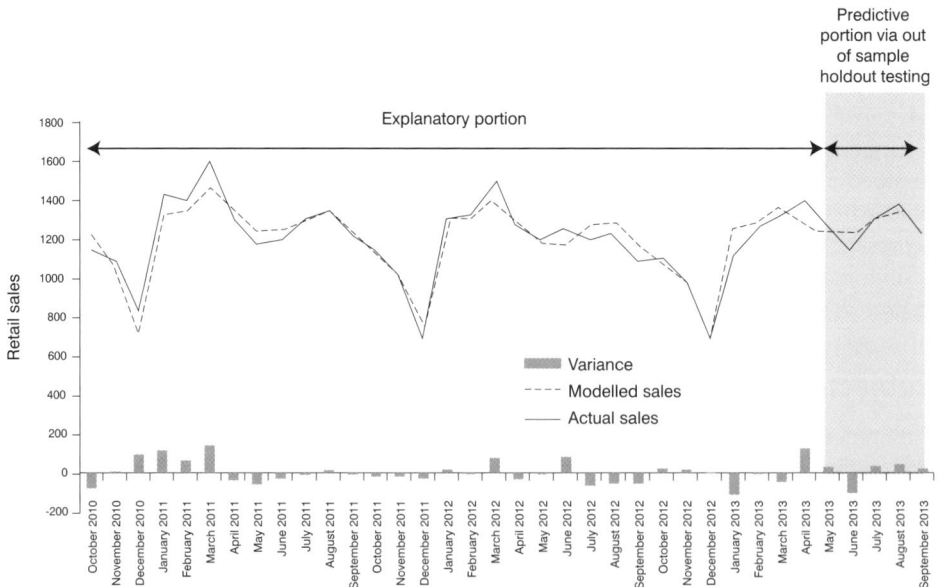

■ *The positioning of econometricians.* The position of econometricians matters. The majority of econometricians operate either within independent mix shops, client-side or media-buying agencies. Some media-buying agencies have been charged, rightly or wrongly, with marking their own homework. This is a debate that splits opinion of course, but does not seem to go away. One of the good things about media-buying agencies is that they generally have access to most of the data required for econometrics and can remove a lot of the upfront pain in collection. However, others have consistently argued this to be a form of market failure as a small number of media-buying agencies monopolise the econometrics space even when the revenue gained from econometrics (which they refer to as post-buy analysis) represents a tiny fraction of their total management fees.

## Measuring the quality of messages and customer engagement within models remains an opportunity

Whilst measuring the effectiveness of media channels is crucial in terms of future placement of marketing budget, understanding the efficacy of communications messages is given less formal treatment. In an age where supposedly content is king, ensuring your communications messages cut through and resonate with the target audience is imperative. Sadly, this has been and is still left out of most econometrics exercises, which focus solely on media channel effectiveness. Introducing the creative quality of messages into econometrics would allow the creative agencies to get more actively involved in brand planning and communications strategy.

Customer engagement measurement comes in many forms. Trended survey-based customer metrics can be used directly within econometric modelling. The other option is to score social media commentary to capture consumer engagement through the language used. Once trended, this can also be incorporated into an econometric model.

## Final thoughts

Econometrics will always rest on advanced statistical modelling, tempered by some degree of art. The art element is only problematic when it is unsupported by external evidence. Clear leadership is required to bring about transparency, via a diagnostics template that is easy to assess externally. This effort may already be underway at the IPA. In bringing about clarity, it should avoid the risk of inadvertently stifling the innovation and renewal within the MMM space. Rather, the focus could be on a set of common diagnostic metrics that are produced, regardless of the actual method used to model.

Increasingly, modelling will need to address ever more challenging business issues and complexities in the customer journey, so innovations in metrics, algorithms and techniques will necessarily become more complex. Future complexity around econometrics should not be met by a Greek chorus crying 'black box'. Advertisers, strategic planners and marketers would most certainly benefit from a basic understanding of statistical terminology.

This is not to suggest everybody needs to train as econometricians, but a broad-based understanding of basic statistical concepts and terms may stem the divergence between end users who want clarity and transparency versus econometricians that are being forced to think outside of the box and broaden their knowledge of the businesses they model. On this latter point, econometricians could benefit from getting involved in the projects early on, so to fully understand the businesses and campaigns undertaken. This will ensure the econometrics projects are not merely transactional (i.e. data modelled with little understanding of the business, market structure and competitive intensity).

The full power of econometrics can be unleashed if we allow it the place it deserves. Econometrics can be used as an evaluative *and* forward-planning tool that is more central to strategic brand planning, message creation, media buying and integrated campaign execution.

# Everest

## Playing the percentages

**By James Price, MBA**
Contributing authors: Ben Hitchcock, Everest; David Walsh and Carl Walsh, MediaCom; James Devon, MBA

In early 2012 Everest, the windows and doors specialist, was struggling with low orders. The market was becoming similar to the sofa sector, with large discounting and price promotions aplenty. This was not an approach Everest wanted to follow, though it was something considered by new owners Better Capital.

In order to grow, Everest looked out of the sector for inspiration – and to the London Olympics. Dave Brailsford (the GB cycling Performance Director) caught the company's attention. Or, more precisely, his self-coined strategy 'the aggregation of marginal gains'. Everest believed it could earn the growth it needed through doing lots of little things a little bit better – finding its '1%s' exploiting them and, crucially, it believed it would make the ideal platform for long-term growth.

Using econometric modelling, it found a number of '1%s' that it could use to boost business performance.

Such 1%s included a rethink on its TV advertising approach. Since going back on TV in 2008 Everest had employed a 'burst' approach with most of its spend deployed in January. Finding its '1%' demanded fresh thinking and this was unearthed through media analysis which identified that switching to an 'always on' approach (flattening its activity across the year) was not only possible, but had the potential to improve the efficiency and effectiveness of its spend – enabling it to reach more people at the right time.

When it came to changing its TV approach, econometric modelling showed that challenging the 'January rule' earned it 1,000 incremental appointments between July and December 2012, equating to 2% more appointments.

Better Capital did look to pursue the 50% discounting approach, concerning the Everest marketing team which thought it would damage the brand. This time the

1% challenge it set itself was to offset the 50%-off headline with value-building messaging and making it part of a bigger story about the value of choosing Everest.

The first phase of TV creative set the offer against the emotional end-benefit, aiming to differentiate away from the competitive discount war. The second phase of TV creative then connected a rational benefit to the emotional benefit, taking viewers up-close and inside the products to show what makes Everest superior.

Between July and December 2012, featuring the new 'up to 50% off' message drove an additional 10,700 appointments.

One area it developed was its use of door drops. It had consistently come across an unusual tension in research – half of those rejecting Everest felt it was too expensive and premium for them, and the other half felt it was too 'uPVC' and downmarket.

Using ACORN profiling it split its door drop postcodes into two groups – one it wanted to talk to about 'style', and one about 'value' and set out to design a bespoke version for each. It also selected a new broadsheet format to test, giving it greater doorstep impact, more space to showcase the products, and a better canvas to pull the two propositions apart.

Without the luxury of major new investment in marketing, its '1%s' strategy was always fundamentally about getting more out of what it was currently spending. The other key measure was its cost-per-appointment (CPA). The average cost-per-appointment in 2011 was £115. By June 2013, with all the gains it had made in efficiency this was down to £100. Meaning Everest was getting a 'free' appointment for every 10 it was getting before.

Further 1%s – outlined in the full case study – contributed to £1,836,872 incremental margin. It also improved ROMI by 15% from £2.38 to £2.74.

# McDonald's

## McDonald's Virtual Coins: from launch to effective platform

**By Kim Bagdonas Jørgensen, OMD Denmark; Christian Budtz, DDB Copenhagen**

Back in 2011, McDonald's Denmark faced a new generation of teens with a wide range of other alternatives to choose from. So the well-established tactical 'Coinoffers' concept which purely focused on low price needed rethinking. Additionally the concept appeared out of sync with the rapidly evolving mobile and digital consumer behaviour and SOV had dropped to 60% due to increased activity from competitors with more aggressive marketing.

To hit the challenges head-on, McDonald's introduced a new virtual currency named 'Coins', which its customers could collect directly from its ads across various media platforms using a special developed smartphone app. Overall, McDonald's Denmark wanted to get 15–19-year-olds to feel more a part of its brand while instilling the message of everyday affordable value. The key insight behind the previous 'Coinoffers' work – 'Teenagers always feel broke' – was still to be at the heart of the creative idea. The strategy was to invent a mobile-led loyalty scheme that leveraged the well-established 'Coinoffers' equity. The chain introduced a whole new virtual currency called 'Coins' with the anchor point of the campaign a free smartphone app. The Coinoffers app is simple. It works like a personal bank account where consumers can collect and save virtual McDonald's Coins and redeem them at McDonald's in exchange for real food.

It developed uniquely designed McDonald's QR pixel codes, depicting the real Coinoffers products, and spread the virtual coins across various media such as print, digital display and YouTube. Consumers could retrieve a Coin simply by scanning the Coin code with the app's incorporated scanner. Each QR code held the value of 1 virtual coin – worth DKK 1 at McDonald's – as did the special Coin sound codes it used on TV, radio and cinema. When consumers had collected a minimum of 10

Coins, they could redeem their virtual coins in the restaurant for real Coinoffers products.

A prerequisite for success was that the target group would quickly download the app, so that they could start scanning Coins. McDonald's went into broad media with the story that it had spread one million virtual Coins across Denmark.

The task in Phase 2 was to capitalise on the successful launch and keep driving the level of traffic to the stores, but at a lower media investment to reduce costs. Phase 3 saw it using 'gaming' as a target group passion point to be leveraged in the creative solution. Now, the target group should not only be able to search and find Coins – it wanted them to be able to play and win extra Coins. McDonald's restaurants were transformed into 'JackpotZones', where customers could activate the app through their smartphone's GPS, which could localise the zone and activate the game. Finally, at Phase 4 the gaming element continued with an in-app game called 'CoinTune', and furthermore, a democratic banner format, which allowed people to embed a McDonald's Coin-banner on their blog or website to boost traffic, was invented. Thereby McDonald's users got the opportunity to click through an eco-system of Coin banners while scanning Coins along the way. In this way, bloggers and charity sites would get increased traffic, users would get 'Coins-for-Clicks' and McDonald's would get free media exposure. A real win-win-win solution!

The app became the fastest ever downloaded app in Denmark, downloaded by 8% of the Danish population. Over four phases McDonald's reduced the cost-per-guest by 21% and achieved an add-on sale of DKK 12.35-19.28 each time a guest redeemed virtual coins. Overall, McDonald's brand favourability amongst 15–19-year-olds increased by 12%, the market share within the quick-service-restaurant category increased by 21% and the campaigns returned a ROMI of 1.49.

# Aviva

## One careful owner

**By Jeff Lush, AMV BBDO**
Contributing author: Ollie Gilmore, AMV BBDO

Being outspent by its two main rivals in the insurance market and with continued competition from price comparison sites, Aviva decided in 2009 to enlist the services of comedian Paul Whitehouse in a bid not only to stand out, but also to ensure its survival in the marketplace.

Choosing not to feature on price comparison websites, Aviva's main challenge was to achieve high saliency and it looked to accomplish this through advertising with a more delicate balance between freshness and consistency.

Determined not to join the commoditised race to the bottom set in motion by the huge-spending price-comparison websites (PCWs), Aviva had to find a new campaign that would produce a step change in efficiency – lower cost per acquisition, through lower cost per quote, through more efficient brand saliency.

To achieve this, Whitehouse appeared in a series of ads as very different characters and by doing so, he was able to deliver different product messages. More importantly however, he provided a balance of continuity and change which – Aviva hoped – would create advertising where both awareness, and brand attribution, would be unprecedentedly high. Known internally as 'Chameleon', it broke in August 2009, with Whitehouse's first character 'Plymouth Phil'. Since then, Whitehouse has promoted car insurance with a total of 11 characters in 14 different ads.

In keeping with the hunt for saliency, all Whitehouse's characters have been rather larger-than-life with narratives playing off nationwide trends and interests. 'Chameleon' enabled Aviva to communicate different car insurance messages at different points: good value, service credentials, innovations and short-term offers.

TV was the main media choice for driving saliency, a choice based on the fact that 80% of broadcast spend in the category was dedicated to this medium. However as Aviva was considerably outspent by direct competitors and PCWs alike, ongoing econometric analysis produced a set of principles which provided the best possible balance of 'consistency' and 'freshness'.

In conjunction with lessons learnt from econometric analysis regarding media principles, qualitative research and neuroscience-based copy testing throughout the campaign have informed creative development – helping to squeeze ever greater efficiency out of the 'Chameleon' vehicle. This has helped make the campaign ever more efficient, dwarfing category competitors by a growing margin.

With the focus on driving advertising efficiency, Aviva's research partners at ICM calculated a measure which they referred to as 'bang for buck'. This took ratings, recognition and attribution levels of Aviva and competitor advertising, and calculated a single measure of how many people remembered seeing an ad, and knew which brand it was for, for each 100 TVRs. This became a key performance measure.

The campaign had an instant and powerful effect on car quotes – rising from an average of around 180,000 a month for the previous three months to over 250,000 in August. Average monthly car quotes for the first six months with 'Chameleon' were in fact 34% higher than for the previous six months (252,910 versus 188,577), and in our last full year of data (2013) are 39% higher than for the last 12 months before the campaign began.

In terms of tracking, measures confirm that the advertising was working as intended, driving more personal associations such as 'has a reputation for looking after customers' well ahead of the price comparison websites.

In terms of 'bang per buck', the 'Chameleon' campaign launch in 2009 was far more efficient than any previous Aviva advertising, and far better than the competition. Crucially, the campaign performed more and more strongly on this measure as each year went by, effectively making it possible for Aviva to continue marketing its own brand in the face of enormous pressure from the PCWs.

# Fairy

## No fairy tale: taking a brand well past the magic 50% share point

**By Fiona Keyte, Lucy Jameson, Matthew Gladstone and Amelia Redding, Grey London**

Contributing authors: Benjamin Cawthray, Kantar Worldpanel; Dominic Hughes, Nielsen

Fairy was one of Britain's first brands to embrace the phenomenon of advertising and has built up a portfolio of memorable advertising assets that have become part of the fabric of the nation. However, Fairy noticed worrying signals in 2008. Brand health was weakening, awareness was falling. Top of mind awareness had fallen by 11 percentage points and by 2008 Fairy had shown no significant or sustained value share growth for many years. Given 2008 was when the recession struck, consumers began to employ recession-coping strategies, like switching to cheaper own-brand products.

In order to get Fairy back on track, it mined its long and rich communication history, looking for clues as to what had helped drive penetration in the past – clues that it could reapply. This review identified three characteristics of Fairy Liquid communication that had helped drive penetration growth: care – both rational and emotional; value – through the long-lasting power of the product; and generating cultural salience – talking to the widest of audiences, the 'national family'. Over its 50 years, Fairy had succeeded in responding to the mood and issues of the day by talking to the national family, not just individual nuclear families.

From 2009 onwards, 'Enduring Care' has been used as the brand's strategic compass, and to give further support to the new strategy in 2009, it nearly doubled its media budget in 2009 from 2008. In 2010 Fairy's anniversary gave it the chance to celebrate the enduring care the brand had offered over the last half century via the 'Heritage' ad, replaying iconic mother and child imagery. In 2011 it introduced 'Molly's Spa' to support the launch of the Clean & Care product now with branded Olay ingredient. This ramped up the care message and deliberately built on the family domesticity that it had used so successfully in the 'Heritage' ad. The success

235

of 'Heritage' also encouraged Fairy to look for other opportunities to tap into the national mood in 2011 and 2012. In 2012, there were two big events that would bring the national family together – the Olympics and the Queen's golden jubilee. Its Olympics campaign played with familiar assets, bringing back iconic long tables and endless plates. Coupled with the voiceover, 'It takes around 20,000 dishes to build an athlete', this communicated value and care. It aired in both 2011 and 2012, in the run up to and during the Olympics. After the Olympics, it reverted to its 'Heritage' execution as this had performed so well for the brand, and most recently in 2014 it created a new value execution 'School Economics'.

Results over this period justified its decision to re-evaluate and refocus its advertising plans. Value share grew from 50% to 60%, with a peak of 65%. Penetration increased overall from 60% to 65%, with a peak of 71%, adding 2 million buyers. Impressively no other brand with 50% or more market share has grown this much. Top of mind brand awareness jumped from 69% in 2007 to 86% in 2010 and remained at 86% into 2013. And this was all achieved despite consumers noticing a price increase of over 15% during first six months of the campaign.

The total average revenue return on marketing investment across the period 2008 to 2011 is over 1: £2.10, and impressively, the long-term revenue ROMI has been estimated to be over £3.50.

# SECTION 6

# New product launches

# In with the new: what can we learn from the newcomer story?

**By Chris Fill**
Director, Fillassociates

The decisions consumers are required to make when assessing an innovation are not simply to adopt or not to adopt. The implications arising from their decision making will frequently require that they have to adapt their behaviour. This might be to learn new behaviours or discontinue an established pattern of behaviour. In addition, consumers strive to calculate the functional and symbolic value a new product might deliver, and this involves judgements about perceived risk and uncertainty.

In 1989, Settle and Alreck conducted research and identified numerous types of perceived risk: performance risk, or the estimation of how useful the product will be; financial risk; physical risk; and psychosocial risks, for example the degree to which a product is socially desirable (under which also comes social/ego risk, the impact which a product might have on an individual's self-esteem or status).

To the above must be added the psychological attachment cost of giving up the familiar, as decision making will frequently require the consumer to adapt their behaviour. Stone and Gronhaug (1993) added time as a further element of uncertainty, an example being the learning cost associated with switching to a new product and learning how to use it effectively (Hoeffler, 2003).

All of these types of risks represent barriers to adoption, yet one of the tasks of marketing communications is to engage audiences in order to reduce relevant risks and provide an open pathway for adoption and customer retention.

The four cases considered in this chapter concern the launch of new products into new or established categories. They all achieved remarkable levels of success and it is evident that marketing communications, and advertising in particular, played a significant role in opening strong, viable pathways. Here we see how they in fact used the very risks that threatened them to frame market entry and in doing so, learn from their success.

239

## Understanding the context of risk

The principal role of communications is to engage consumers. Here engagement is considered to be about stimulating two core responses: thinking/feeling, a combination of both cognitive thoughts and emotional feelings about a brand; and behaviour or brand response. Both of these forms of engagement can be used to reduce risks.

To illustrate our point, consideration is now given to the primary risk and frame that was adopted in four new launch cases.

### Renault – launching Dacia

Renault bought Dacia, a former state-owned Romanian car manufacturer, in 1999 and relaunched it throughout Europe as a value brand. Entering the UK market, with all of its prejudices about low-cost cars, meant that the 'shockingly affordable' positioning used elsewhere was not going to work in the UK.

As part of the contextual analysis the 'stigma problem' was identified. This refers to the relationship people have with cars, exceeding the functional or performance threshold of the car itself. Given that a car says something about the owner, the team also deduced that drivers also make judgements about *themselves*, regarding the car they drive. This insight enabled them to isolate the primary form of uncertainty, namely *ego risk*.

Drivers use post-purchase rationalisation to justify their decision making, which is referred to as an 'intellectual alibi'. To launch the lowest-priced car in the UK the campaign needed to deliver an intellectual alibi that drivers could use to allow them to consider and purchase a Dacia, and side-step the stigma problem. This was achieved by re-engineering the notion of value, by extolling the virtues of having less (fewer features and attributes) rather than more (as with middle- and top-of-the-range cars). In other words, the communications were framed around what smart values should represent to prospective Dacia buyers, as well as the functional value of the proposition itself, and it was this frame that was used to coordinate and deliver the entire campaign.

### Kärcher – the launch of Window Vac

For a significant group of people window cleaning is a despised, even hated, cleaning task. This is not just because of the effort required but also because of the difficulty of getting a satisfactory, streak-free finish.

Kärcher had developed Window Vac, an innovative interior cleaning product, designed precisely to make window cleaning highly effective and one that requires minimal effort.

Kärcher however, had established a strong position across Europe within the high-pressure washer market, but this was thought to represent a significant deterrent to their entry into the UK with Window Vac. The first indication of market uncertainty was seen when retailers refused to list the Window Vac. Although Kärcher had developed strong relationships with key retailers there was significant doubt that this product would be successful.

The risk was embedded within the perceived performance of the product: people simply did not believe that the product would really deliver what it claimed. The solution therefore had to involve challenging these perceptions, otherwise the risk would remain untenable, and once demonstrated the Window Vac was quickly accepted. Therefore, communications were framed around the visible ease with which the product could be used and its ability to deliver a high quality finish.

### McCain – launching Ready Baked Jackets

For people in a hurry, preparing baked potatoes in a microwave speeds up the preparation and consumption time. Unfortunately it seriously reduces the perceived eating experience as both the taste and the quality of the potato are compromised. Therefore, the choice is to either spend time on oven-baking a potato, or compromise on taste by using a microwave. To address this issue McCain created a microwaved jacket potato which was ready in just five minutes, and which had the authentic taste of an oven-baked potato.

McCain had developed a potentially brilliant product, but their challenge was that consumers simply didn't believe that a product that good could exist. In essence there were two risks at play. One concerned performance risk – how could a microwaved frozen jacket potato taste as good as an oven-baked potato? The other concerned time risk – how could this be achieved in just five minutes?

The solution was framed around taste, with a graduated experiential campaign focused on convincing a cynical audience of the flavour, in order to side-step the process element, namely the microwave. The campaign addressed the contextual issues by moving audiences through stages from awareness, to trial and then advocacy.

### Sensodyne – the launch of Sensodyne Pronamel

The condition called acid wear has been known to dentists, but little attention had been given to it. Acid wear results from the acids in our diet weakening and wearing away tooth enamel. The enamel thins, turns yellow, and eventually results in painful, fragile and chipped teeth. Pronamel was developed specifically to address this market need. The product uses a unique formulation allowing minerals to penetrate deep into the weakened enamel surface, actively strengthening it, and preventing further enamel loss.

Launching this product would be challenging. Acid wear is a slow, insidious, and initially a painless condition, which is almost impossible to spot in its early stages with an untrained eye. Most sufferers are unaware that they are affected and therefore don't perceive a need. In addition, dentists were not talking about acid wear, and so people remained unaware of the condition.

Unlike the McCain campaign where consumers understood the issues but didn't believe the quality of the product, the Pronamel context involved a market that was unaware of the condition and saw no need for a product. Communications therefore needed to raise awareness of the problem, and then address the physical risk that arose as a consequence.

The launch of this product differs from the others considered in this chapter because communication was required with two key audiences: dentists and consumers. First, it was necessary to encourage dentists to talk about the condition so that they invested their credibility and authority with regard to acid wear. Consumers then needed to be informed about the condition and presented with Pronamel as a solution.

The frame used for the communications was identified as a result of understanding the target market, namely people who followed healthy diets. High proportions of acid are found within the juices, sports drinks and fresh fruits they preferred. Rather than deter them from their healthy diets and lifestyles (and thereby introducing another risk), the Pronamel campaign was framed around facilitation. The brand was positioned to enable consumers to continue enjoying their healthy lifestyles. It avoided audiences associating acid wear with Pronamel and linking the two through fear, worry or even conflict with their chosen lifestyle.

Pronamel's frame was to facilitate in order to protect. Their media mix was always heavily orientated towards television in order to reach consumers, but it also included press, outdoor, and online. The mix became tailored towards the target market as the campaign developed in order to reach them at relevant times. These included periods when they were considering or consuming acidic foods or drinks, such as in gyms, relevant supermarket aisles, online and in lifestyle press.

Real dentists and real consumers, not actors, were used to provide credibility and relevance for the television work. These opinion formers and leaders helped to reinforce the message that healthy diets cause acid wear and that Pronamel works. They also helped stimulate word-of-mouth communication, especially through social media.

## Observations

In each of the four cases a particular aspect of consumer uncertainty was isolated. With Dacia, it was self-esteem and psychosocial risks. With Kärcher, the risk concerned the performance associated with the effort and outcomes of using a window cleaning system. For McCain the primary risks were both time and performance related, whilst Sensodyne Pronamel determined that the physical risk arising from acid wear was the primary hurdle that communications needed to overcome.

From these insights four campaigns evolved, each rooted in a primary form of consumer uncertainty. There was clearly a structural similarity to the way the brands approached their task. Each of the campaigns were rooted in a rigorous context analysis that had a communications rather than marketing orientation. They each identified a primary perceived risk and used this to frame the communications that followed. Framing in this way has been shown to enhance message reception and effectiveness (Pan and Kosicki, 2001).

The use of media scheduling to demonstrate relevance and heighten consumer experience served to reduce uncertainty during these launch campaigns. Advocacy was also an integral part of all four campaigns; the use of opinion leaders and formers to provide the trust and expertise for the claims being made undoubtedly contributed to reducing consumer uncertainty.

An important question, however, concerns the likelihood that the nature of the primary risk shifts once the launch is complete. Will different risks arise and if so, should the frame change? For example, if psychosocial risks are the primary concern at the birth of a new category, their amelioration will lead to market growth, which normally attracts new competitors. As the new players seek to differentiate their products and highlight different attributes, so consumer uncertainty evolves as they attempt to understand the new offerings. Psychosocial risk gives way to performance or time risk, which will necessitate a new frame if communications are to continue to engage audiences successfully.

These four cases demonstrate that an understanding of the risks perceived by consumers is important if communications are to be effective. However, the dynamic nature of consumer perceived risk suggests that the frame through which audiences are engaged at launch should be reviewed as a market develops.

## References

Hoeffler, S. (2003) 'Measuring Preferences for Really New Products', *Journal of Marketing Research*, 40, (November), 406–421.

Pan, Z. and Kosicki, G. (2001) 'Framing as a Strategic Action in Public Deliberation', in S.D. Reese, O.H. Gandy and A.E. Grant (eds), *Framing Public Life: Perspectives on Media and Our Understanding of the Social World*, Mahwah, NJ: Lawrence Erlbaum, pp. 35–65.

Settle, R.B. and Alreck, P. (1989) 'Reducing Buyers' Sense of Risk', *Marketing Communications* (January), 34–40.

Stone, R.N. and Gronhaug, K. (1993) 'Perceived Risk: Further Considerations for the Marketing Discipline', *European Journal of Marketing*, 27(3), 39–50.

# Dacia

## Making frugality pay

**By Julian Earl, Publicis London**

Contributing authors: Stephen Stokes and Dylan Mouratsing, Manning Gottlieb OMD

Credited companies: Media Agency, Manning Gottlieb OMD; Creative Agency, Publicis London; Econometric modelling agency, The Effectiveness Partnership; Client, Renault UK

### Editor's summary

In mid-2012 Renault announced that it would launch a new car brand into the UK market, Dacia. The premise behind the car was to offer an 'ultra value' proposition which stripped the car of everything that might be deemed unnecessary.

Unfortunately, however, consumers and the media were less than welcoming and this paper tells how the client and agency worked together to overcome the prejudices directed at cheaper cars, especially ones from Eastern Europe. Their idea needed to create social permission and set out to help consumers feel proud to choose Dacia by providing them with an intellectual alibi. They did this through becoming the 'enemy of the unnecessary'; poking fun at traditional car advertising with their 'you do the maths' theme and championing no-nonsense frugality.

Dacia's launch year was the best first-year result ever recorded by a new car brand and the case clearly showed how the UK launch significantly outperformed Dacia's other European launches, selling nearly 22,000 cars, delivering a ROMI of 4.

**The judges were impressed by the scale of the task especially in context of the overall car market and recommended the case for its clear presentation and innovative approach to a significant perceptional barrier.**

## Introduction

In mid-2012 Renault announced that it would launch a new car brand in the UK, something that hadn't been attempted in 17 years, since Daewoo hit the scene. That brand was Dacia.

Eighteen months later, the Dacia launch year was proclaimed the best first-year result ever recorded by a new car brand. Sales outstripped all internal targets and outperformed Dacia's other European launches, hitting 21,852 cars sold and delivering a short-term revenue ROI of four to one.[1]

Dacia was set to be the cheapest car in the UK marketplace. However, we knew that the European launch communication of 'shockingly affordable' would not overcome the engrained prejudice people have towards cheap cars, especially the ones from Eastern Europe. Advertising had to make people proud of, not embarrassed by, their choice. It did this by poking fun at traditional car advertising and by making people realise that they were smart for choosing a car with just the features they needed and none of the ones they didn't. We eschewed the conventional cues of car advertising – a glamorous drive, a young target, lots of gadgets – and championed no-nonsense frugality instead.

## The context

In 2013, a shell-shocked nation was just beginning to emerge from the deepest recession for decades, with new habits of frugality. It was an ideal time for Renault to launch a new, super economical car brand in the UK. Or so you might think.

It hardly needs saying that Britain's economy went through tough times in the years from 2008 to late 2012. Few sectors were untouched by its effects. The car sector was no exception.

Broadly speaking, car buyers saved money, or made their money go further, by adopting one of three strategies.

More people bought top-end, premium brands like BMW and Audi. On the basis that quality lasts, and holds its value, and saves you money in the long run.

More people bought bottom-end 'value' brands like Kia, Hyundai and Škoda, on the basis that cheaper cars cost less in the first place, and save you money right now (Figure 1).

And more people bought second-hand cars, for a combination of reasons one and two. A quality car that lasts – and saves you money straight away (Figure 2).

So those were the winners: expensive cars, cheap cars, and second-hand cars. And the losers? Everybody else, which is to say: mass-market, mid-range brands like Renault.

Renault was suffering. Since its high-water mark in 2004 – when it was the third most popular brand in the UK – sales had fallen by 74%. Renault languished in eighteenth place in the car sales rankings with just 1.99% market share[2] (Figure 3).

But Renault had a plan.

'Value' brands, as we've noted, were increasingly popular, and Renault owned a 'value' brand all of its own. That brand was Dacia, a former state-owned Romanian car manufacturer that Renault purchased in 1999.

## Figure 1: Percentage UK car sales by type

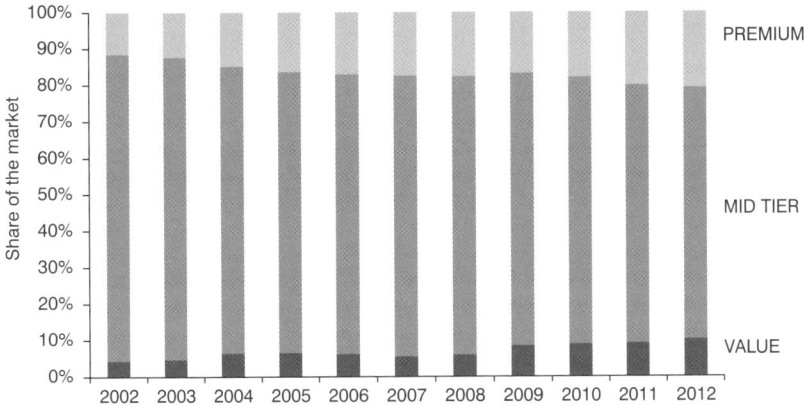

Source: SMMT

## Figure 2: Growth in used car sales

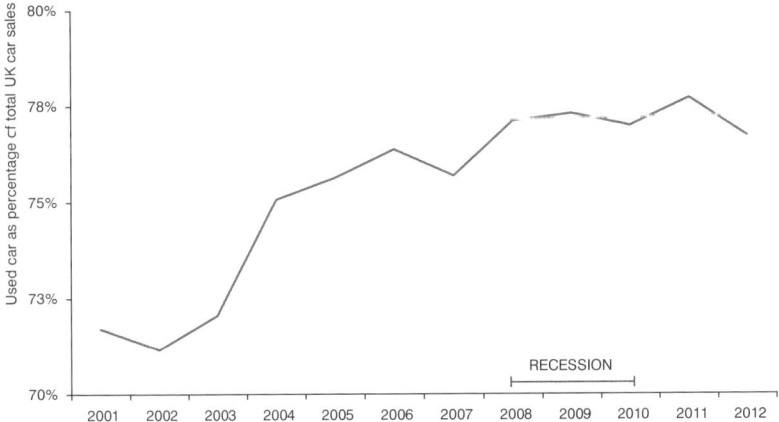

Source: SMMT

## Figure 3: Shrinking Renault UK sales

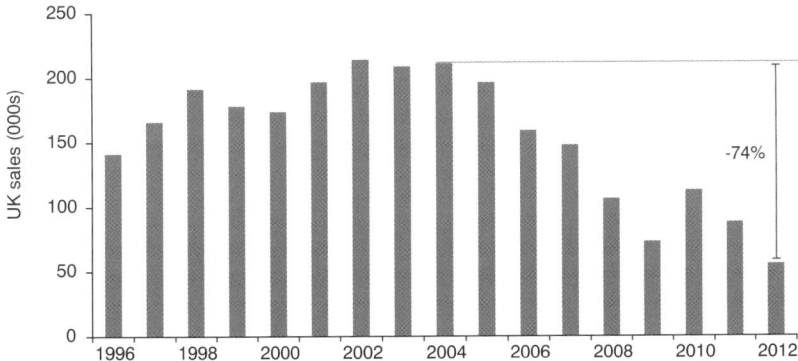

Source: SMMT

Renault's plan was to launch Dacia in the UK – having re-launched the brand throughout the rest of Europe since 2004.

The Dacia Duster would be launched as the lowest-priced SUV on the market, by a long way. It was £5,000 cheaper, at £8,995, than its nearest rival, the Škoda Yeti. And the Dacia Sandero (a five-door hatchback), at just £5,995, would be Britain's cheapest new car of any kind (Figures 4 and 5).

**Figure 4: Dacia Duster SUV**

**Figure 5: Dacia Sandero hatchback**

It appeared to be a sure-fire recipe for success. But appearances, of course, can be deceptive.

## The problem

The stigma problem means that people have a relationship with their cars that goes beyond the purely functional. There is a sense that your car says something about you, and you are judged for it. In the UK, driving a car from an unknown Eastern European brand with bargain-basement prices can attract ridicule and stigma. And jokes were already being made about Dacia.

In the car market, you might think it would be sufficient to have a good product at a great price. But you'd be wrong. People tend to think that the lower the price, the lower the quality and this is where the mockery starts (Figure 6).

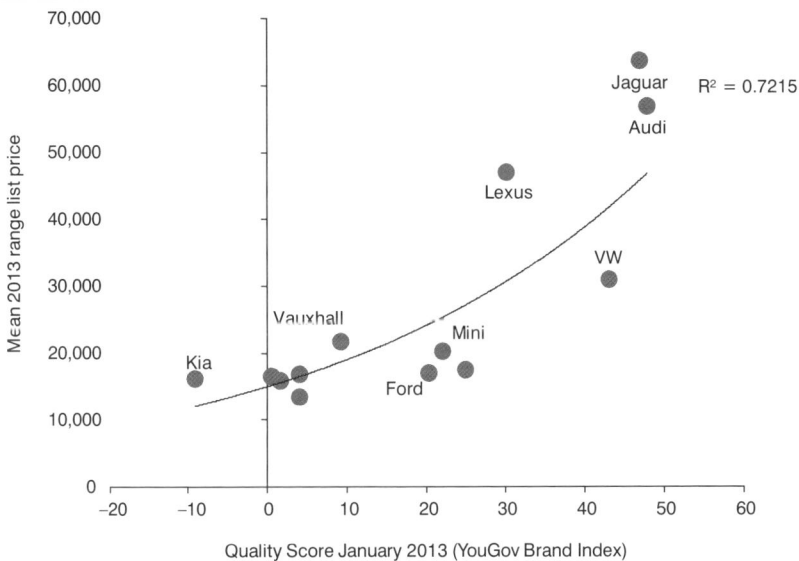

Figure 6: Low price = low quality

Source: YouGov Brand Index, www.carbuyer.couk, www.kia.co.uk, Renault UK

Take Škoda. Back in 1998, this low-priced former Eastern European car brand imagined it had a winning proposition with its new model, the Octavia. It was well-made, well-specified and priced far lower than anything in its competitive set. People who knew about cars rated it positively– it won *What Car?'s* Car of the Year Award. It had a big-budget advertising campaign to trumpet its high specs and low, low prices.

And yet the launch failed. You can read all about how it failed in the winning IPA paper of 2002.[3] In the whole of the launch year, only 2,500 Octavias were sold – which meant that the ad campaign cost £4,000 for each car sold.

You can also read, in the same paper, why it eventually succeeded. The problem was not in quality or pricing. It was a *perception* problem and a stigma problem, summed up by this quote from the Daily Mirror:

*"I see the [Škoda] has been named 'Car of the Year' but I don't think I'm ready to drive one yet. I still think that it›s less embarrassing to be seen getting out of the back of a sheep than getting out of the back of a Škoda."*[4]

Škoda, Lada, Trabant: budget-priced Eastern European car brands had long been the butt of cruel jokes. Dacia was no exception.

Even before the first Dacia hit the UK, presenters on the hugely popular TV motoring show Top Gear had already started to crack jokes about the brand (Figure 7).

Figure 7: Top Gear TV show

*May (mock excitement): Great news!*
*Clarkson: What?*
*May: The Dacia Sandero is almost here.*
*Clarkson: When?*
*May: Next year!*
*Clarkson: Great!*
*Fits of laughter from studio audience.*
*May (head in hands): Oh, bad news!*
*Clarkson: What?*
*May: The Dacia Sandero – it's delayed!*
*Clarkson: Oh no!*
*Fits of laughter from studio audience.*
*May: Great news!*
*Clarkson: What?*
*May: The Dac...(can't speak for laughing)*

So launching in the UK wasn't going to be easy for Dacia. On paper, it all looked so right: great quality and amazingly low pricing in a market crying out for these things. Yet in every other way it was all so wrong, unknown, Eastern European and cheap, already becoming a laughing stock on one of Britain's most-watched TV shows.

To top all that off, Dacia's launch budget was in the same league as its prices: super-low (Figure 8).

## Figure 8: Low Dacia media spend

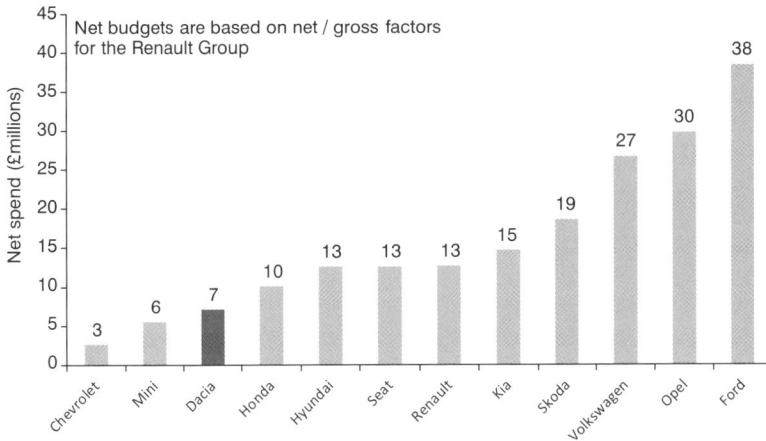

Net budgets are based on net / gross factors for the Renault Group

Net spend (£millions)

Chevrolet 3, Mini 6, Dacia 7, Honda 10, Hyundai 13, Seat 13, Renault 13, Kia 15, Skoda 19, Volkswagen 27, Opel 30, Ford 38

Source: MxPlorer

## The objectives

### Overall objective

- Launch a successful new 'value-brand' for the Renault Group to help plug the gap created by the attrition of mid-range car sales.

### Business objectives

- Base sales target of 9,000 Dacia new cars.
- Stretch sales target of 14,000 Dacia new cars.[5]

Achieving the base target would give Dacia approximately 0.5% share of the UK new car market, placing Dacia just below Chevrolet, a key rival in the value category (Table 1).

## Table 1: New car registrations

|  | 2012 | % Market share |
|---|---|---|
| Volvo | 31,790 | 1.55 |
| Mazda | 26,183 | 1.28 |
| Suzuki | 24,893 | 1.22 |
| Jaguar | 14,109 | 0.69 |
| Chevrolet | 13,476 | 0.66 |
| Lexus | 8,404 | 0.41 |
| Porsche | 7,998 | 0.39 |
| Alfa Romeo | 7,253 | 0.35 |
| Mitsubishi | 6,549 | 0.32 |
| smart | 5,616 | 0.27 |
| Chrysler | 3,333 | 0.16 |

251

Both base and stretch targets were significantly higher than Dacia had achieved in other European markets, in their first year (Figure 9).

## Figure 9: Dacia sales targets compared to other European markets

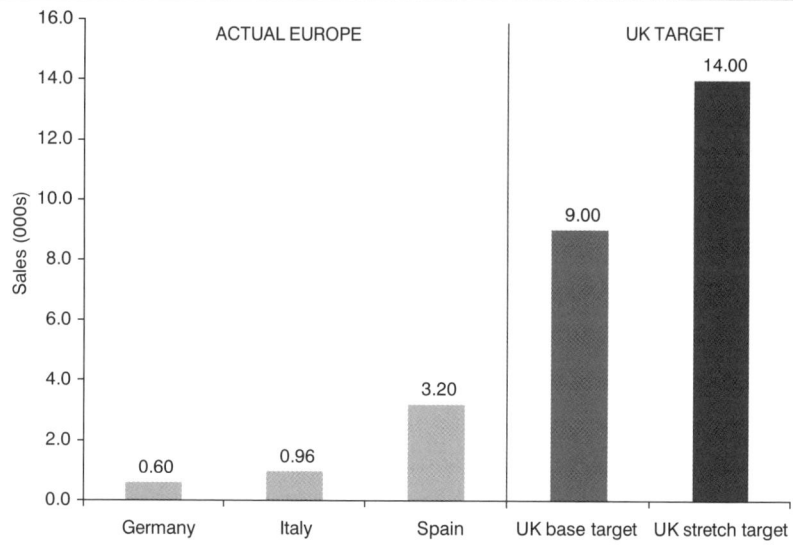

Source: Renault UK

By comparison to Renault sales, Dacia was expected to outsell models like Renault Scénic; if it reached its stretch target, it would need to outsell Renault Mégane, Renault's overall second best seller (Figure 10).

## Figure 10: Dacia sales targets compared to Renault model sales 2012

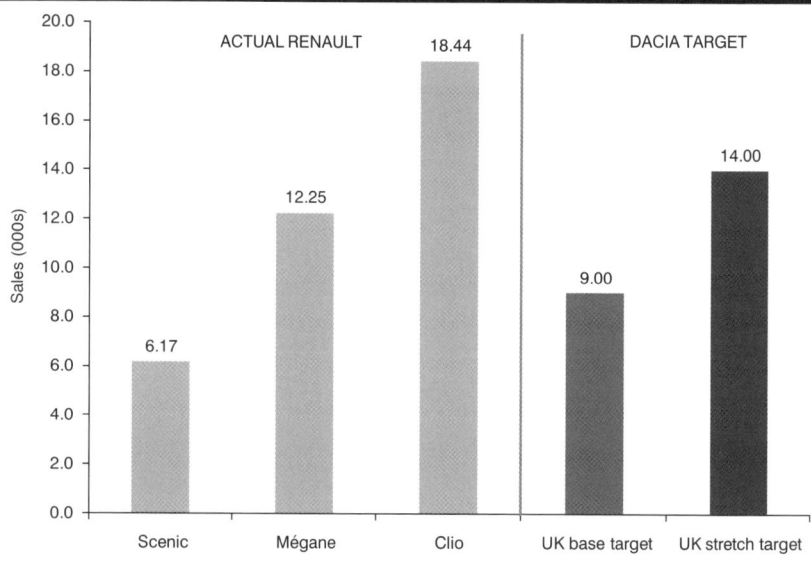

Source: SMMT and Renault UK

### Marketing objective

■ Penetration: To increase the penetration of Renault Group products by drawing incremental customers to Dacia. No more than 10% from current Renault customer base.

### Communications objectives

■ Awareness: To achieve 60% awareness of Dacia in the first year.
■ Persuasion: To make sure that Dacia's good quality/low price proposition hits home and is not dogged by the ridicule and stigma that killed launches like that of the Škoda Octavia.

The objectives are summarised in Table 2.

| Table 2: Summary of objectives | | |
| --- | --- | --- |
| **Area** | **KPI** | **Detail** |
| Business | Sales | 9,000 new car sales with 14,000 stretch target |
| Marketing | Penetration | No more than 10% from current Renault customer base |
| Communication | Brand awareness | 60% |
| | Persuasion | Good brand image |

## The insight

'*Intellectual alibi*' is a term coined by French psychoanalyst Clotaire Rapaille to describe the reason people give to themselves and to others for doing what they do. If Dacia buyers were going to find themselves the butt of jokes from the likes of Top Gear, then they needed a damn good, fool proof alibi to retain their dignity and their belief in having made the right choice.

Speaking to car owners in qualitative research[6] it soon became clear that the reasons given for choosing a particular car were often rationalisations rather than literal truths. For example, SUV drivers often described why they really, *really* needed four-wheel drive and chunky tyres, even though they lived in a town and mainly used their car for the school-run. Other drivers would describe how they paid extra for a higher-range model because of certain features and buttons – and yet when you probed how often they used these features and buttons, it turned out that the answer was mostly 'seldom or never.'

Rapaille had been conducting similar investigations with car buyers in the US and elsewhere: he commented on New York SUV drivers, giving 'the difficulty of parking in snow' as one of their main reasons for choice.[7]

He recognised that these justifications are fig leaves that provide an acceptable, rational gloss on deeper, often emotionally driven reasons and he gave them the term 'intellectual alibi'.

We were sure that people really did want to save money, especially in the aftermath of a recession and with newly ingrained habits of thrift. But we were also aware of the strength of the emotional connection between people and their cars, and the degree to which cars make social statements about their owners.

So we knew that the one thing the launch campaign should do, above all else, would be to provide a really good intellectual alibi to make you feel good, not shoddy, for choosing Dacia, and to rebut the likes of Jeremy Clarkson or his proxies in your home town.

## Creating the campaign

Our solution was to reframe the concept of value in the car market and to extol the virtues of having less rather than more. It provided the perfect intellectual alibi to silence any Clarkson wannabe straight away.

How could we make people feel good about choosing a Dacia? The approach taken by the competition was to communicate generosity and to pack in as many extras (e.g. body colour bumpers, electric windows with auto up and down driver controls, daytime running lights) into the price as possible. Consumers had been conditioned into thinking that value was about getting more for less.

The likes of Škoda's advertising celebrated all the gadgets you got thrown in (Figure 11).

Figure 11: Competitor advertising

Dacia took a different path. The basic models on sale had no gadgets at all – no cup holders, no electric door mirrors, no tinted glass, no sat-nav, not even a radio. The car was stripped down to the bare essentials needed for a comfortable, safe drive from A to B.

This truth gave us our creative starting point and the reason why Dacia UK couldn't simply follow the European launch campaign: placing full emphasis on the 'shockingly affordable' low price (Figure 12).

Figure 12: Dutch TVC for Dacia

Instead we would challenge the idea that more is better and show up the unnecessary extravagance of paying for things you do not need. Good value would be about paying for what you really need in a car and saving on things you don't.

We would target people who get a kick from saving money by cutting out unnecessary frills. We would make them feel that they'd got absolutely everything that matters in a car, but that they'd been clever enough to save thousands by not paying for all of the superfluous stuff that other people get sucked into by sharp-suited salesmen.

The brief positioned Dacia as the enemy of the unnecessary. The campaign that answered this brief, and embodied the insight that went into it, did it all in just four words. Which, if we're talking about economy and cutting out the unnecessary, is something of an achievement in itself. Those four words were:

*You do the maths*

The essence of the campaign can be paraphrased like this: 'Look, here's what you actually want from a car. Now, you can get all that in a car costing £30,000. Or you can get the exact same things in a car costing less than £10,000. So which would you choose? In fact, which would anyone in their right mind choose? You do the maths.'

Different executions featuring the two main models (Duster and Sandero) tackled the message from different angles. Some playful, some straight, some mocking other car brands' ways of doing things, some casting a Dacia eye over topical issues like the way footballers are bought and sold. But all coming back to the same point, the same alibi. You don't choose Dacia because you're hard up, or struggling, or because you can't afford a well-known brand. You choose Dacia because you're smart, because you're savvy, and because you're not taken in by the expensive hype that fools so many other people.

## The media strategy

Major brands in the car market follow very familiar conventions in media. The desire to inject dynamism into their brands and a near incomprehensible obsession with chasing audiences younger than the majority of new car buyers translate into typical *confident and youthful* media behaviour. This manifests itself with the likes of big event and TV sponsorships;[8] heavy weight and long time-length TV in big-rating TV programmes; glossy, intrusive showy press and an obsession with digital media innovation. All are underpinned with similar optimised retail media, all chasing many of the same prospects.

Dacia couldn't play that game, nor wanted to. It was time to call time on the category behaviour. To be truly seen as a fresh face in the car category it needed to back up its anti-frivolity positioning with the way it behaved in media and in who it targeted. This meant targeting prospective new and second hand car buyers who had a budget of around £6–20k, who were smart in their approach to spending and who shunned choosing a car based on its badge. We defined them as in Table 3.

### Table 3: Targeting profile

| | |
|---|---|
| 1 | People looking to buy a new or second-hand car in the next two years |
| 2 | With a budget of £6–20k |
| 3 | Whose reason for purchase isn't brand image |
| = | 2 million people, who we dubbed 'savvy spenders' |

This also meant a whole set of new, smarter rules that were contrary to the category conventions, as illustrated in Table 4.

Dacia's identified media target audience had, on average, a lower income, were older (with an emphasis on people over 55) and more likely to live in rural areas (Figure 13).

### Figure 13: Dacia's identified media target audience vs the average new car buyer

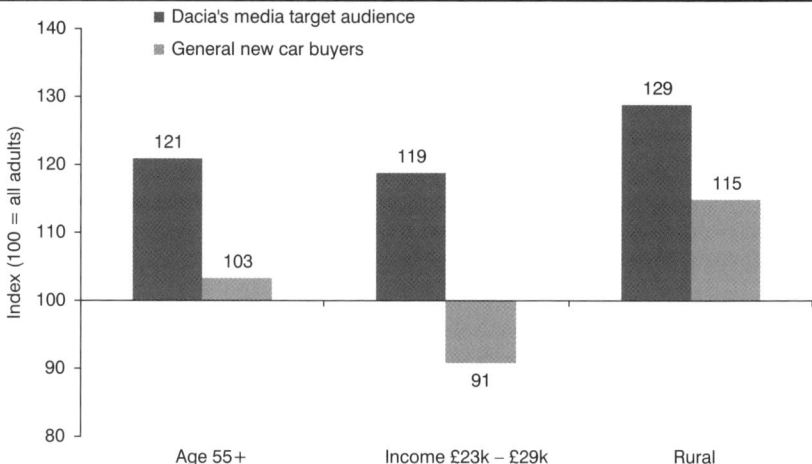

Source: Renault UK and TGI 2014

## Table 4: Automotive media conventions vs Dacia plan

| | Category Conventions | Dacia's Launch |
|---|---|---|
| Target Audience(s) | Broad approach: New car buyers and younger brand opinion formers | Single-minded approach: Smart, savvy new and second-hand car buyers |
| Comms Imperative | Glamorise the drive | Overtly challenge frivolity |
| Media Behaviour | Media that injects youthful lifestyle appeal combined with the need for stature and scale. Often appearing out of sync with reality of the brand. | Unpretentious and smart straight talking. Dacia's point of view on the car category implying where it's gone wrong. |
| Media Implications | Big TV and Cinema. Wide reaching expensive event and youthful TV. Cinema often an essential ingredient. Heavy weights of 500+ TVRs prior to pre-registration periods (March and Sept). Longer time-lengths play important role (22% of TVRs were 40" or longer). Borrowed interest via sport and film sponsorships. | Smart TV Talk to smart, savvy, new car buyers in their smart, savvy, down to earth programming. Up-weighting months away from major competitive peaks (E.g.: Jan vs. Feb-March and June vs. Jul-Sept) ensuring higher SOV (7.4% in Jan and 10.7% in June vs. 2.9% year average). No extravagant time-lengths or big sponsorships. |
| | Glossy Press Lifestyle press and supplements. Double page spreads playing key role. | Point of View press Simple, clear, proud media in intelligent titles. Pages in early main news. Media partnership with two core older titles (Daily Telegraph and Daily Mail). |
| | Big broad digital and vanity innovation Home page take-overs across major sites. Digital innovation such as Shazamable ads! | Smart targeted digital Home page take-overs only car sections of intelligent, savvy sites. Obviously no digital media innovation distractions. |
| | Facebook as broadcast channel Wide reaching ads in news-stream. | Facebook to build community of interest Organically build Facebook group around the appeal of Dacia's attitude, turning them into top DR prospects (achieving the highest performing car DR rates on Facebook). |
| | Wide reaching retail Saturated National press and radio with offer based advertising. Cost per lead drives digital DR and search. | Smart steal the sale retail Comprise hit list of 20 competing cars that Dacia could best present itself against, with savvy comparative claims that steal the sale at the end of buyer's purchase journey. Using specific Google search, digital around specific car reviews. Additionally we exploited under-utilised opportunity in second hand car sites, targeting specific cars and £6–12k buying budgets. |

And this translated into the media plan in Figure 14:

### Figure 14: 2013 Dacia media plan

| Dacia media laydown 2013 | Jan | Feb | Mar | Apr | May | Jun | Jul | Aug | Sep | Oct | Nov | Dec |
|---|---|---|---|---|---|---|---|---|---|---|---|---|
| TV (30" TVRs) | 307 | 185 | | | 151 | 335 | | 30 | 174 | | 171 | |
| Press | | | | | | | | | | | | |
| Press partnerships | | | | | | | | | | | | |
| Radio | | | | | | | | | | | | |
| Online | | | | | | | | | | | | |
| Search | | | | | | | | | | | | |

## Examples of creative work in media placements

**Figure 15: TVC on terrestrial and satellite announcing Dacia's launch**

Hello, we're Dacia. We don't do frivolity. Function is our thing. It's how we keep prices low, and quality high.

But research suggests a touch of frivolity may make a car seem more appealing.

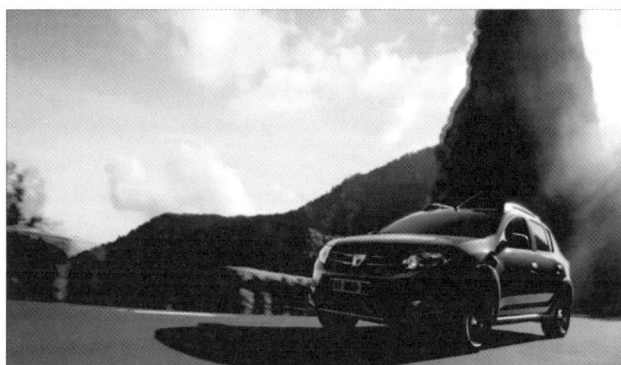

So, just in case …

– *Music* –

Happy?

The Dacia range. From just £5,995.

You do the maths.

## Figure 16: Christmas press

## Figure 17: Press advertising in daily nationals celebrating Dacia's awards

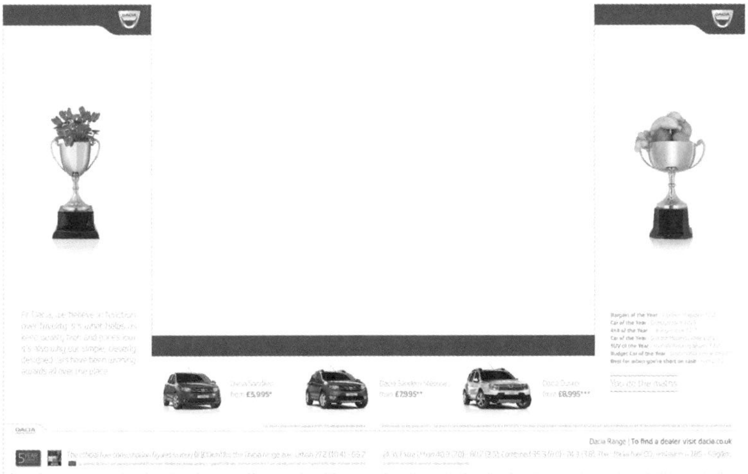

Figure 18: Online display banner MPU demonstrating Dacia's stance on frivolous spending

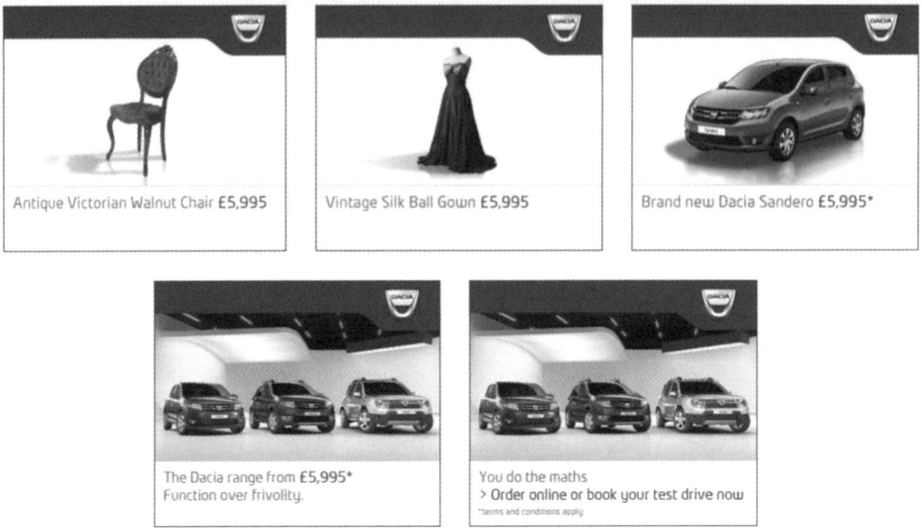
Antique Victorian Walnut Chair £5,995
Vintage Silk Ball Gown £5,995
Brand new Dacia Sandero £5,995*
The Dacia range from £5,995*
Function over frivolity.
You do the maths
> Order online or book your test drive now
*terms and conditions apply

Figure 19: Twitter post demonstrating Dacia's stance on frivolous spending

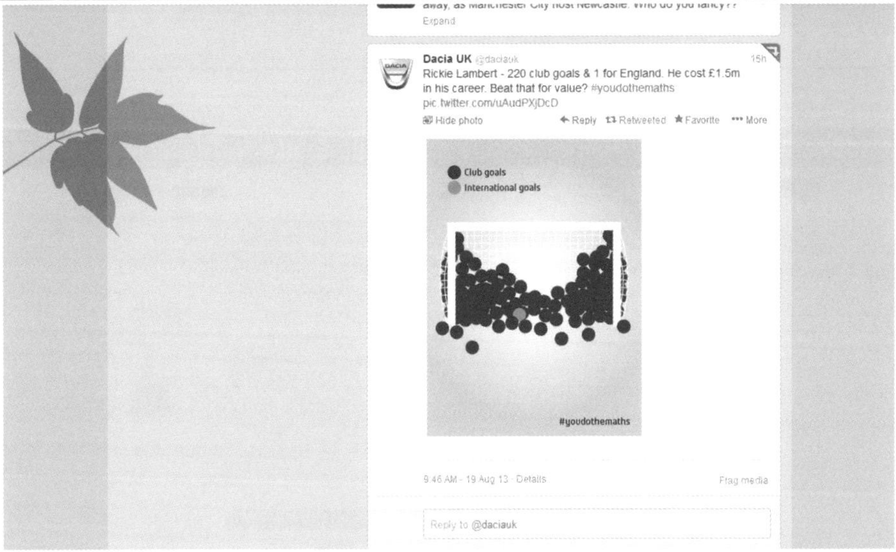
Expand
Dacia UK @daciauk
15h
Rickie Lambert - 220 club goals & 1 for England. He cost £1.5m in his career. Beat that for value? #youdothemaths
pic.twitter.com/uAudPXjDcD
Hide photo
Reply
Retweeted
Favorite
More
Club goals
International goals
#youdothemaths
9:46 AM - 19 Aug 13 · Details
Flag media
Reply to @daciauk

# The results

Did Dacia succeed in its ambitions? Well, Autocar[9] declared that Dacia's achievement in 2013 was the best first-year result *ever* recorded by a new car brand. And this was followed by accolades from other automotive journalists, including AutoExpress[10], stating that 'Dacia has been confirmed as the fastest growing car brand *ever* to hit the UK'.

These are grand statements but what about the specifics, and what role did communications play in this undoubted success?

## What happened?

By the end of its first year, Dacia had sold 17,263 new cars,[11] far surpassing its base sales volume target and also exceeding its stretch target.

By month 15, sales had risen to 21,852.[12]

With this sales success, Dacia reached 0.76% total market share by the end of 2013, and in turn 30% of Renault market share, even though Renault sales also experienced year on year growth (Figure 20).

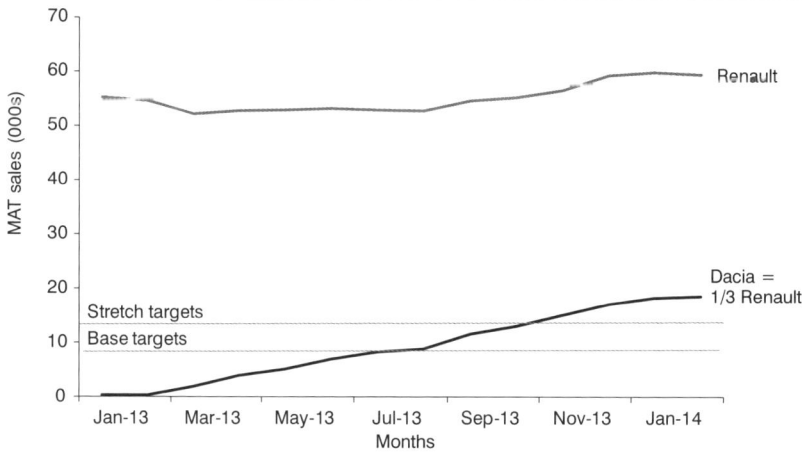

Figure 20: Exceeding sales targets

Source: Renault UK and SMMT

These sales didn't all come from current Renault owners or prospects. Whilst purchasing a Dacia, only 9% of the other brands on consumers' consideration sets were Renault (Figure 21).

## Figure 21: Whilst purchasing a Dacia, only 9% of the alternative brands people considered were Renault

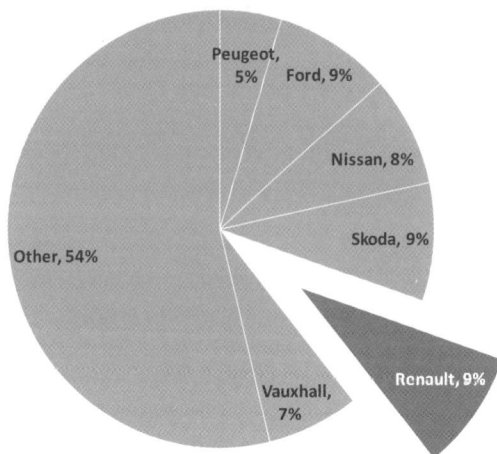

Source: Renault Group survey Apr 2014, question was 'What other car brands did you consider before purchasing your Dacia? If none, leave blank' and base is 1,694 Dacia owners.

### How does this success compare?

Comparing to previous new car launches, Dacia has outperformed the average UK model launch over the first 12 months and continues to do so, even though Dacia only launched with two models, adding a third half way through the year[13] (Figure 22).

## Figure 22: Average sales performance from launch: average Dacia model vs average 'value' competitor model

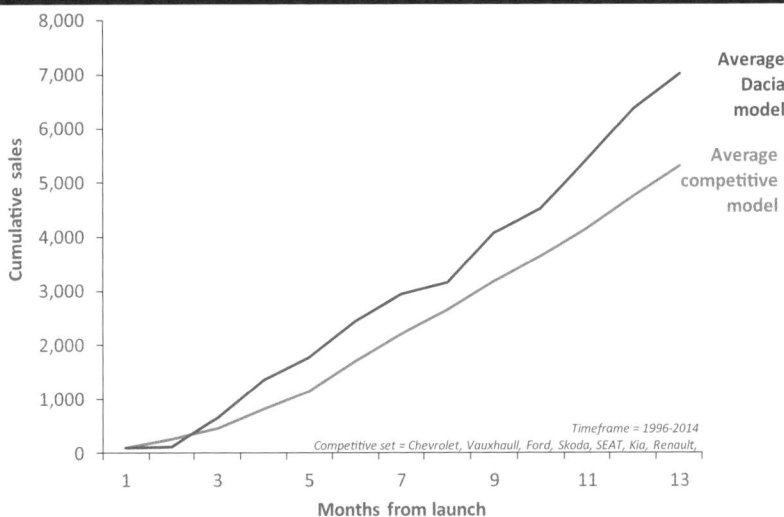

Source: Renault UK and SMMT

We can also compare Dacia's success against other European launches. Dacia UK outstripped launches in all other European countries outside of Dacia's home nation of Romania. Astonishingly, by March 2014, Dacia UK had outsold Dacia in France where sales have been buoyed by the prominence of Renault (Figure 23).

## Figure 23: Outperforming Europe

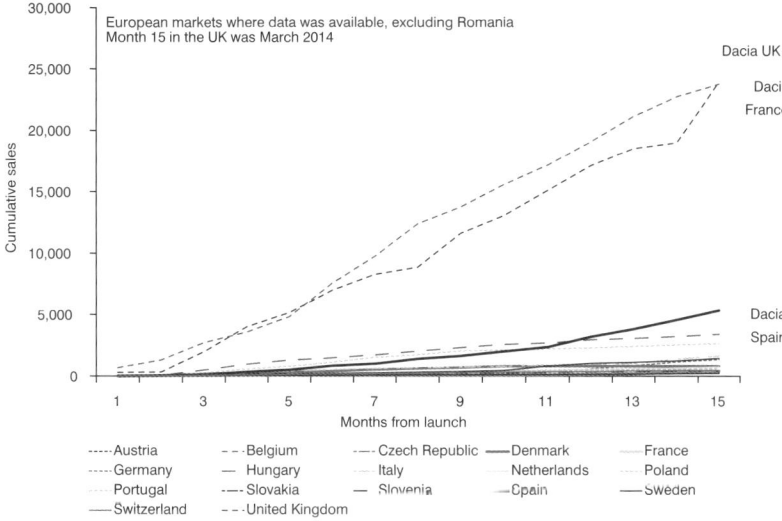

European markets where data was available, excluding Romania
Month 15 in the UK was March 2014

Source: Renault UK and ACEA

This success isn't just due to the size of the UK market. Dacia UK also achieved, by month 15,[14] the highest market share of any European market (Figure 24).

## Figure 24: Market share by month 15

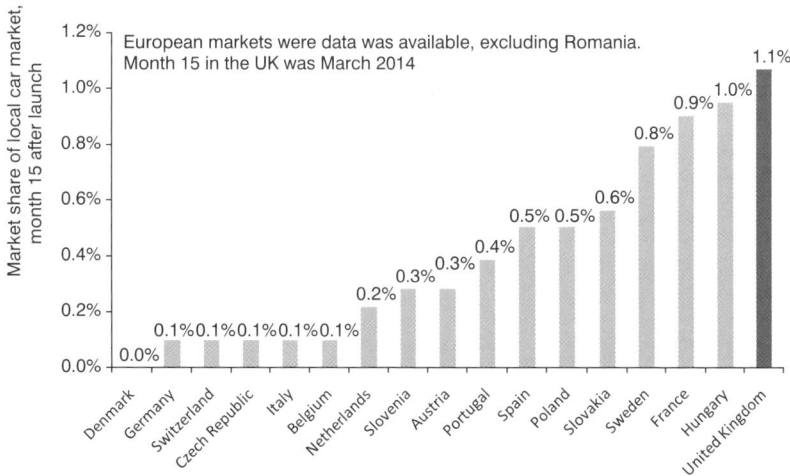

European markets were data was available, excluding Romania.
Month 15 in the UK was March 2014

Source: Renault UK and ACEA

## Attributing success to communications

In this section, we will explain how the communications worked to drive awareness, generate interest in the car, build credibility and ultimately attract a new audience to the value sector. We will also show how other factors within the marketing mix and the broader economy could not fully explain the astonishing success of Dacia UK. Finally we will estimate the payback from communications.

### The campaign got noticed

Research among Dacia owners tells us that the communications resonated with this audience. In fact, 84%[15] of Dacia owners remembered seeing the advertising, compared to 15.5%[16] of all people in the market for a new car.[17]

And 96% Dacia owners say the ads appealed to them.[18]

Moreover, TV awareness was three times that of the average marque: more memorable than advertising from all of our competitive set (Figure 25).

**Figure 25: Ad awareness per market share point to control for the Rosser Reeves Fallacy[19]**

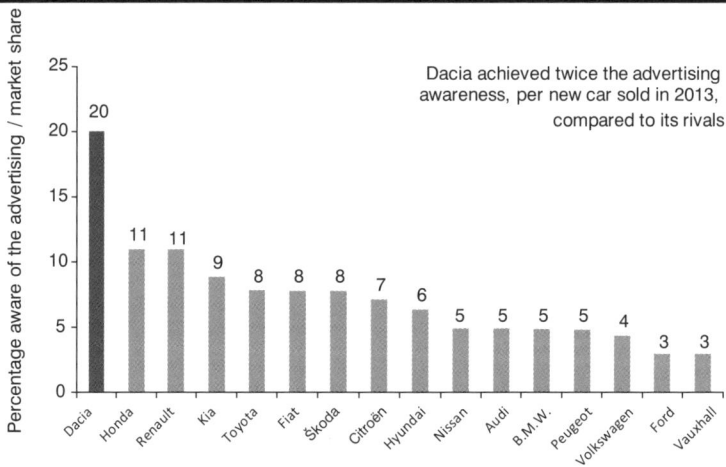

Source TNS Brand tracking Survey (Base: all adults in the market for a new car) & SMMT

### Brand awareness built, in line with communications

Awareness accelerated from 30% to bang-on target of 60% by the end of 2013 (Figure 26).

## Figure 26: Rising brand awareness

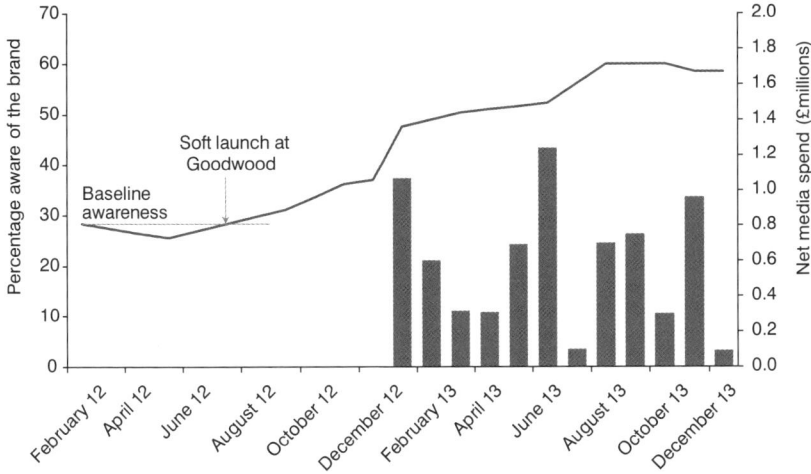

Source: TNS Brand Tracking Survey (Base: all adults in the market for a new car) & Manning Gottlieb OMD

## Communication drove further interest in the brand

Furthermore, evidence shows that there is a high correlation between media spend and consumer behaviour. Overlaying TV spend with visits to Dacia.co.uk and sales leads, shows a strong positive relationship (Figures 27 and 28).

## Figure 27: Correlation between web visits and media spend

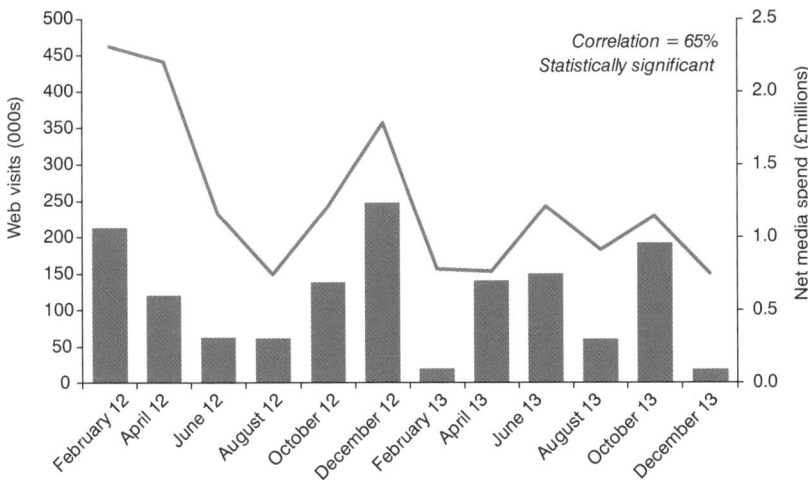

Source: Renault UK & Manning Gottlieb OMD

265

## Figure 28: Correlation between leads and media spend

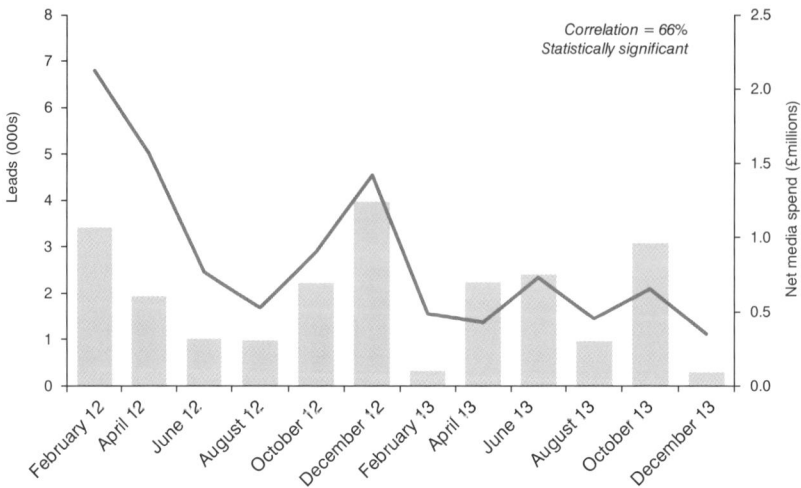

*Correlation = 66%*
*Statistically significant*

Source: Renault UK & Manning Gottlieb OMD

This wasn't simply a function of seasonality. Media spend in the car market traditionally peaks around the key sales periods of March and September. The above graphs clearly show peaks for Dacia outside of these key periods, clear result of Dacia's media planning (Figure 29).

## Figure 29: Dacia media spend by month

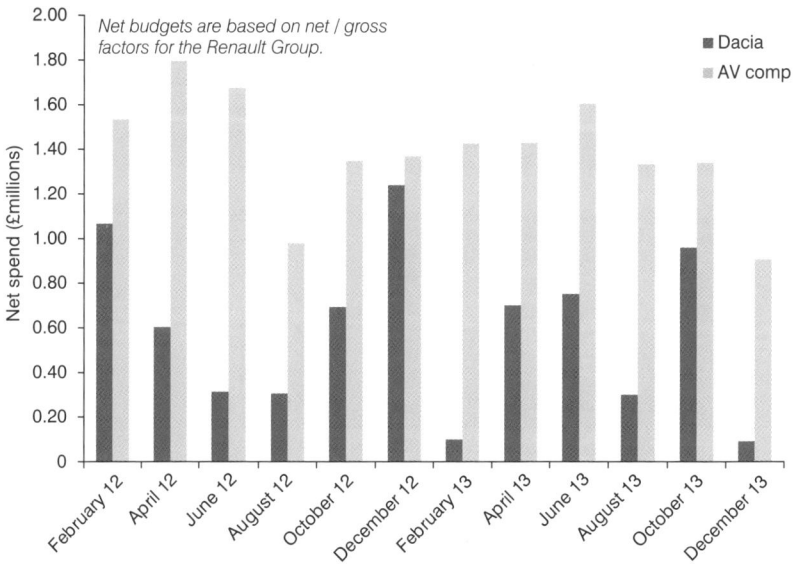

*Net budgets are based on net / gross factors for the Renault Group.*

■ Dacia
■ AV comp

Source: Manning Gottlieb OMD & MxPlorer

## Communications legitimised the purchase of a Dacia

Brand tracking evidence shows that Dacia was portraying itself in a positive and credible way (Figure 30).

**Figure 30: Dacia increases the % agreeing it is a car they'd be proud to drive when media weights are high**

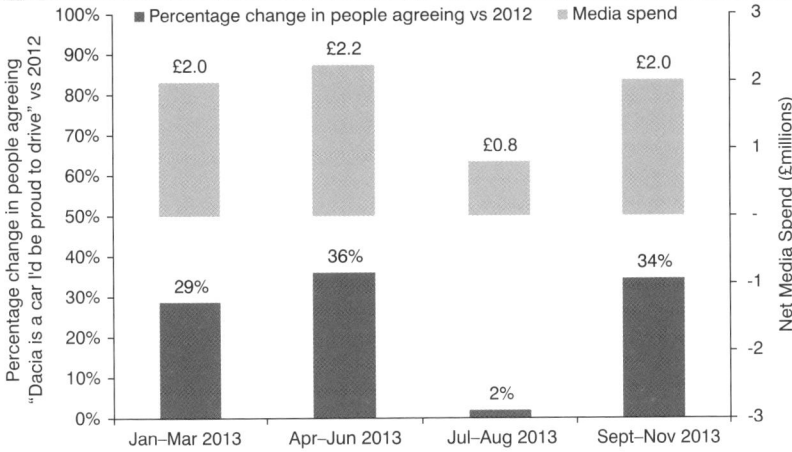

Source: TNS Brand Tracking Survey Q4 2013

## We set out to attract a different type of car buyer, and we did

Further evidence showing the success of the media can be seen in the type of people attracted to Dacia. Our customers match our target audience and are very different to the average new car buyer (Figure 31).

**Figure 31: The Dacia profile is similar to our target audience but differs from an average new car buyer**

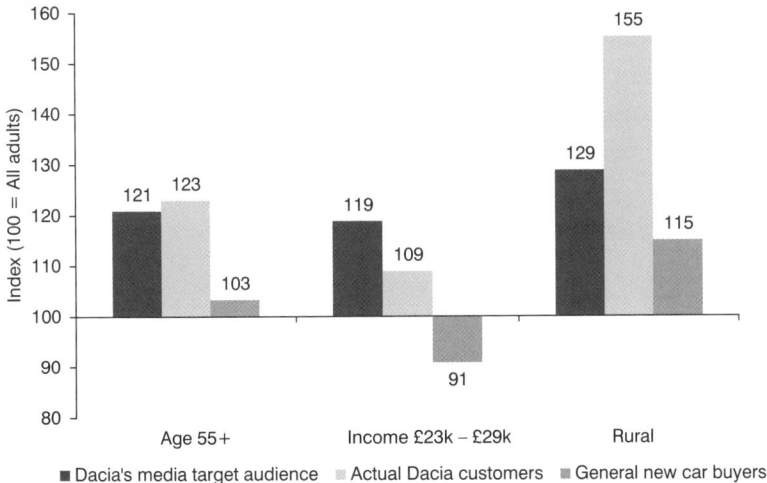

Source: Renault UK and TGI 2014

If these results were driven by price, we'd expect to see a similar profile to the average 'value' car buyer. However, Dacia customers display a very different Mosaic profile (Figure 32).

### Figure 32: Distinct Dacia buyer profile

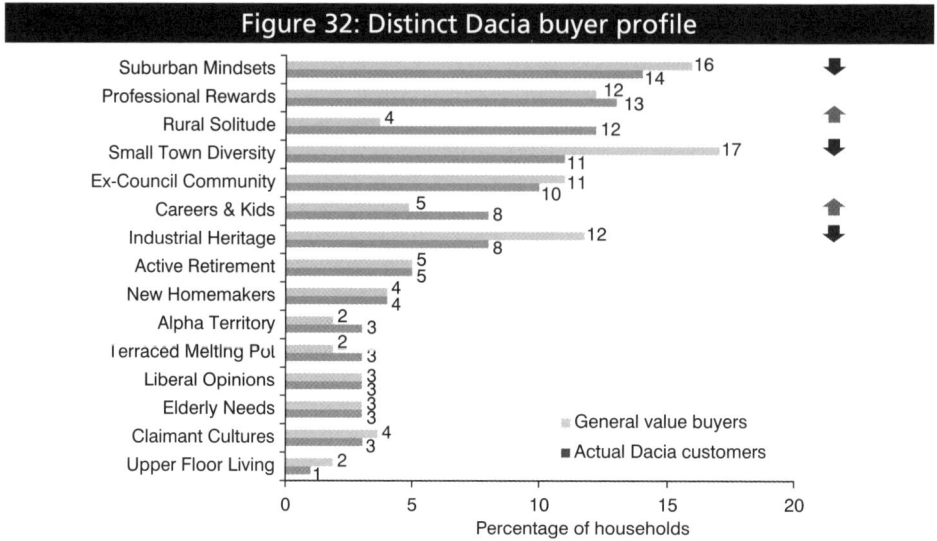

Source: MOSAIC, Renault UK

Indeed, it appears that sales didn't just come from other value brands, which continued to grow throughout 2013[20] (Figure 33).

### Figure 33: Dacia sales relative to competitors

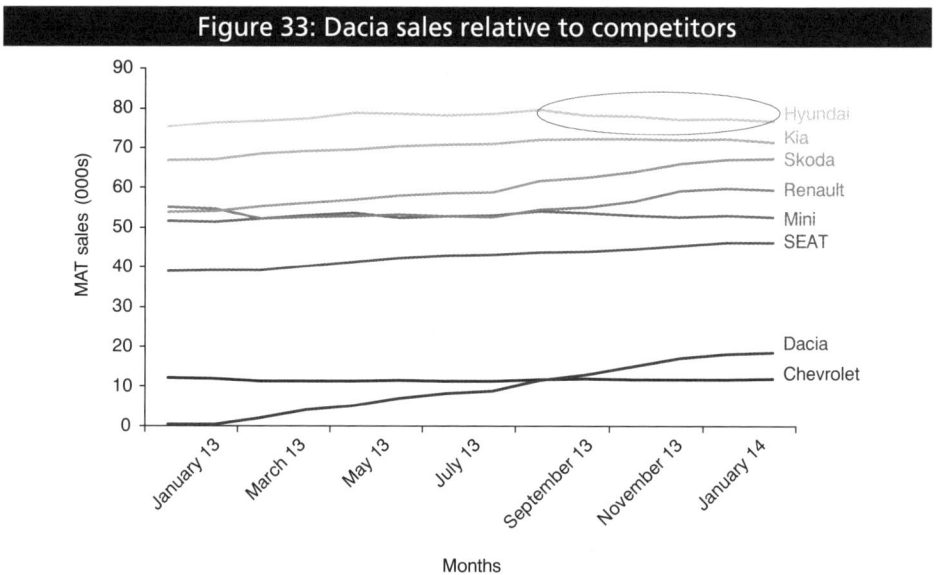

Source: Renault UK & SMMT

Instead sales have come from the used car market (a direct result of Dacia's used car media targeting). Our research shows that over a quarter[21] of Dacia owners actively set out to buy a used car but ended up buying a Dacia.

This result is corroborated with a decline in second hand car sales at the time of Dacia's launch (Figure 34).

## Figure 34: Decline in used car market sales

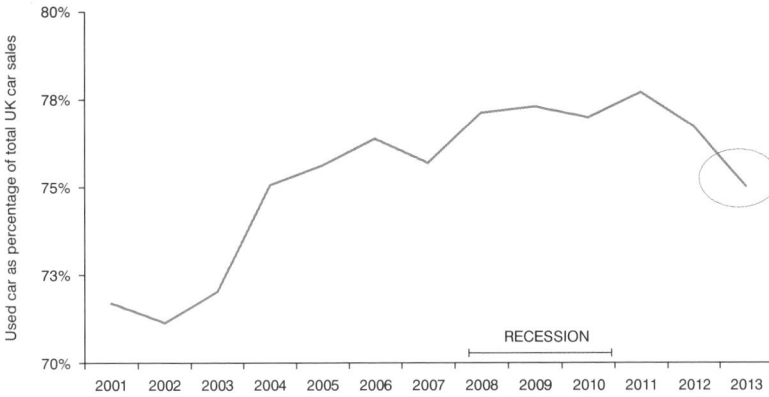

Source: SMMT

## Models with high support outperformed model with no support

Finally, we can see the impact of the media through the popularity of the models featured in the communications: Duster and Sandero. Both outperformed their respective category launch averages (Figure 35):

## Figure 35: Featured models outperform model not featured in advertising

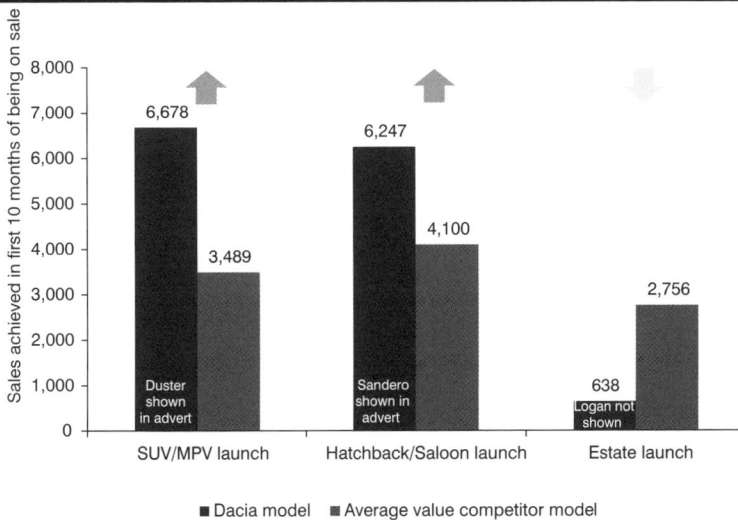

Source: SMMT

Whereas the model not featured in the main advertising (Dacia Logan) did not outsell its category average launch.

So we can conclude that the communications resonated with our target audience, were acted upon directly, attracted the desired consumer profile, and the models featured in the communications enjoyed greater sales success than the one that didn't.

In short, Dacia met all its objectives (Table 5).

## Table 5: Recapping the objectives

| Area | KPI | Detail | Met? |
|------|-----|--------|------|
| Business | Sales | 9,000 new car sales with 14,000 stretch target | YES |
| Marketing | Penetration | No more than 10% from current Renault customer base | YES |
| Communication | Brand awareness | 60% | YES |
| | Persuasion | Good brand image | YES |

## Eliminating other factors

Are there other factors that better explain the success of the launch?

The low price of Dacia was certainly important but it doesn't explain the whole success. The price differential between Dacia and the next lowest priced rival, Škoda, was matched in other European countries and yet the Dacia UK launch outstripped other European launches (see Figures 23 and 24). So the UK success isn't just because Dacia is cheaper than its competitors (Table 6).

## Table 6: Comparing price differentials

| Country | Dacia Duster Price 000€ | Skoda Yeti Price 000€ | Dacia price index |
|---------|------------------------|----------------------|-------------------|
| UK | 1.2 | 2.0 | 60 |
| France | 1.2 | 2.0 | 59 |
| Spain | 1.1 | 1.7 | 62 |
| Germany | 1.1 | 1.9 | 55 |

Source: www.Dacia.co.uk, www.Dacia.fr, www.Dacia.es, www.Dacia.de, www.Skoda.co.uk, www.Skoda.fr, www.Skoda.de, www.Skoda.es

Equally, the state of the UK economy doesn't explain Dacia's success. By the end of 2013, the economy was officially out of recession. However, our econometric modelling explains there's a negative relationship between value brand sector sales and GDP growth. So ending recession actually means that Dacia sales should tail off as consumer confidence grows.

We can also rule out the impact of recession in general. Dacia launched in other European markets in more austere times and didn't match the UK performance of 0.76% market share: Portugal launched in 2008 and achieved 0.3% market share in the first year; Sweden launched in 2009 and achieved 0.5%.

Neither can the success of the launch be attributed to SOV. As we've shown, Dacia's 2013 media spend was low compared to other marques.

Additionally, the success is not a result of market seasonality. We have seen that web visits and leads correlate highly with media spend, but the Dacia media strategy involved deliberately avoiding peak car advertising periods.

PR can't solely explain success either. From launch, Dacia cars, like other marques, have received their fair share of reviews in the press and on television. It's fair to say that most reviews have been positive. However, they have never been positive in the extreme – with many journalists giving the cars middling scores (Figure 36).

## Figure 36: Dacia Duster reviews

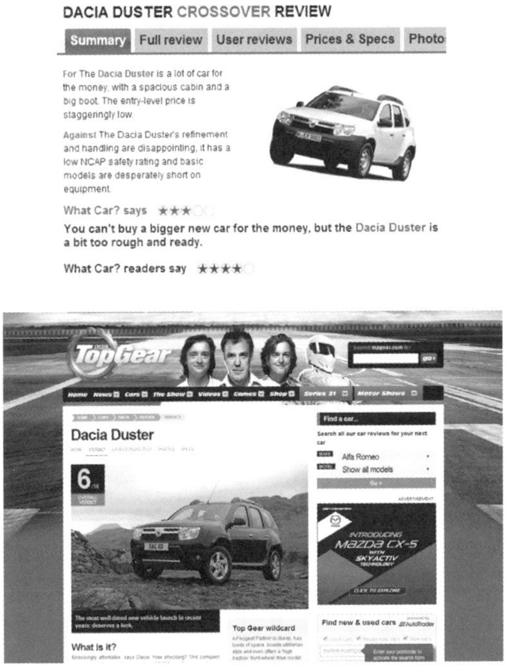

Source: www.whatcar.com , www.topgear.com

Was it Renault? Did the parent company influence results? Obviously Renault played a key role, however only 29% of Dacia customers say Renault's involvement strongly influenced their decision to buy a Dacia.[22]

Finally we can discount the impact of the value brand segment. Between 2008 and 2012 this segment of the market experienced 10% growth. Not including Dacia sales, the value segment continued to grow at the same rate (11%) in 2013.[23] There was no dramatic change for Dacia to ride the wave of. In fact, Dacia brought new people into this sector from the used car market – people who had previously been immune to the lure of value brands.

## Payback

Calculating a robust payback for a car brand that is only 15 months old is always going to be tricky. But when you also consider how important price is in driving Dacia sales, and the fact it launched with only three models (vs. an average of nine models for competitors), you realise this payback is doubly hard.

So the main payback figure we quote is obtained by modelling European Dacia market share, a tried and tested approach in car IPA papers. But we are still left with the problem of very few data points on UK performance. Therefore, we also ran a UK analysis to ensure our main ROI was not overestimated.

### Method 1: European analysis – main approach

We use econometrics to model annual market share across Europe. With this approach, we can reliably control for price in the media payback calculations, as Dacia has the same relative price across Europe. Our model takes account of the influence of the Renault parent brand, changes in the economy, changes in the Dacia price and the number of years since Dacia launched in each market. Ultimately this allows us to isolate the role of media in each of the countries.

All else being equal, the model finds that media has delivered almost twice as many sales per euro spent in the UK, as the average European market.

If we consider this average European payback as a base level of media effectiveness[24] and only attribute the incremental sales to the UK communications planning, we see the 'You do the maths' campaign created around 4,400 sales.

We are unable to provide the actual price paid for a model, so we have used a conservative unit price of £8,220.[25] This shows we delivered a very respectable revenue ROI of 4.1 in the UK. Due to confidentiality, we are unable to disclose profit margins (Table 7).

### Table 7: ROI method 1

| | 2013 |
|---|---|
| Total incremental sales (from model) (000s) | 8.6 |
| Incremental sales over and above European average (000s) | 4.4 |
| Revenue (@£8,220 less VAT per car) (£m) | 29.9 |
| Media + production (£m) | 7.3 |
| Revenue ROI in year one (over and above average European payback) | 4.1 |

### Method 2: UK analysis – sense check

In this method we look at UK model sales, to take account of the differences in size of range between competitors. We go some way to eliminate the role of price, as we only consider 'value' brands, but it can't fully account for the role that price has played.

We've compared the average sales a new model achieves in year one with how much was spent supporting that launch in year one. It shows a very strong correlation: the line of best fit tells us that, on average, you achieve 1,000 sales in year one for every £1.3m spent on media (Figure 37).

## Figure 37: UK model sales and media spend

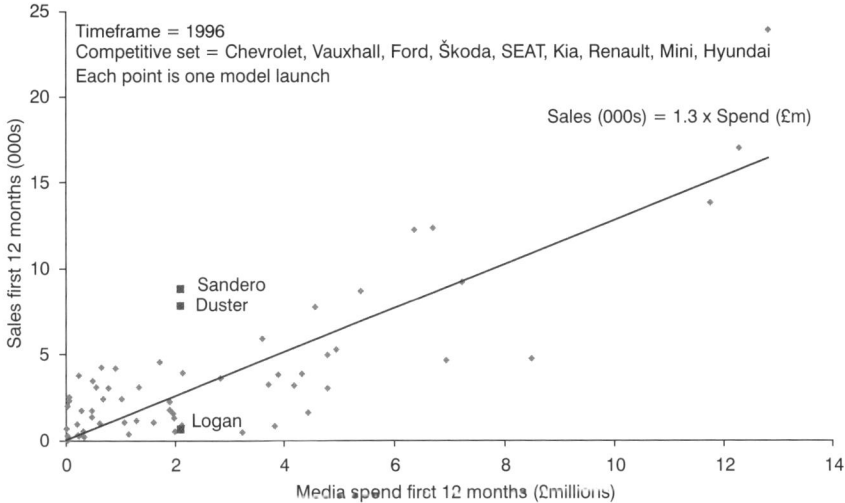

Timeframe = 1996
Competitive set = Chevrolet, Vauxhall, Ford, Škoda, SEAT, Kia, Renault, Mini, Hyundai
Each point is one model launch

Sales (000s) = 1.3 x Spend (£m)

Source: SMMT & MxPlorer

From this equation we can estimate the launch payback for Dacia and compare it to the payback a UK 'value' car manufacturer would expect to achieve.

This approach tells us that Dacia should only have made 9,100 sales (based on its media investment in year one). This suggests that the media campaign *could* have accounted for 8,000 incremental sales. This is higher than the payback obtained in the first approach, so we feel comfortable that the European analysis isn't overestimating the payback in any way (Table 8).

## Table 8: ROI method 2

|  | 2013 |
| --- | --- |
| Expected Dacia sales total (000s) | 9.1 |
| Actual sales (000s) | 17.1 |
| Total incremental sales (000s) | 8.0 |
| Revenue (@£8,220 less VAT per car) (£m) | 54.8 |
| Media + production (£m) | 7.3 |
| Revenue ROI in year one (over and above average UK model launch payback) | 7.5 |

*Long term*

It's worth noting that neither of these payback calculations takes account of the longer term revenue impact. Assuming that Dacia owners follow a similar pattern of loyalty to other Renault owners, then at least 35% will go on to repurchase another Dacia car. This would boost the revenue figures higher and deliver increased payback – as well as a platform for the future stability of Dacia in the UK.

Furthermore, 96%[26] of Dacia owners would recommend Dacia to a friend, so the media driven sales will carry on reaping their reward through brand advocacy.

## Conclusion

After achieving its sales targets and fulfilling its part role in Renault's long term recovery plan, there was one final hurdle to overcome: persuading the Top Gear crew that Dacia is a credible player in the UK car market.

So it's fitting to note that in episode 3 of series 21, James May elected to drive a Dacia across Ukraine in a Top Gear challenge. Of all the small cars available to choose from, he trusted the Sandero more than any other to get him across the entire breadth of the country and through the still radioactive zone of Chernobyl.[27] Dacia has gone from being a joke to the smart choice. Good news, indeed, Jeremy!

## Notes

1   Renault UK was unable to disclose profit margins.
2   SMMT, 2012.
3   WARC IPA Effectiveness Award 2002, 'It's a Škoda Honest – the profitable return on brave communication'.
4   *The Mirror*, February 2000.
5   The sales target is derived from average performance of previous UK model launches (across all 'value' competitors). Renault's aim was to re-enter the top 10 best-selling car manufacturers. To do this, Dacia would need to achieve a stretch target of 14,000 new car sales in year one.
6   Research project among new car buyers (Simpson Carpenter, 2013).
7   From *The Culture Code*, Clotaire Rapaille, Crown Business 2006.
8   E.g. Kia and Hyundai sponsor the World Cup and Ford have been Premier league sponsors for more than twenty years.
9   Autocar.co.uk, January 2014.
10  Autoexpress.co.uk, January 2014.
11  SMMT, Jan 2013 to December 2013.
12  Latest data point is March 2014 (SMMT).
13  Average models for Dacia plotted against average competitor model sales from month one of launch, for the first 13 months.
14  March 2014 is latest data point available.
15  Source: Renault Group survey Apr 2014. The question was: '8. Do you recall ever having seen a Dacia ad?'. The base was 2,168 Dacia owners.
16  Source: TNS Brand Tracking Survey 2013.
17  We are aware that this doesn't imply causality but is still strong evidence that Dacia customers bought as a result of the media.
18  Source: Renault Group survey April 2014. The question was: '9. On a scale of 1–5 (1= very unappealing, 5=very appealing), to what extent did it appeal to you?' The base was 2,168 Dacia owners scoring 3, 4, 5.
19  We needed to take the market share into account because of the relationship between brand size and ad awareness (Rosser Reeves Fallacy – https://www.warc.com/Blogs/Mythbuster_The_Rosser_Reeves_Fallacy.blog?ID=1805).
20  The exception to this was Hyundai.

21  A share of 26% of Dacia customers were looking to buy a second-hand car. Source: Renault Group survey Apr 2014. The question was: 'When you purchased your Dacia, were you mainly looking to purchase a new car or a second-hand car?'. Base is 2,168 Dacia owners, scoring 1–5.
22  Source: Renault Group survey Apr 2014. The question was: '10. On a scale of 1–10 (1 = not at all, 10 = entirely), to what extent did the fact that Renault owns Dacia affect your decision to buy a Dacia car?'. The base was 2,168 Dacia owners scoring 9 or 10.
23  SMMT annual registration data.
24  We do this, on the assumption that price still plays a role in the communication success as, unlike the UK, most European creative focuses on the low price point.
25  The entry price weighted by sales across the models.
26  Source: Renault Group survey Apr 2014. The question was: '7. On a scale of 1–10 (1 = very unlikely, 10 = very likely), how likely is it that you would recommend Dacia to a colleague or friend?'. The base was 2,168 Dacia owners.
27  'Top Gear', BBC, 2014.

# McCain Ready Baked Jackets

## A hot potato

**By Rebecca Clay, PHD Media**
Contributing author: Simon Harwood, PHD Media

Consumers love the taste of an oven-baked potato but they take far too long to make. Looking to capitalise on this opportunity, McCain developed an oven-baked jacket potato which was ready from frozen in just five minutes in the microwave.

McCain found that consumers currently either compromised on time by having to wait over an hour for an oven-baked jacket or compromise on taste by having to microwave a fresh potato. However, one of the biggest barriers to uptake was that consumers felt the new product was simply too good to be true, that a compromise had to have been made somewhere. Our strategy consisted of three key strands:

- Driving appetite appeal
- Driving trial 'tasting is believing'
- Harnessing the power of advocacy.

Consumers' taste expectations of this product were low, driven by general negative associations with pre-prepared and microwaved food. Research showed that driving appetite appeal around the product would help to counter this. It wasn't enough to just tell lots of people, we also needed them to understand and desire the product. Media selection was driven by what would make its audience salivate most, creating a genuine appetite for the product delivered at scale.

A post-9pm time was identified when a cynical audience would be much more open to the concept of a five-minute jacket; when it was too late to bake one from scratch for an hour in the oven, a significant amount of TV ads were therefore delivered at this time. To inject more salience into the outdoor campaign we incorporated over 20 large-format digital screens that switched on at 4pm each evening, targeting home-time.

During product trials, McCain saw significant shifts in agreement to the statements 'tastes really delicious' and 'tastes the same as a jacket made in the oven' after actually trying the product. Tasting really was believing, this led to a mass trial driving part of the launch plan which included couponing, promotions and digital media targeting shoppers at point of purchase.

The power of advocacy was highlighted for this product in concept testing. Positive recommendations and comments from those who had tried the product were shown to be more motivating to sceptics than advertising alone. Therefore a solid part of the launch plan harnessed this advocacy. PR coverage saw established food critics review the product and it was tested live on-air by Matthew Wright on Channel 5's *The Wright Stuff* and by Holly Willoughby and Philip Schofield on ITV's *This Morning* – all reacting positively. All of this positive sentiment worked hand-in-hand with the paid-for advertising to encourage a cynical audience to give the product a try.

Finally, one part of the campaign was devised to capitalise on all of the insight gathered. A larger than life size McCain Jacket Potato was built into a bus shelter. This was designed to drive appetite appeal and trial by incorporating multi-sensory elements and couponing. At the press of a button consumers were able to smell and feel the warmth of a freshly cooked jacket as well as collect a 50p-off coupon. This was the first campaign of its kind in the UK. The special bus stop executions captured public imagination and proved a phenomenal success. Over a two-week period 27,000 coupons were distributed, and earned media that they generated was huge. The story was picked up by over 140 publications including *The Sun* and *The Guardian*.

Kantar Worldpanel heralded McCain Ready Baked Jackets as the most successful FMCG launch of 2012. Penetration rocketed by 52% after the first month of advertising and after six months the product had already reached 12.7% penetration equating to 3.3m UK households. By December 2012 cumulative penetration had reached 15.6% with the product having been bought by 4.1 million households. This beat the Year 1 target by 50%.

# Sensodyne Pronamel

## Gaining and maintaining a first-mover advantage: the launch of Sensodyne Pronamel

**By Rachel Walker, Grey London**

Contributing authors: Lucy Jameson, Grey London; Claire Taylor, MediaCom Business Science; Matthew Gladstone and James Appleby, Grey London; Mita Shaha, GlaxoSmithKline

In 2006 and 2007 GlaxoSmithKline (GSK) faced a number of challenges when launching Sensodyne Pronamel toothpaste in the UK and US to combat Acid Wear. First, this was a new category, so the brand took the risk of being a first mover and had the arduous task of raising consumer awareness (which was virtually non-existent) about the condition. This condition had become more prevalent over recent years because of the rise in healthy eating, with many healthy foods and drinks in modern diets being acidic.

Communication challenges included the fact that dentists weren't telling their patients about Acid Wear, that people thought they were doing enough already when it came to oral hygiene, and that the product was premium priced.

So GSK needed to simultaneously achieve multiple objectives: create condition awareness, educate about causes, help consumers identify with the problem, and establish Sensodyne Pronamel as the solution.

Campaign Phase 1 ran from 2006 to 2009 with the main objective to raise condition awareness. The brand communicated directly to dentists, who would become crucial allies passing on our messages to their patients. Once this groundwork was begun, consumers became the main target through a media campaign. Spearheaded by TV activity in the style of a public health announcement which put dentists at its heart, it was accompanied by long-copy print ads which gave consumers hints for starting conversations with their dentist on the subject. Communications included a 'Torch Test' – this visually demonstrated what only dentists can see in the early stages of Acid Wear – thin and translucent enamel.

While GSK had the market to itself, it built awareness of this initially invisible condition of Acid Wear. However by 2009 rival brands began to offer their own enamel-care products. GSK used its greater consumer understanding to good effect, spotting three opportunities to protect and cement their lead: become more relevant; become more targeted; and embrace people's love of healthy foods. It achieved this with the help of a segmentation study which identified a sizeable group of 'Healthy Balancers' who have healthy diets and lifestyles and are highly engaged in oral health. To increase the relevancy of its message, TV ads now included real consumers, reinforcing the news that healthy diets high in, for example, citrus fruits can cause Acid Wear. However it evolved to reach 'healthy balancers' at relevant times, whilst considering or consuming acidic foods or drinks – in and around gyms, in aisles of acidic food and drink in supermarkets, and in relevant lifestyle press.

The campaign was a clear success, on both sides of the Atlantic. With 2013 penetration levels at 6% and 7% in the UK and US respectively, 10 million people in these two countries alone are now less likely to experience the effects of Acid Wear.

Dentists found it helpful and were influenced by it, it was noticed by consumers – ad awareness reached peaks of 42% in the UK, and 35% in the US – and consumers say advertising encouraged them to buy in the category for the first time. Deeper UK research revealed the campaign's communication was clear with up to 95% agreeing the advertising was easy to understand, while up to 96% appreciated that Sensodyne Pronamel helped protect teeth against Acid Wear.

Additionally, econometrics from MediaCom UK reported the UK campaign contributed approximately 30% to the total revenue of the Sensodyne Pronamel brand and helped launch the Enamel Protect category, worth over £32m in the UK. Away from the UK and US, positive progress has been made globally, with 2.6% value share, and 1.3% volume share of the global toothpaste market, despite a staggered launch over three years between 2010 and 2013.

# Kärcher UK

## Transforming a business by making the UK's most hated chore fun

**By Phil Springall, Kärcher UK; Sotiris Migkos, Holmes & Cook**

Contributing author: Louise Cook, Holmes & Cook

Alfred Kärcher's focus is on exterior cleaning, so sales are highly seasonal. In 2011 pressure washers accounted for 87% of Kärcher's UK home and garden turnover, though this was starting to suggest vulnerability as much as success.

Kärcher had developed an innovative interior cleaning product – the Window Vacuum – designed to make window cleaning effective and effortless. It had been launched in France and Germany in 2011 with a small amount of media support and been modestly successful, but these were markets with much greater awareness of Kärcher, both also ranking Kärcher as first choice brand for electrical cleaning products. In the UK, Kärcher was not even in the top five in 2012. Therefore the ultimate business objective was to create a new and sustainable product category, which would reduce the reliance on pressure washers. The target for Year 1 was to sell 300,000 Window Vacs which would represent 15% of Kärcher's total turnover. Communications therefore needed to build both awareness of Window Vac's existence and a clear understanding of what it offered – streak-free windows with minimal effort.

Focus groups carried out in November 2011 provided some key insights into issues the advertising should address. Shine PR found window cleaning to be the most consistently hated cleaning task and, because it was so difficult to get an expert finish, 75% of UK households actually outsourced their window cleaning. Cleaning windows with a Window Vac needed to appear effortless and enjoyable and this was achieved with a battle of the genders in a TV ad.

The qualitative research showed that the target audience cleaned their windows in spring with a major trigger being the move to British summer time. The shock of seeing a winter's worth of grime in broad daylight goaded many into action.

There were several ways to reach the female ABC1C2 30+ target, but only £951,000 with which to do so. The impact had to be visual and strong enough to influence not just consumers, but also retailers. The strategy was to condense the TV into a four-week period from March 2012 with the 30-second ad appearing in hand-picked peak programming from Wednesday to Sunday each week mirroring footfall uplifts in key retailers. Press, radio, online and VOD were used to provide more detail and increase OTS. Press was highly targeted via niche magazines and supported by digital advertising. Radio was timed to reach consumers in their cars or at the weekend, when they were most likely to be visiting outlets which stocked Window Vac.

The success of this first burst of activity, notably the effectiveness of TV, led to three further TV bursts in 2012 and 2013. As soon as TV aired in 2012, sales responded enthusiastically, to the extent that Kärcher risked investing part of the pressure washer budget (held over due to the hosepipe ban) behind Window Vac. From selling an average of 1,600 units per week, Kärcher sold an average of 17,300 over the 10 weeks on air. This was equivalent to a weekly turnover of £865,000 at RSP. An entire year's target of 300,000 units had been exceeded by the end of May. As a result of its outstanding success in 2012, Window Vac was allocated two further bursts of TV in April and September 2013. From launch to October 2013 when the models were last updated, Window Vac had sold 830,000 units, over 80% of these directly attributable to the campaign. Sales to date are 1.024m units. Window Vac's success has transformed Kärcher's business. In 2011, 87% of Kärcher's revenue derived from outdoor products. In 2013 it was almost evenly split indoor and outdoor, reducing the risk of poor summer weather ruining the whole year's sales.

# SECTION 7

# Content

# Advertising ideas versus ideas worth advertising: is content the new weapon of choice?

**By Kevin Sutherland**
Strategy Director, Seven

In 2014, for the first time, many of the IPA Effectiveness Award entries are content-led, based around an *entertainment* or *service* idea rather than an *advertising* idea.

Take Mercedes-Benz, who changed the entire body language of the brand to tackle its image as 'the stuffy one in the prestige sector' and the 'choice of the older driver'. It took more than just a strong advertising idea to shift the entrenched perception that the brand was 'balm' in a sector where buyers are looking for excitement. Rather than Mercedes simply *saying* something new, a series of campaigns changed the entire *behaviour* of the brand and built momentum via mass interactive experiences and smart, real-time execution. As a result, the perceived age of a Mercedes driver has dropped and sales grew by over 45%.

Or Mattessons, who successfully advertised via social media a meat snacking brand, Fridge Raiders, and effectively built a new snacking category. The agency identified a core target audience of after-school gamers for the product but recognised that traditional advertising wouldn't work with them. As the 2011 Deloitte Shift index quoted in their entry says:

> *[younger consumers] generally rely less on brand names as an indicator of product reliability, turning instead to the internet for product and service information, user reviews and feedback.*

Or Deutsche Telekom AG, that retained the market-leadership spot in Germany from Vodafone (which had near-identical products and tariffs), not with a traditional campaign but through innovative content that let people experience the innovations of mobile internet, and share it.

These examples, plus others in this section and elsewhere in this book are truly diverse in strategy, concept and execution. Budgets, in particular, range from multi-million pounds to hundreds of thousands of dollars. However, each goes further than the traditional advertising-led campaign approach, by incorporating content marketing to prove that the brand promise stands up. And each has delivered the rigour and the results we expect to see from an IPA winner: strong, clear evidence of how content-led ideas achieve reach, engagement, brand impact and conversion. The results delivered are often greater than advertising-led ideas of the past, and many have been achieved at lower cost, further increasing ROMI.

## A new approach?

The only real surprise is that this development has taken this long. At the risk of undermining the hypothesis in the title of this chapter, content and content's role in brand communications isn't especially new.

The general consensus is that the first mainstream example of content marketing is 'The Furrow' launched in 1895 as a magazine by John Deere as a way of reaching, engaging and building a relationship with farmers. It is still going strong today, using multiple content formats across multiple channels.[1]

Or how about the now-famous Michelin Guides, originally published to inspire early motorists to try the finest dining across the country, incidentally speeding up the repurchase cycle as drivers naturally wore out their tyres en-route.

Or General Mills' Betty Crocker brand, which launched a national baking competition back in 1921 and ended up publishing a recipe book as a result. This was followed by the 'Betty Crocker Cooking School of the Airwaves', taking advantage of emerging platform of the wireless in the 1930s.[2] Help remains in the brand's DNA to this day and it continues to focus more on helpful, how-to videos for the most popular baking search-queries, rather than traditional advertising.

## A new weapon?

As the case studies here show, content-led ideas are incredibly impactful and effective. But content shouldn't be considered a weapon – unless you count something that only really works when people *choose* to spend time with it, or even pay for it, as a weapon.

The content-led campaigns featured in this section have not explored content as an additional paid-for revenue stream (perhaps because at present even established media owners are ad-funded). However as more and more media owners erect paywalls for access to their original, high-quality content we can perhaps expect to see brands exploring this to generate significant additional revenue streams.

There is historical precedent for paid-for content from brands, e.g. the Michelin Guides mentioned above and more recently Sainsbury's Magazine, which launched in 1993, retails for £1.80 and sells over 200,000 copies per month.[3] Both are great examples of content from brands that people will pay for.

So what is content? And why have so many of this year's entries been content-led?

## Defining content

*Content Marketing is the only marketing that's left.*

Seth Godin

*Social media – the thing that killed everything – is now itself officially dead. It is survived by its twin brother, Content.*

Bob Hoffman, *The Ad Contrarian*

The marketing community's customary desire to define and codify extends to content and, as the two quotes above demonstrate, there are clearly deeply held and differing points of view.

However, much of the surrounding debate – even amongst those who are pro-content – is like listening to Monty Python's People's Front of Judea splitting hairs with the Judean People's Front. So let's consider the views of the leading content-marketing associations in the UK and US:

*Content marketing is a marketing technique of creating and distributing valuable, relevant and consistent content to attract and acquire a clearly defined audience – with the objective of driving profitable customer action.*

Content Marketing Institute (US)

Nothing controversial in that but simply switch the word 'content' for 'advertising' in the quote above and it's not really clear how this definition helps to distinguish between an advertising idea and something content-led.

The UK Content Marketing Association goes further:

*Content marketing is the discipline of creating quality branded editorial content across all media channels and platforms to deliver engaging relationships, consumer value and measurable success for brands.*

Content Marketing Association (UK)

Note the reference to 'editorial' as a distinction from an 'advertising' approach to delivering success for brands.

For now, perhaps the best, and simplest, articulation of content comes from Sainsbury's Marketing Director, Sarah Warby, who says:

*Sainsbury's promise to help you Live Well for Less. The role of content is to evidence that. Content is stuff that people choose to spend time with [so] it's got to be entertaining, useful or teach them something. Preferably all three.*

So, content is stuff people choose to spend time with. It has editorial thinking at its heart, it's the stuff that makes the brand promise believable, achievable and real, and it needs to deliver real utility by being either entertaining or useful.

## What's driving the change?

In a word, people.

1.  People doing things in subtly but significantly different ways, embracing new devices, channels and platforms as they come along.[4]
2.  People having higher expectations of the brands they choose to do business with. Not just in the things they say, or the way they say it, but how they behave. It's for this reason that so many of the IPA Effectiveness Award entries this year talk about transparency, authenticity, and the effort to engage in legitimate conversations. As stated above, this isn't about deploying a new weapon. To stick with the military analogy, it's about winning hearts and minds.[5]
3.  People expecting more from their interaction with brands. Advertising in all its various forms has always been a value exchange: here is something useful or entertaining to encourage you to watch, read or listen to, and, in return, here is what we would like you to know, to think or do. Content is the same, only more so. Because we are usually asking for *more* of someone's time and attention. The vocabulary of marketing has for so long been focused on value for *money*. With content, in all its forms, brands have got to deliver value for *time* and value for *attention* too.[6]

## Advertising so good, it's a service

And why not? As our historical examples show, there's a long history of brands providing both entertainment and utility (or both). Many of this year's entries continue that tradition, with the user-generated and user-inspired movies from both Sainsbury's in the UK and Deutsche Telekom in Germany, both achieving critical reviews and audience numbers as good as, if not greater than, contemporary mainstream cinema releases. But success relies on more than just the quality, originality and relevance of the content idea. Maybe that's why the film industry, the news industry and the TV industry spend so much time advertising their high-quality editorial content.

The idea that content marketing's reach and engagement could be achieved organically, simply due to the relevance and quality of the content, is naïve – especially in light of recent algorithm changes and the social networks' evolution into fully-fledged ad networks.

Then there is a problem that at our agency we call the infinite content continuum: the sea of content from media owners old and new, from users and increasingly from brands grows at a phenomenal rate *every day*. So, without advertising support, the chances of someone finding, liking and sharing your idea is minimal, negligible, even if you are a brand that has built a significant following already.

Hence the title of the chapter: these are not ideas that replace the need for advertising. They are ideas that deserve to be advertised. Because the audience gets more than they can from just brand and product advertising alone: entertainment, education, usefulness. By getting this right, brands are delivering advertising as a service, not just an interruption.

## Fad or permanent shift?

So much has been written, researched, presented and blogged about in 2014 on the subjects of (brand) authenticity and transparency, and the need for a human-to-human or person-to-person approach to brand comms. Various research studies and benchmark indices have been developed.[78]

This month, in the fiftieth anniversary edition of *Admap*, Neil Dawson writes:

> *Brands must shift the focus ... from 'the invasion of privacy' to the exchange of value and trust, based on transparency, consent and 'trust in intent'.*[9]

Being more open, transparent and human is part of an ongoing journey that brands and their agencies have been on for some time. The step-change from advertising ideas to ideas worth advertising simply marks the latest stage in that journey.

This is, of course, easy to say but much harder to do for long-established brands and their agencies as it marks a significant shift from the brand comms model that both were built on. Even brands and agencies that are products of the era of digital and social media can find this a challenge.

For instance, in an article entitled 'The post-disruptive advertising era' in the same issue of *Admap*, Gareth Kay, partner at San Francisco agency Zeus Jones, argues that the language and approach of modern advertising, which aims to make brands appear more human, is not working. 'The disruptive advertising model has to change to help build brands that are more useful to humans', he asserts. That will require 'a reboot of the advertising model, one that understands that culture has changed, and with it how the brands of today are being built.

Whilst this is more than a passing fad, it's fiendishly difficult to achieve. The award winners in this section are the notable exceptions, examples of brands – and agencies – that are doing this well. So what are they doing? How are they getting it right?

## Common 'content' themes from this year's winners

The entries that are content-led are truly diverse, spanning the auto, telco, FMCG and retail sectors. They cover the UK, Ireland, Germany and Malaysia. Budgets range from the very large to very small, and yet there are observations about content that are common to most or all.

*Adopting a content-led approach inspires brands to rip up the rulebook and create unfair advantage.*

Deutsche Telekom realised that building sustainable market leadership relied on creating real distinctiveness for their brand. So, unlike Vodafone, which uses a traditional advertising approach to stir people's emotions, Telekom sought to break new ground. 'Life is for sharing' was more than just a strapline or a flat brand promise. It became a galvanising platform to let people *experience* the innovations of mobile internet and share that experience with others. (This is also typical of successful content-led ideas. They may be more multi-faceted and complex than the activation of most traditional advertising ideas, but each still ladders-up to a clear, unifying goal.)

### Content-led ideas rely on advertising to be successful.

It's true that many of the brands here were able to spend less on media than previously, but it was still an essential ingredient in the mix. Whether it was the trailers for Sainsbury's 'Christmas in a day' movie both on TV and online, or the real-time ads created by Mercedes, broadcast on ITV during *X-Factor* ad breaks – or even the cost of building 'Twisted Football' goals in public parks in Malaysia by choco-malt drinks brand Milo, all relied on the reach and momentum delivered by advertising or promotional spend. In short, there are no free rides. Or rather, a free ride only gets you so far.

### Content-led ideas require bravery.

Honesty, transparency, authenticity are all evident – in many examples it's true to say that the idea is far bigger than the brand. In contrast to the point above, it's about more than just advertising. People choosing to spend time with your content-led idea relies on it delivering value for time, value for attention. Sharing it demands even more: authenticity and cultural relevance. All of these brands, from Mattessons Fridge Raiders to Mercedes, achieved this by being honest about their internal and external challenges. Success came from focusing on real evidence and genuine insight about their audiences and from being obsessive about putting *their* wants and needs ahead of the brand priorities.

### Content-led ideas are rooted in emotional truths.

The link between emotional impact and ad effectiveness is well documented[10] and this extends to content and content-led ideas too. Even the more practical and functional ideas here had a strong emotional element in their success. For instance, Aldi's 'Swap and Save' is rooted in pure logic: the more you swap your shopping to Aldi, the more you save. And yet Aldi had a higher proportion of top-up or secondary shoppers than the market average due to concerns about limited range and emotional unease about what it says when you buy most of your shopping at a discounter. Cue a hugely successful content-led idea that showed the experience of 'people like me' shopping at Aldi, contributing to the brand's success as the fastest-growing supermarket in the UK and Ireland.

### Expert, editorial experience and cultural expertise is essential.

The content-led ideas here relied on significant input from true content and cultural experts. Each of the brands relied on their agencies either having or hiring-in editorial expertise. Both Deutsche Telekom and Sainsbury's hired recognised Hollywood talent to give their films credibility, whilst Mattessons partnered with online gaming celebrity and YouTuber Tom Cassel. As the marketing director of a national brand said to me recently, he regards his job as being more like that of a newspaper editor than the historical marketing director role and readily admits that his training and experience hasn't prepared him for that. He therefore relies on editorial support from his content agency.

*Content-led campaigns can effectively measure and demonstrate significant ROMI.*

Historically, measuring content marketing effectiveness and ROMI has been difficult. There were three main reasons for this. First, many early content marketing initiatives (from customer magazines to microsites and email newsletters) were often not fully integrated with above the line brand campaigns. Therefore, the reach these activities achieved was often too small to be effectively tracked on brand trackers or via econometric analysis. Second, whilst it has increasingly been possible to isolate awareness and engagement metrics for content marketing activity, it has not always been possible to attribute or quantify its contribution to sales conversion. And third, in contrast to direct marketing, paid search, and OLA investment, the most effective content marketing, especially organic content in digital and social media, supports the customer journey but is not necessarily focused on delivering an immediate, observable direct response. What unites all of the case studies here is that content effectively is the campaign, or at least forms the greatest part of it. That, coupled with the significant reach achieved through an integrated approach and significant paid media investment, means that the performance data is detailed, transparent and ultimately attributable to the content-led activities in question.

## What does this mean for the brand, the CMO and agencies?

*Marketing can no longer be a brand's clothing. It must be its skin.*

Richard Eyre, Chair, IAB

As the case studies in this section prove, this is certainly the case for successful content-led ideas. Understandably this poses a big challenge for most brands, marketers and their agencies, as it requires significant change not just in what they say, but also where and how they say it. And it's not just a case of allocating budgets differently. For instance, the award entry for Sainsbury's 'Christmas in a Day' campaign lists 390 people who were involved in making it happen. This requires greater inter-departmental cooperation and agency collaboration, which often means evolving internal structures and external processes.

The brands here have embraced these changes, not just for a single campaign, but as part of a fundamental shift in the way they behave, the experiences they create for people to enjoy and the value for time they deliver. For instance, Mercedes talked about changing the brand's entire *body language*.

According to the winning case studies here this new content-led value exchange appears to be working. The results for ideas worth advertising speak for themselves.

## Notes

1  The Content Marketing Institute: contentmarketinginstitute.com/2012/02/history-content-marketing-storytelling
2  The Betty Story: http://www.bettycrocker.co.uk/the-betty-story
3  ABC Jan–June 2014
4  OFCOM: http://stakeholders.ofcom.org.uk/market-data-research/other/media-literacy/media-lit-research/adults-2013/

5  Google / Zero Moment of Truth: www.thinkwithgoogle.com/collections/zero-moment-truth.html
6  Seven / ISBA Converged Media 2013: http://blog.seven.co.uk/research/convergedmedia
7  FleischmanHillard / Lepere Analytics Authenticity Gap: http://lepereanalytics.com/authenticity-gap.html
8  Lippincott's Human Era Brand Index: www.lippincott.com/en/insights/welcome-to-the-human-era
9  www.warc.com/Topics/AdmapAt50.topic
10 Brainjuicer / IPA: http://www.brainjuicer.com/xtra/Research_Measuring_Emotion.pdf

# Mercedes-Benz

## How a change in body language transformed the fortunes of Mercedes-Benz

**By David Edwards and Ollie Gilmore, AMV BBDO**

Credited companies: Creative Agency, AMV BBDO; Media Agency, Maxus; Digital Agency, Digital Annexe; Digital Agency, Weapon7; Client, Mercedes-Benz

## Editor's summary

For decades, Mercedes-Benz's image was regarded as staid, sedate and conservative in the prestige sector, the choice of the older driver. However, with the introduction of personal contract purchasing in 2010 the entry cost for buying a car was significantly reduced. Mercedes therefore needed a brand refit to exploit this new opportunity.

They set out to attract younger drivers to help them break through the 100k sales mark, and because these drivers weren't visiting show rooms, decided to take the driving experience to them.

They used communications to provide mass, interactive experiences which restyled Mercedes as dynamic, jeopardous and stimulating. Each campaign saw improvements in efficiency and payback, and over three-and-half years, Mercedes has gone on to become the fastest-growing car brand in the prestige sector, registering a 45% increase in annual sales, a campaign ROMI of 1.11 and a new brand model fit to make considerable further gains.

**The judges appreciated the challenge in attracting a young audience whilst not alienating current buyers; the authors proved how a sustained shift in position could significantly reposition the brand to unlock significant growth.**

## Introduction

This is the story of how, over the last three and a half years, Mercedes has gone from being the 'stuffy' choice compared with Audi and BMW, to being the fastest-growing car brand in the prestige sector.[1]

With annual sales up 45% to more than 108,000 per year – and brand tracking figures reaching record heights – this is the story of how a change in 'brand body language' has made Mercedes unprecedentedly dynamic, exciting and profitable.

To explain how this has been achieved, we begin with the 'six-figure target'.

## Background: hitting 100,000

In 2010, Daimler AG outlined an ambitious objective for Mercedes in the UK: to increase annual sales from their current level of approximately 75,000 per year, to over 100,000, by the end of 2013.

This 'six-figure target' was considered a key developmental milestone for the UK business and held considerable symbolic value.

Achieving a 33% increase in sales, in just over three years, would require considerably accelerating sales growth – which at the time, was almost exactly flat – and competing more aggressively with the other two German prestige sector brands: BMW and Audi.

This would, in turn, require tackling a brand image problem that had plagued Mercedes for decades.

## Mercedes: the 'stuffy one' in the prestige sector

The prestige end of the car market is particularly driven by image concerns. Buyers of the German 'Prestige 3' (Mercedes, BMW, Audi) are most concerned with brand reputation and exterior styling/appearance (Table 1).

| Table 1: Most important factors in vehicle choice for prestige buyers | |
| --- | --- |
| Ranking in terms of importance | Factor in vehicle choice (Mercedes, BMW, Audi buyers) |
| 1 | Exterior styling / appearance |
| 2 | Reputation |
| 3 | General durability |
| 4 | Equipment level |
| 5 | Fuel consumption |

Source: NCBS 2012

This has presented a long-running problem for Mercedes, because for decades, its image has been that of 'the stuffy one' in the prestige sector: staid, sedate, conservative … the choice of the 'older driver'.[2]

There are numerous historical records of this perception. In the 1980s, cultural commentators saw BMW as the choice of 'dynamic trend-setters… to Mercedes-Benz trend-followers'.[3] The following decade, brand consultants noted that Mercedes 'needs to turn from being the reward after a successful career, to being a companion during it.'[4] Continuing the theme: after the turn of the millennium, research respondents were explaining that the problem with Mercedes is that 'it is a badge that says you've made it, but you're putting the brakes on.'[5]

In 2010, around the same time as the new business target was set, Mercedes commissioned updated research into the brand's image. The conclusion: little had changed. Mercedes drivers were considered rich and probably powerful, but also likely to be older and allegedly lacking the dynamism and excitement of BMW and Audi owners (Figure 1).[6]

## Figure 1: Summary of brand image problem, 2010

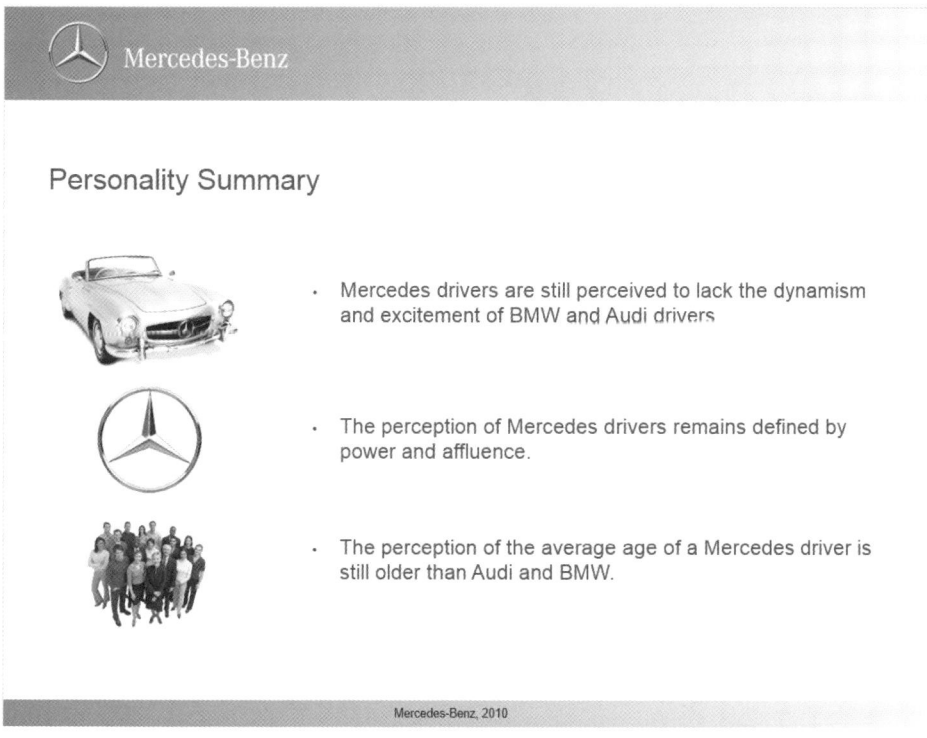

Mercedes-Benz

Personality Summary

- Mercedes drivers are still perceived to lack the dynamism and excitement of BMW and Audi drivers

- The perception of Mercedes drivers remains defined by power and affluence.

- The perception of the average age of a Mercedes driver is still older than Audi and BMW.

Mercedes-Benz, 2010

Reflecting this: Audi and BMW owners in research made this image board of Mercedes drivers (Figure 2):[7]

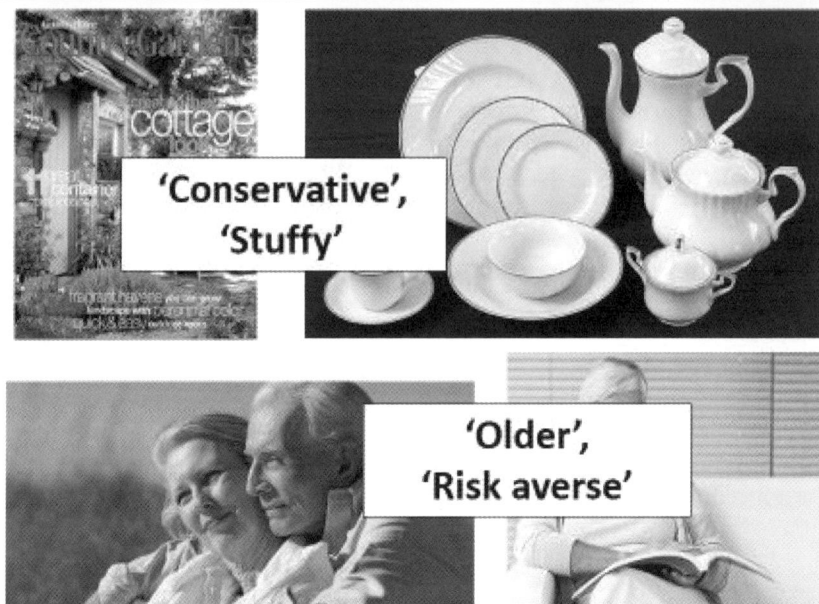

Figure 2: Driver image board

'Conservative', 'Stuffy'

'Older', 'Risk averse'

In short: the brand had an age-old problem of being too old-age.

This image problem would always have ramifications. But it was of particular concern at this point, because the UK car market was going to be transformed by a new type of payment plan.

## The cool guys in the prestige sector are about to become the rich guys in the prestige sector

Towards the end of 2010, UK car companies began widely introducing Personal Contract Purchase (PCP) plans. Under this system, buyers pay a small proportion of the car's cost up front, before paying a monthly fee (typically in the low hundreds of pounds) each month for the next three (or four) years. At the end of this period, they either pay the remaining sum to buy the car outright, or 'trade in' the equity gained to get a reduced price on an upgrade from the same manufacturer. The result? The entry cost for buying a car is significantly reduced.

PCP has not only helped keep the total UK car market buoyant, it has also – as predicted in 2010 – allowed more buyers to consider 'trading up' to the prestigious German marques. As it stood back then, these people would most likely turn to the supposedly more dynamic, exciting brands: Audi and BMW.

In sum: PCP now meant that even more was at stake.

So if ever there was a time for Mercedes to shed the image as the 'stuffy one' amongst the 'Prestige 3', this was it.

## The end of convention

We needed to do things differently. In assessing the brand's historic comms through the lens of some new research, it became apparent what should change.

First, Mercedes advertising in the UK had historically emphasised product quality, focusing on suspension systems, aerodynamic design and such-like (Figure 3).

**Figure 3: Historic 'product quality' advertising**

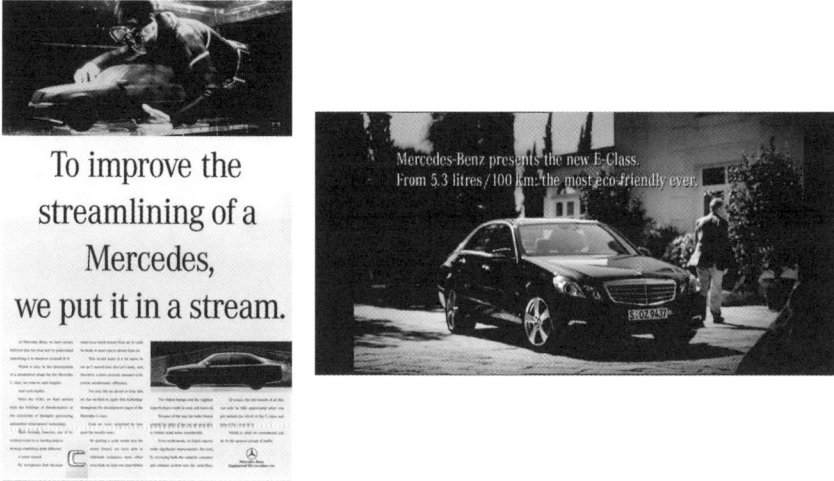

These ads failed to address the image problem and at worst reinforced an impression of exclusivity that exacerbated it.

Second, a lot of historic Mercedes advertising had talked about safety (Figure 4).

**Figure 4: Historic safety advertising**

Our research suggested this was having a negative effect. In recurring qualitative groups, we heard 30/40/50-something drivers proudly referencing jeopardy-laden experience to prove they were still spirited, daring and young(ish): adventure holidays, extreme sports, even risk-laden business deals. Despite – or more likely, because – reality was more humdrum, they wanted to be associated with a degree of jeopardy. And, even more stridently: they wanted other people to know about it.

Third, historic Mercedes advertising had emphasised the cars' ability to take away life's stresses. This implicitly positioned the brand as 'balm' (Figure 5).

### Figure 5: Historic stress-relief advertising

Fast effective relief from stress.

In contrast, we found that BMW and Audi drivers fondly talked about their brands as being 'sporty' and 'dynamic'. As above, these people had a desire for – or at least *wanted to give the impression they had a desire for* – objects/hobbies/brands that raised their pulses, rather than the other way.

The objectives are summarised in Figure 6.

### Figure 6: Campaign objectives

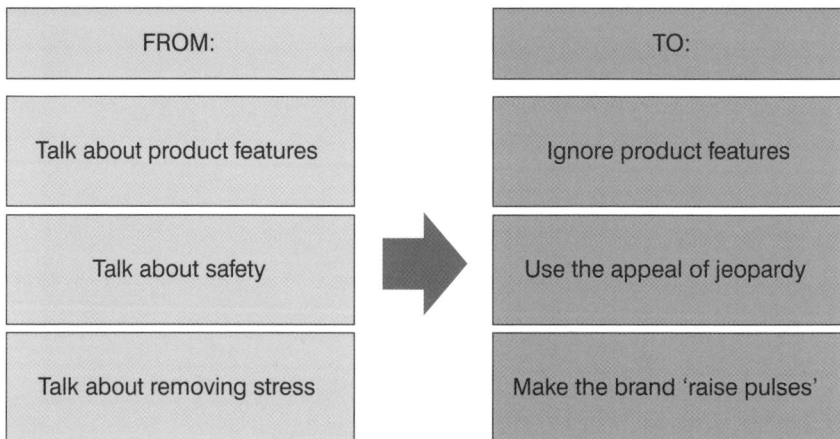

| FROM: | TO: |
|---|---|
| Talk about product features | Ignore product features |
| Talk about safety | Use the appeal of jeopardy |
| Talk about removing stress | Make the brand 'raise pulses' |

The move away from these three conventions was accompanied by a final, significant strategic shift.

## New 'body language' that encourages 'mass, interactive experience'

Historically, Mercedes comms had emphasised the brand's distinctiveness and separation – owning a Mercedes was portrayed like an 'otherworldly dream' (Figure 7).

### Figure 7: Historic 'dream' advertising

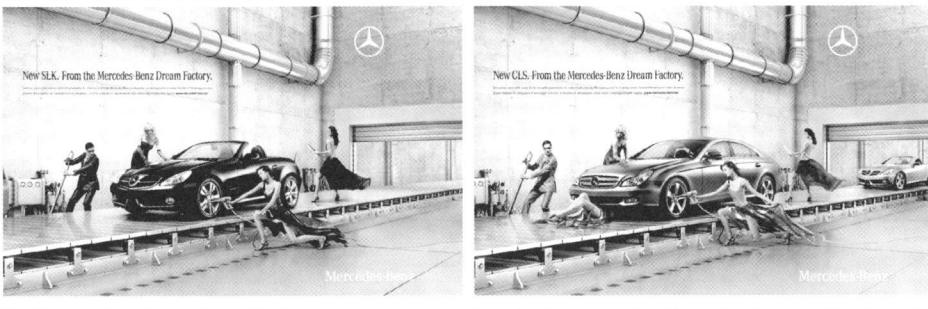

In media terms too, Mercedes had always been distinct and removed: adhering to traditional, non-interactive channels. We believed this should change. We felt Mercedes' 'brand body language' should now become much more accessible and interactive.

Consequently, we did not focus on developing a particular new advertising idea or evolving a certain art direction. That felt insufficient. We wanted to change the brand's *entire behaviour*.

More specifically: with insufficient people visiting Mercedes retailers, we now aimed to take a more exciting Mercedes experience to them.

This was a more open (and less stuffy) position for the brand to take. It also put the focus on *the experience* of Mercedes that people would be given, rather than a message.

This emphasis on experience reflected recent lessons from neuroscience (that behavioural change precedes attitudinal change) and age-old lessons from the dealership floor ('let them hear the engine roar… then see what they say').[8] In other words: create the environment, for the behaviour, that will change attitude.

This thinking had a set of media implications. It would mean putting the brand in unprecedented 'prime-time' environments, offering interaction to a mass audience. And it would mean embracing a range of interactive channels, that – as we come on to show – would ultimately shape campaigns in unprecedented ways.

Consequently, this strategy did not lead to a new advertising end-line. Instead, it articulated *a new role* for the brand's advertising defined in Figure 8.

**Figure 8: Role of brand advertising**

# Provide mass, interactive experience of Mercedes-Benz

The experience should feel:

- *Dynamic*
- *Jeopardous\**
- *Stimulating*

## Communications

From January 2011 onwards, the strategic thinking above was incorporated into Mercedes UK comms wherever possible. Below, however, we focus on the three biggest campaigns that have taken place during this period. There are a few reasons for this.

These campaigns were the biggest change in the '2011-onwards' world of Mercedes UK. A consistent 'bed-rock' of spend on tactical press and direct marketing continued as before, which continued to use Mercedes' European creative visuals.[9] But these campaigns were a clear change.

Equally, these campaigns are what distinguish Mercedes UK from the rest of Europe. And we'll later compare results across countries as evidence of the UK's comms effect.

More specifically: as we come on to show, there is considerable evidence that these campaigns specifically had the most impact in terms of achieving the image change objective.

The timing of these campaigns was as follows.

### Escape the Map (October 2011–March 2012)

We knew we'd need an audacious idea to challenge Audi and BMW driver's deeply entrenched view of Mercedes – an idea that would break the mould for both the category and the brand's communication and behaviour.

Our creative idea was to take a virtual driving experience – as a proxy for a test drive – to where young conquest drivers were spending their time, namely online and on mobile devices. The interactive 'test drive' turned participants into active protagonists in an online drama, designed to play out seamlessly across multiple interactive channels. Communications driving mass participation took the look and form of an action movie launch.

The interactive drama was centred around a character stuck within a dystopian parallel digital world. Encouraged by a promotional film that 'premiered' as a YouTube takeover before appearing in the X-Factor ad break, participants were invited online to take her car keys, solve various challenges and help her 'Escape the Map'. Participants were put in control of their own narrative experience, aided by interactive press and posters, as well as game-play-triggered phone calls direct to players' mobiles (Figure 9).

Figure 9: 'Escape the Map' creative

#### #YouDrive (October 2012–February 2013)

The success of 'Escape the Map' (covered in further detail, below) led us to take the principles of mass, interactive drama to another level.

Tapping into the existing dual-screen behaviour of our audience, #YouDrive was the world's first television commercial where social interaction drove broadcast action in real time.

The drama was an exciting cat and mouse caper during which a music superstar tries to evade police with the help of a female professional driver – and her Mercedes A-Class – in order to get to his secret gig. Sensation, danger, self-expression ... all within a framework that invited a mass audience to play.

Viewers were able to steer the story by tweeting the hashtag assigned to the action they'd prefer to see next. The nation's favourite plotline was played out in a subsequent ad break, eventually revealing a complete viewer-defined narrative (Figure 10).

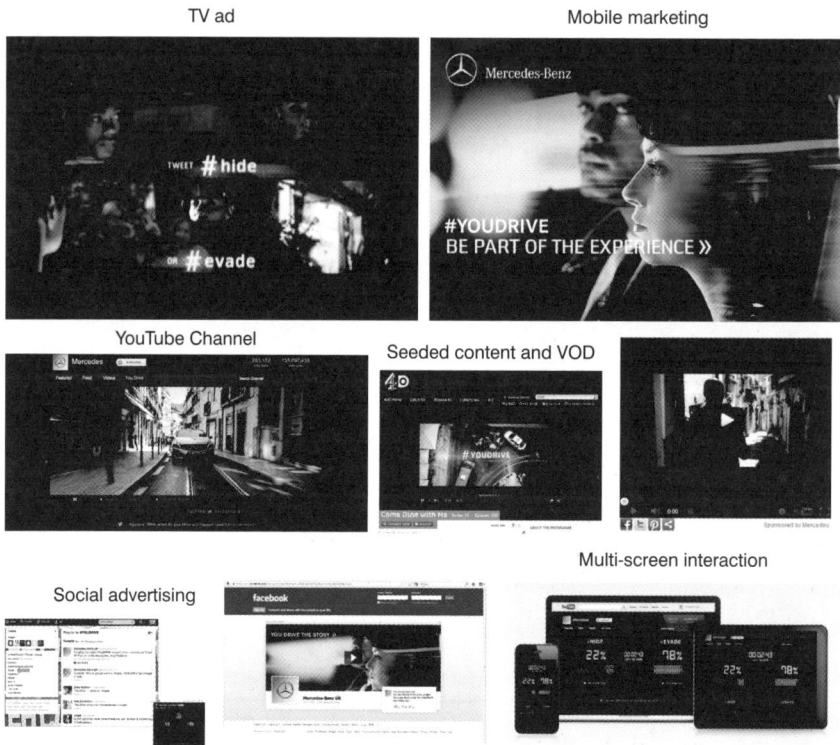

Figure 10: '#YouDrive' creative

There is no automated connection between social networks and broadcasters, but we wanted to give active participants and passive viewers alike a visceral sense of dynamism and jeopardy. And that would mean real-time response. So a team from AMV sat at ITV to aggregate voting via Twitter and manually input real-time dynamic data into the 'winning' ad revealing the percentage who voted for each chosen option.

This was the 'decision architecture' – put another way: a rather unconventional TV media plan (Figure 11).

## Figure 11: '#YouDrive' decision architecture

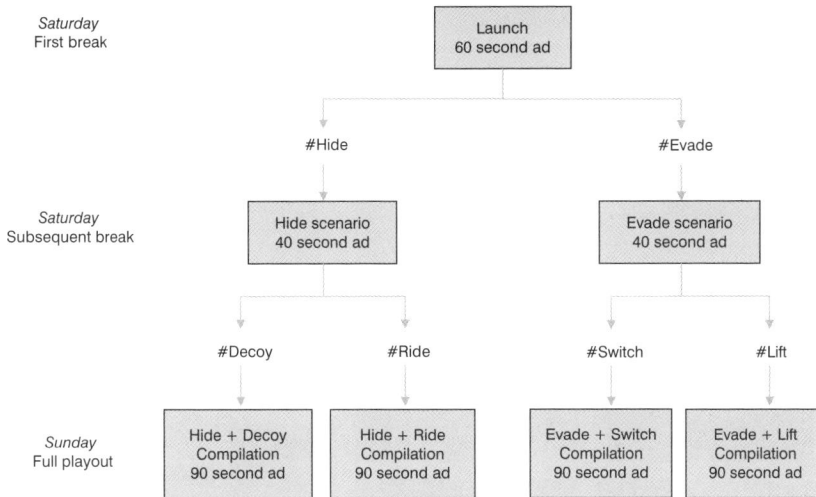

*Saturday First break* — Launch 60 second ad

#Hide · #Evade

*Saturday Subsequent break* — Hide scenario 40 second ad · Evade scenario 40 second ad

#Decoy · #Ride · #Switch · #Lift

*Sunday Full playout* — Hide + Decoy Compilation 90 second ad · Hide + Ride Compilation 90 second ad · Evade + Switch Compilation 90 second ad · Evade + Lift Compilation 90 second ad

Over the following weeks, alternative endings were broadcast, and people were invited online to create their own versions of the story-line, using unseen footage.

### Sound with Power (October 2013–February 2014)

'Sound with Power' made stimulating sensation its centre-point. Building on Mercedes' evidence – found through biometric testing – that the sound of their cars instantly provokes a strong emotional and physical response in drivers, this campaign aimed to demonstrate how powerful sounds can trigger emotions.

But in keeping with our principles, we didn't want to simulate the experience. So, we invited people to play with the emotive power of sound first-hand.

We created an interactive 'mash-up' tool – available on desktop, tablet or mobile – that allowed users to build, layer upon layer, their own personal audio and video 'mash-up' using a range of sounds but all featuring the exhaust notes and other sonic elements of the E63 AMG. The sound bites were specifically chosen for enabling self-expression and their ability to stimulate an emotional response in the end user. Users were then invited to share their 'mash-up' on social networks, using #soundwithpower, for a chance to have their version air on TV.

This was launched with a unique TV campaign showing the real responses of one man to a variety of emotionally resonant sounds. Wearing a specially adapted suit which lights up in response to physical and neurological reactions, the viewer sees how this man reacts to a 'mash-up' of sounds, before being invited to create their own (Figure 12).

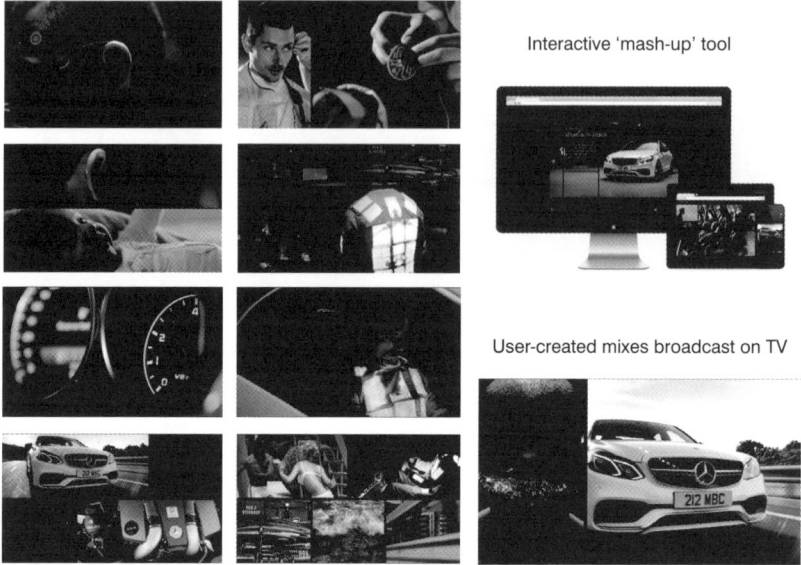

Figure 12: 'Sound with Power' creative

Launch TV ad

Interactive 'mash-up' tool

User-created mixes broadcast on TV

*Comms summary*

Mercedes' business objective was to be selling 100,000 cars annually in the UK, by 2013. To help achieve this, our communications aimed to challenge the long-running perception that Mercedes is the 'stuffy' choice in the prestige sector. We did this by making the role of our communications to provide mass, interactive experiences of Mercedes. These experiences were intended to feel dynamic, jeopardous, stimulating.

We will now go on to show how this approach has paid back for the business.

## Sales results

The most important months of the year for car retailers are March and September, when sales typically peak with new registrations. Mercedes' figures for these 'bi-annual moments of truth' have got increasingly strong. During the last one referenced in this study – September 2013 – monthly sales reached 21,112, continuing an accelerating ascent seen since that start of 2011 – with the implementation of the new comms approach (source: Mercedes-Benz UK, 2011–14).

In turn, Mercedes' annual volume sales are now 45% higher than they were in 2010. As a result, the target of 100,000 annual sales was surpassed last year. Looked at in the context of annual sales results for some preceding years, the marked change in trajectory is evident (source: Mercedes-Benz UK, 2008–14).

This success is out-pacing the growth of competitors. If we index Mercedes' sales against the average of competitors BMW and Audi from the start of 2011, it is evident that during the peak registration periods, Mercedes is growing at a faster rate, with the gap widening over time (source: Mercedes-Benz UK, 2011–14).

Consequently, Mercedes has grown its share of the prestige car market. This metric was affected in 2011 when Audi entered the smaller, cheaper, mini-segment with the A1 – a car that neither BMW or Mercedes had (or have) a direct competitor with.[10] Despite this, Mercedes' share of this sector is now set to be exactly 4 percentage points greater at the end of 2014, than it was in 2010. At current market volumes, this is equivalent to 17,454 cars in a single year. At Mercedes' current average price, this is equivalent to £606,226,085 in extra revenue (source: Mercedes-Benz UK, 2010–14).

And for greater context, this success now means that Mercedes is set to achieve 5% share in the total car market. An achievement that seemed a long way off in 2010 (source: Mercedes-Benz UK, 2010–14).

## Demonstrating the contribution of communications

The contribution of communications to this success can be seen in a number of ways.

### Campaigns have achieved the objective of being 'mass, interactive experiences' and generated significant interaction with the brand

Campaign metrics are of course not evidence of revenue, or commercial effectiveness. However, a snapshot of campaign metrics indicates their success as 'mass, interactive experiences' and shows that significant levels of interaction with the brand (beyond just the campaign) were an almost immediate result.

This is evident in Table 2.

### Table 2: High levels of consumer interaction with major campaigns

**Escape the Map**

- 838,441 people visited the campaign website.
- Visits to the Mercedes website during the campaign rose to four times their monthly average, in a single day.

**#YouDrive**

- 3.8 million people visited the YouDrive YouTube channel in the first three weeks of the campaign.
- More than 40,000 people engaged with the #YOUDRIVE during the Saturday evening launch event. As a benchmark, 312,000 people tweeted about the X Factor itself during the same period.

**Sound with Power**

- 354,219 visits to the website in first three months of campaign.
- Record 'online engagement' (including all likes, shares, comments, posts in all platforms) during campaign, including Twitter engagement +564% vs same period one year earlier.

Using a range of metrics – and looking at timeframes in a variety of ways – we can show how sizeable and dramatic this interaction has been.

For example, monthly visits and unique visitors to the Mercedes website immediately following the launch of 'Escape the Map' vastly exceeded the peaks from new registrations in the preceding March and September (source: Omniture for Mercedes-Benz UK, 2010–11).

Demonstrating a similar point – this time, looking at timescales by the hour – we can show that #YouDrive also had an immediate and dramatic impact on Mercedes site visits during the weekend when the campaign launched within 'X-Factor' (source: Omniture for Mercedes-Benz UK, 2012).

Looking at campaign-related search volume on a daily basis also shows the positive level of consumer interest that '#YouDrive' achieved (Figure 13).

### Figure 13: Uplift in campaign-related search volume for #YouDrive

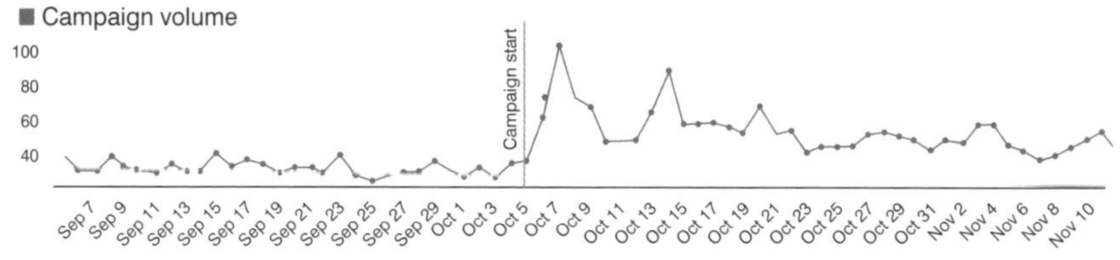

Source: Google, 2012

Finally, to use a suite of measures to illustrate this point across campaigns: below is Mercedes' Facebook 'Organic reach' – showing how many people the brand will have reached through organic consumer links, likes, comments etc. In the month following the launch of 'Sound with Power', this figure was almost *1,000%* greater than pre-campaign (source: Facebook, Holler, 2013).

*Campaigns have successfully communicated the intended brand associations*

These campaigns did not just generate high levels of interaction. They also communicated the right things about the brand.

Below are two 'word clouds' showing the impression that people had of Mercedes from 'Escape the Map' and '#YouDrive'. In the first case, the most common responses were that Mercedes seemed 'for young people', 'sporty', 'recommendable' and 'exciting' (Figure 14).

### Figure 14: Word cloud of responses to 'Escape the Map'

Source: GfK Tracking, 2012

Similarly, those responding to '#YouDrive' thought the brand seemed 'young/for young people', 'fast', 'modern' and 'trendy'(Figure 15).

Figure 15: Word cloud of responses to '#YouDrive'

Source: GfK Tracking, 2013

Unfortunately, we do not have a word cloud diagram for 'Sound with Power'. However, separate research found, akin to the out-takes above, that 'Sound with Power' strongly conveys a *modern, edgy, trendy, younger brand image*.[11]

Another strong indication that viewers took out the right impression of the brand – and that advertising helped shape impressions beyond the cars themselves – is the drop in perceived age of a Mercedes driver for the models featured in advertising, before and after advertising exposure. Below are the scores for '#YouDrive' and 'Sound with Power' (Table 3).

Table 3: Decrease in perceived age of model driver, following ad exposure

| Campaign | Mercedes-Benz model featured | Perceived age of driver | | |
| --- | --- | --- | --- | --- |
| | | Pre ad exposure | Post ad exposure | Effect |
| #YouDrive | A-Class | 43 | 34 | –9 years |
| Sound with Power | E63 AMG | 43 | 37 | –6 years |

Source: GfK Tracking, 2013

Unfortunately, tracking for 'Escape the Map' was slightly different – so we do not have the same measure. However, of everyone who saw this campaign, 60% came away with an increased perception that 'Mercedes-Benz cars are driven by younger people, not just older people'. This figure rose to over 70% when measured purely amongst 20–40 year olds, and reached 77.1% amongst existing Audi/BMW drivers. These scores matched the benchmark top figures for any Mercedes communication on record.[12]

Brand image has improved over time, strengthening relative to prestige competitors, with notable uplifts coinciding with major campaigns.

Taking the longer view, we can see that Mercedes' brand image has improved during this entire period, strengthening relative to prestige competitors BMW and Audi, with significant increases concomitant with major campaigns. (In the charts below, quarterly scores for all brands are indexed to Q4 2010 – the last set of data before Mercedes' new comms approach was adopted.)

Closely reflecting the words in our strategy, Mercedes is now increasingly seen as a 'brand for exciting/dynamic people'.

Echoing this: Mercedes' overall sense of brand momentum – a particularly useful metric for its close correlation with sales, and minimal 'quarter-by-quarter' variation – shows increases for Mercedes associated to major campaigns, and the brand now having 'clear headway' in relative strength versus key competitors.

### Mercedes' sales uplifts during this period have been greater than in other major European markets

To help isolate the impact of comms – and Mercedes' related improved brand image – we can compare UK sales results with the other major European markets: France, Germany, Spain and Italy, countries where product launches and the portfolio range were the same as in the UK. (Note: contrary to common assumption and Eurozone headlines, Mercedes' sales growth in southern European markets Spain and Italy during this period was in fact slightly higher than in France and Germany.)[13]

Indexing sales across these countries, we can see that Mercedes has fared considerably better in the UK than elsewhere.

This pattern is not just due to the slightly slower overall growth of European car markets. To prove this, we can compare market share results across these countries – where once again, Mercedes has fared better in the UK.

### Mercedes' success cannot be explained by any other factors

#### New product launches

Product launches and changes to the portfolio range were the same in all the major European markets. Yet, Mercedes' sales have grown faster in the UK, suggesting that new and/or improved models cannot solely explain this success.

#### Personal contract purchase (PCP) plans

As predicted in 2010, PCP plans have proven popular. The level of appeal of these plans has been almost identical for buyers of Mercedes, BMW and Audi.[14] However, the feared 'step-gain' by rivals with the introduction of PCP has not materialised. On the contrary, Mercedes' share of the prestige market has grown since 2010. So with PCP equally popular amongst prestige brands in the UK, but Mercedes fairing comparatively better, something else was evidently having effect.

#### Prices

The average cost of a Mercedes has increased during this period, so reduced prices cannot be responsible for this success.[15]

Furthermore: Mercedes has maintained its premium versus Audi/BMW since 2010.[16]

## Distribution

The number of Mercedes retailer sites has risen marginally during this period: from 123 in 2010, to 125 in 2014. Such small increases, over this timeframe, would not account for this success.

Equally: Mercedes have not opened up any other form of retail channel – online or offline – during this period.

## Growth in the prestige sector, or the total car market

As shown in charts above, Mercedes has grown its share of both the prestige sector, and the total car market, during this period. So the brand's success cannot be attributed to category trends.

## The calibre of prestige competition

BMW and Audi have remained very strong competitors. Their models have been consistently well reviewed, they have retained competitors to Mercedes in every segment of the market and their strength as brands is renowned.

If anything, this competition has got fiercer. As mentioned above: Audi introduced the new A1 to much fanfare in 2011 – a car in the smaller, cheaper mini-segment that neither BMW or Mercedes had (or have) a direct competitor with. The A1 became (and remains) the cheapest new car that can be bought from one of the 'Prestige 3' brands.[17]

## Share of voice

Mercedes' share of voice has not increased significantly since the new comms approach was implemented. Compared with key rivals, Mercedes' spend through this period has stayed reasonably consistent.

Similarly, Mercedes's share of voice has stayed flat against the total car market. This figure has registered 3%, for every full year, from 2010 to 2013 – and also 2014 so far.[18]

### *Return on marketing investment*

To quantify the effect of Mercedes communication during this period, we can compare Mercedes' share in the UK versus share in other major European markets. This removes variations in product range, the impact of PCP in the UK and the slightly slower overall growth of European car markets. The only significant difference here has been communications.

By calculating the volume that Mercedes would have gained had it followed the same share growth as the rest of Europe, and comparing this with the actual UK share achieved, we can work out the incremental volume in the UK from communications.

This equates to 36,697 extra models sold. Which, based on average price during these respective years, is equivalent to additional revenue of £1,275,783,437.

Communications spend (media, production and agency costs) during the period totalled £92 million.

This means that every £1 spent on communications produced £13.87 in extra revenue.

In terms of profit, Mercedes' margin figures are confidential. However, a number of automotive sector analysts predict the figure to be between 8.0 and 9.4%.[19] Using the lowest figure for our calculation, this equates to a profit of £102,062,675 and therefore a *profitable return on marketing investment of 1.11:1*.

Note: this calculation does not include projections of future customer loyalty sales, even though Mercedes' research suggests that 49% of an incremental sales cohort will generate one further purchase.[20] Nor does this calculation include any future aftersales value, which has been calculated by Mercedes to be worth £160 in revenue over the course of a new car's life.[21] If such figures were included, the final revenue return would be 21:1 – a significant achievement in a relatively short time-frame, in a category not famed for radical transformations.

## Conclusion: the power of 'body language'

Mercedes has achieved record success by having the courage to think differently, challenge norms and confound expectations.

In particular, it has benefited from thinking beyond just an advertising message, and considering the whole 'body language' of the brand. Not just what it says – which was intentionally very little – but how it does so.

Academics refer to this as 'analogue communication'. The things we convey, imply, or demonstrate without precise verbal reference.[22]

Though perhaps the final word belongs to a man who intuitively grasps the importance of non-verbal cues. To take a few lines from the Mercedes fan featured on our cover, Tinie Tempah: 'There ain't nobody fresher... 20 lightbulbs around my table on my dresser... Just in case that don't impress her... (Mercedes) CLC Kompressor.'[23]

## Notes

1  Figures from Mercedes-Benz, UK. Claim based on sales results from January 2011 onwards. (Though the full brand name is 'Mercedes-Benz', this paper typically refers to the brand in its more common, short-hand: 'Mercedes').
2  AMV BBDO research, 2010.
3  Horx and Wippermann, cited in Leslie Butterfield's *Enduring Passion: The Story of Mercedes-Benz* (John Wiley & Sons, 2005).
4  Leslie Butterfield, in *Enduring Passion*.
5  AMV BBDO research, 2007.
6  HPI research, 2010.
7  AMV research, 2010.
8  The Neuroscience point has been made in several places, including: *Searching for Memory: The Brains, The Mind, and the Past*, Schatchter, D. (Basic Books, 1997); *Descartes Error; Emotion, Reason and the Human Brain*, Damasio, A. (Harper, Perennial, 1995). The dealership quote comes from AMV industry research, 2011.
9  In 2010 and beyond, spend in tactical channels made up approximately 40% of Mercedes' total comms spend.
10  See *Audi A1 – A Big Idea Condensed*, IPA Awards, 2012.
11  Murmur research, 2013.
12  GfK tracking research, 2012.
13  Mercedes-Benz, 2010–14.
14  According to the most recent figures, 48% of Mercedes cars have been bought using PCP. For BMW the figure is 47%, and Audi 46%. Source: NCBS, 2013.
15  We do have 2014 data, as this has not been released by NCBS, yet.

16   We do have 2014 data, as this has not been released by NCBS, yet.
17   See Audi.co.uk; Bmw.co.uk; Mercedes-benz.co.uk.
18   Fuel/ZenithOptimedia.
19   Bloomberg (2012), Credit Suisse (2011), Reuters (2014).
20   NCBS.
21   Mercedes-Benz research.
22   See Paul Watzlawick, *Pragmatics of Human Communication* (W. W. Norton & Company, 2011).
23   Tinie Tempah, Lyrics taken from 'Pass Out' ('Disc-Overy', Parlophone Records, 2010).

# Deutsche Telekom

## Move On

**By Gordon Euchler and Daniela Hofmann, DDB Tribal Group**

Contributing authors: Jens Doege, Deutsche Telekom; Eric Schoeffler, DDB Tribal Group

### The heavyweights Telekom and Vodafone go head to head

In the German mobile internet market the two biggest brands Vodafone and Telekom fight for market leadership: with similar market share, similar products and similar tariffs. Yet at the beginning of the year Vodafone announced that it captured the market leadership.

### The difference is in the brand: 'Life is for sharing'

As the difference between the products and services is hardly tangible, it is key to leverage the power of Telekom's brand promise 'Life is for sharing'.

### From 'traditional campaign' to 'innovative content'

With its traditional campaign, Vodafone stirred people's emotions. But for an innovative product like mobile internet, Telekom aspired to go beyond traditional and break new grounds. Telekom decided to leverage the power of their brand promise 'Life is for sharing', for an innovative approach – to create ownable content and use it to turbocharge product communication.

### Bring Telekom back to market leadership

Branded content should help to make Telekom's product communication more innovative and ultimately more successful – so it would beat Vodafone in the race for market leadership.

313

## Experience more on the go

The beauty of mobile is that it brings the internet from the computer screen exactly where people's lives are happening – into the real world and wherever people go. In consumer research one thing became clear: even in normal everyday trips, the most memorable, exciting experiences are those they didn't plan for. The experiences that happen off the beaten track. That is when they truly experience more on the go. People love these surprising experiences so much that there is an entire Hollywood genre dedicated to them: road movies. With the use of mobile internet, we could take this much loved genre to the next level.

## Move On: the first Hollywood-like road movie for everyone to join in

In May 2012 the campaign started with a call-to-participation in the style of a film trailer. During the activation phase, a campaign platform and mobile app offered people from 11 European markets almost 100 ways to inspire the project via mobile internet: from proposing street names, posters or the get-away car, to applying for supporting roles.

To turn the uploaded content into a proper road movie, Telekom enlisted heavyweight professionals for the project: Cannes-winning actor and James Bond baddie Mads Mikkelsen and Hollywood director Asger 'Man on a Ledge' Leth.

In July, Leth chose the winners who were to take part in the movie, and the film crew started off on a journey across Europe. The internet blogger Kitty de la Beche provided continuous behind-the-scenes reports from the shoot to the steadily growing fan community via YouTube. Six weeks, 8,000 km and 400 winning entries later, *Move On* was released in October in eight action-packed online episodes.

On 4 November, *Move On* premiered as full-length film at Cinema International in Berlin with red-carpet appearances of all lead actors and participants from Telekom's 11 European markets. In December, *Move On* exposure culminated in primetime television airing on Pro7, one of Germany's biggest TV channels.

The road movie theme was leveraged to dramatise and enrich the product communication on all levels: Maria Lara, the German lead actress from *Move On*, played the main role in the advertisements, linking product communication and branded content to greater effectiveness.

## Marketing not a cost but an investment

The campaign spread fast and wide: more than 512,000 people saw the call to participation trailer, it generated 231,000 unique visits to the brand's website and created 2.7 million page impressions – 1.2 million above objective. Altogether, more than 1.5 million people watched the road movie, helping Telekom's market share grow by 4% during the campaign, while Vodafone lost 7%, thus relinquishing market leadership to Telekom by Q4 2012. As such, *Move On* generated 23,000 new or renewed subscriptions from postpaid and 10,000 from prepaid customers. This led to a net profit of €3.8 million, the profit generated over a normal Telekom investment in real terms.

# Aldi

## Aldi UK and Ireland: the 'Swap & Save Challenge' campaign

**By Amanda Jones and Brenda Imeson, McCann Manchester**

Contributing author: Chris Burt, Ohal

In 2012, Aldi's share was still only 6% in Ireland and just 3.8% in the UK despite the success of its 'Like Brands' campaign. However, few customers were prepared to do their main shop there. It turned out that there were still two further problems: a limited range perception and a degree of lingering social stigma associated with being seen to shop at a 'discounter'.

Research showed that consumers felt that if visitors came to their house and saw their fridge and cupboards stacked with Aldi own-brand products, they'd feel judged for it, and they'd be embarrassed.

A simple, yet powerful activation idea that complemented the 'Like Brands' campaign was chosen to address these issues. It used behavioural 'nudging' to quickly establish new shopping habits and it used aspirational 'real shoppers' to make it socially acceptable to be an Aldi shopper. Thus the creative solution was the 'Swap & Save Challenge' – that consumers should challenge themselves to swap their main grocery shop from their regular supermarket, and see how much they save. The rational message was that the more you swap, the more you save. You can fill your trolley at Tesco or Sainsbury's and it will cost you a hundred euros/pounds or more. Or you can fill it equally well at Aldi, and you'll pay less than half the price.

To push the aspirational angle, in Ireland for example it used shoppers from affluent south Dublin to be its first challengers, setting them the task of getting their main grocery shop from Aldi for four weeks. It followed them on their shopping trips and recorded their experiences using them as the basis of a multi-platform launch campaign.

In both the UK and Ireland, TV and press were supported by digital media as the lead 'Swap & Save' channels. In addition the 'Swap & Save' campaign was supported through POS, social media, PR and in the UK out of home. TV delivered a more detailed and emotional message to the consumer and post-Christmas was an obvious month to support, as the consumer tends to be feeling the pinch, and this is traditionally a time when change occurs. In addition to the post-Christmas burst, three further bursts were delivered.

Facebook was used to further embed the 'Swap & Save' message in the mind of the consumer. The UK Facebook campaign alone reached 1,512,125 people, with over 27,000 likes for Aldi UK content. A 'Swap & Save' competition which ran for a week during the launch received 10,827 entries.

Aldi planned to increase revenue by 20% in the UK and Ireland in the year 2012–13. In fact, revenue grew by 34.3% in Ireland and by 35.7% in the UK. To put this in context, in the previous year 2011–12, when Aldi was running 'Like Brands' but not 'Swap & Save', revenue grew by 19.3%.

The campaign improved Aldi's market share by 1% point of the £153bn UK market and 1% point of the €14.3bn Irish market; Aldi's share of the grocery market rose in both markets, in the UK from 3.5% to 4.5% and in Ireland from 5.6% to 7.1%.

It also boosted Aldi's market position. At the start of 2013 Waitrose's share was 5%, while Aldi stood notably behind at 3.9%; by October Aldi's share had climbed to 5.1% taking it level with Waitrose. In Ireland, Aldi overtook Lidl to become Ireland's fourth largest retailer.

It increased basket size both in terms of actual items and increase in spend while its loyalty rate has increased to 9.6%, as 21% of our shoppers are now classed as high loyals, i.e. they spend over 20% of their grocery budget with Aldi.

# Mattessons/Fridge Raiders

## The MMM3000: how the world's first meat snacking helmet proved that social can pay its way in the real world

**By William Poskett and Enni-Kukka Tuomala, Saatchi & Saatchi**

Contributing authors: Tom Callard, BBH; Spencer Lucas, Brightblue Consulting

This is the story about how the world's first meat snacking helmet created by teenage gamers proved that highly creative social media campaigns are a viable, and sometimes a more efficient, alternative to TV.

In 2012 sales of Mattessons were declining. Looking to reverse this, Mattessons decided to expand its footprint into new product categories and eating occasions. Fridge Raiders, a bitesized chicken snack, was launched as a way into the hugely profitable snacking market.

The ambition was to take on snacks and grow the meat snacking category, not an easy task for a small player like Fridge Raiders. The category was almost non-existent and Peperami had dominated what little existed of that category for years. Furthermore, Fridge Raiders decided to take on the most popular snack in the UK, crisps, in the after school occasion.

The business challenge was to increase volume and value sales of Fridge Raiders to grow category penetration (by getting teens to choose Fridge Raiders instead of crisps after school). The communications needed to make the brand cool and famous amongst teens.

The strategy was to infiltrate teen culture by associating Fridge Raiders with something 9/10 teens love: gaming. Knowing that 61% of teens were gaming after school and 2/3 of them were snacking whilst playing, Fridge Raiders was re-positioned as the ultimate gaming snack.

Fridge Raiders knew traditional advertising ideas wouldn't work with teens (they are more likely to trust people than brands), it needed an idea worth advertising. So the 'MMM3000' – a social co-creation project with teenage gamers – was born.

317

Research showed that salty and greasy crisps were making gaming messy. To help solve this 'messy finger syndrome', Fridge Raiders asked gamers to design the world's first hands-free meat snacking device.

To build credibility, Fridge Raiders partnered with one of the biggest gaming vloggers called 'The Syndicate Project' – the first brand partnership of this kind and a practice later successfully adopted by brands such as Monster, Uncle Ben's and Pepsi.

The MMM3000 campaign ran in five key phases, with Syndicate Project launching the challenge to his 3m subscribers with a video of him opening a mystery box from Fridge Raiders that invited him and his fans to become a part of the MMM3000 project. He asked his fans to submit their best ideas on the Fridge Raiders Facebook page. Some paid media raised awareness of the campaign further.

Once the ideas were received (15,000 in total), the best suggestions were made into prototypes and shared with the community. The campaign reached a peak when the finished meat snacking helmet was delivered to Syndicate Project by the Royal Marines and shared with his fans in an unboxing video in true gamer style.

Sales volume for Fridge Raiders increased by an average of 20% versus base sales over the campaign period. As a result retail sales value of Fridge Raiders grew by £1.78m (£560,000 more than the previous Hank Marvin TV campaign). And importantly the campaign built significant brand love amongst the 'below 18-years-old' audience. Facebook fans grew by 78% (+127,641 fans), while video content was viewed over 3.2m times, with over 131,000 YouTube likes.

In terms of pure profit the MMM3000 campaign delivered an ROI value of £2.03:1: for every £1 spent the campaign generated £2.03. The total profit generated was worth £864,780 (£2.03 x £426,000). When discounting the total cost of the £426,000 campaign, it is evident it generated £438,780 of absolute net profit. Had the MMM3000 social activity not run, Mattessons would have lost out on £438,780 in incremental profit.

This proves that highly creative social media campaigns can pay their way in the real world.

# MILO

## MILO Cans: new growth for an old brand

**By Andrew Cone, Anthony Wong, Tim Broadbent and Farris Baharom, Ogilvy & Mather**

Contributing authors: Arvind Srivastava and Nizwani Shahar, Ogilvy & Mather

MILO, the powdered choco-malt beverage was, and had always been, a kids' brand in Malaysia. With 1.7 servings per day and 87% incidence, by 2012 the brand had arguably saturated kids' share of drinks in the country. As Malaysian kids grew up, they gradually reduced drinking MILO powdered beverages. On average two out of five would stop drinking MILO altogether, as they became teenagers and young adults.

To migrate kids to stay with MILO, Nestlé sold canned, ready-to-drink MILO in convenience stores and kiosks. Distribution-led expansion ran its course, and MILO Cans were not growing in sales anymore. Teens who had not tried MILO Cans told researchers that they loved MILO for its taste, but it was not something they would readily admit to in public, or be seen with when with friends.

Increasing the challenge, Oligo, a MILO-replica brand, launched cans in 2010 at a lower price which by 2011 successfully eroded 7% of MILO Cans' business away from Nestlé, while Coke invested 54 times more in media than MILO Cans did in 2012.

For MILO Cans to be socially acceptable among teens and yet true to its brand heritage, it chose to focus on its sports equity, which MILO had used for decades.

So it used a twenty-first century twist to resonate with modern teens – thus came the creative idea, 'Twisted Football'. It was decided that something different was needed to generate interest and excitement in teenagers, so MILO Cans added spectacular new ways one could score a goal, based on teens' crazy ideas shared on social media. Scoring a conventional goal would still earn a goal, but a twisted goal was worth two. 'Twisted Football' had oddly designed goalposts of various shapes, sizes, with add-on baskets to the top or sides – to bring MILO Cans into real Malaysian football fields.

For teens to appreciate that MILO Cans could be a beverage for their active lifestyles and not the same wholesome kids beverage they grew up with, media strategy was to be where their moms were not, focusing on two spaces where teens spent most of their time: online and college grounds.

One night, ten 'Twisted Goalposts' were secretly installed in college football fields. Each goalpost was accompanied by an info-board explaining the rules, with a QR code leading players to branded content and an online video teaching them how to play. They were then directed to a Facebook page to post, share and create content.

As these 'Twisted Football' matches kicked off around Malaysia, the brand invited teenagers to create more 'Twisted Goalpost' designs in a Facebook app. Teens could became fans of MILO on Facebook to share designs and collaborate on ideas with their existing social network, thus recruiting more fans to participate.

The result? 1.4 million more MILO Cans sold in 12 months. MILO flourished after a period of stagnant sales and increased teen trial from 50% to 67% and grew monthly can sales by 17% – in a period of category shrinkage with no significant changes in product, pricing or distribution.

In the six months during the 'Twisted Football' campaign, MILO Cans' average monthly sales grew by 10% to RM3.2 million. By contrast, direct competitor Oligo Cans grew by 2%. In the six months after the campaign MILO Cans' average monthly sales grew by 17% to RM3.4 million while Oligo Cans grew by 6%, meaning it outgrew its direct competitor by about three times as the effect of marketing communications investments reached its peak. Additional communications investment drove new growth for an old brand, resulting in incremental sales payback of 1:7. This case shows how communications can create a new market for an old, established brand with no change to the product or its packaging.

# SECTION 8

# Not for profit

# Profiting from the best of not-for-profit marketing

**By Peter Buchanan**
Owner, PB Consulting

**Carlos Grande**
IPA Consultant

What has not-for-profit marketing ever done for you? As an enlightened reader of *Advertising Works* and a follower of the IPA Effectiveness Awards, you most likely don't smoke or drink-drive, and you could set the clocks by the frequency with which you test smoke alarms. (See 'Fire Safety: How a clock nudged a nation so fire couldn't kill' for why this is a good thing.)

You readily accept that campaigns in all these areas have changed behaviour, reduced harmful outcomes and delivered benefits to society as a whole.

But you might need some more *direct* proof of their relevance to your commercial marketing before being persuaded of the need to sift through multiple IPA Award-winning papers on drink-driving (1998, 2002, 2006 and 2010), smoking (1994, 2004, 2006 and 2010) or fire safety (1992, 1994, 2005 and 2014), looking for inspiration.

If not-for-profit marketing developed from application of commercial marketing techniques to the achievement of goals, it is time for the not-for-profit sector to return the favour.

Below, we identify some attributes of successful not-for-profit cases, particularly from the 2014 IPA Effectiveness Awards, that we believe could be usefully studied by commercial marketers, enabling others to profit from the best of not-for-profit marketing.

For the purposes of this analysis, we have taken not-for-profit campaigns to mean campaigns by public bodies to change behaviour and effect social good and/or initiatives by charities and other not-for-profit institutions to grow funds, awareness or trigger some other type of activity.

## Rigour in briefing and piloting campaigns

Commercial organisations should ask themselves what they could learn from some of the practices found in the not-for-profit sector. It is to be expected that high-profile publicly funded communications initiatives will be subject to particular scrutiny for efficacy and value for money. Commissioning procedures reflect this.

UK public-sector bodies are required to submit detailed proposals on why a campaign is needed, why the public sector should take the lead and the end benefit expected.

It goes without saying that briefs in the public sector must include clear objectives that are achievable on the budget allocated. These objectives should be quantified to guide evaluation and demonstrate return on investment. The best cases show a direct link between the stated objectives and evidenced outcomes.

Reflecting the multi-faceted nature of some campaigns in the not-for-profit space, this initial thinking about objectives can be of great strategic import.

Witness the London 2012 Travel Demand Management campaign. Because of the risk that the London Olympic Games could cause transport gridlock, was the public to be encouraged to reduce travelling, take an alternative route, use a different mode or transport or a mixture of the preceding?

The multiplicity of objectives that formed the eventual campaign necessitated additional thought as to how to evaluate the campaign's contribution to achieving these goals.

In addition, the Public Health England campaign, 'Be Clear on Cancer', is an example of how accountability and value for money can be further served by piloting and evolving activity locally and regionally before rolling it out nationally.

It would be a rare commercial marketing organisation that could not learn something from these approaches.

## Turning limitations into advantages

Not-for-profit campaigns often have to think unconventionally to make small budgets work hard or to reach inaccessible or unreceptive audiences.

On the channel side, this unconventionality may express itself in greater use, compared to mainstream commercial campaigns, of owned and earned media, sponsorship, commercial partnerships and digital properties. But as The Salvation Army case demonstrates, even when a not-for-profit organisation is generating solid returns from a reasonably conventional channel mix, the imperative to make its marketing investment deliver even greater benefits can lead it to make a highly productive revamp of the size and allocation of its media budget.

On the creative front, not-for-profit campaigns may resort to innovation, powerful emotional appeals and shock tactics to deliver objectives in effective, cost-efficient and surprising ways.

The Humanitarian Attention to the Demobilised campaign combined both innovation in channel choice and creative messaging to reach an inaccessible audience on a limited budget.

Interviews with former members of Colombia's FARC guerrilla faction found that the insurgents were most likely to miss their families and civilian life at

Christmas, and any appeal to lay down arms was most likely to be effective at that period.

A series of platforms brought to the jungle the message that at Christmas 'everything is possible' – including demobilisation. These mechanisms included dressing jungle trees as Christmas trees, creating rivers of light in the waterways used by fighters, and dropping personalised letters from the country's President into clearings.

The Pancreatic Cancer Action campaign shows how daring creative can achieve national awareness on a budget of just £78k. In this instance, print and poster ads included hard-hitting facts about the poor survival prospects of pancreatic cancer patients and encouraged people to ask about symptoms in the hope of achieving earlier diagnoses of the condition. The executions powerfully featured real patients, including Kerry Harvey, who died shortly after the launch (and following death threats on Twitter as a result of the controversial campaign).

In the above cases, it could be argued that creativity and risk-taking were stimulated by the limitations of budget or conventional media. This is creativity born of adversity which many commercial organisations could strive to emulate.

As one of the Pancreatic Cancer Action team says in an interview on the IPA website, 'Things can get a bit safe in day-to-day (commercial) brand land'.

## Thinking in numbers

The skill of condensing a complex truth into a simple message is always valuable, whether in the commercial or non-commercial sector. Several award-winning 2014 not-for-profit cases embody a specific aspect of this skill, by using a single, memorable figure as shorthand for the story they were telling, and as a stimulus for action by the target.

The team behind the Heart & Stroke Foundation's 'Make Health Last' initiative calculated for the first time the fact that the *average* Canadian would spend his or her last 10 years in sickness.

This figure was then used as a central part of the campaign to jolt the mass of Canadian baby boomers out of complacency that messages about heart and stroke risks must be aimed at someone else. The statistic emphasised the need for a sustained change in habits to achieve long-term quality of life. A first step was the completion of an online risk self-assessment. Some 200,000 Canadians completed the assessment – 50% above target.

In a similar vein, Pancreatic Cancer Action used an impactful number about the condition – namely 'only 3% will survive, because of late diagnosis' – to explain why sufferers might prefer to contract a cancer with better known symptoms that could be diagnosed earlier, leading to an improved survival rate.

McCain's Ready Baked Jackets launch is a commercial use of this numerical technique. The campaign's ads used the line 'Oven-baked tastiness in 5 minutes', shorthand for communicating the new product's benefit – speediness – to a sceptical public.

In an era where the boundaries between branded content, PR, word of mouth and social are increasingly blurred, opportunities to tell stories effectively in numbers – for use in headlines, infographics and social sharing – should not be overlooked.

## 360-degree evaluation as the norm

One potential difference between the not-for-profit and commercial sectors is articulated by Richard Storey, Global Chief Strategy Officer of M&C Saatchi, in the book *How Public Service Advertising Works* (2008):

> No one is going to criticise the marketing director for pursuing an objective of gaining share, boosting footfall or increasing price premium, even though it might be good practice to consider what particular consumer behaviour may be required to achieve these objectives.
>
> As many commercial marketing campaigns operate in a zero-sum game, their commercial objectives largely feature switched loyalty and substituted behaviour. While these are by no means simple challenges, they are focused on modifying existing behaviours rather than initiating it in the first instance. The public service challenge is often one of creating entirely new behaviours.

To evaluate progress towards initiating new behaviours – such as quitting smoking or adopting a healthier diet – that may require targets to complete several steps, not-for-profit marketers often use multiple proof points, mixing intermediate measures, halo effects and evidence taken from seemingly disparate fields with ROI calculations, to demonstrate whether or not campaigns have succeeded.

Accumulating and analysing a multiplicity of behavioural measures over extended periods may strike a commercial marketer, tasked with hitting hard quarterly targets, as a luxury.

However, the idea of using multiple proof points is endorsed for commercial genres by Les Binet and Peter Field in their IPA report, *Marketing in the Era of Accountability*. Here they observe 'It is not the case that any particular business effect reflects overall performance, but rather the *number* of them'.

Examples such as Aldi's 'Swap and Save Challenge' show what can be done in even the most cut-throat commercial categories. This case study includes a plethora of measures, including changes in shoppers' attitudes and specific behaviour towards the chain (such as sales of Aldi's fresh meat products), as well as hard measures including sales, market share and campaign ROI. These are used as evidence of Aldi's success in convincing consumers that the chain was for people like them and they should move their main shop from rival supermarkets to Aldi.

## Creating personalised journeys for the audience

There are few examples from the IPA Effectiveness Awards of generating a commercial payback by delivering a personalised experience or communications. Honourable exceptions include initiatives by Fiat (2011) and Volkswagen (2006) that enabled car buyers to choose vehicle specifications when they bought cars online. These cases focused on leading users towards the completion of short-term, transactional goals (i.e. completed car orders).

Personalisation can also create longer-term audience journeys and engagement as demonstrated by not-for-profit programmes such as The National Depression Initiative case from New Zealand, 'The Journal'.

The latter case centred on an online self-help tool for people with depression combining the best features of traditional therapy – personal, high-frequency contact – with those offered by online technology, namely, ease of access, individualisation, interactivity and tracking.

It has become something of a cliché in public-health advertising discussions to argue that campaigns succeed when they prompt users to take small, specific steps towards larger goals. While confirming this view, the National Depression Initiative case will reward any reader with the instructive detail it contains on the way the audience was taken on this particular set of journeys. Careful thought was given to the use of a celebrity/guide (see below), the site's structure (which required users to complete small, regular actions), tone of voice, and the way the online platform was reinforced by the user's real world activity and by mainstream advertising support.

In a related fashion, the Heart & Stroke Foundation of Canada campaign created a personalised trajectory, starting with a detailed risk self-assessment that encouraged people to set trackable goals, and then to keep a progress diary, create a time capsule of their future, healthier selves and sign up for email reminders.

These examples may seem highly sector-specific. Is it too much to ask whether other campaigns seeking to build long-term relationships with consumers (in categories such as financial services or related to life stages such as new parenting) – could learn from how these cases used technology, data and an ethos of empowering individuals?

## Surprising uses of celebrity

Of the 35 papers on the 2014 IPA Effectiveness Awards shortlist, only four (Aviva, Lux, Garnier and Premier Inn) were commercial campaigns fronted by celebrities. Brands with a successful legacy of celebrity campaigns either submitted non-celebrity campaigns in 2014 (Sainsbury's and Expedia are examples) or their submission did not make it onto the shortlist (e.g. Lays).

Using celebrities to promote public messages is often a big risk for a charity, whereas using a respected public figure may be less so. However, this year two successful not-for-profit cases used unconventionally chosen celebrities to challenge the preconceptions and inhibitions preventing the aimed-for behaviour.

The British Heart Foundation's choice of the hard-man footballer-turned-actor Vinnie Jones to instruct the audience on cardio-pulmonary resuscitation (CPR) for heart attack victims enabled its 'Hands-only CPR' campaign to use black comedy to tackle the anxiety and ignorance holding bystanders back from intervening if someone had a heart attack.

The resulting ad – set to disco music – was both highly effective at communicating CPR techniques and ideal material to go viral, largely because of its unexpected star. The fame achieved by the campaign is highlighted by the fact that another brand, LEGO, chose to recreate the ad using LEGO figures for Vinnie and his henchmen (see *The LEGO Movie Ad Break,* 2014).

Likewise, the decision to cast John Kirwan, the legendary former rugby All Black, rather than a medical figure or actor, to front New Zealand's National Depression Initiative paid off in several ways.

Kirwan's personality mixed likeability and authority, and his sporting credentials challenged any stigma among male Kiwis that depression was unmanly. The rugby player was a consistent factor in the multi-year initiative – whether the campaign phase was targeting users or doctors. Kirwan's role adapted to the context; sometimes appearing in TV ads simply to exhort people to use the online tool and at other times using the online context to provide more detailed guidance, or narrate his own experiences of depression.

Finally, the Pancreatic Cancer campaign was designed to drive reappraisal by featuring terminally ill patients. Gaining the confidence and permission of someone who is terminally ill to take part in a high profile campaign of this type must have been challenging: but it proved to be a very powerful approach.

## Sharing learnings

Social problems can transcend geographical or political boundaries. As a consequence, ideas and insights that originate in not-for-profit campaigns in one market can be translated for other territories, albeit with localised adaptations.

It is not uncommon that public sector case studies directly reference how evidence from other markets shaped the development of their strategies.

Collecting robust evaluation data from several markets can be difficult for the public sector, given the constraints that result from national borders.

However, it is encouraging to see that the 2014 Awards included cases from Canada, New Zealand and Colombia, as well as from the UK. We believe these cases contain insights that can cross borders.

Commercial organisations tend to avoid overtly imitating the tactics of their adversaries. Could it be that in the commercial space, learnings and tactics with proven efficacy are sometimes too quickly ignored or discarded by brands in the search for a novel solution?

Within commercial marketing, we typically see campaign learnings transferred between markets only when the brand in question is owned by multi-nationals, and better positioned to compare experiences and data from several countries.

We believe that commercial marketers could learn from the not-for-profit sector's willingness to import the best ideas, wherever they come from.

## In conclusion

The not-for-profit sector often turns budgetary and media limitations into advantages, making unconventional decisions about creative or media, and in its use of celebrity or technology.

But there remains one striking overlap between not-for-profits and commercial consumer brand marketing and that is in the shared importance given by both sectors to meeting financial targets.

Whether the targets sought are cost savings to the public purse, or a financial return to the commercial advertiser, robust ROI measures are common currency.

Long may that continue.

# National Depression Initiative (NDI)

## The Journal

**By Carl Sarney, FCB New Zealand**

Contributing authors: Blair Alexander, Brian van den Hurk and Simon Sievert, FCB New Zealand

Credited companies: Creative Agency, FCB New Zealand; Production company, Exposure Films; Others, Mental Health Interactive; Digital agency, Salt Interactive; Client, Health Promotion Agency

### Editor's summary

Depression is an all-too-common mental condition that is expensive to treat and, in the worst cases, costs people's lives. The problem is that too often those with burgeoning problems are reluctant to seek the help that they need in order to work through the problem. In addition, successful treatment often requires ongoing support which can be expensive and is not always timely when provided by doctors. Helping people with depression to do what they could to help themselves became an important goal for the thinking.

To spread awareness and tackle prejudices, the agency therefore created an above the line campaign integrated with an online self-help tool. The whole campaign was fronted by one of the nation's favourite Rugby stars; and The 'Journal' was distributed as a free solution for the public to use and share.

**The adoption of a holistic approach to solving the problem impressed the judges and the ROMI of 5 was applauded. Furthermore, the ongoing relevance of the solution as part of the treatment plans of the New Zealand nation hinted at a much longer term value yet to be realised.**

## Case summary

In 2009 we were briefed to fix a costly problem for New Zealand. Depression is an all-too-common mental condition that is expensive to treat, and in the worst cases, costs people's lives when suicide seems like the only way out.

It's the kind of complex problem that necessitated greater depth than your average public service announcement. We not only created a compelling, above the line campaign to keep the public aware that what they are struggling with might be depression, we also created an online self-help tool to integrate the problem with a solution.

The Journal is a solution that's free for the public to use. It costs much less for the government than subsidising GP visits and medication, and 90% of those who use it are achieving a medically recognised improvement in their condition. In some cases, users have written to us and said The Journal has literally saved their life.

This is a story of how continuous learning is building success upon success. In 2010 The Journal was recognised in the New Zealand Effies for outstanding launch results. In 2011, it continued to exceed expectations, and was awarded Most Effective Campaign that year. In 2013, three years on from its launch, it won the Grand Effie in New Zealand for sustained success.

Now in this IPA paper, we will demonstrate that the National Depression Initiative (NDI) campaign including the TVC, depression.org.nz, and The Journal online self-help tool, has demonstrated its long-term ability to influence behaviour.

Read on to learn how we overcame new challenges that arose year after year, and sustained effectiveness in changing behaviour and saving lives.

### The challenge: a huge problem for New Zealanders, and reluctance to seek help

In 2008, New Zealand had the second highest rate of depression among OECD countries. It was estimated to affect one in five New Zealanders in any given year.[1] By Census 2006 figures, that represents about 562,000 people a year.

Due to the nature of the illness itself, there are significant barriers to getting people with depression to seek help:

- social isolation and stigma, making them reluctant to ask for help;
- poor decision-making abilities, making traditional websites hard to use;
- reduced concentration, making learning harder;
- very low motivation, causing high drop-out rates.

The previous NDI campaign achieved 90% awareness.[2] Most New Zealanders had some understanding of the illness, yet many of those affected remained reluctant to seek *professional help*.[3] Driving people to visit their GP for professional help is not only hard to do, but also has a significant cost in government subsidies for each consultation. Driving people to call the NDI helpline was also not the best option as we didn't want to overwhelm the instantaneous capacity of the helpline.

So the Ministry of Health briefed us to increase the awareness of *self-help* techniques, as an alternative option for New Zealanders suffering from mild to moderate depression. But the challenge involved more than simply raising awareness of self-help options. If you Google 'self-help techniques for depression', you get about 96,000,000 results. Even with all this information, the reader is still required to formulate their own treatment plan. Given a depressed person's difficulty with decision-making and concentration, raising awareness and leaving people to puzzle their own way through would be an ineffective approach.

In 2009 the Ministry of Health had a new vision for public health services: that they would be 'better, sooner, more convenient'. With that brief, our challenge was to figure out a *better* way to get people engaged with self-help *sooner*, by making the techniques much more *convenient* to understand and put into practice.

To prove that a self-help option really is better, we would need robust measurement to determine if people engaging in the campaign were achieving a medically recognised improvement in their depression condition.

To put the budget in an international context, we had around NZ$2m media budget each year, compared with the likes of Vodafone NZ who spend NZ$44m (rate-card March 2013–February 14) and Coca Cola NZ who spend NZ$20m (rate-card March 2013–February 2014).

## Campaign objectives

1. Improve information seeking (increase visits to depression.org.nz and calls to the helpline).
2. Increase the number of people with depression using a self-help alternative to GP visits.
3. Get those who self-help to achieve a medically recognised improvement in their condition. This is measured by the PHQ9 scoring system discussed later in the paper.
4. Deliver effective self-help at a lower cost than GP visits.

Specific details of how these objectives are measured are included in the results.

## Strategic thinking on how to meet the objectives

### Improve information seeking

Although the core target for self-help was men and women experiencing mild to moderate depression, our overall audience included all adult New Zealanders.

Depression is an illness that can be triggered by a number of factors at any time. Depression.org.nz and an online self-help programme (The Journal) would be irrelevant to people, until such a time that depression is triggered – i.e. it was important that all adults knew enough about the condition before it developed, to recognise it and know that depression.org.nz has information to help them. So we took a funnelled approach to get people what they needed at the right time (Figure 1).

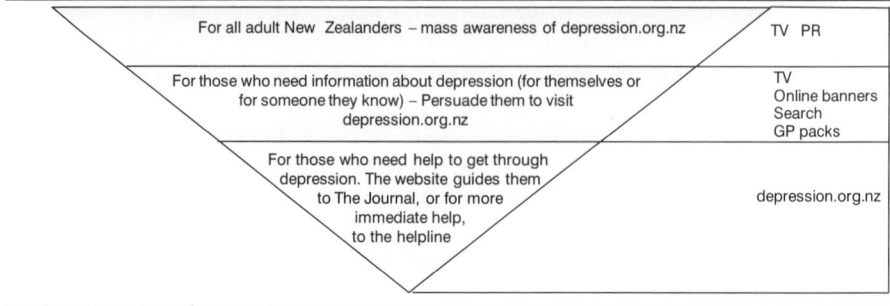

Figure 1: We took a funnelled approach to get people what they needed at the right time

*Increase the number of people with depression who use a self-help alternative to GP visits*

Research showed that people with depression were reluctant to get professional help because:

1.  They are unmotivated so getting out of the house to do anything may be hard.
2.  It costs a lot to go to a GP in New Zealand. Doctors' practices and medical centres are privately owned and set their own fees. If you're enrolled with the GP then the Government subsidises the fee, but a visit to a doctor still costs the user around NZ$40–50 (approximately £23).
3.  Some people still perceive a stigma around depression, so it can be hard to open up and admit you might be depressed to another person.[4]

Converting a clinically based self-help structure to an online format would mean people could get help from the comfort of their own home, it could be provided free of charge, and it could be done alone, without the pressure of having to talk directly to another person.

But an online-only approach would never have worked. We needed the mass reach of TV to normalise help seeking, to create a perception that everyone knows about depression.org.nz and it's a normal, acceptable resource to use.

*Get those who self-help to achieve a medically recognised improvement in their condition*

Lots of careful thought and collaboration with clinical experts went into the design of the self-help programme structure to ensure it would be effective at achieving this crucial objective. Two overarching strategies informed the design of the programme structure:

1.  Make small changes in several areas of their daily lives in order to create a larger overall change.
2.  Use behaviour change principles to ensure users stick with the programme. Details on this are included later in the discussion about creative execution.

*Deliver effective self-help at a lower cost than GP visits*

Right from the outset we were thinking long-term. The longer the programme could sustain its success, the less it would cost to help each subsequent user. The TVC would need to be produced at a level of quality that it could run for years, and the online component would need to be more technically robust than those typically built to support a short-term campaign.

*A crucial insight*

We unlocked the solution to our challenge when we realised *how* the self-help techniques could be taught.

Medical research had proven treatment to be more effective if the patient knows the therapist administering it.[5]

*How could an online programme replicate the intimate relationship between a psychologist and their patient?* The answer we hit upon was to leverage the relationship our NDI campaign frontman John Kirwan had already created with our audience since 2006.

John Kirwan (or JK as he tends to be known) is a former All Blacks rugby hero. A living legend, his total of 199 first class tries remains a New Zealand record. He embodies strength and success in the eyes of New Zealanders. (In NZ's masculine culture, our All Blacks heroes are just as relevant to women as they are to men.)

So in 2006, when JK fronted the previous NDI TV campaign talking about his own experience of the illness, it was the surprising use of a celebrity that shattered misconceptions about depression. Who would have thought that depression could affect a rough and tough All Black like him (Figure 2)?

Figure 2: An All Black talking about his experience with depression shattered misconceptions and made headline news in New Zealand

The New Zealand Herald    Search keywords...    Q

National Video Opinion Business Technology World Sport Entertainment Life & Style Travel Motor

## John Kirwan inspires men to reach out for help

By Martha McKenzie-Minifie

5:00 AM Tuesday Nov 28, 2006

*And it wasn't just men that he inspired* – although it's notoriously hard to get stoic Kiwi men in touch with their feelings, research showed that all groups (even Asian women) were inspired by JK's story.

After that first NDI TV campaign, JK had been voted seventh most trusted person in New Zealand.[6] Combined with the courage he had shown in telling his story to the nation, JK was a unique combination of likeability and authority.

So JK would be a persuasive mentor to coach men and women through the steps of our online self-help tool.

### The big idea

*Evolve JK's role* from empathetic celebrity on TV, *to personal coach online*, delivering self-help in a unique way that would inspire people to practise the skills they need to recover from depression.

## The creative journey and media strategy

Herein lies another key to this campaign's success: collaboration among all the experts involved across multiple communication channels, all overseen by one single creative director.

For example, the digital architect who led the design and build of the online self-help programme worked with the script writers of the TVC to make sure the online product was positioned in the right way.

Similarly, the design of the digital banners and the pack to GPs all happened in collaboration with the same digital architect who created the central online self-help programme. So all the consumer touchpoints have a familiar feel, and seamlessly funnel people to the right place for help.

Plus our media team also sits within the same building and was involved with the design of the campaign right from the beginning.

### Pre-launch 2009

We built The Journal – a private, personalised online programme where JK could inspire people to learn, and more importantly practise, the self-help skills they need. It is a secure section of the main depression.org.nz website.

A key innovation was to combine what works about traditional therapy – personal, high-frequency contact – with the best online features: ease of access, personalisation, interactivity and tracking.

The Journal online interface uses the familiar visual metaphor of a book to create a greater sense of comfort with the technology. Every page features a video of JK and a written summary of the information they need for that lesson. A set of tools built into the book help users plan and execute each task. The Journal also integrates with the Depression Helpline team for seamless, live support from the privacy of the user's home.

A key creative challenge was to keep the user's relationship with JK, balanced between likeability and authority. JK fronts every touchpoint with the user (Figure 3).

1. JK interviews medical experts and translates technical details into his own words;
2. he shares his personal experience before telling our audience what to do;
3. the tasks he sets are very specific (e.g. 'cook two healthy meals this week');
4. every communication, tip, and technique was given his tone of voice and personal sign-off.

## Figure 3: depression.org.nz homepage

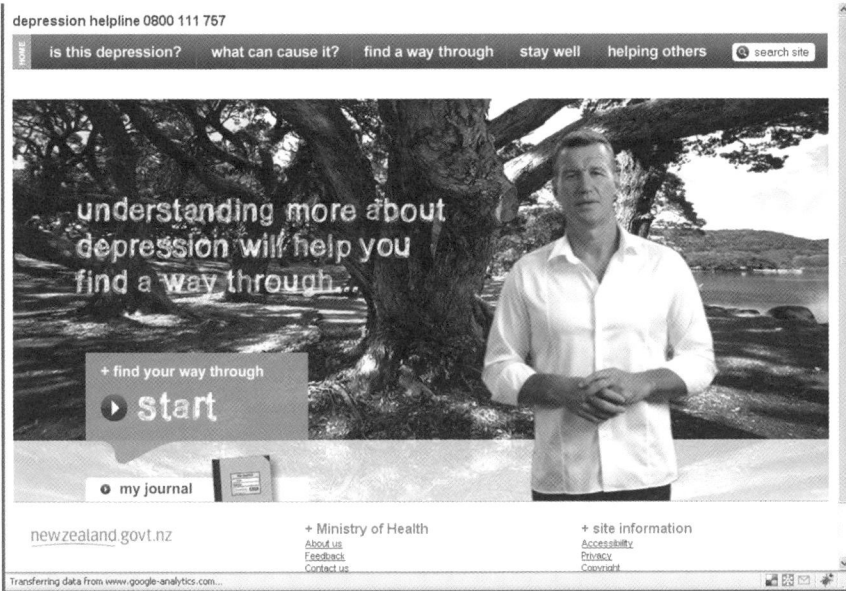

*The Journal was designed in accordance with behaviour change principles*

Chunking: a set course of six 'lessons' that limited decision-making required by the user (Figure 4).

## Figure 4: The Journal contents page chunks the course down into six 'lessons'

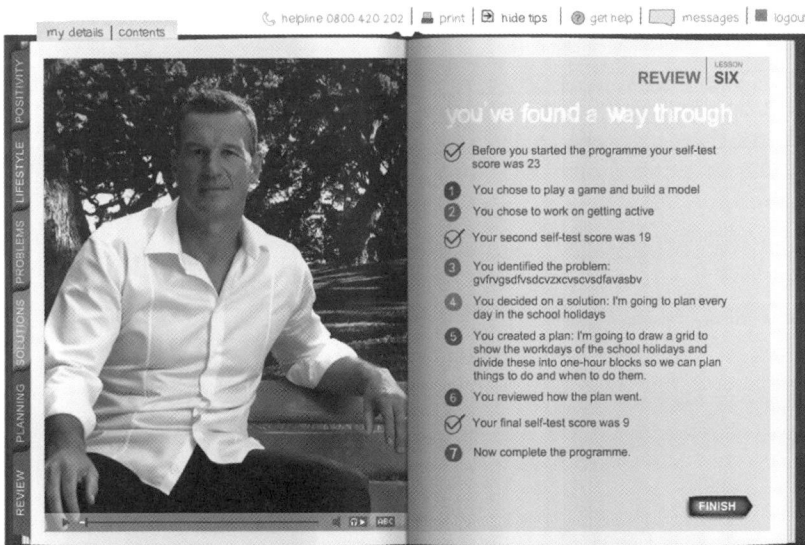

Repetition: a consistent structure to each lesson made The Journal easier to use (Figure 5).

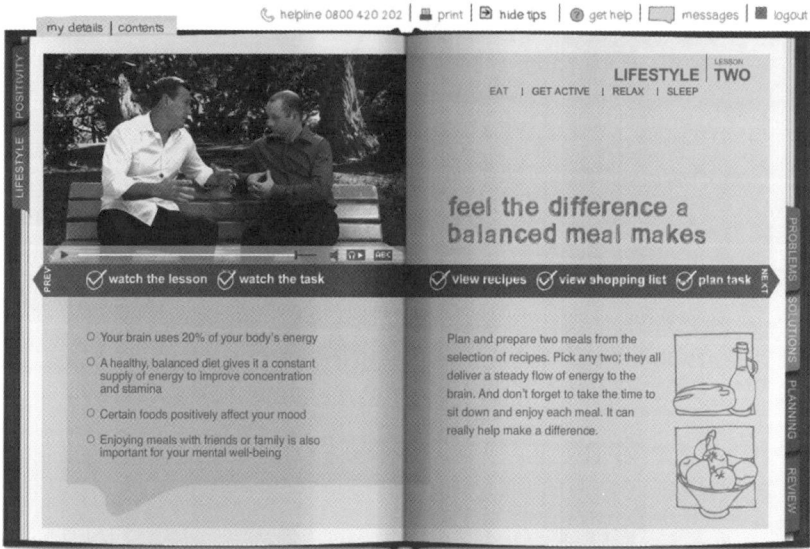

**Figure 5: An example of one of the lessons – Includes video of JK talking with clinicians**

Goal-setting: each skill is broken down into smaller, more simple steps, and we gave people all the tools and information they needed to complete each task.

Planning: a calendar triggered personalised reminder messages 'from' JK to keep the user motivated (Figure 6).

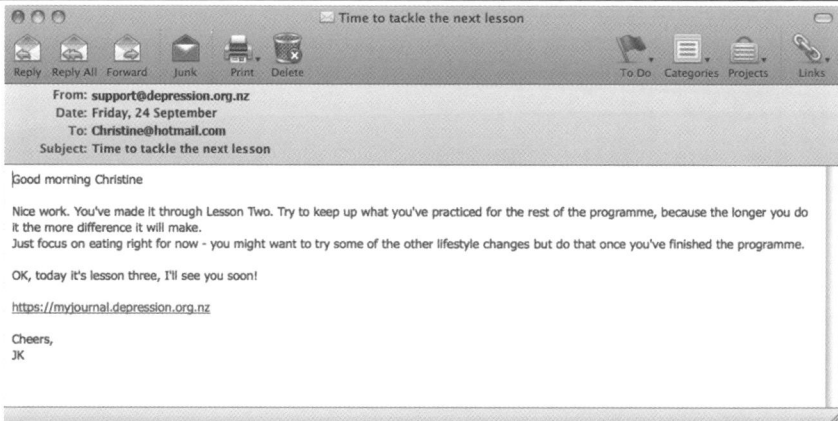

**Figure 6: An example of an email sent to users 'from' JK to keep users motivated**

Practise: real-world tasks encouraged users to set goals to practice the skills they learn, and contextual feedback on their progress reinforced positive behaviour (Figure 7).

**Figure 7: An example of a text message sent to users, encouraging them to put skills into practice**

## Year 1: Reposition JK as a mentor (2010–2011)

We created a 45-second TVC that was half about engaging a mass audience with the issue of depression, and half about the call to action – driving direct response from those who were experiencing depression and seeking help.

We portrayed JK in his authoritative rugby coach role. He uses a sporting analogy to make the point that having a plan helped him get through depression, and that at depression.org.nz he can help you make your own simple plan to help you get through depression too (Figure 8).

**Figure 8: JK portrayed in his rugby coach role in the TVC**

Figure 9: End-frame from the TVC

depression.org.nz

depression
there is a way
through it
0800 111 757

New Zealand Government

Importantly, we chose not to try and explain what The Journal was in the TVC because it would sound complicated and put people off. Instead, JK simply signs off with the call to action: *'depression.org.nz. I'll see you there.'*

Building on the insight that treatment is more effective if the patient knows the therapist administering it, this sign-off deliberately set up the expectation that JK would be there with you all the way through this challenging journey of recovery.

Once on the website, the audience was guided towards signing up to The Journal self-help option. And again, JK intentionally uses language that reassures the user that he'll be with them all the way: *'Let's get started'*, *'I'll be right here while you do that'*, *'Come on, let's keep going'*.

Sufficient TV weighting was used to establish the fact that JK could now help you make a plan to get through depression at depression.org.nz.

We noticed that we were getting more sign-ups during the day than when we ran the TVC in primetime spots in the evening. This is a similar pattern to direct response TV, so we up-weighted daytime spots to catch people at moments when they were more likely to take action and visit the site. Sign-up activity was continuously monitored to help us find the right balance between day-time and evening spots.

Online banners that could be clearly linked with the TVC were also developed to drive response and prompt people to click through to depression.org.nz directly (Figure 10).

Figure 10: An example of an online banner ad

to tackle depression
you need a plan

New Zealand Government

From 2010 on, depression.org.nz, The Journal self-help tool, and the TVC have remained unchanged.

To sustain the effectiveness of the campaign, JK's role evolved across other touchpoints.

### Year 2: Use JK to prompt action (2011–2012)

We knew that JK's familiar face would prompt recall of the TVC, but we needed to figure out where and when to use JK in supporting touchpoints to prompt action at moments when people were most likely to engage.

*TV* continued to air at slightly lower weights, now that awareness levels were tracking well.

*Online banner ads* continued in the channels achieving the best click-through rates.

*PR activity* was carried out to give further prominence to JK's likeability and authority. It was crucial that as many of our target as possible would look up to him and respect him enough to be motivated to follow his advice and check out depression.org.nz.

*An extensive search engine optimisation audit* was carried out to identify the most effective keywords. Subsequent search activity saw increased rankings on those keywords, leading to increased site traffic. Prior to the campaign, 96,000,000 results would come up in a search, leaving people with depression feeling like self-help is confusing and too hard. Now depression.org.nz (where JK said he'd see you) is the first result and in one click you're ready to start The Journal (Figure 11).

**Figure 11: depression.org.nz positioned as the obvious option to try first, among millions of search results**

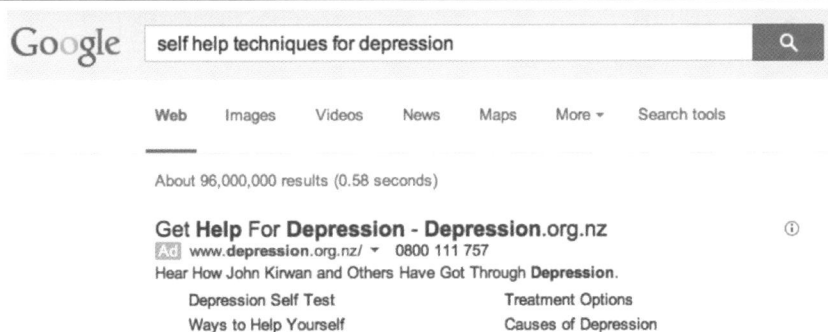

Google   self help techniques for depression   🔍

Web   Images   Videos   News   Maps   More ▾   Search tools

About 96,000,000 results (0.58 seconds)

**Get Help For Depression - Depression.org.nz**   ⓘ
Ad www.**depression**.org.nz/ ▾   0800 111 757
Hear How John Kirwan and Others Have Got Through **Depression**.

Depression Self Test      Treatment Options
Ways to Help Yourself      Causes of Depression

### Year 3: Use JK to recommend the programme to medical professionals (2012–2013)

In Year 3, our media budget was reduced due to changing priorities of the Government. All the learning we had gained so far was put to use to find new opportunities to boost overall effectiveness, and further fine-tune the media mix.

TV, online, and the most effective supporting media were continued, and the remaining budget was utilised for one of the opportunities identified – GPs.

In the first instance, The Journal was designed as an alternative to GP visits for those with mild to moderate depression who were reluctant to visit a GP. However, it could also be complementary to GP visits for those who had already made a GP their first port of call.

So we evolved JK's role again, by creating a direct mail campaign targeted at GPs that included a case study outlining how The Journal is helping people achieve a medically recognised improvement in their depression condition, and could be incorporated into their overall treatment plan. Print advertising in magazines for GPs supported the DM.

This converted GPs into an additional and highly effective communications channel in their own right (Figure 12).

## Figure 12: DM pack sent to GP practices

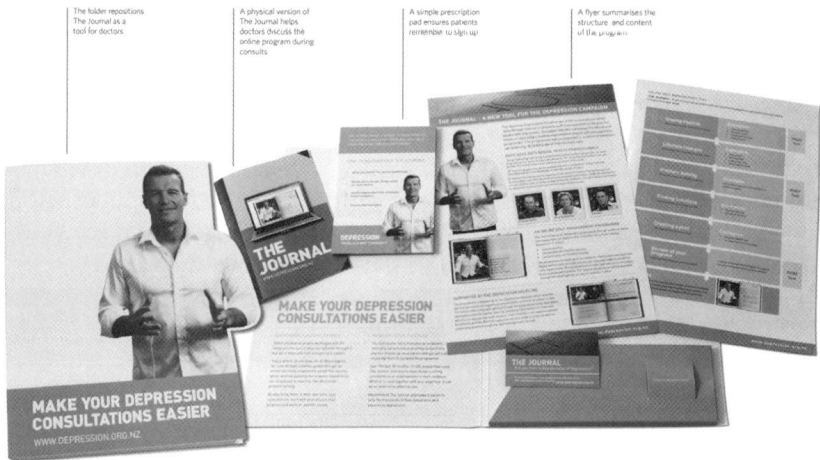

### Results summary

Over three years this campaign has achieved *80% unprompted awareness,*[7] and persuaded more than *1.2M people to seek information* from depression.org.nz. These unique site visitors (as measured by Google Analytics) are equivalent to over a quarter of the 4.4m national population.[8] This reflects the statistic that one in five New Zealanders are affected by depression in any given year, including friends and family of those directly experiencing depression.

This campaign has sustained an average of *600 new people per month signing up* to The Journal (Figure 13). That means every month for three years we exceeded our original monthly target by 200 users.

*A medically recognised improvement is achieved by 90%* of people who complete The Journal, as measured by the PHQ9 score.

The average cost per user for the Government to deliver The Journal is just $172 – a *saving to the Government of $1,036 per patient*, compared to subsidising professional fees and medication.

**Figure 13: The Journal sustained an average of 600 new users every month**

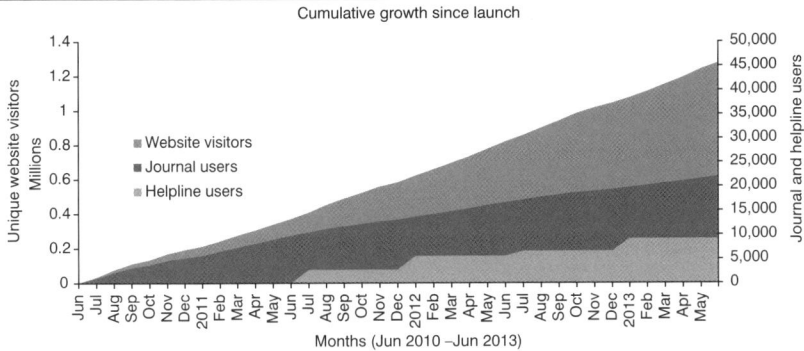

Cumulative growth since launch

Sources: Website – Unique users per month, Google Analytics; Journal – unique users per month, Google Analytics; Helplinesix-monthly helpline traffic, Lifeline (note only data from June 2011 available)

## Results against objectives in detail

*Improve information seeking (visits to depression.org.nz and calls to helpline)*

Our 2009 benchmark was 140,000 total visitors to depression.org.nz and 10,984 calls to the helpline. Our specific targets were to increase visits to the website by 100% in the first year (target: 280,000) and to maintain the same number of calls to the helpline (as it was already near capacity).

The results are shown in Table 1:

**Table 1: Information seeking improved each year**

|  | 2009 (pre The Journal) | 2010 | 2011 | 2012 |
|---|---|---|---|---|
| Total Website Visitors | 140,000 | 426,672 | 539,515 | 619,873 |
| Total Helpline Callers | 10,984 | Not reported | 12,878 | 18,437* |

*NB: in 2012 the provision of texts, email and messenger services are included as people were seeking alternative methods of contacting the Depression Helpline.
Source: Google Analytics and Helpline Tracking

*Increase the number of people with depression using a self-help alternative to GP visits*

This is important because getting people to use a self-help alternative overcomes many people's reluctance to use professional help, and therefore it is an opportunity to help more people get through depression. (Some may also have used The Journal as complementary support to GP visits.)

Our 2009 benchmark was the 4,659 new cases of depression GPs reported in 2009 (*about 400 new patients per month*).[9] Our specific target was to get the same number of people using GPs to sign up to The Journal each month – 400 users per month.

Result: we exceeded this target by 200 new users per month, every month for three years.[10]

### Get those who self-help to achieve a medically recognised improvement in their condition

We measured this by using a standard medical questionnaire (PHQ9) at three stages throughout The Journal programme. The PHQ9 questionnaire is built into The Journal so we could directly compare our results against the targets set for traditional treatment.

Traditional treatment with a course of medication has a target decrease of 6 points. We wanted to achieve the same with The Journal.[11]

Results:

- users of The Journal achieved an average decrease of 8.9 points over the course of the programme;
- 83.5% of The Journal users decreased their score after just two lessons;
- 90.1% of people completing the whole programme decreased their score;
- these results remain consistent three years on.

**Figure 14: Showing users the improvements in their scores**

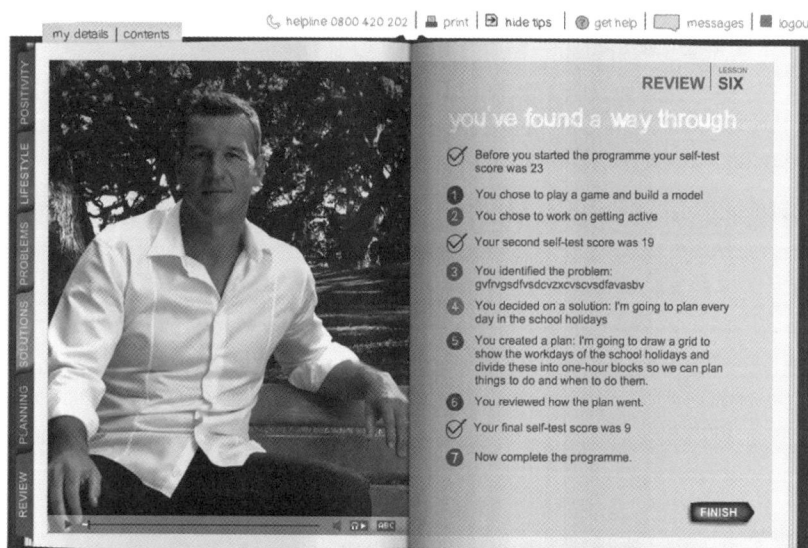

*Deliver effective self-help at a lower cost than GP visits*

As a benchmark, we used an economic report prepared by an associate professor of the University of Auckland Business School. The report looked at the costs of a primary care intervention for depression by a GP, taking into account the typical five consultations required for an early depression intervention, the 2009 costs of subsidies paid for each consultation, plus the average cost of pharmaceuticals prescribed to depression patients. The report established the average costs per patient to deliver treatment via a GP was NZ$1,208.

Our specific target was to deliver The Journal for a lower cost per user than treatment via a GP, including developing the programme, building the online tool, and media costs.

Results: compared to the cost of delivering treatment via a GP, The Journal saves the Government more than NZ$1,000 per user;

*ROMI:*

- ROMI = 5:1.

*Global effectiveness*

The sustained effectiveness of The Journal has been gaining attention around the world:

- it's been put through clinical trials at Ottawa University;
- it's the subject matter for a study at St Michael's hospital in Toronto;
- Harvard University has studied The Journal as part of their research for NASA.

*A final few words from The Journal users and Sir John Kirwan*

Q: In what ways has The Journal been helpful?[12]

*Helped me to accept I had depression in the first place.*

*JK is awesome; his approach, delivery, personality, positivity, kept me coming back for the next lesson.*

*Found it more beneficial than talking to a counselor.*

*Have been able to come off medication.*

*Has motivated me to carry on with life.*

*I'm contacted daily by people with depression and I can't count the number who have said the program has literally saved their life – it's very humbling.*

Sir John Kirwan, June 2013

*New learning for advertisers*

We built The Journal so that our audience could put the campaign's call to action into action, and make a personalised plan to get through depression. It's effective because it integrates awareness and normalising of a problem through the mass reach of TV, with a solution to the problem online.

Taking a long-term approach from day one ensured that each touchpoint was built to last. This not only had cost efficiencies, but also sustained a consistently high level of sign-ups month after month for three years and counting.

Strong integration across all touch points was achieved through a close collaboration between all disciplines involved in creating the campaign.

Using the power of JK's celebrity in a surprising way helped to create fame for the campaign, resulting in high levels of engagement. We also discovered that the familiarity a celebrity has amongst their audience is powerfully reassuring for people in need of a mentor to coach them through behaviour change.

## Notes

1   Ministry of Health survey, 2008.
2   NDI 3 Year Evaluation, 2009, Phoenix Research.
3   NDI 3 Year Evaluation, 2009, Phoenix Research.
4   2009, Phoenix Research.
5   'Therapist Success and Its Determinants'. Retrieved from: http://archpsyc.jamanetwork.com/article. aspx?articleid=493591.
6   Readers Digest New Zealand, *Most Trusted People Survey*.
7   Phoenix Research NDI Tracking, April 2013.
8   Retrieved from worldbank.org.
9   NDI 3 Year Evaluation, 2009, Phoenix Research.
10  Unique users per month, Google Analytics.
11  PHQ9 treatment response table, The MacArthur Initiative on Depression and Primary Care website.
12  NDI 3 Year Evaluation, 2009, Phoenix Research.

# Pancreatic Cancer Action

## Giving a voice to a silent killer

**By Nick Radley and Greg Phitidis, Team Darwin**

Contributing authors: Ali Bucknall, Ali Bucknall Planning and Research

Credited companies: Creative Agency, Team Darwin; Media Agency, Media Q; Research Agency, Neuro-Insight; Client, Pancreatic Cancer Action

### Editor's summary

Pancreatic cancer is the fifth biggest cause of cancer death in the UK: only 3% survive. Pancreatic Cancer Action wanted to start to change these statistics, but with only a small budget of £78k.

Working with Team Darwin, they launched a heavily researched campaign based around the idea of 'I wish I had a more survivable cancer', an insight gleaned from real pancreatic cancer sufferers, which brought to life the horrific realisation that for the majority, by the time they were diagnosed, it was already too late.

The campaign relied on press and outdoor media coverage to get the best visibility, generated awareness in over a quarter of the adult UK population, and secured PCA an audience with the Health Secretary. The campaign could deliver a potential ROMI of 4000, saving the NHS millions of pounds.

**Winning both Gold and Best Small Budget awards, the campaign for Pancreatic Cancer Action clearly demonstrated how insight and courage were a key ingredient of success at lower budget levels. Bold creativity helped them leverage a wealth of earned media with more than a quarter of the population newly recognising the symptoms of pancreatic cancer.**

## Introduction

### A story of David and Goliath

This is a story that demonstrates how a tiny budget is no barrier to ambition, or more importantly, to effectiveness. Above all, it's a story of passion, conviction and a desire to challenge the status quo of ignorance of the symptoms of the fifth biggest cause of cancer death in the UK. And it's a campaign born of bitter experience. We'd personally lost people to the disease and our client is one of the 3% (yes, 3%!!!) of people who survive pancreatic cancer. We were determined to start changing this shocking statistic by drawing attention to pancreatic cancer's signs and symptoms – to empower people to ask the questions that could save lives. This is exactly what we did: turning a meagre budget of £15k into publicity that was worth over £1m through creative work that demanded attention, generated campaign awareness among over a quarter of the adult UK population and secured our client an audience with MPs. Our model suggests we will save the NHS a minimum of £3.1m (and probably much more) and importantly it will save lives too.

### But first – a disclaimer

This is not a typical IPA entry paper – we don't have an econometric model or reams of data to demonstrate that our campaign (and not the media budget) was responsible for the effect. What we will demonstrate is that when passion, conviction and neuroscience come together with amazing creativity, things change – and that small budgets can really punch above their weight. What more can you ask when it's people's lives at stake?

## The background

### Why does pancreatic cancer need help?

*Any* diagnosis of cancer is life-changing, but what's particularly horrific about pancreatic cancer is its survival rate. Just 3% of those that are diagnosed with it will survive past five years[1] and most will die within four to six months.[2] This is the worst survival rate of all the 22 common cancers[3] and compares with 97%, 85% and 66% survival for testicular, breast and cervical cancers respectively.

Pancreatic cancer is almost always diagnosed too late to be treated effectively (only 10% are diagnosed in time for surgery, which gives them a 30% chance of surviving past 5 years[4]). In fact 50% of those diagnosed with the disease find out about it in hospital A&Es[5]. The reason for this is that the symptoms are not well known by either patients or doctors and symptoms are easily confused with other less serious ailments (e.g. upset tummies and back pain). Many sufferers had been going to the doctors repeatedly with symptoms, in some cases, for years.

The result is that pancreatic cancer is the fifth biggest cause of cancer death in the UK and it is set to become the fourth biggest by 2030[6] as other cancers' survival rates continue to improve. The survival stats have not changed in over 40 years and there has been precious little advancement in trying to treat or cure the disease (Figure 1).

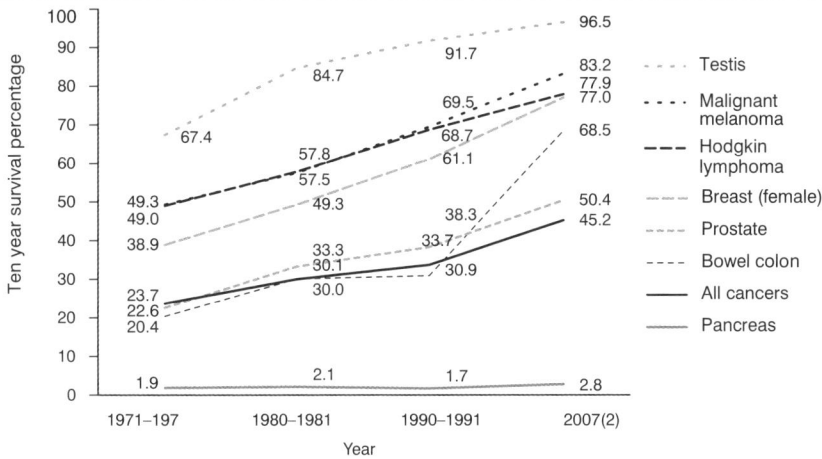

Figure 1: Survival trends for selected cancers

Source: Cancer Research UK

In 2012 the total spend on pancreatic cancer research was £4.4m. That may sound like a lot – but it's less than 1% of all cancer research funding.[7]

So this is a cancer that needs to be moved up the agenda, otherwise over 8,000 lives will be lost every year to this so-called 'silent killer'.

## The importance of awareness

It may seem obvious, but knowledge really is power. The more you know, the more likely you are to act. There is a lot of documented evidence showing that greater awareness and understanding of cancer symptoms can lead to early detection – and better outcomes. As the World Health Organisation states:

*Increased awareness of possible warning signs of cancer, among physicians, nurses and other health care providers as well as among the general public, can have a great impact on the disease.*

Previous 'Be Clear on Cancer' advertising campaigns in the UK, analysed by the National Cancer Intelligence Network (NCIN), show a strong link between awareness and increases in the number of diagnosed and ultimately saved lives.

For example, for bowel cancer, increased awareness of its two key symptoms of 15% and 13% led to a 30% increase in GP visits among the target audience and a 40% increase in suspected bowel cancer referrals.[8] This led to 11.5% more people being diagnosed.[9]

So increased awareness saves lives. It can also save the NHS money – diagnosing the 50% of pancreatic cancer sufferers through A&E (rather than through GPs) costs the NHS nearly £5,000 per patient[10] or nearly £21m per year.

*The charity/client – who is Pancreatic Cancer Action (PCA)?*

PCA is a charity set up four years ago by Ali Stunt – herself one of the 3% to survive pancreatic cancer beyond five years. The charity exists primarily to improve survival for pancreatic cancer patients by focusing on early diagnosis. This is achieved by raising awareness of the disease and its symptoms. So PCA raises money that can then be spent on trying to increase awareness amongst the public and the medical profession and also on lobbying for increased research funding into better diagnoses and treatments.

## Developing the campaign

*Our mission – increase awareness and understanding*

The objectives of this campaign were very simple.

- Make a quantum leap in the awareness of the disease and its symptoms.
- Spark a conversation.
- In essence, put the disease on the map.

Overall, our ambition was to arm the public with the awareness and knowledge of what pancreatic cancer is and how to spot its symptoms. This would allow people to be diagnosed earlier and therefore ultimately save lives as well as NHS money.

To maintain the purity of the awareness objective we did not directly ask for donations. However we knew there would likely be an increase in donations because there is a correlation between awareness and likelihood to donate.

*Developing the strategy – some big hurdles to overcome*

The objectives were clear but the task was far from easy – for the following reasons.

### We were up against some very big hitters

The UK charity sector is crowded and highly competitive. There were 164,415 registered charities in the UK as of March 2014.[11]

- The ad spend for Britain's charity sector in 2013 was £394m.[12]
- Three of the top six spenders are generic cancer charities making it even harder for us to cut through (620 cancer charities in total).

### There is increasing 'cause fatigue' amongst the British public

Recession, rising costs, government cut-backs, more charities, falling incomes are all making people think twice about what they give and to whom. Getting noticed, cutting through and being heard was getting harder and harder. As a result overall donations to UK charities are in decline. In 2012 we gave £9.3bn to charity, which was a £2.3bn decrease in real terms versus 2010/11.[13]

### We had little or no awareness or knowledge to build on

Pancreatic cancer has a hard time getting on the map. This is not surprising, given that 87% of people are unaware of where their pancreas is and only a vague idea of what it does (one third have no idea at all).

And although 66% of people have *heard* of pancreatic cancer, they don't think of it as one of the big cancer killers and know almost nothing about it. Most people are also unaware of the symptoms that go along with pancreatic cancer – nearly half can't name a single one.[14]

This is rather surprising as many famous people have died of it and others have tried to raise awareness of it in the past. Steve Jobs, Patrick Swayze, Roger Lloyd-Pack (Trigger from 'Only Fools and Horses'), and Luciano Pavarotti have all died from it and yet it has still failed to enter our collective consciousness.

### Finally, we had a pretty hefty budgetary constraint

The entire budget for marketing was £78k – how on earth do you do any real good and achieve a real shift in public awareness for a budget of £78k?

To put that in context over the course of a year, that represents 0.0198% of the total spent on charity advertising (let alone the rest of UK ad spend). And even in the month we were live, our campaign was 0.23% of total charity advertising expenditure (Figure 2).

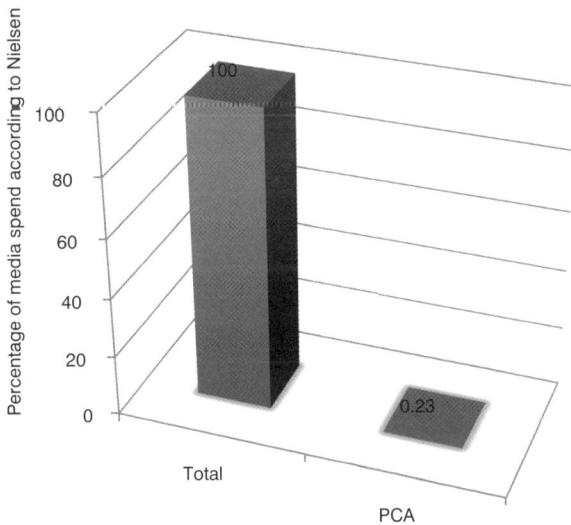

**Figure 2: Charity spend in month of PCA campaign**

### The strategy – a no-holds-barred approach to generate massive awareness

Given the difficulties mentioned above, we had to punch above our weight to find a way to cut through more effectively.

A polite, reasoned campaign that explained the symptoms was unlikely to shout louder than its media budget and, in fact, it could under-perform as people actively ignore messages about difficult topics like cancer.[15]

So the strategy was to present the genuinely shocking statistics around pancreatic cancer in as arresting a way as possible. To shake people out of their apathy, make them feel compelled to find out more, and give them the information they need to do so.

Through initial qualitative research we also knew that putting shock, facts and symptoms into a single ad, overloaded the communication and increased the likelihood of people ignoring the message altogether. This led to a risky decision to divide the campaign into two phases:

1. create impact to make people sit up and take notice;
2. expand and explain in order to drive action.

Neither would do a good enough job on its own – generating the shock and interest wouldn't deliver a message about symptoms and a simple message about symptoms wouldn't get the attention.

So all rested on Phase one, delivering earned media so that the campaign would get repeated beyond the print media it was scheduled in. This meant actively courting controversy, but without stepping over the line – causing a justifiable amount of offence/shock, otherwise not enough people would notice Phase two.

### Phase 1: The starting point – creating an impact

We uncovered a powerful insight that generates real empathy and a desire to find out more.

The core insight in the campaign came from our conversations with real pancreatic cancer sufferers. It was the moment when the reality of their situation dawned upon them:

*When I heard the word cancer I thought I'd at least have a fighting chance, so to find out you basically don't was shocking.*

*Anything but this, I wish I had a different disease, a different cancer – at least they have a higher survival rate.*[16]

This led directly to our ad – 'I wish I had a [more survivable] cancer' – which brought to life the horrific realisation that for the majority, by the time they were diagnosed, it was already too late.

### Phase 2: Expanding and explaining

Having created an impact and courted a degree of controversy, the idea was to use the interest generated to deliver the symptoms information. This in part through a modified version of the original campaign but also through resource on PCA's website and, crucially, through PR where symptoms were provided as part of the initial press release.

### Smart research to ensure the right level of offence for Phase 1

The decision to run this campaign was not taken lightly and it was not done without a fair amount of research to understand the likely reaction. We genuinely didn't want to cause serious and widespread offence, but we did want people to think 'You can't say that!', and then find out why we had.

We wanted to do more than gauge what people *said* they were feeling; we wanted to see it for ourselves. So, in addition to qualitative and quantitative research, we commissioned neuro-research to enable us to literally track what people saw and how it affected them neurologically.

The research helped us in two ways:

- it enabled us to prove that we were jolting people – but not offending them;
- it enabled us to maximise the effectiveness of the campaign by fine-tuning the campaign so that maximum long-term memory encoding was achieved (LTME).

As well as checking the overall concept, revealing that there were no gross negatives, the research highlighted areas where the campaign could be improved. For example, the chart below illustrates how respondents reacted to the original adcepts. From this, we knew we had to use younger patients and shoot them face on. Other learnings informed which cancers and which type of patients would illicit the greatest response. This insight allowed us to tune each execution for maximum engagement and emotional attachment (Figure 3).

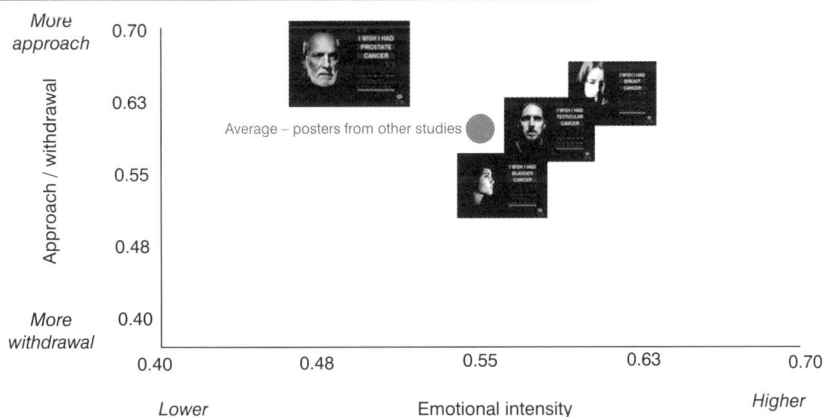

Figure 3: Overview of results

### The media strategy

Given the arresting headlines, we needed a medium where people could be stopped in their tracks and spend time making sense of the shocking headline. Print delivered that opportunity better than any other medium. TV (apart from not having the budget) doesn't offer dwell time. However, we did produce a YouTube film to aid any TV coverage of the campaign. And the Internet is full of sensational headlines that have little weight and are quickly forgotten. Also we knew we couldn't expect much in the way of direct social shares as the campaign carries too much personal social risk. The print budget was strategically split between the two phases.

## Phase 1

We wanted maximum reach in the quickest time frame for the least money. High circulation papers in the two biggest cities was the best way to achieve this. The budget for this phase was set intentionally low at £15,000 as we knew the campaign would either be picked up by the media within a few days, or not at all.

## Phase 2

This was where the bulk of the budget went (£63,000). The aim was to deliver the symptoms information efficiently to capitalise on any coverage. We chose 48 sheet cross track sites on 25 London Underground stations, and 200 tube car panels. This was based on the following:

Highly visible campaign to capitalise on the recognition generated in Phase 1. The un-ignorable poster format to add impact to a less impactful execution.

Dwell time so the symptoms information could be properly absorbed. A full two-week presence plus overspill due to posting cycles.

*Final costs and timings*

| Table 1: Media plan and total campaign costs | | |
|---|---|---|
| | | **Cost** |
| Phase 1 | Press: | |
| | Four insertions 25 x 9 (half page) in full colour in four publications (Evening Standard, London Metro, Manchester Metro, Manchester Evening News) | £15k |
| | Total of 16 half pages 4 February 2013 | |
| Phase 2 | London Underground x 2,000 tube car panels (TCP) 2 weeks – including production of three sets of artwork | £63k |
| | W/C 10 February 2013 | |
| | General distribution cross track 48 sheets x 25 London Underground – including production of three sets of artwork | |
| | W/C 10 February 2013 | |
| Agency | Fee and Production | Waived |
| Research | Neuro-insight costs | Waived |

*Summary – the campaign model*

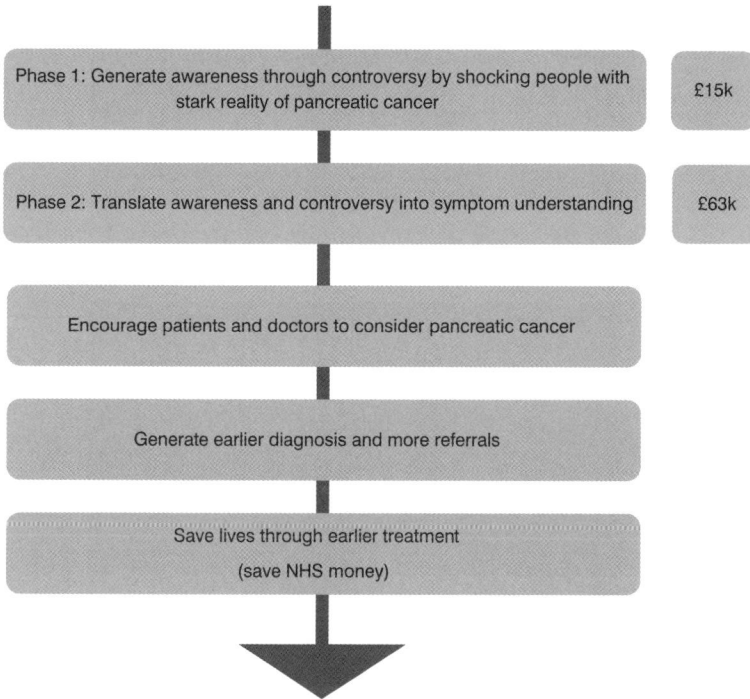

Figure 4: Overall model of how the campaign is intended to drive awareness and ultimately save lives

Phase 1: Generate awareness through controversy by shocking people with stark reality of pancreatic cancer — £15k

Phase 2: Translate awareness and controversy into symptom understanding — £63k

Encourage patients and doctors to consider pancreatic cancer

Generate earlier diagnosis and more referrals

Save lives through earlier treatment
(save NHS money)

# The campaign

*Phase 1*

The campaign depicted three real sufferers of pancreatic cancer saying that they wished they had another, more survivable form of the disease. The insight was so accurate that all three patients thought the campaign had come directly from something they had said themselves[17].

The campaign was formed of a print campaign and a YouTube video (Figure 5).

Figure 5: Phase 1 campaign

## Phase 2

Building on the awareness of the original campaign, Phase 2 was designed to focus more specifically on the symptoms. In terms of creative strategy, we kept the same images as we knew recognition would drive people to the messages (Figure 6).

## Figure 6: Phase 2 campaign

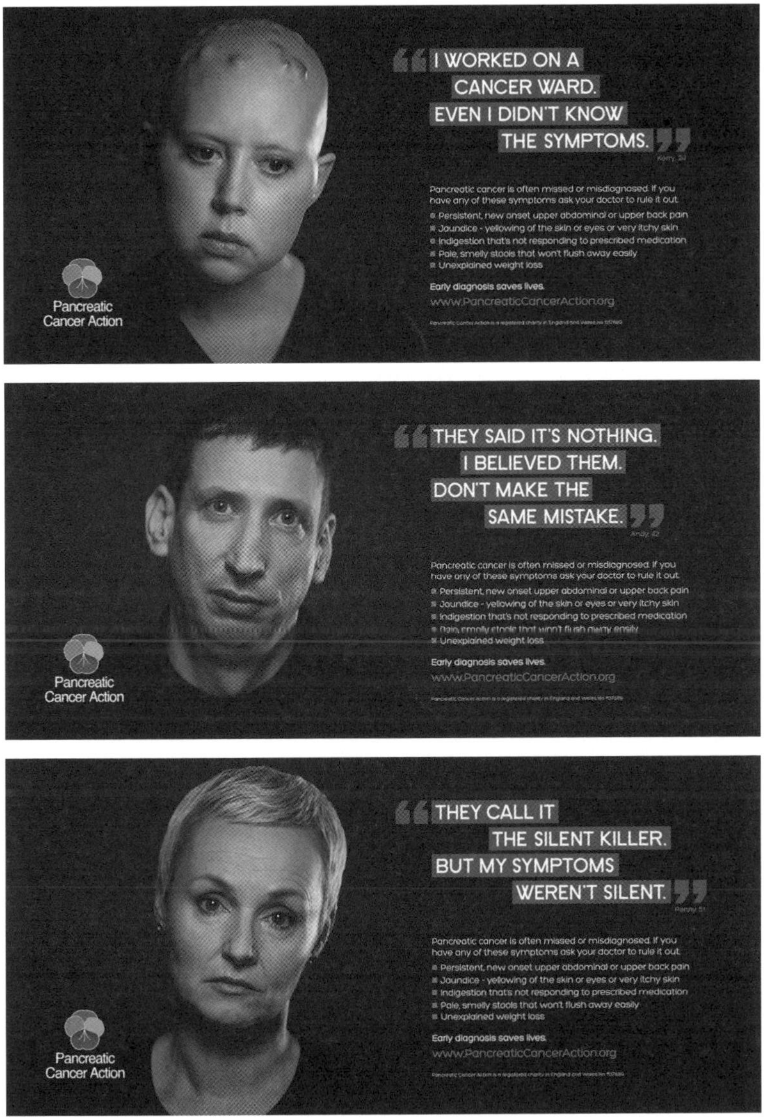

## The results

The campaign had a powerful and immediate impact and received unprecedented coverage – smashing its objectives.

### *It was noticed and it got people talking*

- Discussed on all major TV channels (and many minor ones), e.g. BBC's 'Newsnight', ITV's 'This Morning' (twice), SKY news (every hour for a whole day);
- picked up by all major newspapers (*The Daily Mail*, five times);
- most news websites carried stories about the campaign;
- it provoked fierce debate on social media: a *Mail on Sunday* article, on 8th February, received 1,142 shares;
- Twitter mentions of pancreatic cancer went up 69% from previous month[18] (Figure 7);
- over £1m of highest quality earned media from £15k Phase 1 spend (and this underestimates it as all media was editorial);
- over 100 pieces of media coverage relating to the advertising in the UK alone; two months after the campaign ran, it was being discussed on US Doctor's TV;[19]
- head of PCA invited to talk to MPs and held a separate meeting with Health Secretary Jeremy Hunt about increased funding. The issue is being referred to the Chief Medical Officer.

**Figure 7: The campaign provoked fierce debate on social media**

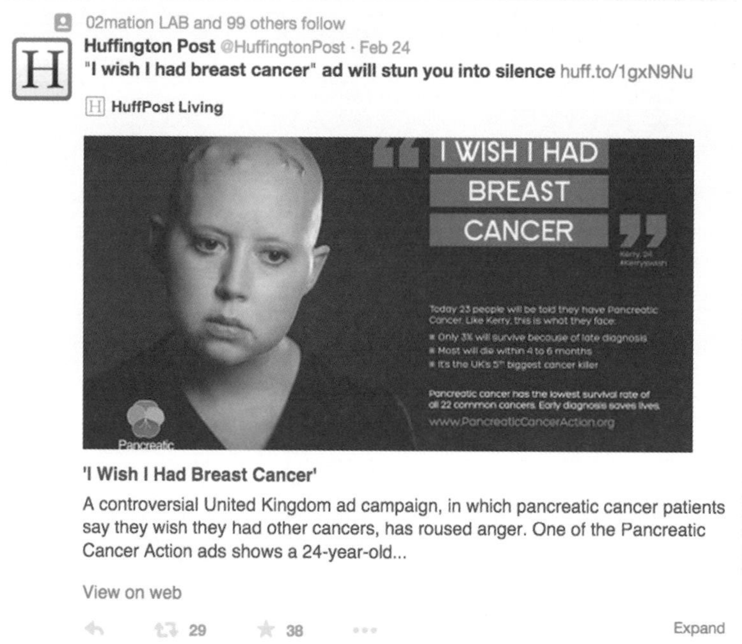
02mation LAB and 99 others follow
H
Huffington Post @HuffingtonPost · Feb 24
"I wish I had breast cancer" ad will stun you into silence huff.to/1gxN9Nu
HuffPost Living
I WISH I HAD
BREAST
CANCER
Today 23 people will be told they have Pancreatic Cancer. Like Kerry, this is what they face:
Only 3% will survive because of late diagnosis
Most will die within 4 to 6 months
It's the UK's 5th biggest cancer killer
Pancreatic cancer has the lowest survival rate of all 22 common cancers. Early diagnosis saves lives.
www.PancreaticCancerAction.org
'I Wish I Had Breast Cancer'
A controversial United Kingdom ad campaign, in which pancreatic cancer patients say they wish they had other cancers, has roused anger. One of the Pancreatic Cancer Action ads shows a 24-year-old...
View on web
29
38
Expand

## Figure 8: The campaign featured heavily on news media

Cancer 'envy' campaign criticised

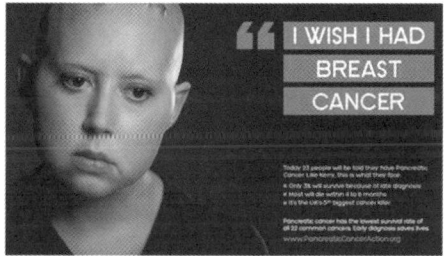

A campaign to raise awareness of pancreatic cancer has been criticised for suggesting patients wish they had other forms of the disease.

Related Stories

Pancreatic cancer charity's new ad slogan causes outcry

A pancreatic charity's new campaign slogan has been condemned as "repugnant" after the ads showed patients wishing they had other 'less lethal' cancers instead

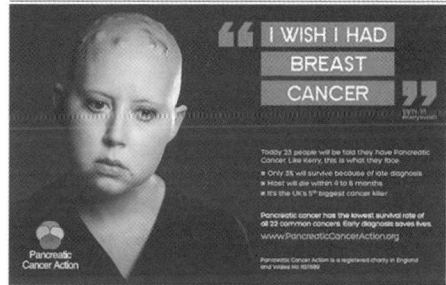

Emotive posters show a young pancreatic sufferer called Kerry next to a quote saying: 'I wish I had breast cancer'.

*It got people to do something*

- Traffic on explanatory page of PCA website up 963%;[20]
- donations to charity up 60% on same period last year;
- home page visits up 1,204%;
- symptoms page up 291%.

*It increased awareness*

- Prompted awareness of the campaign was 27% for all UK adults;[21]
- among people that saw our ad, 72% think the survival rate for pancreatic cancer is low (22% higher than for people who hadn't seen our campaign);
- among people who'd recognised our campaign, 43% are more aware of the symptoms of pancreatic cancer than they were 6 months ago; this compares with 16% who don't remember seeing the campaign.

*And it will save lives and money*

- Our model (see below) suggests pancreatic cancer diagnosis increased by 14%.
- The model also suggests it could save as many as 34 lives.
- This would create a potential saving for the NHS between £3.1m and nearly £8m!

### Figure 9: Most stories included the symptoms

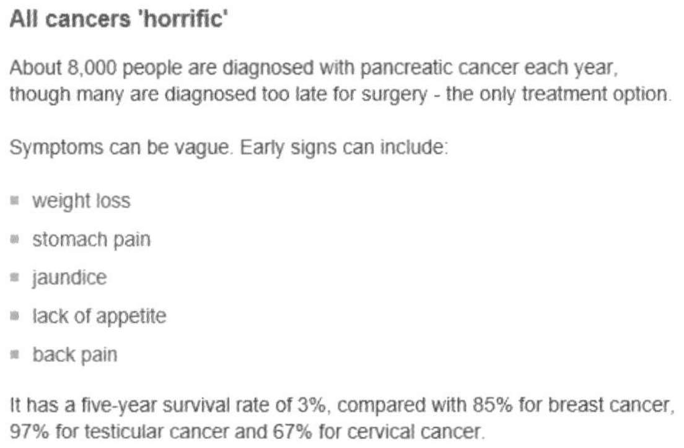

**All cancers 'horrific'**

About 8,000 people are diagnosed with pancreatic cancer each year, though many are diagnosed too late for surgery - the only treatment option.

Symptoms can be vague. Early signs can include:

- weight loss
- stomach pain
- jaundice
- lack of appetite
- back pain

It has a five-year survival rate of 3%, compared with 85% for breast cancer, 97% for testicular cancer and 67% for cervical cancer.

## Why it worked

*As intended, Phase 1 of the campaign generated strong interest and debate.*

Initially reaction was led by *The Daily Mail* and cancer charities (especially breast cancer ones) who were quick to criticise the campaign. This generated media interest across the globe. Crucially, most of the coverage also included the symptoms of pancreatic cancer. Very quickly, the vast majority of people (who'd by now read the body copy) became more supportive of the approach and *The Daily Mail* now ran articles in support of the strategy. The patients in the ads also stepped up to defend the campaign on TV, radio and in print. As the debate went on, more and more people were exposed to the campaign. Then tragically, three weeks after the campaign launched, Kerry Harvey died, which inevitably generated more news stories.

## The right amount of offence

Most online articles received widespread coverage from the number of shares. The top-rated comments on many articles are positive. This one below received 3,023 likes versus 47 dislikes.

> *The survival rates for pancreatic cancer are exactly the same as 20 years ago when my sister died of it leaving behind two young children. If shock tactics are what is needed to help find cures for this dreadful disease then that cannot be wrong.*
>
> *Mail Online*

PCA had a huge amount of supportive messages sent to it via social media and e-mail.

They have also received high profile support in the media, including articles written by Anne Widdecombe,[22] Jenni Murray[23] and Dr Miriam Stoppard.[24]

From our point of view, if Jenni Murray says it's OK then it must be!

## Could anything else have caused this?

As we said, famous people have died of it before with little impact on awareness.

Weeks before the campaign there was a 'Coronation Street' story line about pancreatic cancer and the recent death of Roger Lloyd-Pack. But ultimately the social and media conversation was dominated by our campaign.

Of all the people who are now more aware of the symptoms of pancreatic cancer, the awareness of those who'd seen the campaign is 268%[25] higher than those who claim not to have done. And the Twitter stats show the increases in mentions of pancreatic cancer correlate with our campaign.

## Earned media

Our most conservative estimate is over £1m based on:

- TV – £530k
- print – £153k
- online – £350k
- radio – £6k.

However, this underestimates the value of the media as the campaign was discussed in editorial contexts – it wasn't 'just an ad'. Nevertheless it still represents a media uplift of 6,900% using the £15k Phase 1 spend (this is based on the fact that all media coverage focused on the 'I wish I had' ads). Even if we include all the spend it's still an uplift of 1,282%.

## Developing a model to estimate ROI

Although the campaign was developed purely to raise awareness, we felt it important to attempt to attribute a value to that awareness, so we've built an assumptive model to give an idea of the campaign's real world effect.

### Basis for model

Previous studies show that there is a strong link between generating awareness of symptoms through advertising campaigns and diagnosis of cancer. We can use these figures to model a relationship between awareness uplifts and increases in diagnosis (see Figure 10).

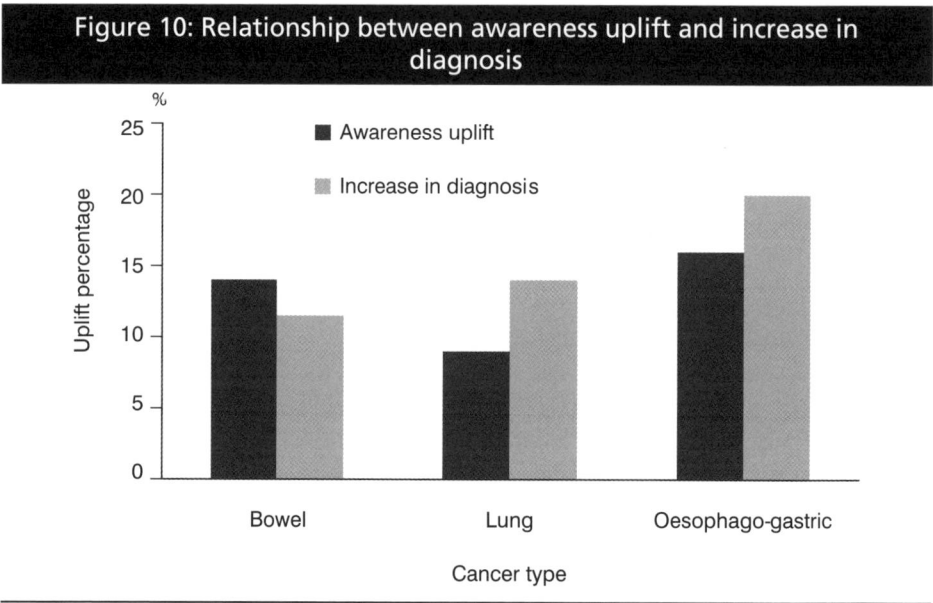

Figure 10: Relationship between awareness uplift and increase in diagnosis

Taking the mean of the ratios reveals that for every 1% uplift in awareness, you can expect an increase in diagnosis of 1.21%.

Working this through from the awareness our campaign generated, projects an increase in diagnosis of 14.05% or 1,194 people.

### Putting a value against these numbers

### Saving to the NHS of these extra diagnoses not going through A&E

We know that the 50% that get diagnosed through A&E cost the NHS £4,848 per patient.

Using this cost as a model and assuming half of our new diagnoses would otherwise have been diagnosed through A&E,[26] gives a saving to the NHS of £2.89m.

This would deliver a campaign ROI of 3,705%.

### But there's also a saving in lives saved

Through a calculation based on numbers being diagnosed and survival rates, we can estimate that our campaign will save an additional 34.7 – call it 34 lives. What's the value of these lives?

In the US the EPA values a life at $9.1m and the FDA says $7.9m[27]. A far simpler figure is provided by the NHS (and NICE) who are prepared to spend between £20k and £30k to keep you alive for one year.[28] This values one of our additional survivor's lives at a minimum of £100–£150k (since they live past five years).

So our five-year survivors are worth at least £3.4m–£5.1m in NHS terms. This from a £78k investment: an overall ROI of between 4,359% and 6,538%. Combining the savings, the best case gives a total of £2.89m + £5.1m = £7.99m. An ROI of 10,243%!

Even if we are very conservative and divide the worst cases by two, it's still an ROI of 4,032% or a saving of £3.1m.

### Conclusions

For us this campaign is about intelligent bravery, about setting out to shock in order to get attention and then using that attention to deliver the message. It's about using smart research to get the best out of a strategy. But most of all it's about not being put off by the impossible and being prepared to take a calculated risk.

> *I saw your campaign and it made me ask my doctor to consider pancreatic cancer.*
>
> Anonymous call to Pancreatic Cancer Action enquiry line

## Research projects and further analysis

- Discussions with sufferers conducted in December 2012 by Team Darwin;
- rudimentary Qual and Quant carried out from January to February 2013 by Team Darwin;
- neuroscience project carried out on 5–6th March 2013 by Neuro Insight;
- further Quant into campaign carried out in January 2014 By Atomik research;
- post-campaign Omnibus carried out on 26–27th February 2014 by Populus;
- Twitter analysis conducted by Trigger Social;
- media analysis conducted by TTMV.

### Media calculation

Working out a value attached to this is not straight forward. The approach we've taken is as follows.

We've tried to calculate the approximate value of the media where there is a direct comparison, by asking how much it would cost to buy, for example, ten minutes of time on 'This Morning'. We've also had to apply similar approximations for shows like 'Newsnight' by asking ourselves how much it would cost to buy that audience at that time.

What is extremely difficult to put a value on is the digital content, for example the *Mail Online*'s coverage, the comments that people have made and the number of times they have been shared.

Our most conservative estimate is £1m based on the following:

- TV – £530k
- print – £153k
- online – £350k
- radio – £6k.
- Example calculations for TV are shown in Table 2.

## How we modelled the effect

### Developing a model to estimate ROI

Although the campaign was developed purely to raise awareness, we felt it important to attempt to attribute a value to that awareness, so we've built an assumptive model to give an idea of the campaign's real-world effect.

### Table 2: Example calculations for TV

| TV Show | Channel | TV Market | Aired | Length | Adult TVRs | Univ | Imps | CPT | 30" equiv | Value @ station price |
|---|---|---|---|---|---|---|---|---|---|---|
| Newsnight | BBC 2 | UK National | 6 Feb | 05:00 | 0.01 | 49806 | 498 | £7.71 | 10 | £38,400 |
| Daybreak | ITV | UK National | 4 Feb | 10:00 | 0.015 | 49806 | 747 | £7.71 | 20 | £115,201 |
| This Morning | ITV | UK National | 12 Feb | 10:16 | 0.024 | 49806 | 1195 | £7.71 | 20.5 | £188,930 |
| This Morning | ITV | UK National | 4 Feb | 01:43 | 0.024 | 49806 | 1195 | £7.71 | 3.5 | £32,256 |
| The Wright Stuff | Channel 5 | UK National | 4 Feb | 10:00 | 0.0064 | 49806 | 319 | £7.71 | 20 | £49,153 |
| ITV News* | ITV | UK National | 7 Feb | 00:49 | 0.02 | 49806 | 996 | £7.71 | 1.65 | £12,672 |
| NBC Bay Area News at 11AM | KNTV-SF (NBC) | San Francisco | 5 Feb | | | | | | | |
| RTV 6 News at 11:00 | WRTV-IN (ABC) | Indianapolis | 5 Feb | | | | | | | |
| Fox8 News at 6:00PM | WGHP (FOX) | Greensboro | 9 Feb | | | | | | | |
| Good Morning Quad Cities | WQAD-DAV (ABC) | Davenport | 10 Feb | | | | | | | |
| Nine Melbourne | | Melbourne | 6 Feb | | | | | | | |
| Sky News | Sky News | UK National?? | 15 Feb | 02:26 | 0.048 | 49806 | 2391 | £7.71 | 5 | £92,161 |
| | | | | | | | | | | £528,774 |

* based on lunchtime news due to timing of post on website

Previous studies show that there is a strong link between generating awareness of symptoms through advertising campaigns and diagnosis of cancer. We can use these figures to model a relationship between awareness uplifts and increases in diagnosis (see Table 3 below).

**Table 3: Results of 'Be Clear on Cancer' ad campaigns show how awareness translates into increased diagnosis.**

| Type of cancer | Awareness uplift | Increase in diagnosis | Awareness uplift to diagnoses ratio |
|---|---|---|---|
| Bowel | | | |
| Symptom 1 | 15% | 11.5% | 0.82% |
| Symptom 2 | 13% (average is 14%) | | (11.5/14) |
| Lung | | | |
| Symptom 1 | 9% | 14% | 1.56 |
| Symptom 2 | 3%* | | (14/9) |
| Oesophago-gastric | | | |
| Main symptom | 16% | 20% | 1.25 |
| | | | (20/16) |

*NB: We've removed the Symptom 2 awareness uplift for lung cancer as this looks like an outlier and might unfairly bias the results in our favour.

Taking the mean of the ratios reveals that for every 1% uplift in awareness, you can expect an increase in diagnosis of 1.21%.

To calculate a number for our campaign we know that 27% of the population saw our campaign and that of them 43% are more aware of the symptoms. This gives the results shown in Table 4.

**Table 4: Relationship between awareness and potential diagnosis**

| Awareness uplift as a result of our campaign | Projected increase in diagnosis |
|---|---|
| 11.61% (43% of 27%) | 14.05% (11.61% × 1.21%) |

## Putting a value against these numbers

There were 8,500 people diagnosed with pancreatic cancer in 2010[29]; 14.05% equates to 1,194 more people being diagnosed as a result of our campaign.

We know that diagnosing pancreatic cancer through A&E cost the NHS £14.65m for the patients diagnosed that way. This study concluded that each of these patients equated to £4,848 extra. Using this cost as a model and assuming half of our new diagnoses would otherwise have been diagnosed through A&E,[30] gives a saving to the NHS of £2.89m.

This would deliver a campaign ROI of 3,705%.

## But there's also a saving in lives saved

Three percent of pancreatic cancer sufferers survive.

Let's assume that 3% of the extra 1,194 people diagnosed would have survived anyway. That leaves 1,158 people whom we would not expect to survive had their diagnosis not been brought forward by our campaign.

Now let's assume that despite their diagnosis being brought forward, the same survival rate applies. This would equate to 34.7 lives saved (3% of 1,158) – call it 34.

## What's the value of a life?

In the US the EPA values a life at $9.1m and the FDA says $7.9m. We could use the saving to the NHS of the earlier treatment plus the on-going tax contributions. But these methods require too many assumptions. We can put a minimum value on the price of one year of human life based on the maximum amount the NHS (recommended by NICE) is prepared to spend to keep you alive for 1 year. This figure is between £20k and £30k for each year of life.

We know that 3% survive past 5 years so at the very least we can call the value of one saved life at £100k–150k.

So our five year survivors are worth at least £3.4m–£5.1m in NHS terms.

This from a £78k investment. An overall ROI of between 4,359% and 6,538%.

Combining the savings, the best case gives a total of £2.89m + £5.1m = £7.99m An ROI of 10,243%!!

## Notes

1   Office for National Statistics, Statistical Bulletin 'Cancer Survival in England'. Patients diagnosed in 2005–2009, followed up to 2010. Accessed 20 April 2012. Welsh Cancer Intelligence and Surveillance Unit (2011), 'Cancer in Wales: A comprehensive report', September. ISD Scotland – patients diagnosed between 2003 and 2007. Northern Ireland Cancer Registry Cancer Statistics, Pancreas. http://www.qub.ac.uk/research-centres/nicr/CancerData/OnlineStatistics/Pancreas/.
2   Spalding and Williamson (2007) Pancreatic Cancer, Medicine Vol 35, pp 325–329.
3   http://www.cancerresearchuk.org/cancer-info/cancerstats/survival/common-cancers/#Five-year.
4   Ghaneh et al. (2008), 'Neo-adjuvant and adjuvant strategies for pancreatic cancer', *European Journal of Surgical Oncology*, 34, pp. 297–305.
5   NCIN (2012) *Routes to Diagnosis 2006–2008*, England Information Supplement.
6   Mistry M., Parkin D., Ahmad A., Sasieni P. (2011) 'Cancer incidence in the UK: Projections to the year 2030', *British Journal of Cancer*, Vol 105, pp. 1795–1803.
7   NCRI Data package 2012 http://www.ncri.org.uk/what-we-do/research-database.
8   http://www.cancerresearchuk.org/cancer-info/spotcancerearly/naedi/beclearoncancer/background #evidenceandevaluation.
9   http://www.cancerresearchuk.org/prod_consump/groups/cr_common/@nre/@hea/documents/ generalcontent/cr_113267.pdf.
10  https://www.pancreaticcancer.org.uk/media/450955/elm_policybriefing_final.pdf.
11  http://www.charitycommission.gov.uk/about-charities/sector-facts-and-figures/.
12  Nielsen charity spend data from 1 January 2013 to 31 December 2013.
13  http://www.ncvo.org.uk/policy-and-research/giving-and-philantropy/what-research-tells-us.
14  PCA Research Findings: Ipsos Mori, October 2012.
15  Team Darwin qualitative research.
16  Taken from Thinkbox presentation 'The Winning Formula: Creativity and effectiveness'
17  http://www.dailymail.co.uk/news/article-2554820/I-dont-regret-saying-I-wish-I-breast-cancer-Id-better-chance-live-Star-repugnant-charity-ad-defies-death-threats.html.
18  Online fieldwork survey of 1,051 respondents, who are a representative sample of the population, carried out by Populus on 26–27 February 2014.
19  Analysis conducted by Trigger Social.
20  Google analytics, comparing February 2013 with February 2014.
21  Online fieldwork survey of 1,051 respondents, who are a representative sample of the population, carried out by Populus on 26th/27th February 2014
22  http://dexpr.es/1kAj9Vs.
23  http://dailym.ai/1hOIcRD.
24  http://bit.ly/1dC96Lt.
25  See Note 18.

26  https://www.pancreaticcancer.org.uk/media/450955/elm_policybriefing_final.pdf.
27  NCIN: NCIN (2012) Routes to Diagnosis 2006–2008, England Information Supplement
28  http://www.care2.com/causes/epa-puts-the-value-of-human-life-at-9-1-million-fda-says-7-9-million. html.
29  ONS Cancer Statistics Registrations England (Series MB1 – No 41 2010). Released 13 June 2012.
30  NCIN: NCIN (2012) Routes to Diagnosis 2006–2008, England Information Supplement.

# Group of Humanitarian Attention to the Demobilised

## At Christmas everything is possible

**By Juan Pablo Garcia, Lowe-SSP3; Mihir Warty and Jane Dorsett, Lowe Counsel; Maria Alejandra Urbina, Lowe-SSP3**

The Fuerzas Armadas Revolucionarias de Colombia, or FARC, are the largest and oldest insurgent group in the Americas. FARC conduct bombings, unlawful killings, mortar attacks, kidnappings, forced displacement, extortion and hijackings. It is considered a terrorist group by the Colombian government, the United States Department of State and the European Union.

Since 2002, the GAHD (the Colombian Ministry of Defence's Group of Humanitarian Attention to the Demobilised) have strived to promote guerrilla demobilisation and enable a return to conventional, civilian life.

Due to the sensitive nature of the subject and the constantly changing landscape, the GAHD has never set numeric targets for the number of the guerrillas that should quit as a result of their activity. However, by 2010 their ambition – and therefore the campaign challenge – was to stem the recent decline in demobilisations and reach an increasingly remote – and hard to convert – audience.

Despite the difficulties involved it was recognised early on that insight from ex-guerrillas was needed in order to formulate an effective campaign. Consequently group sessions were held to identify key insights that could be utilised. The major theme that emerged was that in this highly religious Catholic society, Christmas is the time when many guerrillas think seriously about the idea of quitting.

In December 2010, 'Operation Christmas' featured two professional anti-guerrilla contingents and two Black Hawk helicopters venturing to the remote jungle FARC strongholds, in order to cover 75-foot trees with 2,000 Christmas lights. Adjacent to each tree, military light mechanisms were installed that detected the guerrillas' movements and thus lit the trees as they approached. Beside each tree, large banners proclaimed an emotive message:

'If Christmas can come to the jungle, you can come home. Demobilise. At Christmas everything is possible.'

The successful installations led to a TV commercial being produced of the activity, subsequently broadcast on primetime Christmas television.

In November 2011, 'Operation Rivers of Light' invited people from all over the country to send a Christmas message, note or even a small gift to their loved ones in the jungle. The army delivered these messages for them by floating them in lit plastic balls along the river routes frequented by FARC guerrillas. 6,823 messages and gifts were received from friends and relatives inviting their loved ones to demobilise. Even the President, Juan Manuel Santos, his family and the entire cabinet of ministers sent their own messages. Once again coverage of the delivery operation was filmed and broadcast in a commercial spot, thus widening the impact of the activity.

Finally, in 2012 'Operation Bethlehem' involved powerful light reflectors being installed in towns with a known guerrilla presence. Once lit, they cast shafts of light into the sky to guide the demobilising guerrillas out of the jungle. The Minister of Defence lit the final beacon on 17 December. Simultaneously, Colombian forces dropped hundreds of LED lights into the depths of the jungle, lighting paths home for demobilising guerrillas. The installation of jungle billboards with glow-in-the-dark ink also provided exhortation and guidance.

Over three Christmases, and on a small budget of just $1m USD, this powerful and timely messaging encouraged 711 FARC guerrillas (out of a total 8,000) to demobilise and re-enter society. The combined reduction in guerrilla numbers is estimated to return over $8.6m to Colombian government through tax receipts, an $8.31 return on marketing investment. At a wider level, the benefits to Colombian society and the economy through a reduction in FARC's illegal 'fund raising' are estimated to be in excess of $5m. And looking even more broadly, the innovative concepts and their collective impact gained huge awareness, both within Colombia and internationally.

# The Salvation Army

## Bringing transformational growth to best of breed fundraising

**By Mike Colling, Mike Colling & Co; Helen Weavers,
Real World Planning**
Contributing author: John Eversley, WPN Chameleon

The heart of The Salvation Army's fundraising is a six-week marketing campaign before Christmas, during which it recruits all its donors and spends 70% of annual marketing budget. It also asks existing donors to give again.

In spring 2008 the Salvation Army approached MC&C with an exciting brief: could it help them recruit significantly more new donors? No charity can keep asking the same pool of people for donations, since response wanes over time, donors die or become less able or inclined to give so it needed to increase its donor pool.

However the agency faced two specific challenges:

- the recruitment of new donors needed to continue to pay back immediately (i.e. a short-term ROME of at least 1%);
- the new donors must have a similar profile to current donors so that subsequent requests for donations would continue to achieve ROME figures of at least 1,000% (£12 donated for every £1 spent).

To understand how to recruit more, the agency profiled the donor database using Acxiom Behaviour Bank data.

In 2008 it kept targeting, messaging, call to action and the bulk of the communications schedule exactly as per 2007 – but made two major changes: it added a DRTV campaign as a stand-alone media channel and it deployed an unusual pattern of investment. TV campaigns typically start with a bang, building coverage quickly and then continuing at lower weights. It reversed this norm, starting at low weights and building to a peak on Christmas Eve as people become more inclined to give the closer to Christmas it gets.

It added paid search as another stand-alone media channel, enabling those donors who did want to give online to do so more easily and efficiently.

Year 1 results were extremely pleasing. For only a modest increase in spend, 27% more new donors were recruited reversing the decline seen previously.

The 2009 plan was somewhat conservative: almost the same as Year 1 but with TV spend doubled. It also added radio, to further increase reach and unweight the key days running up to Christmas Eve.

The charity was rewarded with another leap in the number of new donors recruited, further reduction in cost of acquisition, more income and better returns.

The following year spend on TV was doubled again. Its more unconventional move was to invest more in cold addressed mail and door drops. Models showed strong interactions between TV and addressed/unaddressed mail, implying that TV 'primes' people to give when prompted by mail. So as TV spend increased in 2010 it felt there was an opportunity to increase investment in mail too.

It decided to change the timing of door drop activity from its traditional position early in the campaign to much later, in the last week before Christmas. All in, this revised approach bore real fruit with 100,000 more new donors recruited.

For both 2011 and 2012, investment in television and cold mail was increased even further, by 45% and 22% respectively, while it moved door drops earlier in the campaign. In both years it achieved record results. The 2012 campaign delivered 131,367 new donors.

By 2012 the campaign was attracting 37% more response in total than in 2007. As new donors come in, the pool from which to solicit future donations grew, driving up the number of existing donors who could be asked to give the following year. Over the five years 493,694 new donors have been recruited. 242,659 of these are due to the improvement in campaign effectiveness cited here. The active donor base (defined as those who have given during the last two years) has grown by a net 191,000.

# Heart & Stroke Foundation of Canada

## Make health last

**By Liam Brown, Jonathan Daly and Laura Davis, Lowe Roche**

Contributing author: Jane Dorsett, Lowe Counsel

Heart disease and stroke are two of the three leading causes of death in Canada, accounting for 29% of all deaths and killing more than 69,500 Canadians every year. Research revealed that the five major risk factors associated with heart disease and stroke – poor nutrition, obesity, smoking, binge alcohol consumption, and stress – now made nine out of ten Canadians susceptible to heart disease and stroke in their older, and even younger, years. While these were alarming facts, the reality was that Canadians were constantly inundated with facts and figures about their health. Thus the challenge became how the Heart & Stroke Foundation of Canada could turn the facts into a focused and compelling message that would bring new relevance for both the disease and the foundation itself.

So in February 2013, it launched its 'Make Health Last' campaign, focusing on the baby-boomer target to trigger action using a three-pronged approach: 'Wake Them' to understand the current reality; 'Shake Them' to see that there was hope; and 'Make Them' inspired to facilitate the simple daily changes to their health behaviour that would ensure they lived healthier, longer lives.

With these three core factors in mind, a personalised health-education platform, MakeHealthLast.ca, was designed featuring an online risk assessment, as well as interactive monitoring and record-keeping tools. The programme experience built around the site served as the final destination point for the campaign, and provided the foundation with a means to have an ongoing, life-changing conversation with visitors well beyond the campaign's initial run.

Through mass-media vehicles, including national provocative TV spots, the 'last 10 years in sickness' fact was highlighted and promised that change was indeed possible if Canadians made a choice today. The TV spot used a split-screen narrative to follow the life of a man through two possible fates: on the left, a life filled with vitality; and on the right, a life defined by sickness and disease, asking the audience 'What will your last 10 years look like?'

Earned media was generated with journalists and key media influencers, and driving social word-of-mouth. The campaign's reach was extended by placing the 'Make Health Last' film on both YouTube and the foundation's Facebook page.

But providing the facts and offering Canadians a choice to change their fates was not enough. In order to 'make them' move toward greater health, it offered the means and tools to facilitate change via the campaign microsite, MakeHealthLast. ca. The user-friendly site immediately offered first time visitors the opportunity to completely customise their experience. The journey began with the user encouraged to take a seven-minute medical survey that effectively determined their major risk factors based on their current habits, hereditary considerations, and previous medical history. Once the assessment was completed, the site adjusted to offer up only the simple tips, tools, and content most relevant to their personal results. Users could set simple and trackable goals, create a progress diary and share information with loved ones via social media.

The results to date have far exceeded expectations despite limited budgets in paid media. The foundation delivered a memorable TV commercial to drive mass awareness with 62% recall among baby-boomers and raised awareness among this demographic to the realities of heart disease and stroke. As well as impressive digital results – including 1.7m views of the spot on YouTube – the campaign gained major PR coverage across online and offline national media channels including the *Huffington Post*. The foundation garnered over half a million users to MakeHealthLast.ca and traffic to the site surpassed the +20% target after the first two months. While such statistics are impressive, the true value of the campaign will only be felt when baby-boomers reach their last ten years of life, which could be anywhere between now and 25 years.

# How to access the IPA Effectiveness Awards Databank

The IPA Databank represents the most rigorous and comprehensive examination of marketing communications working in the marketplace, and in the world. Over more than 34 years of the IPA's Effectiveness Awards competition, we have collected over 1,400 examples of best practice in advertising development and results across a wide spectrum of marketing sources and expenditures. Each example contains up to 4,000 words of text and is illustrated in full by market, research, sales and profit data.

## IPA Effectiveness Awards Search Engine (EASE)

You can use the EASE search engine at www.ipa.co.uk/ease to interrogate over 1,400 detailed case studies from the IPA Databank. You can search the case studies by keywords and/or filter by any parameter from questions asked in the Effectiveness Awards Entry Questionnaire. EASE is free to use and is the first search engine on the web which allows you to do this. IPA members can also contact the Insight Centre directly where more complex searches can be commissioned and the results supplied by e-mail.

## Purchasing IPA case studies

Member agencies can download case studies from www.ipa.co.uk/cases at a discounted rate of £25 per case study. Alternatively members can sign up to warc. com (see overleaf) at a beneficial IPA rate and can then download case studies as part of that subscription. Non IPA members can purchase case studies from the IPA website (www.ipa.co.uk/cases) at £50 per copy.

## Further information

For further information, please contact the Insight Centre at the IPA, 44 Belgrave Square, London SW1X 8QS
Telephone: +44 (0)20 7235 7020
Fax: +44 (0)20 7245 9904
Website: www.ipa.co.uk/insight
Email: insight@ipa.co.uk

## warc.com

Warc is the official publisher of the IPA Effectiveness Awards' case histories. All IPA case studies are available at warc.com, alongside thousands of other case studies, articles and best practice guides, market intelligence and industry news and alerts, with material drawn from over 50 sources across the world.

Warc.com is relied upon by major creative and media agency networks, market research companies, media owners, multinational advertisers and business schools, to help tackle any marketing challenge.

IPA members can subscribe at a 10% discount. To find out more, request a trial at www.warc.com/trial.

## www.ipa.co.uk/effectiveness

On our dedicated hub where you can find out everything you need to know about the IPA Effectiveness Awards competition, including how to enter, how to get mentored, how to calculate ROMI and who's won what since 1980.

As well as viewing case study summaries and creative work, you'll also find a series of over 30 brand films from over three decades of the Awards including:

- HSBC
- John Lewis
- Marmite
- Yorkshire Tea
- Cadbury Dairy Milk
- Walkers
- PG Tips

You will also find links to publications and blogs on effectiveness from around the world.

# IPA Databank case availability

* Denotes winning entries
** Denotes cases published in *Area Works* volumes 1–5
ˢ Denotes cases published in *Scottish Advertising Works* volumes 1–4

NEW ENTRIES 2014
2014    Aldi UK & Ireland*
2014    Aviva*
2014    Blue Dragon
2014    British Heart Foundation*
2014    BT
2014    Cancer Research UK
2014    Colombian Ministry of Defence's
        Group of Humanitarian Attention
        to the Demobilised*
2014    Cuprinol*
2014    Dacia*
2014    Deutsche Telekom AG*
2014    Doritos
2014    easyJet*
2014    EDF Energy*
2014    Enterprise Rent-A-Car
2014    Everest*
2014    Expedia*
2014    Fairy Liquid*
2014    Fire Safety*
2014    first direct*
2014    Ford
2014    Foster's*
2014    Garnier Ultralift*
2014    Gillette
2014    Groupe Média TFO
2014    Health Promotion Board of
        Singapore
2014    Heart and Stroke Foundation of
        Canada*
2014    IKEA
2014    ITV
2014    Kärcher Window Vac*
2014    KitKat
2014    Lay's Global
2014    Lay's US
2014    The LEGO Movie
2014    Lidl
2014    Lifebuoy
2014    Lux*
2014    Maaza

2014    Mattessons Fridge Raiders*
2014    McCain Ready Baked Jackets*
2014    McDonald's Sponsorship London
        2012
2014    McDonald's Virtual Coins*
2014    Mercedes*
2014    MILO*
2014    MINI UK
2014    Missing People
2014    National Depression Initiative
        (NDI)*
2014    National Lottery
2014    New York Bagel Company
2014    O₂
2014    Olympic Delivery Authority/
        Transport for London*
2014    ONLY*
2014    Paddy Power
2014    Pancreatic Cancer Action*
2014    Pedigree
2014    Petplan
2014    PowerPacq
2014    Premier Inn*
2014    Public Health England*
2014    QualitySolicitors
2014    Range Rover Sport
2014    Sainsbury's
2014    Salvation Army, the*
2014    Sensodyne Pronamel*
2014    Specsavers*
2014    Sprite
2014    Supermalt
2014    Tide Naturals
2014    Toyota Daihatsu
2014    Twix
2014    Virgin Trains

NUMERICAL
2003    55 Degrees North**
2006    100.4 smooth fm
2000    1001 Mousse*
2012    2011 Census

| | | | |
|---|---|---|---|
| 2010 | Barclays Wealth* | 2006 | Branston Baked Beans* |
| 2002 | Barnardo's* | 1980 | Braun Shavers |
| 2012 | Barnardo's | 1982 | Bread Advisory Council* |
| 1994 | Batchelors | 1982 | Breville Toasted Sandwichmaker |
| 1998 | Batchelors Supernoodles* | 2002 | Britannia Building Society* |
| 2005 | Baxters Soup$^S$ | 1994 | British Airways* |
| 2008 | BBC iplayer | 1996 | British Airways |
| 2004 | Beck's Bier (Australia) | 2004 | British Airways* |
| 2005 | Belfast City | 1984 | British Airways Shuttle Service |
| 2001 | Belfast Giants** | 1994 | British Diabetic Association* |
| 1998 | Bell's Whisky | 1980 | British Film Institute* |
| 2002 | Benadryl* | 2012 | British Gas* |
| 2006 | Bendicks | 1994 | British Gas Central Heating |
| 2009 | Benecol | 1988 | British Gas Flotation* |
| 1986 | Benylin* | 2006 | British Heart Foundation* (Anti |
| 2010 | Berocca* | | Smoking) |
| 2006 | Bertolli | 2009 | British Heart Foundation – Watch |
| 2007 | Big Plus, The (Improving Scotland's | | Your Own Heart Attack* |
| | adult literacy and numeracy) | 2009 | British Heart Foundation – Yoobot* |
| 1990 | Billy Graham's Mission 89 | 2014 | British Heart Foundation – Stayin' |
| 1986 | Birds Eye Alphabites* | | Alive* |
| 1992 | Birds Eye Country Club Cuisine | 1988 | British Nuclear Fuels |
| 1994 | Birds Eye Crispy Chicken | 1988 | British Rail Young Person's Railcard |
| 1982 | Birds Eye Oven Crispy Cod Steaks | 1982 | British Sugar Corporation |
| | in Batter* | 1980 | British Turkey Federation |
| 1999 | Birmingham, City of** | 2005 | Broadband for Scotland*$^S$ |
| 1988 | Birmingham Executive Airways | 2006 | Brother |
| 2010 | Bisto* | 2007 | Brother* |
| 1990 | Black Tower | 1992 | BT |
| 1996 | Blockbuster Video | 2008 | BT |
| 2005 | Blood Donation* | 2009 | BT |
| 2014 | Blue Dragon | 2010 | BT |
| 1982 | Blue Riband | 2012 | BT* |
| 2000 | Bluewater* | 2014 | BT |
| 2005 | bmi baby | 2004 | BT Broadband* |
| 1994 | BMW* | 2005 | BT Broadband (Consumer) |
| 2004 | BMW Films – The Hire* | 1994 | BT Business |
| 1994 | Boddington's* | 1996 | BT Business* |
| 2012 | Bombay Sapphire | 2000 | BT Business |
| 2008 | Bonfire Night | 1992 | BT Call Waiting* |
| 2003 | Bonjela** | 2002 | BT Cellnet* |
| 1994 | Book Club Associates | 1986 | BT Consumer* |
| 2012 | Boots* | 2001 | BT Internet (Northern Ireland)** |
| 1998 | Boots Advantage Card | 1999 | BT Northern Ireland** |
| 1988 | Boots Brand Medicines | 1986 | BT Privatisation* |
| 2004 | Bounty (paper towels)* | 2002 | BT Retail* |
| 1994 | Boursin | 2007 | BT Total Broadband |
| 1998 | Boursin | 2010 | BT Total Broadband* |
| 1986 | Bovril | 1998 | Bud Ice |
| 2000 | Bowmore | 1988 | Budweiser |
| 2008 | Bradesco | 2002 | Budweiser* |
| 1986 | Bradford & Bingley Building | 2006 | Bulldog 2004 |
| | Society* | 1980 | BUPA |
| 1990 | Bradford & Bingley Building | 2000 | BUPA |
| | Society | 2002 | BUPA |

| 2004 | Co-op Food Retail |
| 1994 | Cooperative Bank* |
| 1996 | Cooperative Bank |
| 1990 | Copperhead Cider |
| 2007 | Cornwall Enterprise |
| 2010 | Corsodyl* |
| 1982 | Country Manor (Alcoholic Drink) |
| 1986 | Country Manor (Cakes) |
| 1984 | Cow & Gate Babymeals* |
| 1982 | Cracottes* |
| 2004 | Cravendale (Milk)* |
| 2000 | Crime Prevention |
| 2003 | Crimestoppers Northern Ireland** |
| 1980 | Croft Original |
| 1982 | Croft Original |
| 1990 | Croft Original* |
| 2011 | CrossCountry Trains |
| 1999 | Crown Paint** |
| 2002 | Crown Paint |
| 2003 | Crown Paint** |
| 2000 | Crown Paints* |
| 2004 | Crown Paints |
| 1990 | Crown Solo* |
| 1999 | Crown Trade** |
| 1999 | Crown Wallcoverings** |
| 1984 | Cuprinol* |
| 2014 | Cuprinol* |
| 2007 | Curanail |
| 1999 | Cussons 1001 Mousse** |
| 1986 | Cyclamon* |
| 2009 | Cycling Safety* |

**D**

| 2014 | Dacia* |
| 1996 | Daewoo* |
| 1982 | *Daily Mail*\* |
| 2002 | Dairy Council (Milk)* |
| 2000 | Dairylea* |
| 1992 | Danish Bacon & Meat Council |
| 2008 | Danone Activia* |
| 2012 | Danone Activia* |
| 1980 | Danum Taps |
| 2003 | Data Protection Act |
| 1990 | Data Protection Registrar |
| 2008 | Dave* |
| 1980 | Day Nurse |
| 1994 | Daz |
| 2006 | Daz* |
| 2008 | De Beers* |
| 1996 | De Beers Diamonds* |
| 2002 | Debenhams |
| 1980 | Deep Clean* |
| 2005 | Deep River Rock - Win Big |
| 2000 | Degree |
| 2003 | Demand Broadband** |

| 2011 | Department for Transport |
| 2012 | Department for Transport* |
| 2011 | Depaul UK* |
| 2006 | Dero* |
| 2008 | Dero |
| 1980 | Dettol* |
| 2014 | Deutsche Telekom AG* |
| 2009 | Dextro Energy |
| 2002 | DfES Higher Education |
| 2010 | DH Hep (C) |
| 1984 | DHL Worldwide Carrier |
| 2012 | Digital UK* |
| 1998 | Direct Debit |
| 2004 | Direct Line* |
| 1992 | Direct Line Insurance* |
| 2008 | Direct Payment* |
| 2007 | Direct Payment (Department of Work and Pensions)* |
| 2006 | Disability Rights Commission |
| 2003 | District Policing Partnerships (Northern Ireland) |
| 1990 | Dog Registration |
| 2006 | Dogs Trust |
| 2000 | Domestic Abuse* |
| 2002 | Domino's Pizza* |
| 2009 | 'Don't be a Cancer Chancer'* |
| 2014 | Doritos |
| 2011 | Doro Mobile Phones |
| 2008 | Dove* |
| 2012 | Dove* |
| 2010 | Dove Deodorant* |
| 2012 | Dove Hair* |
| 2002 | Dr Beckmann Rescue* |
| 2001 | Dr Beckmann Rescue Oven Cleaner** |
| 1980 | Dream Topping |
| 1988 | Drinking & Driving |
| 1998 | Drugs Education* |
| 1994 | Dunfermline Building Society |
| 1980 | Dunlop Floor Tiles |
| 1990 | Duracell Batteries |
| 1980 | Dynatron Music Suite |

**E**

| 1988 | E & P Loans* |
| 2007 | E4 Skins (Channel 4)* |
| 2011 | East Midlands Trains* |
| 2004 | East of England Development Agency (Broadband)* |
| 2000 | easyJet* |
| 2014 | easyJet* |
| 2009 | Eden and Blighty* |
| 2014 | EDF Energy* |
| 1994 | Edinburgh Club* |
| 1990 | Edinburgh Zoo |

| | | | |
|---|---|---|---|
| 1986 | GLC's Anti 'Paving Bill' Campaign* | 1982 | Henri Winterman's Special Mild |
| 2000 | Glenmorangie*S | 1996 | Hep30 (Building Products) |
| 1995 | Glow-worm Boilers (Hepworth Heating)** | 1990 | Herta Frankfurters |
| | | 1992 | Herta Frankfurters |
| 1996 | Glow-worm Central Heating | 2008 | Hewlett Packard Personal Systems Group (PSG) |
| 2001 | GoByCoach.com (National Express)** | 2005 | Hidden Treasures of Cumbria* |
| 1996 | Gold Blend* | 2005 | Highlands and Islands Broadband Registration Campaign |
| 1988 | Gold Spot | | |
| 1984 | Golden Wonder Instant Pot Snacks* | 2011 | Hiscox |
| 1980 | Goodyear Grandprix | 2007 | Historic Scotland* |
| 2012 | Gordon's* | 2006 | HM Revenue & Customs (Self Assessment)* |
| 1984 | Grant's Whisky | | |
| 1992 | Green Giant | 1980 | Hoechst |
| 1988 | Green Science | 1992 | Hofels Garlic Pearles |
| 1988 | Greene King IPA Bitter | 1984 | Hofmeister* |
| 1990 | Greenpeace | 1982 | Home Protection (Products) |
| 2014 | Groupe Média TFO | 1984 | Home Protection (Products) |
| 2012 | Gü* | 2006 | Homebase |
| 1982 | *Guardian, the* | 2012 | Homebase |
| 2004 | *Guardian, the* | 1990 | Honda |
| 1990 | Guinness (Draught) in Cans | 2004 | Honda* |
| 1996 | *Guinness Book of Records* | 1986 | Horlicks |
| | | 1994 | Horlicks |
| **H** | | 2006 | Horlicks |
| 1990 | H. Samuel | 1986 | Hoverspeed |
| 1992 | Haagen-Dazs* | 1992 | Hovis |
| 2009 | Halifax* | 1996 | Hovis |
| 2006 | Halifax Bank of Scotland | 2002 | Hovis* |
| 1982 | Halifax Building Society | 2010 | Hovis* |
| 1992 | Halifax Building Society | 2010 | HSBC* |
| 1994 | Halifax Building Society | 1984 | Hudson Payne & Iddiols |
| 2002 | Halifax Building Society* | 1996 | Huggies Nappies |
| 1980 | Halifax Building Society Convertible Term Shares | 1994 | Hush Puppies |
| 1994 | Halls Soothers* | **I** | |
| 1982 | Hansa Lager | 1996 | I Can't Believe It's Not Butter!* |
| 1999 | Hartley's Jam** | 2012 | IBM* |
| 2007 | Hastings Hotels | 2008 | Iceland |
| 2002 | Hastings Hotels (Golfing Breaks)* | 1992 | Iceland Frozen Foods |
| 2001 | Hastings Hotels (Golfing Breaks in Northern Ireland)** | 1980 | ICI Chemicals |
| | | 1984 | ICI Dulux Natural Whites* |
| 2000 | Health Education Board for Scotland | 1992 | IFAW* |
| | | 2014 | IKEA |
| 2012 | Health Promotion Board Singapore* | 1998 | Imodium |
| | | 2001 | Imperial Leather** |
| 2014 | Health Promotion Board of Singapore | 2002 | Imperial Leather |
| | | 2003 | Imperial Leather** |
| 2014 | Heart and Stroke Foundation of Canada* | 2004 | Imperial Leather* |
| | | 1990 | Imperial War Museum |
| 1994 | Heineken Export | 1998 | Impulse |
| 2010 | Heinz* | 1988 | *Independent, the* |
| 2008 | Heinz Beanz Snap Pots | 2006 | ING Direct* |
| 1980 | Heinz Coleslaw | 1998 | Inland Revenue Self Assessment |
| 1984 | Hellman's Mayonnaise* | 2005 | Inland Revenue Self Assessment* |

| | | | | |
|---|---|---|---|---|
| 1980 | Levi Strauss UK | | 2003 | Magna Science Adventure Centre** |
| 1992 | Levi Strauss UK* | | 2007 | Magners Irish Cider* |
| 1988 | Levi's 501s* | | 1999 | Magnet Kitchens** |
| 2014 | Lidl | | 2004 | Magnum |
| 2014 | Lifebuoy | | 2012 | Magnum Gold?!* |
| 2005 | Lift Off | | 2014 | Mattessons Fridge Raiders* |
| 2012 | Lights by TENA | | 2009 | Make Poverty History |
| 1990 | Lil-lets* | | 2006 | Make Poverty History (Comic Relief) |
| 1996 | Lil-lets | | 1990 | Malibu |
| 1996 | Lilt | | 2006 | Manchester City* |
| 1992 | Limelite* | | 1999 | Manchester City Centre** |
| 1980 | Limmits | | 2001 | Manchester City Centre** |
| 1999 | Lincoln Financial Group** | | 2002 | Manchester Evening News (Job Section)* |
| 2000 | Lincoln Insurance | | | |
| 2000 | Lincoln USA | | 2003 | Manchester Evening News Job Section** |
| 1980 | Lion Bar | | | |
| 1988 | Liquorice Allsorts | | 2003 | ManchesterIMAX** |
| 1992 | Liquorice Allsorts | | 1982 | Manger's Sugar Soap* |
| 1980 | Listerine | | 1988 | Manpower Services Commission |
| 1988 | Listerine* | | 2011 | Marie Curie Cancer Care* |
| 2004 | Listerine | | 1994 | Marks & Spencer |
| 1998 | Littlewoods Pools | | 2006 | Marks & Spencer* |
| 2011 | Liverpool ONE | | 2004 | Marks & Spencer Lingerie* |
| 1984 | Lloyds Bank* | | 1998 | Marmite* |
| 1992 | Lloyds Bank | | 2002 | Marmite* |
| 2010 | Lloyds TSB* | | 2008 | Marmite* |
| 1999 | Local Enterprise Development Unit (NI)** | | 2011 | Marmite XO |
| | | | 1998 | Marmoleum |
| 1990 | London Buses Driver Recruitment | | 1988 | Marshall Cavendish Discovery |
| 2009 | London Business School* | | 1994 | Marston Pedigree* |
| 1982 | London Docklands | | 2001 | Maryland Cookies** |
| 1984 | London Docklands* | | 2006 | Mastercard |
| 1990 | London Philharmonic | | 2008 | Mastercard |
| 1992 | London Transport Fare Evasion | | 2009 | Maximuscle* |
| 1986 | London Weekend Television | | 1986 | Mazda* |
| 1980 | Lucas Aerospace* | | 1986 | Mazola* |
| 1996 | Lucky Lottery | | 2008 | McCain |
| 1980 | Lucozade* | | 2012 | McCain |
| 1992 | Lucozade | | 2011 | McCain Wedges* |
| 2008 | Lucozade Sport* | | 2014 | McCain Ready Baked Jackets* |
| 1988 | Lurpak | | 1996 | McDonald's |
| 2000 | Lurpak* | | 1998 | McDonald's |
| 2008 | Lurpak | | 2010 | McDonald's |
| 2014 | Lux* | | 2012 | McDonald's* |
| 2012 | LV=* | | 2008 | McDonald's Eurosaver |
| 2002 | Lynx* | | 2014 | McDonald's Sponsorship London 2012 |
| 2011 | Lynx* | | | |
| 2004 | Lynx Pulse* | | 2014 | McDonald's Virtual Coins* |
| 1994 | Lyon's Maid Fab | | 1980 | McDougall's Saucy Sponge |
| 1988 | Lyon's Maid Favourite Centres | | 1988 | Mcpherson's Paints |
| | | | 1990 | Mcpherson's Paints |
| **M** | | | 2000 | McVitie's Jaffa Cakes |
| 2014 | Maaza | | 2004 | McVitie's Jaffa Cakes |
| 2004 | M&G | | 2010 | Medicine Waste |
| 1988 | Maclaren Prams | | | |

| | | | |
|---|---|---|---|
| 1980 | *Observer*, the – French Cookery School Campaign | 2000 | Persil* |
| | | 2006 | Petits Filous |
| 2002 | Ocean Spray* | 2014 | Petplan |
| 1988 | Oddbins* | 1990 | PG Tips* |
| 2012 | Odol-med3 | 2000 | PG Tips* |
| 1998 | Olivio* | 1996 | Philadelphia* |
| 2002 | Olivio/Bertolli* | 1994 | Philadelphia |
| 2014 | Olympic Delivery Authority/ Transport for London* | 1988 | Phileas Fogg |
| | | 1988 | Phileas Fogg |
| 1998 | Olympus | 1994 | Phileas Fogg |
| 1982 | Omega Chewing Gum | 2010 | Philips |
| 1998 | One2One* | 1980 | Philips Cooktronic |
| 2005 | onlineni.net | 1980 | Philips Video |
| 2014 | ONLY* | 2003 | Phoenix Natural Gas |
| 1992 | Optrex* | 2003 | Phones 4u** |
| 2010 | Oral-B | 1998 | Physical Activity Campaign (HEB Scotland) |
| 2005 | Oral Cancer* | | |
| 1996 | Orange* | 2009 | Pilgrims Choice |
| 1998 | Orange* | 2007 | Pilkington Activ* |
| 2010 | Orange* | 1990 | Pilkington Glass |
| 2000 | Orange International | 1992 | Pilsner |
| 2000 | Orange Just Talk* | 1986 | Pink Lady |
| 1984 | Oranjeboom | 1984 | Pirelli |
| 2007 | Organ Donor Recruitment (Scottish Executive)* | 1986 | Pirelli |
| | | 1990 | Pirelli |
| 2011 | Organ Donor Register* | 1996 | Pirelli |
| 2007 | Original Source* | 1994 | Pizza Hut |
| 1990 | Otrivine | 1996 | Pizza Hut |
| 2001 | Our Dynamic Earth Visitor Attraction** | 1998 | Pizza Hut* |
| | | 1990 | Plax |
| 2011 | Ovaltine* | 2010 | Plenty |
| 1988 | Oxo | 1980 | Plessey Communications & DataSystems |
| 1990 | Oxo | | |
| 1992 | Oxo* | 1998 | Polaroid* |
| 1998 | Oxo Lamb Cubes | 2007 | Police Community Support Officers |
| | | | |
| **P** | | 1994 | Police Federation of England and Wales |
| 2007 | P&O Cruises | | |
| 2007 | P&O Ferries | 2004 | Police Officer Recruitment (Hertfordshire Constabulary)* |
| 2014 | Paddy Power | | |
| 1986 | Paignton Zoo | 2002 | Police Recruitment* |
| 2000 | Pampers South Africa* | 2002 | Police Recruitment (Could You?) |
| 2011 | Panasonic Toughbook | 2002 | Police Recruitment Northern Ireland |
| 2014 | Pancreatic Cancer Action* | | |
| 1988 | Paracodol* | 2001 | Police Service of Northern Ireland** |
| 1984 | Paul Masson California Carafes | | |
| 2005 | Payment Modernisation Programme | 2007 | Police Service of Northern Ireland (Recruitment) |
| 1982 | Pedal Cycle Casualties* | | |
| 2014 | Pedigree | 1996 | Polo Mints |
| 1998 | Penguin | 1984 | Polyfoam |
| 1994 | Peperami* | 2007 | Pomegreat |
| 2011 | PepsiCo Walkers* | 1986 | *Portsmouth News* |
| 1994 | Pepsi Max | 2002 | Post Office* |
| 1986 | Perrier | 2012 | Post Office |
| 1990 | Perrier | 1980 | Post Office Mis-sorts |

| | |
|---|---|
| 2004 | Safer Travel at Night (GLA)* |
| 1996 | Safeway |
| 2002 | Sainsbury's* (Jamie Oliver) |
| 2002 | Sainsbury's* (Promotion) |
| 2006 | Sainsbury's |
| 2008 | Sainsbury's* |
| 2010 | Sainsbury's* |
| 2012 | Sainsbury's |
| 2014 | Sainsbury's* |
| 2008 | Sainsbury's magazine |
| 2001 | Salford University** |
| 2003 | Salvation Army, the** |
| 2014 | Salvation Army, the* |
| 1996 | Samaritans |
| 1980 | Sanatogen |
| 1986 | Sanatogen |
| 1988 | Sandplate* |
| 1986 | Sapur (Carpet Cleaner) |
| 1992 | Save the Children* |
| 1988 | Schering Greene Science |
| 2001 | Scholl Flight Socks** |
| 2000 | scoot.com* |
| 1980 | Scotcade |
| 2005 | Scotch Beef S |
| 1984 | Scotch Video Cassettes |
| 1992 | Scotrail |
| 1992 | Scottish Amicable* |
| 2008 | Scottish Government: Teacher Recruitment |
| 2005 | Scottish Power* |
| 1998 | Scottish Prison Service |
| 2005 | Scruffs Hard Wear |
| 2002 | Seafish Industry Authority |
| 2006 | Seeds of Change (Masterfoods) |
| 1980 | Seiko |
| 2010 | Self Assessment* |
| 1992 | Sellafield Visitors Centre |
| 2001 | Senokot** |
| 2002 | Senokot |
| 2005 | Senokot |
| 2014 | Sensodyne Pronamel* |
| 1999 | Seven Seas Cod Liver Oil** |
| 1980 | Shake 'n' Vac |
| 1984 | Shakers Cocktails* |
| 2012 | Shangri-La Hotels & Resorts* |
| 2009 | Shell |
| 2002 | Shell Optimax |
| 1999 | Shippam's Spread** |
| 1980 | Shloer* |
| 1986 | Shredded Wheat |
| 1990 | Silent Night Beds* |
| 2005 | Silent Night My First Bed*S |
| 2009 | Simple |
| 2002 | Skoda* |
| 1982 | Skol |

| | |
|---|---|
| 1992 | Skol |
| 2008 | Sky |
| 2012 | Sky |
| 1999 | Slazenger (cricket bats)** |
| 2009 | Slendertone* |
| 1980 | Slumberdown Quilts |
| 1990 | Smarties |
| 1980 | Smirnoff Vodka |
| 1980 | Smith's Monster Munch |
| 1982 | Smith's Square Crisps |
| 1992 | Smith's Tudor Specials |
| 1992 | Smoke Alarms |
| 1994 | Smoke Alarms* |
| 2011 | Smokefree North West |
| 2012 | Snickers* |
| 1996 | So …? (Fragrance) |
| 2006 | Sobieski (Vodka) |
| 1986 | Soft & Gentle |
| 1996 | Soldier Recruitment |
| 1995 | Solpadol** |
| 1994 | Solvent Abuse |
| 1996 | Solvite |
| 1999 | Solvite** |
| 2000 | Solvite* |
| 1988 | Sony |
| 1992 | Sony |
| 2006 | Sony BRAVIA |
| 1992 | Sony Camcorders |
| 2006 | Sony DVD Handycam |
| 2006 | Sony Ericsson K750i/W800i* |
| 2004 | Sony Ericsson T610* |
| 2014 | Specsavers* |
| 1996 | Springers by K (Shoes) |
| 2006 | Sprite |
| 2014 | Sprite |
| 1984 | St Ivel Gold* |
| 2004 | Standard Bank (SA) |
| 2005 | Standard Life S |
| 2009 | Stanley Tools UK |
| 2000 | Star Alliance |
| 1992 | Stella Artois* |
| 1996 | Stella Artois* |
| 1998 | Stella Artois |
| 2000 | Stella Artois* |
| 2002 | Stella Artois* |
| 2002 | Strathclyde Police |
| 1994 | Strepsils* |
| 2010 | Stroke Awareness* |
| 1990 | Strongbow |
| 2009 | Strongbow |
| 2007 | Subway* |
| 1982 | Summers the Plumbers |
| 1980 | Sunblest Sunbran |
| 1990 | Supasnaps |
| 2014 | Supermalt |

| | |
|---|---|
| 2001 | Vimto** |
| 1986 | Virgin Atlantic |
| 2008 | Virgin Atlantic* |
| 2010 | Virgin Atlantic* |
| 2012 | Virgin Atlantic* |
| 2012 | Virgin Media |
| 2004 | Virgin Mobile* |
| 2004 | Virgin Mobile Australia* |
| 2004 | Virgin Trains* |
| 2006 | Virgin Trains* |
| 2010 | Virgin Trains |
| 2012 | Virgin Trains* |
| 2014 | Virgin Trains |
| 1994 | Visa |
| 2006 | Visit London |
| 2012 | VO5 Extreme Style* |
| 1986 | Vodafone |
| 1998 | Volkswagen* |
| 2002 | Volkswagen (Brand)* |
| 2004 | Volkswagen Diesel* |
| 2006 | Volkswagen Golf* |
| 2006 | Volkswagen Golf GTI Mk5* |
| 2002 | Volkswagen Passat* |
| 2012 | Volkswagen Passat |
| 2008 | V-Power |
| 1992 | VW Golf* |

**W**

| | |
|---|---|
| 1980 | Waistline |
| 2002 | Waitrose* |
| 2007 | Waitrose* |
| 2008 | Waitrose* |
| 2012 | Waitrose* |
| 2003 | Wake Up To Waste (Northern Ireland)** |
| 1992 | Wales Tourist Board |
| 2010 | Walkers |
| 2012 | Walkers* |
| 1996 | Walkers Crisps* |
| 2002 | Walkers Crisps* |

| | |
|---|---|
| 1980 | Wall's Cornetto |
| 2006 | Wall's Sausages |
| 1984 | Wall's Viennetta* |
| 1996 | Wall's Viennetta |
| 1998 | Wallis |
| 1984 | Walnut Whips |
| 2003 | Warburtons |
| 1990 | Warburtons Bread* |
| 2005 | Waste Awareness |
| 1984 | Websters Yorkshire Bitter |
| 2004 | Weetabix* |
| 2007 | Weetabix* |
| 1988 | Weight Watchers Slimming Clubs |
| 2002 | West End Quay |
| 2005 | West Midlands Hub of Museums* |
| 1990 | Westwood Tractors |
| 2012 | Which?* |
| 1992 | Whipsnade Wild Animal Park* |
| 1980 | Whitegate's Estate Agents* |
| 2010 | Wickes |
| 1990 | Wilson's Ultra Golf Balls |
| 1988 | Winalot Prime* |
| 2010 | Wispa* |
| 2006 | Women's Aid* |
| 1994 | Wonderbra* |

**Y**

| | |
|---|---|
| 2000 | Yellow Pages Norway |
| 1980 | Yeoman Pie Fillings |
| 1980 | Yorkie |
| 1982 | Yorkshire Bank |
| 2002 | Yorkshire Forward/Yorkshire Tourist Board |
| 2012 | Yorkshire Tea* |
| 2008 | Yorkshire Tourist Board – Make Yorkshire Yours |

**Z**

| | |
|---|---|
| 1984 | Zanussi* |
| 1994 | Zovirax |

In compiling this list the IPA has made every effort to ensure an accurate record of all cases currently available in the IPA Databank. However, there may be instances where cases are currently missing from file and as a result have not been listed here.

# Index